Google Cloud Platform for

– From Beginner to Data Engineer using Google Cloud Platform

Copyright © Alasdair Gilchrist 2019

Table of Contents

Part 1 – An introduction to Data Engineering

Chapter 1: An Introduction to Data Engineering

A Professional Data Engineer enables data-driven decision making by collecting, transforming, and publishing data. A data engineer should be able to design, build, operationalize, secure, and monitor data processing systems with a particular emphasis on security and compliance; scalability and efficiency; reliability and fidelity; and flexibility and portability. A data engineer should also be able to leverage, deploy, and continuously train pre-existing machine learning models. (Google)

In recent years data engineering has emerged as a separate and related role that works in concert with data analysts and data scientists. Typically, the differentiator is that data scientists will focus on finding new insights from a data set, while data engineers are primarily concerned with the technologies and the preparation of the data such as: clean, structure, model, scale, secure, amongst others.

As a result data engineers primarily focus on the following areas:

Clean and wrangle data

However, it is not all about playing with technology and connectors as there is a lot of time spent cleaning and wrangling data to prepare it for input into the analytical systems. Hence, data engineers must make sure that the data the organization is using is clean, reliable, and prepped specifically for each job. Consequently, a large part of the data engineer's job is to parse, clean and wrangle the data. This important task is about taking a raw dataset and refining it into something useful. The objective is to restructure and format the data into a state that is fit for analysis and can have queries run against it.

Build and maintain data pipelines

It will be the responsibility of the data engineer to plan and construct the necessary data pipelines that will encompass the journey and processes that data undergoes within a company. Creating a data pipeline is rarely easy, but at big data scale it can be challenging as it requires integrating data I/O from many different big data technologies. Moreover, a data engineer needs to understand and select the right tools or technologies for the job. In short the data engineer iş the subject matter expert (SME) when it comes to technologies and frameworks so they will be expected to have in-depth knowledge of how to combine often diverse technologies in order to create data pipelines solutions, which enable a company's business and analytical processes.

What does a data engineer need to know?

According to Google, and as this book is ultimately about data engineering on the Google Cloud Platform – so who better to ask – the required body of knowledge expected of a certified data engineer is as follows:

1. **Designing data processing systems**

1.1 Selecting the appropriate storage technologies. Considerations include:
- Mapping storage systems to business requirements
- Data modelling
- Trade-offs involving latency, throughput, transactions
- Distributed systems
- Schema design

1.2 Designing data pipelines. Considerations include:
- Data publishing and visualization (e.g., BigQuery)
- Batch and streaming data (e.g., Cloud Dataflow, Cloud Dataproc, Apache Beam, Apache Spark and Hadoop ecosystem, Cloud Pub/Sub, Apache Kafka)
- Online (interactive) vs. batch predictions
- Job automation and orchestration (e.g., Cloud Composer)

1.3 Designing a data processing solution. Considerations include:
- Choice of infrastructure

- System availability and fault tolerance
- Use of distributed systems
- Capacity planning
- Hybrid cloud and edge computing
- Architecture options (e.g., message brokers, message queues, middleware, service-oriented architecture, serverless functions)
- At least once, in-order, and exactly once, etc., event processing

1.4 Migrating data warehousing and data processing. Considerations include

- Awareness of current state and how to migrate a design to a future state
- Migrating from on-premises to cloud (Data Transfer Service, Transfer Appliance, Cloud Networking)
- Validating a migration

2. Building and operationalizing data processing systems
2.1 Building and operationalizing storage systems. Considerations include:

- Effective use of managed services (Cloud Bigtable, Cloud Spanner, Cloud SQL, BigQuery, Cloud Storage, Cloud Datastore, Cloud Memorystore)
- Storage costs and performance
- Lifecycle management of data

2.2 Building and operationalizing pipelines. Considerations include:

- Data cleansing
- Batch and streaming
- Transformation
- Data acquisition and import
- Integrating with new data sources

2.3 Building and operationalizing processing infrastructure. Considerations include:

- Provisioning resources
- Monitoring pipelines
- Adjusting pipelines

- Testing and quality control

3. Operationalizing machine learning models

3.1 Leveraging pre-built ML models as a service. Considerations include:
- ML APIs (e.g., APIs such as Vision API, Speech API)
- Customizing ML APIs (e.g., customising AutoML Vision, Auto ML text, or others)
- Conversational experiences (e.g., Dialogflow)

3.2 Deploying an ML pipeline. Considerations include:
- Ingesting appropriate data
- Retraining of machine learning models (Cloud Machine Learning Engine, BigQuery ML, Kubeflow, Spark ML)
- Continuous evaluation

3.3 Choosing the appropriate training and serving infrastructure. Considerations include:
- Distributed vs. single machine
- Use of edge compute
- Hardware accelerators (e.g., GPU, TPU)

3.4 Measuring, monitoring, and troubleshooting machine learning models. Considerations include:
- Machine learning terminology (e.g., features, labels, models, regression, classification, recommendation, supervised and unsupervised learning, evaluation metrics)
- Impact of dependencies of machine learning models
- Common sources of error (e.g., assumptions about data)

4. Ensuring solution quality

4.1 Designing for security and compliance. Considerations include:
- Identity and access management (e.g., Cloud IAM)
- Data security (encryption, key management)
- Ensuring privacy (e.g., Data Loss Prevention API)
- Legal compliance (e.g., Health Insurance Portability and Accountability Act (HIPAA), Children's Online Privacy Protection

Act (COPPA), FedRAMP, General Data Protection Regulation (GDPR))

4.2 Ensuring scalability and efficiency. Considerations include:
- Building and running test suites
- Pipeline monitoring (e.g., Stackdriver)
- Assessing, troubleshooting, and improving data representations and data processing infrastructure
- Resizing and autoscaling resources

4.3 Ensuring reliability and fidelity. Considerations include:
- Performing data preparation and quality control (e.g., Cloud Dataprep)
- Verification and monitoring
- Planning, executing, and stress testing data recovery (fault tolerance, rerunning failed jobs, performing retrospective re-analysis)
- Choosing between ACID, idempotent, eventually consistent requirements

4.4 Ensuring flexibility and portability. Considerations include:
- Mapping to current and future business requirements
- Designing for data and application portability (e.g., multi-cloud, data residency requirements)
- Data staging, cataloguing, and discovery

However, with the explosion in interest and adoption of big data analytics over the last decade or so a data engineer's required body of knowledge is rapidly expanding. Currently a data engineer will be expected to have a good general knowledge of the different big data technologies. But these technologies fall under numerous areas of speciality, such as file formats, ingestion engines, stream and batch processing pipelines, NoSQL data storage, container and cluster management, transaction and analytical databases, serverless web frameworks, data visualizations, and machine learning pipelines, to name just a few.

A holistic understanding of data is a prerequisite. But what is really desirable is for data engineers' to understand the business objectives – the purpose of analytics - and how the entire big data operation works to deliver on that goal and then look for ways to make it better. What that means is thinking and acting like an engineer one moment and as a traditional product manager the next.

Data Engineering is not just a critical skill when it comes to advanced data analytics or Machine Learning every data scientist should know enough about data engineering to be competent in the skill of evaluating how data projects are aligned with the business goals and the competency of their company.

Furthermore, the topic of generic data engineering skills is also a crucial element in the certification exam. Therefore, in this section of the book we will provide a detailed introduction to the concepts and principles behind data engineering from a vendor agnostic perspective. If you are a beginner, you will certainly need to know this, as Google assumes you have at least one year's practical experience, so if you are pursuing a career in the discipline or are looking to take the certification exam we recommend you read through Part 1 to get familiar with the concepts and terms you will need to know later on.

The topics we will cover in this the first part of Data Engineering for the Google Cloud Platform will deal with the generic and platform agnostic principles of data engineering. If you already have a good back-ground in the following topics:

- Types of Data
- Data Modelling
- Types of OLTP and OLAP systems
- Data Warehousing
- ETL and ELT
- Machine Learning models, concepts and algorithms
- Big Data ecosystems (Hadoop, Spark, etc.)

You may want to skip this section and go straight to part II Google Cloud Platform Fundamentals.

Data is dumb, it's not about the data it's about the information (Stupid).

Data in itself is meaningless without either context or processing upon which it becomes information. That is the common explanation of data's value and why we need to process it so that it will transform into information. An example of this could be the stream of data contained within computer logs, which to the untrained eye the data is meaningless:

127.0.0.1 user-identifier frank [10/Oct/2000:13:55:36 -0700] "GET /apache_pb.gif HTTP/1.0" 200 2326

It is only when that log snippet is placed in context as being the output from an Apache Web Server log that we can actually gain any understanding from it. Then we can gain information such as the local address of the server, the identifier of the person making the request and the resource they requested. Hence we have transformed raw data, the log, into information by applying context. And this relationship between data and information is the foundation of what is called the Data/Information/Knowledge/Wisdom or DIKW pyramid.

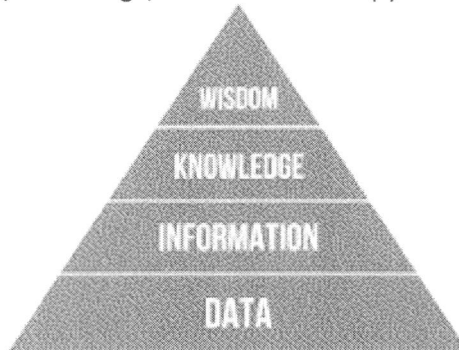

The DIKW pyramid refers loosely to a class of models for representing purported structural and/or functional relationships between data, information, knowledge, and wisdom.

The principle of the Data, Information, Knowledge, Wisdom, hierarchy was introduced by Russell Ackoff in his address to the International Society for General Systems Research in 1989.

The DIKW sequence as it became known reinforces the premise that information is a refinement of data and to be more precise that information is the value we extract from data. The DIKW sequence has been generally accepted and taught in most computer science courses. However, some have a problem with this sequence, specifically the middle steps in the sequence between information and knowledge. The general consensus however is that at least the first sequence is correct; as from data we derive information and so that part is accepted.

In order to be able to understand the complex domain of Data Analytics or Business Intelligence and all it entails we need to start by having a good understanding of the basic elements – data.

Data can be defined as discrete, raw or unorganized pieces of information, such as facts or figures. Data is ambiguous, unorganized or unprocessed facts. When a system or process handles data and arranges, sorts, or uses data to calculate something, then it is processing the data. Raw data, which is the term for unprocessed data, are the raw material used to make information. Unprocessed data is the input to an information system that the system organizes and processes. Raw data is fed into a computer program as variables, or strings, that these can be the binary representation on a computer disk, or the digital inputs from electronic sensors that themselves collect data in the form of analogue signals from their environment.

Data can be qualitative or quantitative; the difference being quantitative data – which is measured and objective - can be represented as a number so can be statistically analysed, as it can be represented as ordinal, interval or ratio scales. Qualitative data – subjective and opinion based – cannot be a number, so it is represented on a nominal scale such as likes or dislikes, etc.

Data can be represented in many formats, but as distinct pieces of information formatted in a specific way such as; character, symbols, strings, numeric, aural (Morse code) and visual (frames in a movie.) Data can also have many attributes, unverified, unformatted, unparsed. It may also have attributes regards its status; verified, unreliable, uncertified or validated.

Quantitative Data: Continuous Data and Discrete Data

There are two types of quantitative data, which is also referred to as numeric data: *continuous* and *discrete.* As a general rule, we consider *counts* to be discrete and *measurements* are continuous.

For example, discrete data is a count that can't be made more precise. Typically it involves integers and exact figures. For instance, the number of children in your family is a set of discrete data. After all there are no half children, they are or they are not.

Continuous data, on the other hand, could be granular and reduced to finer and finer levels of grain. For example, you can measure the time taken to commute to work in the morning.

Continuous data is therefore valuable in many different kinds of hypothesis tests when comparing figures. Some other analyses use continuous and discrete quantitative data at the same time as it may reveal performance such as time over distance. For instance, we could perform a regression analysis to see if the speed over per meter (continuous data) is correlated with the number of meters run (discrete data).

Qualitative Data: Binomial Data, Nominal Data, and Ordinal Data

We commonly use quantities and qualities to classify or categorize something, and it is easy to categorize quantity – but if you have to relate to *Qualitative* data it is not so easy. There are three main kinds of qualitative data.

1. There is the case where results are displayed as Binary data and this is when output is one of two mutually exclusive categories: right/wrong, true/false, or accept/reject.
2. There is also the situation when we are collecting unordered or nominal data, and we assign individual items to named categories that do not have an

implicit or natural value or rank. For example, if I went through a list of results and recorded each that would be nominal data.

3. However we can also can have ordered or ordinal data, in which some items are categorized so that they do have some kind of natural order, such as "Short, Medium, or Tall."

Importantly, there are also three types of Data structure which we should know about:

Structured data: This is data, which is relational and can be stored in a database such as SQL in tables with rows and columns. They have a relational key and can be easily mapped into pre-designed fields. Unfortunately, most data is not structured, and the level of structured data collected by organizations represents only about 5% to 10% of all business data.

There is of course another type of data called semi-structured data, which is information that doesn't reside in a relational database, due to its lack of correlation but nonetheless does have structure and organizational properties that make it easier to analyse. Some examples of semi-structured data are: XML and JSON documents which are semi structured documents that do not fit an exact data type, NoSQL databases are considered as semi structured data stores.

But what is surprising is that data stored as semi structured data again only represents a small minority of business data (5% to 10%) so the last data type is the most prevalent one: unstructured data.

Unstructured data represent around 80% of all collected data in today's business. It has become so prevalent it will often include video, voice, emails, multimedia content, music, social media chats and photos amongst many other formats. Note that while these sorts of files may have an internal structure, they are still considered to be unstructured, because the data they contain doesn't fit neatly in a database schema. Actually, unstructured data is everywhere and is not just ubiquitous it is in fact the way most individuals and organizations conduct their work and social communications. After all social media chat, voice, text and video are the way that most people live, and they interact with others through exchanging unstructured data. However, to confuse things, as with structured data, unstructured data can be further classified to be either machine generated or human generated.

Here are some examples of machine-generated unstructured data:

- Computer Logs: these contain information without knowledge unless you understand the context.
- IoT sensors: these will provide streams of binary data from a wide variety of machine or environmental sensors
- Satellite images: These include weather data or satellite surveillance imagery.
- Scientific data: This includes seismic imagery, atmospheric data, and without context it's difficult to extract any meaning?
- Photographs and video: This type of information includes security, surveillance, and traffic video.
- Radar or sonar data: This technology allows autonomous vehicles, to take advantage of visual, audio, meteorological, and oceanographic seismic profiles.

The following list shows a few examples of human-generated unstructured data:

- Chats, e-mails, documents, and even verbal conversation.
- Social media data: This source of data is generated from the social media platforms such as YouTube, Facebook, Twitter, LinkedIn, and Flickr.
- Mobile data: This includes shadow IT where users store data, text messages and location information in the cloud.
- Website content: This comes from any site delivering unstructured content, like YouTube, Flickr, or Instagram.

The unstructured data group is a vast source of raw data and it is growing quickly and has become far more pervasive than traditional forms of documented text based files. Unstructured data can be a problem with regards security as it is easily leaked out with the business boundaries but that is not the real issue. Social media and unstructured data such as You Tube videos, chat texts, and social media comments, are typically easily accessed but they actually allow data miners to determine the poster's attitudes and their sentiments. Indeed analysis of social media comments for sentiment is a valuable form of information which could help in business decision making.

Another important distinction we must make when evaluating the business is what type of data we are storing and processing. There are typically a few categories of data that have very distinct characteristics and therefore we must be able to identify them and cater for their specific requirements. In most business use cases where data is being or planned to be analysed for Business Intelligence purpose data will fall into one of three types:

- Transactional data: this type of data is derived from application web servers, they may be on-premises, web, mobile or SaaS applications and they will be producing data base records for transactions. These transaction focused systems are data write optimised in order to support high throughput of customer transactions whether that be sales on an ecommerce web server or process transactions on an industrial robotic controller. Their purpose is to record transactions by creating and storing data. A preferred collection and processing method for transactional data is in-memory caching and processing while being stored on SQL or NoSQL databases.
- Data Files: this type of data category relates to log files, search results and historical transactional reports. The data is relatively large sized packets and is slow moving so can be managed with traditional disk/writes and database storage.
- Messaging & Events: This type of data known as data streams consist of very small packets in very high volumes and high velocity which, require real time handling. This type of data

can come from IoT sensors or the internet but is typically collected and managed by using Publish/Subscribe queues and protocols. Data streams may require specific storage requirements if they are related to industrial application that require real-time handling, such as stream enabled tables in NoSQL databases, or stream optimised databases that are designed for stream management, storage and processing.

In addition data also has other important attributes that we need to consider such as it can have velocity where it is fast moving and may be short lived, i.e. has very high entropy where it loses its value very quickly. For example, the revolutions per second reading obtained from a machine sensor. On the other hand some operational data is slow moving but of potentially long term value such as monthly sales figures. We can categorise these types of data as being hot or cold respectively and how we store them will depend on our design trade-offs. Generally speaking hot data is streaming data, which is processed in real-time and processed in-memory or in-cache for fast and efficient processing times. Examples of streaming data would be industrial sensors and other IoT alarms and publish/subscribe messages used to control industrial equipment and operational processes. Hot data's value is measured in milliseconds and requires immediate processing.

Cold data on the other hand has high durability very low entropy and can be stored for long periods. Examples, of cold data would be file data particularly historical data like reports and previous year's transaction data which is stored and used for reference. Another characteristic of cold data is it may require only infrequent access and this is important to consider when designing appropriate storage.

A summary of the qualities of Hot and Cold data is shown in the table, with some of their respective operational qualities – some data such as transactional data will fall somewhere along the spectrum within the warm area.

	Hot	Warm	Cold
Volume	MB-GB	GB-TB	PB-EB

Item size	B-KB	KB-MB	KB-TB
Latency	ms	ms, sec	Min, hrs
Durability	Low-high	High	Very High
Request rate	Very-high	High	Low
Cost/GB	$$-$	$-cc	c

As we have seen there are several types of data which we are required to manage and handle proficiently and that requires an understanding of several components. Firstly we should consider the data structure, for example does it have a fixed schema which makes it suitable for standard relational SQL or is it JSON (schema free) or Key/Value style unstructured or semi-structured data in which case NoSQL or in-memory storage or processing will be the appropriate method. We will discuss this further later on, but for now all we need to understand is that we must make the correct choice that matches our requirements. Therefore there is a need to plan how often we will require to access the data and with what latency, and this will depend on the data's characteristics, i.e. whether it hot, warm or cold. As a general rule we should always store the data in the same method we wish to access it, i.e. if we only require infrequent access store in cold or warm storage. Lastly, and very importantly we should ensure that we handle and manage the data in the most cost effective manner that meets our operational requirements – there can be significant unnecessary costs if you choose an inefficient or inappropriate method. We will go into all of these design choices much later when we consider cloud deployments and the plethora of tools and choices we have to fit our design requirements in a design efficient and cost effective manner.

Chapter 3 – Deriving Knowledge from Information

The European Committee for Standardization's official "Guide to Good Practice in Knowledge Management" says: "Knowledge is the combination of data and information, to which is added expert opinion, skills and experience, to result in a valuable asset which can be used to aid decision making."
In the introductory chapter to this book we saw that Information can be distilled from raw data but we did not examine in any depth how we manage this feat. The answer is of course through the application of the techniques and the subject of this introduction – data analytics.

Data Analytics

In this section we will investigate the data analytical methodologies and technologies that are feasible for SMEs in the pursuit of business intelligence. Most small medium enterprise businesses still run on spreadsheets and that isn't an issue as they perform more than adequately for the consumers of strategic, tactical and even operational information. Indeed so successful are spreadsheets that you will find weaning executives, managers and decision-makers of their favourite analytical tools is easier said than done.
Spreadsheets provide a way for managers and executives to analyse data and importantly get that data away from the control of IT. Spreadsheets allow managers to do their own data preparation and analysis. It also provides a means of self-sufficiency and the ways that spreadsheets can accomplish this feat are through:

- Financial Modelling: Spreadsheets are great for the kind of assumptions and testing needed to put together month-by-month forecasts of financial performance.

- Hypothesis testing: Spreadsheets are fast and easy to use so are perfect for on the spot calculations or hypothesis checking on a new data set.
- One-Time Analysis: Spreadsheets are great for one-time modelling as you can quickly load source data, run an analysis, and draw conclusions quickly.

There are several types of data analytics that are commonly used in business. Descriptive analysis is the first type of data analysis that is usually conducted as it describes the main aspects of the data being analysed. For example, it may describe how well a certain model of mobile phone is performing by contrasting its number of sales compared to the norm. This allows for comparisons to be made among different models of phones and helps in decision making as it aides in predicting what stock holdings are required per model.

There is another common type of data analysis which is called exploratory analysis and here the goal is to look for previously unknown relationships. This type of analysis is a way to find new connections and to provide future recommendations and is commonly used in supermarket basket analysis to find interesting correlations between the products bought by a customer on a specific visit.

Predictive analysis as the name suggests predicts future happenings by looking at current and past facts. This sounds very grand but can also be as simple as trending analysis which graphs performance against time so that a researcher can see straightaway if there is a recognisable and predictable pattern or not.

There is also inferential analysis where a small sample is used to infer a result from a much larger sample, this method is commonly used in the analysis of voters in exit polls. Causal analysis is used to find out what happens to one variable when you change some other variable. For example, how are sales affected if a product is placed in a different location, adjacent to another product or on a higher/lower shelf?

Evaluating Information

Gaining information through data analytics however, may be a better basis for decision making than nothing – or just gut feeling – but it isn't at this level really knowledge as some quantity of that was required to understand the problem initially. Furthermore, knowledge was required to comprehend what data would be required to provide the information to prove or disprove a hypothesis, and then knowledge had to be referenced in order to comprehend and validate the information. Hence, we can consider that although Knowledge may sit above data and information in the DIKW pyramid it may not be a perfect fit. It may be considered to be an actionable component derived from the original data and information. However for now the focus is on data and most importantly how we derive information from the raw data that we collect, sometimes not just from the by-products of our operations but by the social interactions with our customers.

There has recently been an epiphany regards the worth of data and its value to an organisation. Data is something most companies, even SME's have potentially vast quantities off, typically they have no use for it so they have previously only stored what was necessary for historical reporting and ditched the rest due to the high costs associated with storage. Over the last decade, the cost of storage has plummeted and with the advent of Big Data and cloud storage it became both possible to store and analyse vast quantities of all sorts of data. Moreover, cheap cloud storage supplemented with new analytical techniques and tools, which promise to reveal insights mined from this data through predictive and proscriptive analytics have changed executive thinking. Now there is potential value to even the small business in the collection, storage and analysis of data based on predictions and trends. Consequently, business and technology leaders have begun the process of building data warehouses and even in some cases data lakes in order to harvest and hoard this precious commodity of raw data.

An interesting aside though is that although just over 52% of SME companies that have actively pursued a BI or data analytics program say they derived benefits few seem so far to have generated quantifiable success. This of course may be down to the fact that only around 1% of all data they harvest is actually analysed.

For several years the procedures and techniques of data mining or the manipulation of Big Data was perceived to be the domain of big enterprises with big budgets. However, open source tools allied with cloud computing services have brought data analytics into the reach of even the most financially constrained SME. Also for SME to succeed in such an endeavour requires that they understand what data is, how it is analysed, for what purpose, and very importantly how it is managed. This is because for all the rhetoric data analytics is only as good as the data you feed it. With data analytics the computer maxim of garbage in, garbage out is a certainty and if we are looking for quality information then we need to ensure quality data at the source. In addition, we also need to know the right questions to ask of our data, and that is where most companies stumble – as they just don't actually know what they want.

The Information that SME businesses require comes from many sources and has many characteristics some of these may be desirable, essential, comprehensive and accurate but others may not be so; for example the information derived may well be incomplete, unverified, cosmetic or extraneous. In order to evaluate the differing characteristics of information when considering its value we have to have a process to put that information through in order to characterize its attributes as valid information. Today we have vast amounts of new information that is being sourced from data collected from many diverse sources such as social media, online news sites and forums as well as coming in many formats such as video, text, memes or photographs and these are not so easily classified and verified especially when we are doing text or sentiment analysis.

To complicate matters further the marketplace is changing due to the advent of social media and ubiquitous mobile communication, which make customers far better informed. This proliferation of information comes about through active collaboration as customers will provide product reviews and exchange views on goods and services with potential customers on social media sites. As a result, customers are making more informed decisions based upon data that they feel they can trust, which ultimately makes retaining customers more difficult. Indeed many customers in retail are now actively targeting retaining customers through improved goods and services by taking a more proactive position on social media marketing.

Therefore when we are evaluating the credibility, veracity and quality of the information we must also consider its provenance or source especially if it is coming from the internet. There are several key areas to consider:

- Authority of the source or the publisher (this is especially important when taking data from social media sources)
- Objectivity of the author (again social media sources can be difficult to verify and objectivity or bias hard to quantify)
- Quality of the information
- Currency of the information
- Relevancy of the information

These were the generally accepted steps taken to verify and authenticate information in the pre-internet social media days of the printed press, journals and libraries. However these steps are just as important today when we have to authenticate information from the internet. For instance when we evaluate authority we have to ask several questions of the source, and this does not just apply to social media authors as data can come from many diverse locations such as sensors, servers, third party distributors/aggregators and the Internet of Things, and any of these can be fraudulent;

- Who is the source?
- What are their credentials?
- What is the sources reputation?
- Who is the publisher, if any?
- Is the source associated with a reputable institution or organization?

To evaluate objectivity we ask the following questions, especially of data obtained through third party brokers;

- Does the author of the data, information or algorithm exhibit a bias?
- Does the information appear valid and true?

To evaluate quality;

- Is the information well structured?
- Is the information source legitimate?
- Does the information have the required features and attributes?

In addition we may take into account the Information characteristics themselves, for example, is the information;

- Accurate
- Comprehensive
- Unbiased
- Timely
- Reliable
- Verifiable
- Current
- Valuable
- Relevant

These are all characteristics we should check for when dealing with information especially when sourced from the internet. Information coming from the internet especially should be checked for being timely and current and hence relevant. One of the issues with search engine algorithms is that they typically rate the most popular relevant entries, but these cannot be the most timely and current. Hence you may end up supporting your hypothesis with data that is ten years old.

Bias and completeness should also be considered, as often information is supplied in social media sites, in a one sided manner, in order to support the publisher's agenda. This phenomenon isn't particularly new as traditional printed media were at this game for centuries but it has become more pronounced and prevalent where social media on the internet is concerned. The concept of an echo chamber is how it is best described where like-minded individuals congregate and exchange their similar views, which is not a bad thing – but it is when it is to the exclusion of any opposing point of view. Of course this isn't a healthy environment and it is a Petri dish for cultures of false news and the propagation of deliberate falsehoods to support an agenda. This appears to have exacerbated the all too human condition, best explained in the Simon and Garfunkel song The Boxer, "All lies and Jest, still a man hears what he wants to hear and disregards the rest".

We must be careful how we handle Information as can be seen through the proliferation and perceived damage cause by 'fake news' as it can have many characteristics.
Within a business or organization, information may come from several sources and be categorized by the role that information will play. Hence, within a SME we may find that some forms of information have roles and can be separated into five main categories;

- Planning - A business needs to know what resources it has (e.g. cash, people, inventory, property, customers). It needs information about the markets in which it operates and the actions of competitors.
- Recording – Financial transactions, Sales orders, stock invoices and inventory all need to be recorded.
- Controlling – Information is required to apply controls and to see if plans are performing better or worse than expected.
- Measuring – Performance in a business need to be measured to ascertain if sales and profits are meeting targets and operational costs are controlled.
- Decision making – Within the decision making group we find subsets of information that further separates information into three classes, operational, tactical and strategic, which is dependent on the information's role and purpose.

(1) Strategic information: this is highly summarized information used to help plan the objectives of the business as a whole and to measure how well those objectives are being achieved. Examples of strategic information include:

- Profitability of each part of the business
- Size, growth and competitive structure of the markets in which a business operates
- Investments made by the business and the returns (e.g. profits, cash inflows) from those investments

(2) Tactical Information: this is used to decide how the resources of the business should be employed. Examples include:

- Information about business productivity (e.g. units produced per employee; staff turnover)
- Profit and cash flow forecasts in the short term
- Pricing information from the market

3) Operational Information: this information is used to make sure that specific operational tasks are executed as planned/intended (i.e. things are done properly). For example, a production manager will want information about the extent and results of quality control checks carried out in the manufacturing process.

Cognitive bias and its impact on data analytics

Cognitive bias is defined as a limitation in a person's objective thinking that comes about due to their favouring of information that matches their personal experience and preferences.

The problem is that while data analytics technology can produce results, it is still up to the individuals to interpret those results. Furthermore they may unwittingly even skew the entire process by selecting what data should be analysed, which can cause digital tools used in predictive analytics and prescriptive analytics to generate false results.

Cognitive Bias is not the only bias we should be aware of as there are several more that can have a telling effect on data analysis and how the results are interpreted:

- Clustering illusion - the tendency for individuals to want to see a pattern in what is actually a random sequence of numbers or events.
- Confirmation bias - the tendency for individuals to value new information that supports existing ideas.
- Framing effect - the tendency for individuals to arrive at different conclusions when reviewing the same information depending upon how the information is presented.
- Group think - the tendency for individuals to place high value on consensus.

Analysts should be aware of the potential pitfalls of deploying and using predictive modelling without examining the provenance of the data selected for analysis for cognitive bias. For example, over the last decade pollsters and election forecasters around the world have deployed predictive analysis models with shockingly poor results. This is due chiefly to an over reliance on weak polling data and flawed predictive models, which resulted in an unpredicted outcome.

In this chapter we have learned that knowledge, information and data differ mainly in abstraction, with data being the least abstract and knowledge the most. Information is data that has been organized for a specific purpose, is deemed timely and accurate and can be presented within a context that give it meaning and relevance that leads to an increase in knowledge. Conceptually information is the message, the message is made up of a sequence of symbols (data), and the message conveys some knowledge to a recipient that can understand it.

However like any other structure the pyramid is reliant on sound foundations. Hence, the importance of managing and assuring the quality of our data is vital. The discipline of Data Governance is outside the realms and capabilities of data engineers, but the requirement to manage data is not.

Chapter 4 –An Introduction to Database Systems

People since the stone ages have been storing and presenting information through cave paintings and carvings in stone tablets. The invention of paper and ink led to a more efficient and user friendly method of storing and presenting information as it could now be stored and consumed in scrolls, manuscripts and later in books. However as we have seen previously information is not all the same, some information requires to be handled differently than other types.

Each database management system, as we have already seen whether it be a relational or non-relational data base, has its strengths and weaknesses. Indeed, it is often the case where a designer, will choose the database system they know or are most comfortable with, and fit the data into that schema. A schema is the blueprint for the database and is the inter-relationships between tables and data. The schema sets out the names for the tables, columns and rows and which data types can be stored in each – a data type could be a small or large integer or a body of structured text such as a date or just a label or body of text such as a name or a description – hence it is a detailed plan of the database. In relational databases there is also the concept of normalisation (3NF), which strives to reduce the instances of redundant data, by moving instances into their own tables, which will improve the database performance and consistency but at the cost of flexibility and added complexity.

However, normalisation has its drawbacks because as the schema becomes more efficient i.e. to accommodate common instances such as customer names, addresses, products, prices, stock numbers, vendors, the list goes on and on so the number of instance of tables grow and grow. The result being is that the schema becomes a labyrinth of interconnected relational tables which only the database designer can possibly understand.

Furthermore, most organisations do not have just one vast database system that controls all business operations as typically there are several each with their own area of responsibility. For example there would be a separate database system for CRM, ERP, HR or ecommerce all heterogeneous (dissimilar and incompatible) systems that cannot naturally integrate and share data and this creates what is known as silos of information.

To compound the problem often these systems will have different underlying databases one might be MySQL another Oracle and a third PostGRES and of course they will have their own unique data schemas as they host applications that perform completely different tasks. But of course often reports need to be run, which will require access to data from several applications hosted on different databases. The SQL query will collect and then collate the retrieved data from several of these systems, and that makes writing report queries extremely complicated. These unfortunate disparate structures arose from the fact that several applications would favour and come preinstalled upon different databases, such as CRM on MySQL, ERP on SQL Server, or PeopleSoft on Oracle and there was nothing that could be done about that. However the problem that could be addressed was that they would each have their own analytic and reporting infrastructure that would have to be queried in turn when building a report.

A new thought-process surfaced that suggested that instead of fitting the data to the database schema, what if we let the database schema fit the data? So instead of juggling several diverse schemas, across several physical servers and then have to start joining tables from dissimilar applications we could build a central database with a schema that would accept data from all the other application databases. Hence, there would be the possibility of perhaps connecting all those troublesome data silos. And what if we just got rid of these disparate reporting servers altogether and formed a single warehouse for analytics and reporting that held a repository for all the aggregated data?

Database models

To understand how this problem was resolved and how data warehousing came into being we need to understand how database models are designed to work in more detail. However, this is not intended to be a database tutorial or primer instead it is simply a high level introduction to the underlying technologies and database concepts, so that you will be familiar with the terminology when it arises later in the book. Hence, if you are comfortable with OLTP and OLAP databases and schemas, you can skip most of the next two chapters.

A Data base "Model" refers to how a database stores and organizes the data it has been given and this term is synonymous with a schema. The design of the schema is based typically on the relationship between categories of data, such as Sales, Products, Price and Date and these are referred to as dimensions. Therefore the schema is concerned with how one dimension (a column) interacts with the data stored in a row and how that can be retrieved via a query language.

The relational model

If we initially take a look at the Relational paradigm, which is by far the most common in SMEs, as these are the SQL databases underpinning the applications many of us are familiar with. In the relational SQL database the data is stored in tables, where each row column forms a dimension, such as a product, location or cost and each row contains in the intersecting cell a value or a measure and the column represents a particular attribute of the items.

As we have seen, well-designed relational databases conventionally follow third normal form (3NF), in which no data is duplicated or deemed redundant in the system. To accomplish this lack of redundancy, any references to an entity is made using foreign keys. So, for example, in an ecommerce system with an orders table and a customer table, the row referring to a single order will reference the unique ID of the customer, which references the Customer table. This is done so that instead of storing all of the customer's information directly within the Orders table as this would incur many instances of redundant data, we can keep the Customer information in just one table.

Of course that is great when we are writing transaction data into the database as only one instance or location of the data will need updating. However when we come to reporting, the issue is that the order table doesn't have the customer information, so a join is needed to pull that information into one query statement.

Furthermore, due to normalisation the data schema ensures that the order table can't store a list of items in the order; that information is on the order items table. But the order items table only references product keys, so getting details like the name of the product requires looking at the products table. So, for something as simple as just viewing order details, we may have to join across at least five tables. Now we can clearly see why spreadsheets are as popular and prevalent in SME environments as even to construct a simple query requires skill and intricate knowledge of the database schema. The problem is further compounded by the fact that each report or query has to be pre-constructed and even for an experienced DBA (database administrator) this is not a trivial task so it makes business-user ad-hoc queries just about impossible.

However, this deconstruction of information into the relational model has advantages:

- With a homogenous data set, it is highly space efficient. This was an extremely valid point a decade or two ago when local hard disk storage capacity was at a premium. Nowadays disk capacity is vast and cheap but consumption levels are escalating. The more you give a user the more they use.
- The data integrity of 3NF ensures consistency about what is considered "true" in the system. Again a valid reason when hard disk technology performance was an issue, today's solid state drives and in-memory processing – where the entire database is loaded and runs in memory – negates much of this latency issue, but of course these systems are sometimes

out-with the financial budgets of SMBs and even smaller enterprises.

- A well-designed schema, for a domain where such a thing exists, often reveals the shape of the domain and can guide application logic. This is very true but such is the complexity of most schemas it would take a long time of studying to become familiar with the schema let alone have it guide the application logic.

There are disadvantages, too:

- Data integrity requires a high degree of dependency across tables. This can cause scaling problems because 'sharding' across multiple machines may physically separate data tables that have to be joined in a query to be useful. This is only really relevant to very large databases that are distributed across several machines.
- Relational data schemas are complex and hard to change, and have to be designed and implemented before data is added to the system. If you can't predict what the incoming data will look like, it is impossible to create a meaningful schema for it. This can certainly be an issue with in-house applications where updates and custom changes are commonplace.
- There is a mismatch between how data exists in the real world, and how it is stored in the database, and how it is used by any consuming application. This can cause a loss of context and detail, making the data less meaningful.
- The integration of systems also becomes difficult as we cannot just interconnect disparate systems and schemas as we will need to translate data from one system's schema into another schema and format, and that is before we can load it and make use of it in another database or application.

As we can see integrating disparate applications that run upon databases at the backend is not a trivial task. In addition the problem if anything is growing as in order to accommodate the diverse nature and characteristics of data many specialist forms of database management systems have appeared on the scene. There are many types of databases available, which can be categorized by their content or their application;

- *An in-memory database* is a database that primarily resides in main memory, but is typically backed-up by non-volatile computer data storage. Main memory databases are faster than disk databases, and so are often used where response time is critical, such as in telecommunications network equipment

- A cloud database relies on cloud technology. Both the database and most of its DBMS reside remotely, "in the cloud," therefore the end-users access the DB through a web browser and Open APIs. The advent of Cloud databases has radically reduced the total cost of storage of data and created business opportunities for SMEs that previously – only a generation ago – would have not been feasible.

- Data warehouses: These are databases used to aggregate and archive data from operational databases and often from external sources such as social media, data distributors and direct market research firms. The warehouse becomes the central source of data for end-users who may not have access to operational data as running queries and analytics on an operational database can have a profound detrimental impact. Some basic applications of data warehousing include archiving, analytics and presentation of data which, includes the tasks of retrieving, analysing, mining, transforming, loading and the management of data. The purpose is to archive and manipulate data to make them available for further use.

- A distributed database is one in which both the data and the DBMS span multiple computers, we will see these later in the case of the Hadoop distributed file-system ecosystem for handling Big Data and vast data sets across an array of physical servers.

- A document-oriented database is designed for storing, retrieving, and managing document-oriented, or semi structured data. Document-oriented databases are one of the main categories of NoSQL databases and we will see several of these and other popular Cloud NoSQL databases when we take a look at cloud storage solutions.

- An embedded database system is a DBMS, which is tightly integrated with application software that requires access to the stored data in such a way that it is transparent to the end user. However embedded databases are also common in Retail POS systems and lately have become popular in IoT and industrial systems but they retain the same characteristics of transparency and light-weight design.

- End-user databases consist of data developed by individual end-users. Examples of these are collections of documents, spreadsheets, presentations, multimedia, and other files.

- Hypertext databases: In a hypertext or hypermedia database, any word or a piece of text representing an object, e.g., another piece of text, an article, a picture, or a film, can be hyperlinked to that object. This type of database is particularly useful for organizing large amounts of disparate information. For example, they are useful for organizing online encyclopaedias, where users can conveniently jump around the text. A perfect if extremely large version of a distributed hypertext database is the World Wide Web.

- A knowledge base is a special kind of database for knowledge management, providing the means for the computerized collection, organization, and retrieval of knowledge. Also a collection of data representing problems with their solutions and related experiences as often used by Call Centres and Technical Support.

- A mobile database can be carried on or synchronized from a mobile computing device such as a mobile phone or tablet.
- Operational databases store detailed data about the transactional operations of an organization. They typically process relatively high volumes of transactions which entail updates of a data base using many small 'write' procedures. Examples of operational or transactional data bases (Online Transaction Processing) include customer relation databases (CRM) that record contact, credit, and demographic information about a business' customers, ecommerce data bases that record online sales transactions, enterprise resource planning (ERP) systems that record details about product components, parts inventory, and financial databases that keep track of the organization's production, logistics, inventory and assets, accounting and financial transactions.
- Probabilistic databases employ fuzzy logic to draw inferences from imprecise data. Real-time databases process transactions fast enough for the result to come back and be processed immediately.
- A spatial database can store the data with multidimensional features. The queries on such data include location based queries, like "Where is the closest hotel in my area?"
- A temporal database has built-in time aspects, for example a temporal data model and a temporal version of SQL. More specifically the temporal aspects usually include valid-time and transaction-time.

As can be seen from the list the one significant driver than has changed the way we need to store data within databases has come from the types of data available. There are three types of data that we work with:

1. Structured – relational data that is easily stored within a relational database (approx. 10%)

2. Semi-structured – Data that has some relational structure but does not readily conform to the relational database schema, XML or CVS for example (approx. 10%)

3. Unstructured – Videos, Photographs, and social media chats, etc. (approx. 80%)

Therefore we have to find suitable storage and processing methods for all of these types of data and this is especially important as the most troublesome of the three, which is unstructured data, consists of approximately 80 per cent of the data that organizations collect and now require to analyse. Previously relational databases using structured data only accounted for 10% of the data that we are now required to handle, process, analyse and store securely. Consequently in recent times there has been a shift towards non-relational databases or NoSQL databases especially in the fields of data analytics and large scale cloud data storage across distributed systems.

Non-relational models (NoSQL)

In addition to having to compensate for the disadvantages of the relational model data engineers have over the last decade needed to solve new sets of problems created by the size and scope of the internet. As a result, a new model for database design has emerged and these are called NoSQL databases, and the most popular NoSQL databases are document oriented.

Document databases

The beauty of NoSQL databases is that they are conceptually easy to understand and use. Hence there common use in what are termed Document databases This type of database is designed to store complete, usually self-contained representations of entities, such as emails, video clips, social media chat, Twitter tweets, and photographs. For most non-technical users accessing and managing the data contained within Document Databases —which includes anything from social media content to medical records — is actual a very straightforward and natural way to approach storing data.

Graph databases

A graph database is not what it initially seems as it holds the mathematical context of a graph which is a model that takes the form of a web of nodes and the inter-connections (called "edges") between them. For example, the graphic mapping of IoT wireless mesh networks and the connectivity of the internet through internet routing protocols such as BGP, which provides the route mapping of the web, have provided a number of important uses for graph databases. Additionally, these Graphic databases are also finding important new environments due to the prevalence of IoT industrial projects that connect wireless devices across remote wide areas and even smart cities. This is because the graph or map they produce can be easily calculated and updated using robust algorithms and they are also easier to visualise as they are the most natural way to model the network of relationships among a collection of entities.

Key-value store

A key-value store is an associative array or dictionary which relies on a unique key to represent a body of data whether that is a video clip, a music file, some chat text or a photograph. This is because data is stored simply as binary code but the key and the metadata makes the entity unique so it can be written and retrieved to and from storage extremely quickly. Of course this is as long as you already know the key of the data file you are looking for as the process of querying by the values is typically very difficult.

Data aggregation

A welcome advancement from the tedious manual aggregation of operational data into a report every month is to aggregating the data into a new database, typically a relational database with a schema designed to answer particular types of analysis questions i.e. a warehouse with an Online Analytical Processing (OLAP) capability. An OLAP as they are termed differs from a standard Online Transaction Processing (OLTP) database due mainly to its data schema being multidimensional as opposed to the traditional 2-dimensional relational data schema. The advantage of this approach is that IT or the database administrator can write scripts to Extract, Transform and Load (ETL) the data out of the other operational systems (CRM, POS, ERP, etc.) into the warehouse, and then pre-prepared reports can be scheduled to run every day or even hour, which ensures that the data in the reports is always fresh. Problems with this approach:

- Defining a schema that will work well for data coming from a variety of sources can be very difficult.
- The ETL process may rob data of its original context and format, which may affect its meaningfulness.
- Like the traditional style reports, the new database will often only be able to answer the types of questions that were thought of when designing the schema.
- Changes in the way data is organized in the originating databases will require changes to the aggregating database.

Multiple models, one database

A multi-model database can solve these problems by providing a single storage solution for all the different types of data an organization handles. A multi-model database supports multiple data models in their native form within a single, integrated back end, and uses data standards and query standards appropriate to each model. Queries are extended or combined to provide seamless queries across all the supported data models. Indexing, parsing, and processing standards appropriate to the data model are included in the core database product.

A multi-model database has relational storage, document storage, graph storage, and key-value storage together in one place. Data does not need to be transformed before it is loaded, and a relational schema does not need to be designed before data is brought in.

The multi-model database allows querying across data of different types, without losing the context and formatting that often gives meaning to individual pieces of information.

The major advantage to the multi-model approach is that it allows you to keep data in the form the data wants to be in, it minimizes or eliminates the need to transform data to fit new formats, and it allows you to consume data before knowing how it will be organized. As we already live in a multi-data model world it makes sense that a multi-model database system can bring that world view into a single application.

Chapter 5 – Data Modelling

Data modelling, a key component of the analytic process comprises many complex steps, which are getting increasingly difficult as new sources of data become available. One of the biggest problems businesses face is that to mine relevant insights from data, companies need to have a clear purpose for running analytics in the first place. Otherwise, useful information may be indistinguishable from vast tracts of irrelevant data. Traditionally, the typical approaches to analytics - those established before the rise of big data platforms and the growing mainstream adoption of technologies like AI, predictive analytics and geo-location intelligence - was accomplished through what was deemed to be passive analytics. Today, businesses are spoilt for choice with an assorted array of high-tech analytics technologies available to them but they often struggle to apply those advanced analytical techniques effectively – i.e. to align them with their business objectives.

Data modelling, therefore, should ultimately be an iterative process that requires collaboration across the business. For example, IT teams capturing the data; the data engineers model the data to create machine learning models; then the business users or subject matter experts validate the methodology and interpret the results.

When we discuss data models we are referring to the mapping of the relationships between data entities and attributes in a way that identifies and captures the business value of data. Data models therefore need to be flexible as an organization's circumstances, objectives and their data changes. Keeping data models up to date and aligned with the business plan and objectives helps ensure that business data remains valid and of value.

That concept applies whether an organisation is using traditional data modelling tools or new cloud platforms as it not always just about the technology. Indeed for successful data analysis we often need to have subject matter experts review the source data and interpret the results. This means that business users should be involved in the modelling process and importantly the model itself should be conveyed at the high-level in common business language that users can understand.

Data engineers will be responsible for constructing the data model but to prevent endless reiteration it is wise to seek stakeholder input and agreement on a reasonable scope. If possible try and start with a draft model and refine it based on business input. By adopting a consensus approach that combines top-down and bottom-up modelling work, will get you consensus more quickly.

Getting that all important buy-in from stakeholders is important in data modelling especially in areas whereby ad-hoc changes can be challenging such as having to restructure the schema of a relational database. Changes will always occur but the goal should be to minimise change by aligning the data models to the business objectives at an early stage.

Database Modelling

Having seen some of the other type of specialized database models available that have flexible or no schema it might seem strange that the most commonly deployed by far in business is still the relational database. The advantages that RDBM databases have over tradition file systems is quite clear and they are typically; speed, efficiency, and cost. In addition, they also provide for improvements in data quality over spreadsheets in their; completeness, validity, consistency, timeliness and accuracy. However, when we consider why relational databases are still used in operational systems, when compared to other types of database. Then we find that RDBM databases can also be optimized for very fast write functions for small portions of data making them extremely efficient for logging high volume transactions where write performance is critical and read less so. These database models are described as being Online Transactional Processing or OLTP databases.

OLTP (Online Transaction Processing)

An OLTP database is generally an SQL relational database manager (RDBM) such as Oracle or MySQL and it stores structured data in a relational 2-dimensional data structures called tables. Although most database systems use a form of SQL, most of them also have their own additional proprietary extensions that provide valuable product differentiation and as such are usually only available for use on their system. However, the standard SQL commands provide all the functionality required such as "Select", "Insert", "Update", "Delete", "Create", and "Drop" and these limited commands can be used to accomplish almost everything that one needs to do with a database. Such are the popularity of SQL databases they are almost always used in transactional operational database systems for SME, Enterprise, Commerce and Business applications such as CRM (Salesforce), ERP (SAP), Finance (Oracle) and HR (PeopleSoft) systems. In addition to providing the back-end storage for business applications there are also embedded and PC based version in retail POS systems and in industrial control systems. Therefore, SQL databases make up the majority of operational databases found in the business and in operational environments, which require an OLTP database.

What makes SQL databases so suitable for OLTP is that they are highly optimized for write processing of transactional data into their 2-dimentional table structures. Visualizing a SQL table is much like looking at a spreadsheet, which consist of Column, Rows, and data fields. The complexity comes with normalization where tables grow rapidly and the interconnections between them grow exponentially creating a complex lattice of many small tables sometimes numbering into the hundreds or thousands.

The databases we have described at a very high level so far are relational databases, which we would commonly see utilized in standard transaction based OLTP data bases. This model of databases are designed for inserting data efficiently by writing data one record at a time albeit extremely quickly. As their name suggests OLTP databases are online and constantly receiving transaction data such as sales records, log files or sensor status updates. However, as we know from everyday experience a database does not just store data it provides views and reports of the input data it holds in the tables. What is more the database can generate its own data through arithmetic techniques such as the SUM and AVG functions. Indeed in SQL databases this set of arithmetic functions termed the Aggregation Functions can generate new data about the stored data in the internal schema tables. By performing these aggregate functions on data gives SQL very powerful reporting and data aggregation and manipulation techniques. Therefore in most SME reporting is done on the OLTP data sources such as the Financial, ERP or CRM databases directly. But in larger organizations or where there is large data sets present, or heavy transactional use it is no longer either feasible or advisable to run SQL Queries on the OLTP data base as it is optimized to write transaction data and not to read and process vast amounts of data as output. Running SQL queries can have a serious negative impact on the OLTP performance and so another solution for reporting is required.

Traditionally, the solution to the burden of reporting and analytics was to pre-process reports and schedule them to run out-off working hours and that is still feasible today. However for many systems there is no quite periods as they operate 24/7 an example would be an ecommerce website. In this case the solution is to host another server that cloned the transactional database via either a cluster or by data replication on to another server. Using either of these options allowed reports to be run on a slave database thereby mitigating the detrimental effects of overloading the resources of the main transactional database.

Utilizing clusters or through data replication techniques provides another benefit in that it facilitates a live backup of the data. This also mitigates the risk in the case of a primary database crash. Without a clone or online data replication many of the transaction replays would be required to restore a single transactional data base server and consolidate its database. (The issue being if you run an incremental back-up even once an hour, there is a possibility of the backup being up to one hour out of date and the Data Base Administrator would need to manually replay all the transactions missed but logged during that period).

Having dual servers in a cluster or in an online replication configuration is feasible and can even be used on different transactional servers. For example, a slave CRM reporting server can be the slave ERP Reporting server and vice versa and this reduces both the capital and operational overheads. All that is needed then is for the designated slave reporting server to run an instance of the RDBM for each application and hold a copy of the schema for each database. This may be sneered at as just a poor man's data warehouse, but it is perfectly feasible for an SME with limited resources and low transaction rates.

There are some issues with the shared reporting server model as although it seems a good solution for the SME with light workloads across several applications, issues do arise. Online data replication works really well and under light load is both quick and reliable. However the initial issue was that running intensive reports or data analysis on an operational application server may have been detrimental to the application's performance and that was quite true. The issue now was how would running those same reports, but this time for all the applications on just one server, affect the operation of the online replication.

The only other option is to double up each transactional operational server with a slave reporting server and that is not financially feasible for a lot of SMEs, so that wasn't ideal either.

There had to be another solution which would lower both the CapEx and OpEx overheads and provide a reporting and analysis platform that could deal with high transaction workloads without the risk of overloading the transactional servers. Again depending on the workloads two or three instances could be run without any issues but conflict may arise due to the ambiguous nature of the server – is it a reporting server or a backup server?

What was needed to solve these issues was a database architecture that could alleviate some of the inefficiencies of read operation performed on a write optimized platform. The solution was to think out of the box and pivot the tables, so that rows became columns.

Column-Oriented Databases

Increasingly businesses are realizing a one size fits all model isn't working for databases. It seems we can have issues with reporting and analysis performance even on a dedicated reporting server albeit one performing replication and reporting services for several disparate applications. The issue appears to be down simply to the way RDBM servers operate. Interestingly, it didn't need to be this way; by simply pivoting the tables meant that tremendous improvements in performance could be leveraged. For example, when you want to analyse large amounts of data, with analytical queries that span 1000's of rows, column-oriented databases can provide a 100x speedup. Particularly for time-series data, which is transactional data, column-oriented databases have been successfully used to deliver very high performance, fast storage, and quick analysis.

What is a column-oriented database?

Column Orientated Database		
Date	Price	Size
2019-10-02	10.34	10
2019-10-03	11.54	20
2019-10-04	17.68	30
2019-10-05	10.34	40
...		
2019-10-31	15.24	100

A column-oriented database stores each column continuously i.e. on disk or in-memory each column on the left will be stored in sequential blocks.

For analytical queries that perform aggregate operations over a small number of columns retrieving data in this format is extremely fast. This is because of the way that PC computer BIOS and hard disk drive storage is optimized for block access. Simplistically, designers when they were deliberating the read/write operations of hard-disk access on PCs had some performance issues due to the issues of precision. So they decided that once a disk-drive's head was roughly positioned over the track it was to read data from it was easier and quicker to just hoover up all the data as a large block and sort out what was required in memory. This was both simple and brilliant. Therefore, if we take advantage of this and the fact that column data is very often stored beside each other on the hard drive we can exploit the physics of what is termed the locality of reference. On hard disk drives this is particularly important due to their relatively sluggish performance characteristics, due to the mechanical constrains of physically moving the read/write head assembly. Hence, column based databases running on hard disk drives provide optimal performance due to the sequential disk-access limiting the head movement.

Row Orientated Database

Date	Price	Size
2019-10-02	10.34	10
2019-10-03	11.54	20
2019-10-04	17.68	30
2019-10-05	10.34	40
...		
2019-10-31	15.24	100

Table of Data

Date	Price	Size
2019-10-02	10.34	10
2019-10-03	11.54	20
2019-10-04	17.68	30
2019-10-05	10.34	40
...		
2019-10-31	15.24	100

Column Orientated Database

Date	Price	Size
2019-10-02	10.34	10
2019-10-03	11.54	20
2019-10-04	17.68	30
2019-10-05	10.34	40
...		
2019-10-31	15.24	100

To better illustrate the benefit of columns versus rows let us consider the image depicting the Row Orientated Database. The areas that need to be read when performing a query like "average price" for all dates in row-oriented databases would require that large areas of the disk be accessed as we will have to read every single row in order to extract just one field from each – the price and discard all the other data we collect via a read operation. This is very inefficient and consequently it is very slow in large databases with perhaps 10s of thousands of rows.

However, in a column-oriented database the prices are stored as one column and in a sequential region therefore the drive read operation needs only collect data from a single small region. As a result we discover that when we use column-oriented databases for aggregate functions (sum, average, min, max, etc.) within queries they are extremely fast and this is tremendous for reporting and analysis, which rely heavily on these aggregate functions. This of course may well beg the question, why are most databases row-oriented? The answer to that question is due to ease of editing and scaling the schema. If we want to add one row somewhere in the middle of our data for 2011-02-26, on the row oriented database this is not an issue. With a column oriented data base on the other hand we will have to move almost all the data. Fortunately, since we mostly deal with time series new data this requires only appends to the end of the table so is not an issue.

Column-Oriented Vs. Row Oriented Model

Operation	Column-Oriented	Row-Oriented
Aggregate Calculation of Single	Fast	Slow

Column		
e.g. 'avg.' (price)		

Compression	Higher- stores similar data together	-

Retrieval of a few columns from a table with many columns	Faster	Slower

Insertion/Updating of single new record	Slow	Fast

Retrieval of a single record	Slow	Fast

As can be seen from the table Column-based databases are fast and agile when reading data from the database because much of the similar data in grouped together and can therefore be swept up in one disk read operation. Where column-based databases excel is exactly where reporting and analysis functions place the most stress on a database making them a great fit for these use cases.

In-memory database solutions

In-memory databases put the working set of data into system memory, either completely, in the case of solutions such as SAP Hana, or partially, based on the identification of tables that will benefit most from DRAM speed.

There is an obvious performance benefit in the reduced latency which in-memory database solutions bring, even over heavily cached systems as these can only optimise database read requests.

The performance benefits that in-memory databases bring are more subtle than that just read/write performance uplifts. This is because when all the data is kept in memory, the issues that naturally arise from the use of traditional spinning disks disappear. For example, in-memory databases provide an opportunity to optimise the way data is managed compared to traditional databases on disk-based media.

What this means in terms of performance is that, for example, there is no need to maintain additional cache copies of data and manage the synchronisation between them. In addition, the data can also be compressed and decompressed in memory more easily, resulting in the opportunity to deliver both high security performance and space savings over the equivalent disk copy.

Sometimes, we see an attempt to compromise and a data base administrator may create a RAM disk in memory and move the database to this virtual volume in a bid to get many of the benefits of in-memory databases but without the cost overhead.

This can be done, but the performance benefits do not really manifest themselves due to the internal algorithms of the database are still managing the data as if it were on disk —the virtual disk drive is transparent to the algorithms as they should be. Therefore the underpinning database management algorithms still perform tasks such as pre-fetching, caching and lazy writes and that doesn't result in any optimal gains in terms of performance and sometimes they may even use more processor time. Instead, in-memory database solutions have logic specifically adapted to work with data in DRAM.

The biggest problem with in-memory databases is that system memory is volatile, which means in-memory databases only conform to three out of four of the ACID model of database characteristics - atomic, consistent, isolated and durable. Of these, durability cannot directly be served by in-memory database solutions, because data is lost when power is removed from the server.

Overcoming the shortcomings of volatile memory

But there are solutions to the problem. These include keeping additional copies of data in clustered and scale-out databases that allow systems to keep running by replicating updates to one or more standby systems. Some database systems also perform periodic commits-to-disk to maintain state to a point from which recovery can be performed in the case of a server crash. Here there is a trade-off between the time between commits (and subsequent recovery) and the overhead of the commit process on performance.

In-memory database technology has largely been avoided for general OLTP applications due to the lack of durability and instead targeted at specific data types or analytics requirements (including batch analysis and reporting) where re-running transactions can easily be achieved. Having said that, in-memory databases are set to move into the OLTP world as the acceptance and adoption of the technology continues. Indeed a major foothold in the market has been already gained with the release of Microsoft SQL Server 2014, which offered out-of-the-box in-memory capability. SQL Server makes use of "memory optimised tables", which allow portions of a database to be placed into system memory thereby accelerating the performance of analytical calculations.

Storage for in-memory databases

Although the operation of in-memory databases occurs in system memory, there is a need for permanent storage media. There are three main in-memory database storage requirements: first, to provide permanent media to store committed transactions, thereby maintaining durability and secondly, to provide a mechanism for recovery purposes if a database does need to be reloaded into memory, and; thirdly to provide permanent storage to hold a copy or backup of the database in its entirety.

With regard to the requirement to reload databases back into memory, then of all the latest disk drive technology flash is possibly the most beneficial. The issue may come down to cost, and with flash being significantly more expensive than hard disks per gigabyte and, in the case of in-memory database use, the efficiency and necessity of such performance will come into question as the data will be accessed very infrequently. But there is no doubt that reading an entire database into memory from flash will always be much faster than from spinning disk and it is still cheaper than Solid State Drives. Therefore you might want to undertake a cost/benefit risk audit to decide on that all important price/performance balance. However, there are ways around the storage issues such as using clustered or replicated environments, but that will still require significant investment so a shared flash-based storage solution may still be best.

Chapter 6 – Alternative OLAP Data Schemas

Online Analytic Processors (OLAP)

As we have examined in the previous chapters, OLTP database systems typically are designed around the RDBM model which can be readily optimised for efficient transaction handling. We also learned that these types of database were not ideal for reporting and analysis and often the solution was to offload the burden onto another reporting server which held a clone of the operational data. This slave reporting system architecture works well on a one to one basis and is the foundation of the concept of the Data Warehouse.

A data warehouse (DWH) is a system used as a central repository in which to collect data from one or more disparate operational systems in order to collate, transform and store information for use in data analysis and reporting. Data marts are specialized areas of a data warehouses and they can be internal or external to the physical warehouse and they are used to store information needed by a single department or even by an individual power user.

Regardless of the warehouse/mart model deployed there still is the non-trivial problem of moving data from heterogeneous operational systems and physically storing it within a common schema within the central warehouse. In order to accomplish this task requires that data be extracted from each operational systems database and then transformed in order to fit the new schema of the central repository, as this is likely to require table names, columns and data types to be translated or changed to suit before it can be successfully loaded. This ETL process is used to add "new" data to the warehouse system on a regular basis. ETL is an acronym for Extract, Transform and Load and that describes perfectly its functional purpose. As the name hints, we'll extract data from one or more operational databases, transform it to fit our warehouse structure, and load the data into the DWH.

Remember when we spoke about the idea of having the schema fit the data rather that than have our data fit the schema. Well this is where we get the chance as when creating the warehouse we need to consider whether to leave the schema in a 3NR (normalised relational format) schema (lots and lots of tables) or to change the schema to a much simpler structure called a Star schema which is not only simpler, but also not normalised. The downside is it could possibly have some data redundancy and consistency issues. However if we consider that the performance of the technologies available to us today such as very high capacity high performance disk drives, Solid State Drives and In-memory optimised Databases then we might be willing to accept that risk. Therefore, if we consider an alternative schema to get away from the constraints and complexity of the 3NF Relational schema there are several options available to us. Designing the warehouse data schema is described as dimensioning the warehouse or dimension modelling. Dimensional modelling, which is a fundamental and significant part of data warehouse design, results in the creation of the data schema. It is describes as being dimensional modelling because there are two types of tables involved:

- Dimension tables are used to describe the data we want to store. For example: a retailer might want to store the date, store, and employee involved in a specific purchase.
- Fact tables contain the data we want to include in reports, aggregated based on values within the related dimension tables. A fact table has only columns that store values and foreign keys referencing the dimension tables. Combining all the foreign keys forms the primary key of the fact table. For instance, a fact table could store a number of contacts and the number of sales resulting from these contacts.

With this info in place, we can now dig into the star schema data model.

The Star Schema

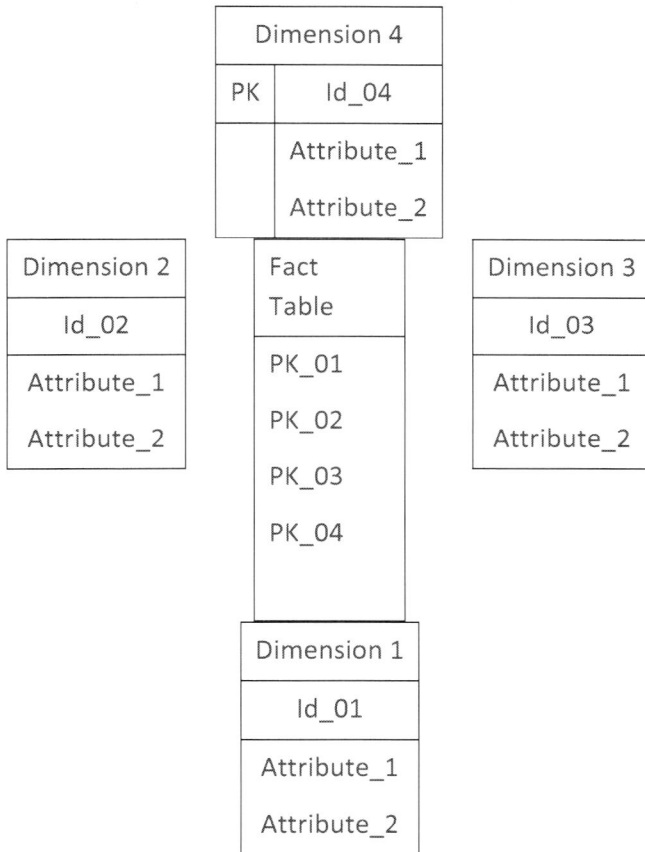

Dimension 4	
PK	Id_04
	Attribute_1
	Attribute_2

Dimension 2
Id_02
Attribute_1
Attribute_2

Fact Table
PK_01
PK_02
PK_03
PK_04

Dimension 3
Id_03
Attribute_1
Attribute_2

Dimension 1
Id_01
Attribute_1
Attribute_2

What is star schema? The star schema architecture is the simplest data warehouse schema. It is called a star schema because the diagram resembles a star, with points radiating from a centre table, which is called the Fact table and the tables at the points of the star are the dimension tables. Usually the fact tables in a star schema are in third normal form (3NF) whereas dimensional tables are de-normalized. The fact that the star schema is the simplest architecture is probably why it is most commonly used nowadays and is recommended by most system integrators and vendors.

Cubes and Multidimensional models

Database systems can be roughly divided into two categories: operational and reporting systems. Operational systems are often called Online Transaction Processing (OLTP) systems. In contrast, reporting and analytical systems are referred to as Online Analytical Processing (OLAP). In almost all cases the OLTP systems support business processes are they are optimised for high consistency and high volume transactions. They are designed to work with "live" operational data, are highly normalized, and manage high volumes and intensity of small write style transactions and in addition they can respond very quickly to user actions. On the other hand, the primary purpose of the OLAP systems is reporting and to a lesser degree analytics. However, OLAP systems are required to perform predominantly read type processes and these are slow on an OLTP system. Consequently, OLAP systems are used to upload or clone and then summarize data, which is usually placed in a denormalized data warehousing structure like the star schema. As we have seen previously denormalization is having redundant data records within tables for the sake of better performance but at the cost of storage and write consistency.

An OLAP cube is a data structure that overcomes the limitations of relational databases by providing rapid analysis of data. Cubes can display and sum large amounts of data while also providing users with searchable access to any data points. This way, the data can be rolled up, sliced, and diced as needed to handle the widest variety of questions that are relevant to a user's area of interest.

As a result an OLAP system often uses a different database model for dimensioning, called a multi-dimension model and these data structures are often represented as cubes. The difference is that the traditional 2-Dimensioned table is replaced by a multi-dimensional cube.

The first question that may arise is what is a multi-dimensional cube? The simplest high-level answer is that a cube is a multidimensional model, and these are constructed using data according to user preferences. This means that multiple tables of interest can be held within the same multi-dimension structure but they are still defined by dimensions and facts, which makes pre-processing easy and queries very efficient. For example, in disciplines such as finance and accounting where reports and analysis tend to follow a classic structure i.e. the information required rarely deviate out with the common range of financial standard reports. This makes it feasible to think ahead and if the cubes are preconfigured by collating all the relevant data tables together it is then relatively easy to pre-process the queries allowing for almost instantaneous retrieval of reports. As a result, multidimensional cubes are optimal where user query reports are standard and predictable as they can be pre-processed. Consequently cubes and multidimensional databases are most commonly used in data warehouses and OLAP systems optimised for reporting and analysis.

To understand cubes, how they operate and how we can configure or query them we need to understand how they came about. Rather strangely they came into being as a result of the need for simplicity. Indeed the issue that cubes resolve - or at least strive to - is that the requirement for technical competency in order to make even a simple database query is not ideal. The relational model for all its worth is rather a poor solution and for the majority of all users within an organization it is a drawback, so the goal should be towards ease of use. The multi-dimensional model, the cube, is important because it enforces simplicity. And, it is that simplicity which allows users to understand the database and for the database system to efficiently navigate and handle the data it contains.

The problem has been that traditionally in relational database analysis there is one basic storage structure, a flat table. This object, the table, takes on many different roles depending on how it relates, or joins, to other tables. Even in a much simplified structure such as a star schema, where fact tables and dimension tables describe the relationship between the various tables within the schema, it can still be confusing.

In multi-dimensional analysis the same basic structures also exist and the fact table is usually the main driver within the query. Indeed, the fact table is referred to as a cube, and the columns within the table are referred to as measures. Each cube has additional structures over and beyond a simple table. The cube has edges, which are referred to as dimensions. Each dimension is a grouping of common or related columns from one or more tables into a single entity. For example a Product dimension could be based on a single or collection of tables containing columns that refer to categories, sub-categories, and products.

All these structures (cubes, dimensions, hierarchies, levels and measures) interact with each other to provide an extremely powerful reporting environment. Each object adds new levels of interactivity when it is fully exploited. (We will discuss cubes in detail later).

Users want to interact with their data using business terms and objects without having to comprehend the underlying storage model. The abstraction of the physical storage model from the logical presentation model is the key to the success of multi-dimensional models.

The benefits on multi-dimensioning are that cubes enable interactive analysis of large quantities of data by rapidly processing the data within the database and providing "just in time" information for effective decision making.

Software vendors or information technology (IT) developers with a working knowledge of OLAP cubes can create management packs to define their own extensible and customizable OLAP cubes.

As we have seen over the course of the chapter there are several alternative schemas we can use for OLAP type reporting and analysis database design. What has become clear though is that for even the SME to collect, process and report on operational data when it is sourced from heterogeneous sources is going to be a serious issue without some central repository for reporting and analysis.

Now that we have had a brief high-level overview of the major architectural design patterns and concepts regarding databases, data warehouses and data marts we can move on to consider the design of a data warehousing model which will provide for an offline solution where reporting, standard and ad hoc queries, analysis and data manipulation or transformation can be performed without any adverse effect on the operations of the real time transactional systems.

Overview of ETL in Data Warehouses

The challenge in data warehouse environments is to integrate, rearrange and consolidate large volumes of data over many systems, thereby providing a new unified information base for business intelligence.

The process of extracting data from source systems and bringing it into the data warehouse is commonly called **ETL,** which stands for extraction, transformation, and loading. Note that ETL refers to a broad process, and not three well-defined steps. The acronym ETL is perhaps too simplistic, because it omits the transportation phase and implies that each of the other phases of the process is distinct. Nevertheless, the entire process is known as ETL.

ETL Basics in Data Engineering

What happens during the ETL process? The following tasks are the main actions in the process:

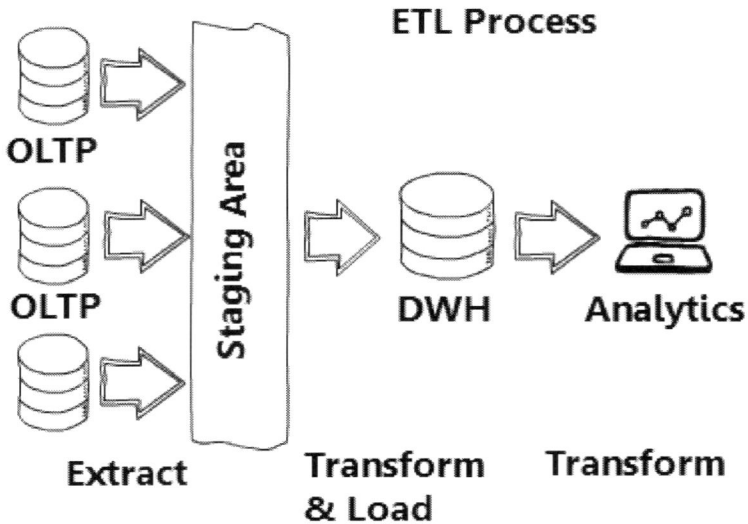

- **Extract**: this is the step where sensors wait for upstream data sources to land (e.g. an upstream source could be machine or user-generated logs, relational database copy, external dataset, etc.). Once available, the process triggers the transport of the data from their source locations for transformation.
- **Transform**: This is the core process of any ETL job, where the appropriate business logic is applied and actions such as filtering, grouping, and aggregation are performed in order to translate the source data format into analysis-compatible datasets. This step requires a great deal of business understanding and domain knowledge.
- **Load**: Finally, we load the transformed data in its new format and transport it to a final destination. Often, this dataset can be either consumed directly by end-users or it can be treated as yet another upstream dependency to another ETL job, forming the so-called data lineage.

During extraction, the desired data is identified and extracted from many different sources, including database systems and applications. Very often, it is not possible to identify the specific subset of interest therefore more data than necessary has to be extracted, so the identification of the relevant data will be done at a later point in time. Depending on the source system's capabilities (for example, operating system resources), some transformations may take place during this extraction process. The size of the extracted data varies from hundreds of kilobytes up to gigabytes, depending on the source system and the business situation. The same is true for the time delta between two (logically) identical extractions: the time span may vary between days/hours and minutes to near real-time. Web server log files, for example, can easily grow to hundreds of megabytes in a very short period.

However, when dealing with very large datasets the ETL system is not always optimum. The reason being is that the transform step can cause delays and even affect the source systems performance. Hence, there is an alternative called ELT.

ELT (Extract, Load & Transform)

When dealing with data pipelines such as in Big Data there needs to be a way to optimise the extraction and loading steps and then performing the transformation. Hence, the ELT is the preferable method in Big Data and Hadoop environments.

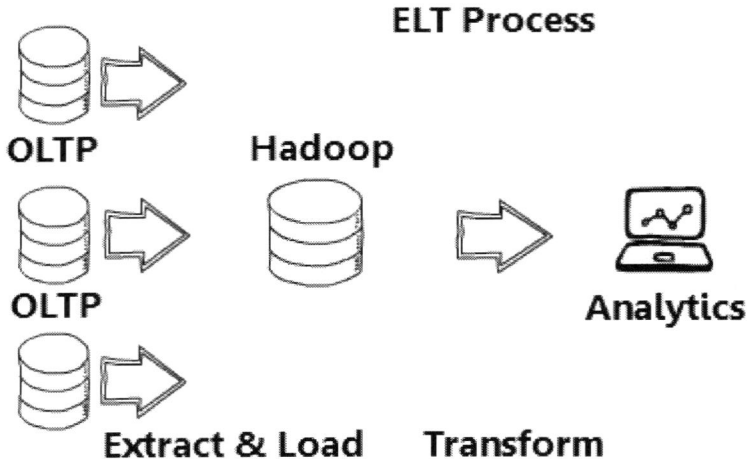

ELT Process

OLTP · Hadoop · OLTP · Analytics · Extract & Load · Transform

OLTP vs. OLAP

OLTP is said to be more of an online transactional system or data storage system, where the user does lots of online transactions using the data store. It is also said to have more ad-hoc reads/writes happening on a real-time basis. OLAP is more of an offline data store. It is accessed a number of times in offline fashion. For example, Bulk log files are read and then written back to data files. Some of the common areas where OLAP is used are Log Jobs, Data mining Jobs, etc. Cassandra is said to be more of OLTP, as it is real-time, whereas Hadoop is more of OLAP since it is used for analytics and bulk writes.

Parameters	ETL	ELT
Use-case	Small amounts of data	High amounts of data

Transformation	Occurs in the staging area	Performed in the target
Speed	Slow as all data is transformed during staging	Fast as data is not transformed during loading
Supports	Relational data	Unstructured data
DWH support	Used in on-premises DWH	Used in cloud DWH
Complexity	High as data needs to be identified beforehand	High as data needs to be identified later at processing
Cost	High for SMBs	Low if using SaaS

ELT should be used, instead of ETL, in these various cases:
- There are big volumes of data
- The source database and the target database are the same
- The database engine is well adapted for that kind of processing, such as a parallel data warehouse (PWH), which is great at loading massive amounts of data very quickly

So in short, when using ETL the transformations are processed by the ETL tools, while in ELT the transformations are processed by the target data source.

ELT has the benefit of minimizing the processing on the source since no transforming is being done, which can be extremely important if the source is a production system where you could be impacting the user experience as opposed to a copy of the source (via replication, database snapshot, etc.). The negative of this approach is it may take longer to get the data into the data warehouse as with the staging tables you have an extra step in the process, and you will need more disk space for the staging tables.

Chapter 8–Advanced Data Analysis & Business Intelligence

Forrester Research Definition: "Business Intelligence is a set of methodologies, processes, architectures, and technologies that transform raw data into meaningful and useful information used to enable more effective strategic, tactical, and operational insights and decision-making."

Business intelligence (BI) is the discipline of creating value for an organization based on facts that we can derive from data. Of course BI has been around for a long time and executives may be quite ambivalent as to its worth as for them gut feelings and hard-nosed business experience trumps most technology predictions. In some cases, executives will openly embrace BI as it provides them with the backup and support for their hypothesis and so long as the results continue to be supportive all is well.

BI was coined by Gartner (Dresner, 1989) as an umbrella term to describe the set of concepts and methods used to improve business decision-making by using fact-based support systems. As a brief step through BI's long history it was around in the 1980's as Executive Information Systems (EIS), in the 1990's, OLAP, followed by scorecards, dashboards, KPIs (key performance indicators), and real time alerts through business activity monitoring. In 2000, BI manifested itself once again through the data mining of Data Warehouses, and since 2010 it has evolved into Big Data, using advanced analytics, AI algorithms and Machine Learning. BI therefore has a long resume with several aliases and has been at the core of business management for decades.

However, no matter how long BI has been around its purpose has remained the same in so much as Business intelligence is not about tools and technologies; rather it is strategies of combining data from various sources with methodologies that derives value in the form of information and business insights. The problem is though that many of the data sources, which we now need to access, have changed to being digital channels. These sources could be web based social media sites, forums or IoT sensor information. Also, these new channels often produce unstructured data such as website click-data, email, text from social media comments, messenger text, and even photographs and video, which present the analysts with issues.

BI is about analysing an organization's performance using data with the purpose to improve its revenue, profits and competitiveness. BI uses a combination of historical information about past transactions or events and reference data about, for example, customers or products, to enable a wide variety of analyses and decision support techniques.

Thus, BI is something organizations, even SMEs, have always been involved with on some strategic level using a combination of historical data, market experience and knowledge and gut instinct. But SME organizations today are doing things a bit more scientifically – or rather that's what they think – by collecting ever increasing volumes of data for the vague purpose of analytics. However, collecting data should have a purpose, an end product in mind and not just be an arbitrary pastime. If not we end up with the collection of data being the project instead of a task within a project. What's more we will end up with a situation where it is no longer possible to analyse such quantities of raw data –even if we could find a purpose - without specialized tools and methods. Therefore it is essential to always keep the focus on the purpose and SMEs especially should have a clear business case for performing business intelligence beyond standard reporting and trend analysis.

The reason for this is not only can the complexity and hence the expenses escalate rapidly once we start to delve into higher levels of data analytics but so does the understandability, and importantly the capability to interpret the results. Consequently, we must never lose track of the purpose of the BI analytics and always ensure that the goals mirror or are tightly aligned with the business objectives so as to justify their existence as well as to increase the potential of ROI (Return on Investment).

The typical BI or DA output that comes from a general analytical project is best described as being represented through:

• Reports: Standard, preformatted templates for 'what happened' style of analysis.
• User-defined analyses: This is a self-service form of limited ad-hoc query but with limited input criteria for example the user can select input

criteria from a "pick-lists" to filter (select) the information they wish to analyse, such as sales for a selected product, region, during a selected month or quarter.

• Ad hoc analyses: This form requires that power users create their own queries to extract self-selected pre-staged information and then use the information to perform a user enabled analysis. This is the most difficult to implement as it requires users who are knowledgeable in both business and database technology as well as an intuitive database schema or pre-processed OLAP cubes.

• Scorecards and dashboards: These predefined visual interactive reports provide up to date business performance metrics regarding key performance indicators. The choice of variables to be displayed can be selected and determined as to whether the scorecard/Dashboard is for strategic, tactical or operational purpose. This type of continuous visual presentation especially if used in large TV screen wallboards is highly effective ways to disseminate important KPI to the organization.

• Multidimensional analysis: Provides the flexible tool-based user-defined analysis of business performance and the underlying drivers or root causes of that performance.

• Alerts & Notifications: Predefined analyses of key business performance variables, comparison to a performance standard or range, and communication to designated business people when performance is outside the predefined performance standard or range.

• Advanced analytics: This is best described as being the application of statistical and/or Operational knowledge and research to historical business information. The idea is to apply knowledge or a hypothesis to large scale historical data in such a way as to characterize a relevant aspect of business performance, thereby proving or disproving the theory.

• Predictive analytics: This is one of the easier business cases to sell as it can have a real impact on operational efficiency and therefore a short or valuable ROI. The principle is to monitor the application of long-established statistical and/or operations data in order to predict an event. In industry predictive analysis is heavily used in predicting maintenance on machinery.

Research methods to historical business information to predict, model, or simulate future business and/or economic performance and potentially prescribe a favoured course of action for the future.

From the preceding list of different approaches to BI we can see that it is primarily about the analysis of data but for diverse purposes. The operational role in a BI strategy is traditionally to collect, monitor/process and store historical operational data and then display it for the subject matter experts in a format they can make use of to make important inferences. Historical reporting by its nature makes the pivoting of any combination of dimensions or attributes within a report or table possible. This is done by "slicing and dicing" the dimensions in the tables or report in order to focus only on the relevant data. An important part of Data Analytics is in presenting data in a format that the experts can use, which requires presenting results in varying levels of granularity and aggregation. Today a plethora of On Line Analytic Processing (OLAP) type data structures provide the ability to drill in, around and through data structures such as multidimensional cubes in order to make sense of the data presented.

While OLAP presents a multi-dimensional highly structured interface to the data the object still remains to dig out interesting details of value. In other words, the technology is less important than the ability to synthesize the data into meaningful bits of information. What is more, the driver for change often comes from the executives' desire to move away from static dashboards and to provide a method to query and analyse the data themselves. Hence, a self-service method of data query has evolved and it comes in a more natural human based language such as in the way we interact with Siri, Alexa and Google personal assistants in the home with "Show me what's wrong" or "Highlight the facts for me," and this was the impetus behind the interactive dashboard and scorecards in today's executive toolkit.

The limitations are that reporting on the past can only show what has happened, and provide some predictions through trend analysis but it cannot predict the future. For that we must combine historical information with real-time data and then using layered predictive analytics so that we can glean the probability or the likelihood of an event happening and we need that in order to have true foreknowledge. This type of analytics comes through data mining, forecasting and this is where other predictive analytics especially those advanced ML algorithms play an important role.

Consequently, the types of data analytics we are now interested in have expanded to include:

- *Prescriptive analytics* is really valuable, but largely not used. According to Gartner, 13 percent of organizations are using predictive but only 3 percent are using prescriptive analytics. Where big data analytics in general sheds light on a subject, prescriptive analytics provides a focus to answer specific questions. For example, in the Insurance industry, it is possible to manage the customer base by using prescriptive analytics to measure the number of drivers who are past claimants, then to add filters for factors like gender, age and even post code to determine the price of a policy, thereby benefiting careful drivers over the unlucky ones that have failed to avoid accidents. However this is categorizing individuals and also encouraging stereotyping. The same prescriptive model is applied in almost all industry to identify desirable or problematic social groups.

- *Predictive analytics* uses big data to identify past patterns to predict the future. For example, companies may well use predictive analytics in generating sales lead scoring. Many SME take this approach as predictive analytics performed over the entire sales process such as when analysing lead source, number of communications, types of communications, social media channels, documents, CRM data, etc. can determine the most valuable low cost customers.

- *Diagnostic analytics* are typically used for as the name suggests discovering why something happened. For example, for a social media marketing campaign, you can use descriptive analytics to assess the number of product reviews, followers, page views, etc. This is because thousands of online mentions can be distilled into a single dashboard that visualizes what marketing techniques work and what didn't.
- *Descriptive analytics* or data mining are often considered to be at the bottom of the big data value chain, but they can still be valuable for uncovering patterns that offer insight. A simple example of descriptive analytics would be assessing credit risk; using past financial performance to predict a customer's likely financial performance. Descriptive analytics can be useful in the sales cycle, for example, to categorize customers by their likely product preferences and sales history.

Today's Business Intelligence tools allow business users to interrogate huge amounts of data in a matter of seconds. That alone is not a result in itself or just down to technology as fast response times are not simply the result of modern hardware and software often the way the data is framed or presented has a greater overall effect on performance. This of course is more the result of operational knowledge and detailed business process planning and they in turn are the product of subject matter expertise.

Chapter 9 - Introduction to Data Mining Algorithms

This section will provide a high-level overview of some of the most common data mining algorithms in use today. Traditionally there were the classical statistical techniques based upon classification and regression but lately newer technologies have become popular so it is fair to say there are two main groups of algorithms:

- Classical Techniques: Statistics, Nearest Neighbour and Clustering
- Next Generation Techniques: Decision Trees, Bayesian Networks and Association Rules

Despite the large number of specific data mining algorithms and patterns developed over the years, there are only a handful of fundamentally different types of tasks these algorithms address.

As a result the six broad classes of data mining algorithms listed above cover most use cases and one of the algorithms from this group of six is almost always used in real world deployments of data mining systems.

An interesting aspect of Data Analytics and data mining is that just about every data-driven business decision-making problem is likely to be unique in so much as it will comprise its own combination of goals, constraints, and desired outcomes. Fortunately they will also be very similar in most of their business goals and attributes so there are sets of common processes that underlie the analytical tasks.

Therefore it is a required skill for data engineer's to recognise and categorise the business problem, then to decompose it into subtasks. It might turn out that some of these subtasks are unique to the particular business problem, but more often than not other sub-tasks are common data mining tasks that have been solved and documented. These common tasks and their solutions are now incorporated into a body of knowledge or framework for decomposing common data mining tasks. Hence, having knowledge of these frameworks and their ability to decompose a data-analytics problem into pieces such that each piece matches a known task is invaluable. After all having the ability to recognize familiar problems and their solutions for which tools, libraries and procedures are available avoids wasting time and resources reinventing the wheel.

Statistical Techniques

The use of Statistical techniques go back hundreds of years but are still relevant as they are data centric and are especially useful in discovering patterns and building predictive models. Indeed there is little practical difference between a statistical technique and a data mining technique, the label has changed more to accommodate the scale of the data analysed and the variety of the source data.

Knowing statistics will help the average business person make better decisions by allowing them to figure out risk and uncertainty when all the facts either aren't known or can't be collected indeed it might be the one thing that defines the gut feeling manager. The better the understanding of statistics, even if it is not recognised as such, the better the decision that can be made. For example, it could be the ancient Egyptians and Greeks knew about probability and statistics long before the field was officially recognized.

Today some of the techniques used in data mining such as CHAID and CART really grew out of the statistical profession more than anywhere else, and the concepts of probability, independence and causality and overfitting are the foundation on which both data mining and statistics are built.

Today people have to deal with terabytes of diverse types of data and they have to make sense of it and glean the important patterns. Statistics can help greatly in this process by helping to answer several important questions about raw data:

- What patterns are in the database?
- What is the probability that an event will occur?
- Which patterns are significant?

- What is a summary of the data that describes what is contained in the database?

The last point is interesting because statistics is concerned with summarizing data, and this has to do with counting. Therefore, statistics can present a high level view of a database that provides some useful information without requiring every record to be understood in detail. Summarization is used in the reporting of important information from which people may be able to make useful decisions such as in strategic or tactical reports.

By presenting summaries of the data in graphical format we can visualise all of the data in the database for a particular predictor or data column. However the important part is that we can also deduce the average, the maximum and minimum. These values are called summary statistics. Some of the most frequently used summary statistics include:

- Max - the maximum value for a given predictor.
- Min - the minimum value for a given predictor.
- Mean - the average value for a given predictor.
- Median - the value for a given predictor that divides the database as nearly as possible into two databases of equal numbers of records.
- Mode - the most common value for the predictor.
- Variance - the measure of how distant the values are from the average value.

Many data distributions are well described by just two numbers, the mean and the variance. The variance uses the square of the distance rather than the actual distance from the mean and the average is taken by dividing the squared sum by one less than the total number of records. In terms of prediction a user could make some guess at the value of a predictor without knowing anything else just by knowing the mean and also gain some basic sense of how variable the guess might be based on the variance. This is because the variance measures the average distance of each predictor value from the mean value over all the records in the database. Therefore, if the variance is high it implies that the values do not have a distinct pattern however if the variance is low most of the data values are fairly close to the mean making predictions more likely. Prediction is a commonly used tool in statistics and is synonymous with regression of some form. There are a variety of different types of regression in statistics but the simplest form of regression is simple linear regression that just contains one predictor and a prediction. The relationship between the two can be mapped on a two dimensional space and the records plotted for the prediction values along the Y axis and the predictor values along the X axis.

The simple linear regression model then could be viewed as the line that minimized the error rate between the actual prediction value and the point on the line (the prediction from the model). Of the many possible lines that could be drawn through the data the one that minimizes the distance between the line and the data points is the one that is chosen for the predictive model.

The actual equation would look something like: Prediction = a + b * Predictor. Which is just the equation for a line Y = a + bx. As an example, for a bank the predicted average consumer bank balance might equal $1,000 + 0.01 * customer's annual income. The trick, as always with predictive modelling, is to find the model that best minimizes the error. The most common way to calculate the error is the square of the difference between the predicted value and the actual value. The values of variables 'a and b' in the regression equation that minimize this error can be calculated directly from the data relatively quickly.

However, regression can become more complicated than the simple linear regression we've introduced so far. For example, when trying to predict a customer response that is just 'yes' or 'no' (e.g. they bought the product or they didn't) the standard form of a line doesn't work. Typically in these situations a transformation of the prediction values is made in order to provide a better predictive model. This type of regression is called logistic regression and because so many business problems are response problems, logistic regression is one of the most widely used statistical techniques for creating predictive models.

Nearest Neighbour

Clustering and the Nearest Neighbour prediction technique are among the oldest techniques used in data mining. Most people have an intuition that they understand what clustering is - namely that like records are grouped or clustered together. Nearest neighbour is a prediction technique that is quite similar to clustering - its essence is that in order to predict what a prediction value is in one record look for records with similar predictor values in the historical database and use the prediction value from the record that it "nearest" to the unclassified record.

The nearest neighbour prediction algorithm simply stated is:

Objects that are "near" to each other will have similar prediction values as well. Thus if you know the prediction value of one of the objects you can predict it for its nearest neighbours.

One of the classical places that nearest neighbour have been used for prediction has been in text retrieval. The nearest neighbour technique is used to find other documents that share important characteristics with those documents that have been marked as interesting.

Unfortunately, just relying on the sole nearest neighbour to the unclassified record can be unreliable, as that may be an outlier that is unrepresentative, so one of the improvements that are usually made to the basic nearest neighbour algorithm is to take a vote from the "K" nearest neighbours.

In cases like these a vote of the 9 or 15 nearest neighbours would provide a better prediction accuracy for the system than would just the single nearest neighbour. The voting mechanism is accomplished by simply taking the majority of predictions from the K nearest neighbours if the prediction column is a binary or categorical or taking the average value of the prediction column from the K nearest neighbours. So basically you are taking the average predication from the K nearest neighbours in order to improve the reliability of the predication.

Another important aspect of any system that is used to make predictions is that the user be provided with, not only the prediction, but also some sense of the confidence in that prediction (e.g. the prediction is defaulter with the chance of being correct 60% of the time). The nearest neighbour algorithm provides this confidence information in a number of ways:

The distance to the nearest neighbour provides a level of confidence. For example, if the neighbour is very close or an exact match then there is much higher confidence in the prediction than if the nearest record is a great distance from the unclassified record.

The degree of homogeneity amongst the predictions within the K nearest neighbours can also be used. If all the nearest neighbours make the same prediction then there is much higher confidence in the prediction than if half the records made one prediction and the other half made another prediction.

Clustering

Clustering is the method by which like or similar records are grouped together. Usually this is done to give the end user a high level view of what is going on in the database. Clustering is sometimes used to mean segmentation where companies have grouped the population by demographic information into segments that they believe are useful for direct marketing and sales.

Sometimes clustering is performed not so much to keep records together as to make it easier to see when one record sticks out from the rest. For instance:

The nearest neighbour algorithm is basically a refinement of clustering in the sense that they both use distance in some feature space to create either structure in the data or predictions. The nearest neighbour algorithm is a refinement since part of the algorithm usually is a way of automatically determining the weighting of the importance of the predictors and how the distance will be measured within the feature space. Clustering is one special case of this where the importance of each predictor is considered to be equivalent.

An important constraint on clustering is that a reasonable number of clusters are formed for example when there are too few clusters (too much generalization) or too many clusters and original records, which is also unacceptable. Many clustering algorithms either let the user choose the number of clusters that they would like to see created as an input the algorithm will then strive to create that number using the data points available.

It is possible to guarantee that homogeneous clusters are created by breaking apart any cluster that is inhomogeneous into smaller clusters that are homogeneous. However this usually means creating too many clusters which defeats the original purpose of the clustering.
For clustering the n-dimensional space is usually defined by assigning one predictor to each dimension. For example, cluster with time, product, sales, colour, price, would be said to be in a 5 dimensional space. For the nearest neighbour algorithm predictors are also mapped to dimensions but then those dimensions are literally stretched or compressed based on how important the particular predictor is in making the prediction. The stretching of a dimension effectively makes that dimension (and hence predictor) more important than the others in calculating the distance.

Hierarchical and Non-Hierarchical Clustering

There are two main types of clustering techniques, those that create a hierarchy of clusters and those that do not. This hierarchy of clusters is created through the algorithm that builds the clusters. There are two main types of hierarchical clustering algorithms:

- Agglomerative - With the Agglomerative clustering techniques the process starts with each record in a cluster, i.e. there are as many clusters as there are records and each cluster contains just one record. This of course defeats the purpose so the clusters that are nearest each other are merged together to form the next largest cluster. This merging is continued until a hierarchy of clusters is built with just a single cluster containing all the records at the top of the hierarchy.

- Divisive - Divisive clustering techniques take the opposite approach from agglomerative techniques. These techniques start with all the records in one cluster and then try to split that cluster into smaller pieces and then in turn to try to split those smaller pieces.

Of the two the agglomerative techniques are the most commonly used for clustering and have more algorithms developed for them. The non-hierarchical techniques in general are faster to create from the historical database but require that the user make some decision about the number of clusters desired or the minimum "nearness" required for two records to be within the same cluster.

Decision Trees

The data mining techniques in this section represent the vast majority of the techniques that are being spoken about and have been developed over the last two decades of research. These techniques can be used for either discovering new information within large databases or for building predictive models.

What is a Decision Tree?

Decision trees are data mining technology that has been around in a form very similar to the technology of today for almost twenty years now and early versions of the algorithms date back in the 1960s.
A decision tree is a predictive model that, as its name implies, can be viewed as a tree. Specifically each branch of the tree is a classification question and the leaves of the tree are partitions of the dataset with their classification. For instance if we were going to classify customers who churn (don't renew their phone contracts) in the Cellular Telephone Industry a decision tree might look something like that found in the following diagram.

50 Churners
50 Non-Churners|

New Technology Phone?

Yes   No

30 Churners
50 Non-Churners|

Customer < 2.3 years?

20 Churners
0 Non-Churners|

Yes   No

25 Churners
10 Non-Churners|

Age < 55

5 Churners
40 Non-Churners|

Yes   No

20 Churners
0 Non-Churners|

5 Churners
10 Non-Churners|

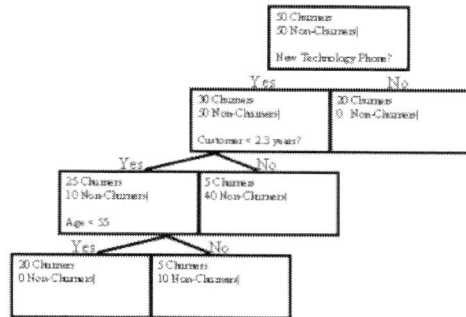

If you look closely, there is something interesting things about the decision tree:

- It divides up the data on each branch point without losing any of the data (the number of total records in a given parent node is equal to the sum of the records contained in its two children).
- The number of churners and non-churners is conserved as you move up or down the tree
- It is pretty easy to understand how the model is being built (in contrast to the models from neural networks or from standard statistics).
- It would also be pretty easy to use this model if you actually had to target those customers that are likely to churn with a targeted marketing offer.

You may also build some intuitions about your customer base.
E.g. "customers who have been with you for a couple of years and have up to date cellular phones are pretty loyal".
From a business perspective decision trees can be viewed as creating a segmentation of the original dataset (each segment would be one of the leaves of the tree). In this case the segmentation is done for a particular reason - namely for the prediction of some important piece of information. The records that fall within each segment fall there because they have similarity with respect to the information being predicted - not just that they are similar - without similarity being well defined. These

predictive segments that are derived from the decision tree also come with a description of the characteristics that define the predictive segment. Thus although the decision trees and the algorithms that create them may be complex, the results can be presented in an easy to understand way that can be quite useful to the business user.

Applying decision trees to business problems

Because of their tree structure and ability to easily generate rules decision trees are a favoured technique when building understandable models. Because of their high level of automation and the ease of translating decision tree models into SQL for deployment in relational databases the technology has also proven to be easy to integrate with existing IT processes.

Where can decision trees be used?

Because decision trees can be used in a wide variety of business problems for both exploration and for prediction within data mining and score very highly for their effectiveness they have been used for problems ranging from credit card attrition prediction to time series prediction of the exchange rate of different international currencies. However, there are also some scenarios and business problems where decision trees will not do as well as other techniques. For example in very simple problems where the prediction is just a multiple of the predictor these can be solved much quicker using linear regression. However, commonly in business predictions the interactions to be detected are much more complex that linear regression can handle and this is where decision trees excel.

Using decision trees for Exploration

The decision tree technology can be used for exploration of the dataset and business problem. This is often done by looking at the predictors and values that are chosen for each split of the tree. Often there are times when these predictors provide insights or propose questions that need further investigation.

Using decision trees for Data Pre-processing

Another way that the decision tree technology has been used is for pre-processing data for other prediction algorithms. Because the algorithm can be run relatively quickly decision trees can be used on the first pass of a data mining run to create a subset of possibly useful predictors, which can then be fed into neural networks, nearest neighbour and normal statistical routines.

Classification and Regression Trees

Classification and Regression Trees (CART) is a data exploration and prediction algorithm. In building the CART tree each predictor is picked as to how well they decrease the disorder of the data. For instance one measure that is used to determine whether a given split point for a give predictor is better than another is the entropy metric.

CART automatically validates the Tree

One of the great advantages of CART is that the algorithm has the validation of the model and the discovery of the optimally general model built deeply into the algorithm. CART accomplishes this by building a very complex tree and then pruning it back to the optimally general tree based on the results of cross validation or test set validation. The tree is pruned back based on the performance of the various pruned version of the tree on the test set data. The most complex tree rarely fares the best on the held aside data as it has been over fitted to the training data. By using cross validation the tree that is most likely to do well on new, unseen data can be chosen.

Association Rule Induction

Association Rule induction is perhaps the form of data mining that most closely resembles the imaginary process of data mining, namely "mining" for gold through a vast hoard of raw data. Rule induction on a data base can be a massive undertaking where all possible patterns are discovered then an accuracy and significance are added to them that indicates how strong the pattern is and how likely it is to occur again. In general these rules (patterns) are relatively simple such as for a supermarket basket database of items scanned at the check-out there might be some interesting correlations such as:

- If bagels are purchased then cream cheese is purchased 90% of the time and this pattern occurs in 3% of all shopping baskets.
- If live plants are purchased from a hardware store then plant fertilizer is purchased 60% of the time and these two items are bought together in 6% of the shopping baskets.

The rules that are pulled from the database are extracted and ordered to be presented to the user based on the percentage of times that they are correct and how often they apply.

The bane of rule induction systems is it retrieves too much data and this overabundance of patterns can also be problematic as there may be conflicting predictions made by equally interesting rules. Therefore there is an active field of research looking at automating the process of culling and combing the recommendations to reduce the output.

Applying Rule induction to Business

Rule induction systems are highly automated and are probably the best of the data mining techniques for exposing all possible predictive patterns in a database. They can be modified for use in prediction problems but the algorithms for combining evidence from a variety of rules comes more from rules of thumbs and practical experience.

What is an association rule?

In rule induction systems the rule itself is of a simple form of "if this and this and this then this". In order for the rules to be useful there are two pieces of information that must be supplied as well as the actual rule:

- Accuracy - How often is the rule correct?
- Coverage - How often does the rule apply?

Just because the pattern in the data base is expressed as rule does not mean that it is true all the time. Thus just like in other data mining algorithms it is important to recognize and make explicit the uncertainty in the rule. This is what the accuracy of the rule means. The coverage of the rule has to do with how much of the database the rule "covers" or applies to.

The rules themselves consist of two halves. The left hand side is called the antecedent and the right hand side is called the consequent. The antecedent can consist of just one condition or multiple conditions which must all be true in order for the consequent to be true at the given accuracy. Generally the consequent is just a single condition (prediction of purchasing just one grocery store item) rather than multiple conditions. Since there is both a left side and a right side to a rule (antecedent and consequent) they can be used in several ways for example we can:

- Target the antecedent. In this case all rules that have a certain value for the antecedent are gathered and displayed to the user.

- Target the consequent. In this case all rules that have a certain value for the consequent can be used to understand what is associated with the consequent and perhaps what affects the consequent.
- Target based on accuracy. Sometimes the most important thing for a user is the accuracy of the rules that are being generated. Highly accurate rules of 80% or 90% imply strong relationships that can be exploited even if they have low coverage of the database and are only likely to appear a limited number of times.
- Target based on coverage. Sometimes user want to know what the most ubiquitous rules are or those rules that are most readily applicable. By looking at rules ranked by coverage they can quickly get a high level view of what is happening within their database most of the time.
- Target based on "interestingness". Rules are interesting when they have high coverage and high accuracy and deviate from the norm. There have been many ways that rules have been ranked by some measure of interestingness so that the trade-off between coverage and accuracy can be made.

Caveat: Rules do not imply causality

It is important to recognize that even though the patterns produced from rule induction systems are delivered as if-then rules they do not necessarily mean that the left hand side of the rule (the "if" part) causes the right hand side of the rule (the "then" part) to happen. This is particularly important to remember for rule induction systems because the results are presented as if-this-then-that as many causal relationships are presented.

The business importance of accuracy and coverage

From a business perspective accurate rules are important because they imply that there is useful predictive information in the database that can be exploited - namely that there is something far from independent between the antecedent and the consequent. The lower the accuracy the closer the rule comes to just random guessing. If the accuracy is significantly below that of what would be expected from random guessing then the negation of the antecedent may well in fact be useful (for instance people who buy denture adhesive are much less likely to buy fresh corn on the cob than normal).

From a business perspective coverage implies how often you can use a useful rule. For instance you may have a rule that is 100% accurate but is only applicable in 1 out of every 100,000 shopping baskets. You can rearrange your shelf space to take advantage of this fact but it will not make you much money since the event is not very likely to happen. The table below displays the trade-off between coverage and accuracy.

	Accuracy Low	Accuracy High
Coverage High	Rule is rarely correct but can be used often.	Rule is often correct and can be used often.
Coverage Low	Rule is rarely correct and can be only rarely used.	Rule is often correct but can be only rarely used.

Rule coverage versus accuracy.

Which Technique and When?

Clearly one of the hardest things to do when deciding to implement a data mining system is to determine which technique to use when. When neural networks are appropriate and when are decision trees appropriate? When is data mining appropriate at all as opposed to just working with relational databases and reporting? When would just using OLAP and a multidimensional database be appropriate?

Some of the criteria that are important in determining the technique to be used are determined by trial and error. There are definite differences in the types of problems that are most conducive to each technique but the reality of real world data and the dynamic way in which markets, customers and hence the data that represents them is formed means that the data is constantly changing. These dynamics mean that it no longer makes sense to build the "perfect" model on the historical data since whatever was known in the past cannot adequately predict the future because the future is so unlike what has gone before.

Balancing exploration and exploitation

There is always the trade-off between exploration (learning more and gathering more facts) and exploitation (taking immediate advantage of everything that is currently known). This theme of exploration versus exploitation is echoed also at the level of collecting data in a targeted marketing system: from a limited population of prospects/customers to choose from how many to you sacrifice to exploration (trying out new promotions or messages at random) versus optimizing what you already know.

Chapter 10 – On-premise vs. Cloud Technologies

With the advent of the WWW came a new source of data, which has led to a huge increase in the dissemination of information worldwide. This era of the Internet and the phenomena of social networking, where people can create, exchange and publish multimedia files on the WWW has created a deluge of information, and it is all information that needs to be stored somewhere.

These new formats of information not only consumes large amount of storage but they also take time to retrieve specific pieces of the information. In order to make these searches more efficient a new framework for storing information is required and this is the non-relational or unstructured database.

An unstructured database or as they are often called a NoSQL database, which is an acronym for 'Not Only SQL' is a database designed to store diverse data objects that do not fit naturally and conveniently into common SQL database schemas. The data types it will typically hold may include the textual contents of email messages, videos, photographs, social media chats, journals, system logs, multimedia objects, Twitter tweets, Facebook posts, Forum comments, etc. The names used to refer to these database types may be misleading since some objects can be highly structured and some do hold relational data in normalized form. What is more, the new type of data is not something our self-service model can readily accommodate as it is almost always in unstructured data. Therefore we need to look at redesigning our self-service SME data analysis model in order for it to accommodate all types of data and from all sorts of sources. For example a design constraint with the retail on-premises BI model is that users Data may require to build reports where the data comes from customer surveys, support call feedback, social media comments, email, Twitter tweets or a myriad of other social media sources. This type of unified communication will provide our earlier BI models with significant challenges and again most likely managers will have to revert to much onerous manual work collating and processing the multitude of data from such diverse sources.

Furthermore the vast majority of this data may well be unstructured data and that will require different analysis techniques which are far removed from our earlier Pivot table analysis.

To address these new and significant challenges we have to look to the cloud for both the infrastructure and the intelligent services we require, but again the premise is not to lose the self-sufficiency and compatibility that we have already achieved. There are good reasons for wishing to maintain our on-premises servers and warehouse as a good maxim is: *Data sourced on-premises stays on premises, Data sourced from the cloud stays in the cloud.*

Furthermore, the web is also a huge source of unstructured data that we can utilize for data analytics and there are no shortages of APIs freely available for us to use in analysing text, reports or even photographs and video. The effects of Big Data and the availability of affordable cloud services are having a profound impact on SME opportunities in almost any industry, allowing companies of all sizes to more effectively serve customers to perform risk-analyses and create new revenue streams.

The IoT will also provide opportunities through the ability to connect devices to each other and to the cloud and this will be essential for businesses of all kinds and their consumers. This is because the IoT combined with the cloud, analytics; mobile and social applications have three major advantages for small and midsize businesses:

1. These technologies allow an SME to go from an innovative idea, a pilot, or a proof of concept to an actual product or service quickly by removing big, upfront capital investments in technology and staff.

2. The technologies remove the barriers to entry so allow businesses to scale up or down quickly, providing flexibility when responding to changing customer demands, which mitigates the risks associated with having to speculate and over provision hardware, networks and capacity.

3. The technologies are global so they remove the geographic constraints and open new markets that previously were not accessible to an SME.

Consequently, bearing that in mind we need to look towards a cloud based solution for managing Internet sourced data.

Building a Data Warehouse

Data engineering when deployed in the context of Business Intelligence and with the purpose of extracting insights from processing very large datasets - typically up to petabytes in size - encounter some unique constraints. At this scale of operation for processing to complete in a timely manner there is a need to deploy distributed systems with the capability for parallel processing and the ability to handle both large-scale batch and low-latency stream processing. However there is also a requirement for a scalable source and destination for the dataset input as well as the derived output. This is what we would call the single source of truth on which our processing will depend and this is where a scalable data warehouse is a necessity.

Data engineers design, build, and maintain data warehouses as they are the source of the trusted – single source of truth - data that enables the higher levels of analytics in business intelligence or machine learning. Hence, without a properly designed data warehouse it is likely that the data engineers might use different source data or worse query against the production database, causing severe performance issues and even outages. Similarly, data engineers need a safe haven for online experimentation and a data infrastructure that can support building labelled training data and running trial feature computations. However, knowing that you need a data warehouse and where you can locate it are two entirely separate things.

Cloud vs. On-premise data storage

The biggest decision is whether to have a cloud-based or on-premise infrastructure and there are many things to consider. The first question is where is your data located? If the majority of your data is on-premises then the second question is how important is availability and reliability to your business? The answers to both these questions will provide good pointers to a solution. The benefits of being in the cloud can far outweigh the additional costs for some businesses of installing direct connections to the cloud provider to transport their data to and from the cloud in a timely manner. Also the inherent resiliency, replication and redundancy that comes with the cloud guarantees increased probability of uptime. Hence, for example, if the business relies on mainly online transactions it will consider uptime an extremely important factor so will likely be willing to pay more for a cloud-based solution. However, some businesses may not be so dependent on online transactions so internet uptime may not be so important to them hence they may be more suited to an on-premises setup.

	On-Premises	Cloud Hosted	Cloud SaaS
Infrastructure Required	High	Moderate	Low
Total Cost of Ownership	High at first large CapEx but low OpEx over time	Low at first then moderate over time	Low to start, but OpEx increases with time
SLA	N/A	Contract based	Contract based on managed service

Upgrades	Your responsibility	12-18 months	Automatically
Security	Your responsibility	Shared responsibility	Managed Service

A third option, however, is hybrid data storage. Rather than choosing between on-premises and cloud solutions, why not take the best of both worlds? Hybrid data storage offers the opportunity for you to take advantage of the prime features of either world yet mitigate the weaknesses by using both storage solutions. A common example of hybrid data storage is when an organization stores its primary data on a local server but stores backup copies on the cloud. Granted, this is more costly than simply choosing a single storage option, but it also protects against unforeseen disasters. If a fire or flood occurs at the organization's server room, it could destroy their locally stored on-premises data. Since the organization's backups are stored on the cloud, however, the business can restore their lost data with limited interruption. However, a thing to bear in mind is to recall how long did it take you to upload those servers and data backups to the cloud? It is going to take that same length of time to download them again when you need them in a big hurry!

There are pros and cons associated with each data storage solution. On-premises require a substantial monetary investment for a green-field deployment but in most cases the infrastructure assets already exist and it also offers the highest level of security and transport speeds up to 10-40 Gbps are commonplace; on the other hand cloud 'cold' storage is very affordable, scalable and can be accessed over the internet but data transfer of large datasets can take days or even weeks over a VPN internet connection; a hybrid solution brings them both together so that they balance out each other's weakness. However, a hybrid solution comes at extra cost and added complexity. Hence, you should consider your organization's short- and long-term needs and choose the data storage solution that best delivers those requirements.

Design Patterns for Data Engineering Frameworks

The automation of key workflows is often a prime task for the data engineer. When contemplating which workflows to automate, the data engineer needs to start by thinking about the end user's experience. There are generally three layers of a well-designed data engineering framework: the input layer, the data processing layer, and the output layer.

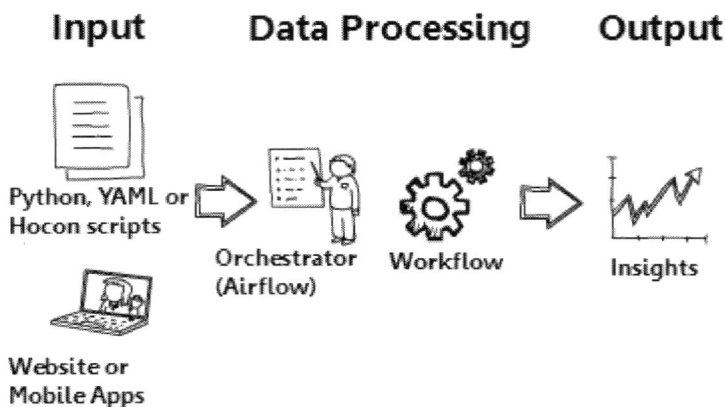

Input   **Data Processing**   **Output**

Python, YAML or Hocon scripts

Orchestrator (Airflow)   Workflow   Insights

Website or Mobile Apps

- **Input layer:** This is the layer where an end user specifies how their DAGs should be configured. User experience really matters here. Typically, the input could be a static configuration file (e.g. Python, YAML or Hocon), or it could be something dynamic such as a web UI. Regardless the objective remains the same; to deliver the user experience through capturing the UI requirements.
- **Data Processing layer:** This is the core of any data engineering framework, as this is where the ETL pipelines are instantiated and the goal is to make this hands-free so it is dynamic. This layer is generally referred to as the *DAG factory*, as the code automates the construction of the pre-designed pipelines just like in a factory.
- **Output layer:** The DAGs generated by the data processing layer create derived data, and the output will typically be output to a downstream Hive table, a UI / visualization layer, or be consumed by another downstream pipeline.

Processing Large scale data

The main goal of Big Data analytics, or Big Data Analysis, is to help provide information to companies for making business decisions using data engineers, predictive modellers and other data analysis specialists. The data sources that will be analysed include; Web server logs, click information, social media content, activity reports of online social networks, messages from customer emails and survey responses, voice recording of customer telephone details as well as data recorded from sensors on connected devices like the Internet of Things.

Big data can be analysed using tools that are widely used such as Hadoop or Spark as they are considered necessary for large scale in-depth analysis, predictive analysis, data mining, text analysis and statistical analysis. However, what hinders many organizations from establishing big data analysis is the lack of understanding and internal skills required to do data analysis. When this is coupled with the high cost of hiring experts with experience in data analysis then the cost can exceed potential benefits. Also, many organisations still fail to grasp the amount of preparation that the data requires. Data needs to be prepared, cleaned, standardised before it is ready to be analysed, which makes data management difficult. Moreover, often the interfacing of the connection between the Hadoop system and the data warehouses is a challenge albeit intermediary software has improved this issue.

The advancements and maturity of cloud based systems such as GCP has mitigated many of the financial risks by reducing the capital investment associated with big data analysis. These high starter costs can now be avoided due to cloud pay-per-use billing models. For data analytics this is a major boon as you only pay for the cost of the running time of the job and then you can shut down the infrastructure. The costs are still not trivial but the insights derived have become increasingly business-critical and valuable. This makes running big data analytics in the cloud very attractive especially on Google Cloud Platform as its compatibility with Hadoop and many of its ecosystem components are built-in. This makes migration to or from the cloud a trivial process.

Hadoop is so important within big data analytics that you cannot hope to understand the subject without a firm grasp of its ecosystem and capabilities. However, Hadoop is a still a specialist Big Data system that few of us are likely to have encountered let alone worked on. Hence, before we go any further we need to understand what Hadoop and its ecosystem of supporting software are and what they do.

The Hadoop Ecosystem Overview

The Hadoop ecosystem is a platform or framework which comprises of different analytical components and services (ingesting, storing, analysing, and maintaining). Most of the services available in the Hadoop ecosystem have been developed to supplement the four main core components of Hadoop which include HDFS, YARN, MapReduce and Common.

How Hadoop Works

At a high-level Apache Hadoop is a set of open-source software utilities. Collectively known as Hadoop they facilitate the optimal usage of a cluster of computers to solve problems involving massive amounts of data. Apache Hadoop is open source software framework originally developed by Google. Hadoop acts to store identical data-blocks across a cluster of backend off-the-shelf servers in a distributed manner and then processes that data in parallel. Hadoop provides; the underlying reliable distributed storage layer – HDFS; a batch processing engine – MapReduce; and an application resource management layer – YARN.
Hadoop's purpose is to perform distributed processing for huge data sets across the cluster of commodity servers and it works across multiple backend servers simultaneously. To initiate the processing action the client submits data and a program to Hadoop. HDFS stores the data across an array of available back-end servers – which also provides for redundancy - before MapReduce processes the data and Yarn divides the application tasks across the cluster.

Hadoop therefore is said to provide a software framework for distributed storage and distributed computing. The advantages of using Hadoop are many as it provides for affordable large scale clustering of low-price commodity computers, which cost effectively delivers massive parallel computing power. Hadoop does this by dividing a file into a number of blocks (each 128mb) and distributes these for storage across a cluster of machines (backend nodes). Hadoop also achieves fault tolerance by replicating the blocks across at least three computer nodes in the cluster. It handles the distributed processing by dividing a job into a number of independent tasks. These tasks run in parallel over the computer cluster.

Hadoop Components and Domains

Hadoop may seem simple enough but to really understand how it works we need to understand how its core components integrate and interact. HDFS – Hadoop Distributed File System provides for the storage of Hadoop. As the name suggests it stores the data in a distributed manner. The file gets divided into a number of equal sized blocks of 128mb (default) which are spread across the cluster of commodity hardware. MapReduce – This is the processing engine of Hadoop. MapReduce works on the principle of distributed processing. It divides the task submitted by the user into a number of independent subtasks. This sub-task executes in parallel thereby increasing the throughput.
Yarn – Yet Another Resource Manager provides resource management for Hadoop. There are two daemons running for Yarn. One is Node Manager on the slave machines and other is the Resource Manager on the master node. Yarn looks after the allocation of the resources among various slaves competing for it.
The way that this works in practice is that there are several critical processes that need to run in the background. The Hadoop Daemons are:-
a) A Namenode – It runs on master node for HDFS
b) A Datanode – It runs on slave nodes for HDFS
c) Resource Manager – It runs on YARN master node for MapReduce
d) Node Manager – It runs on YARN slave node for MapReduce

These 4 daemons need to be running for Hadoop to be functional.

Hadoop under the Bonnet

If we take a deeper dive into Hadoop we can see how the individual components carry out their specific tasks.
i. HDFS
The Hadoop Distributed File System (HDFS) is built on a master-slave topology. It has got two daemons running they are referred to as the NameNode and the DataNode respectively.

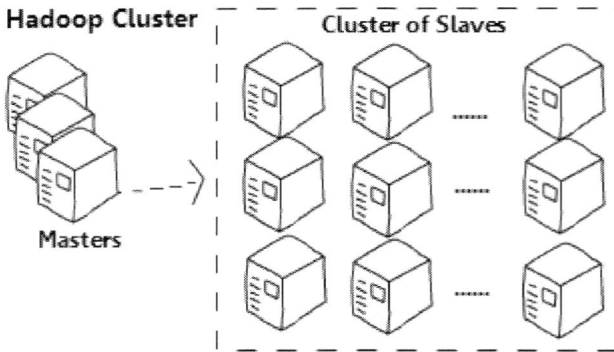

NameNode

NameNode is the daemon running on the master machine. It is the center-piece of the HDFS file system. NameNode stores the directory tree of all files in the file system. It tracks where across the cluster the file data resides. It does not store the data contained in these files only the location metadata.
When the client applications want to add/copy/move/delete a file, they interact with NameNode. The NameNode responds to the request from the client by returning a list of relevant DataNode servers where the data can be found.

DataNode

The DataNode daemon runs on the slave nodes and it stores data in the Hadoop File System. In production and functional file systems the data is replicated across many DataNodes.

On startup, a DataNode connects to the NameNode on the master. Once it has an active connection it keeps on listening for any requests from NameNode to access data. Initially applications do not talk directly to a Datanode but once the NameNode provides the location of the data, client applications can then talk directly to a DataNode. When replicating the data, DataNode instances can talk directly to each other.

Replica Placement

The placement of replicas decides HDFS reliability and performance. Optimization of replica placement sets HDFS apart from other distributed system. Huge HDFS instances run on a cluster of computers spreads across many racks. The communication between nodes on different racks has to go through switches. Mostly the network bandwidth between nodes on the same rack is more than that between the machines on separate racks.

The rack awareness algorithm determines the rack ID of each DataNode. Under a simple policy, the replicas get placed on unique racks. This prevents data loss in the event of rack failure. Also, it utilizes bandwidth from multiple racks while reading data. However, this method increases the cost of writes. Placement therefore requires a trade-off between write performance and read bandwidth.

Summary of how Hadoop works

Step by step:

Input data is broken into blocks of size 128 Mb and then blocks are moved to different data-nodes.

Once all the blocks of the data are stored on data-nodes, the user can process the data.

Resource Manager then schedules the program (submitted by the user) on individual nodes.

Once all the nodes process the data, the aggregate output is written back to HDFS.

Hadoop Ecosystem Overview

Hadoop however consists of many additional software components that have been developed to enhance the framework. The following components, which are often stand-alone applications and systems in their own right, nonetheless are considered to be integral in constructing a complete Hadoop ecosystem.

HDFS (Hadoop distributed file system)

The Hadoop distributed file system is a storage system which runs on Java programming language and is used as the primary storage device in Hadoop applications. HDFS consists of two components, Namenode and Datanode; these daemons or applications are used to store large datasets across multiple nodes on the Hadoop cluster.

NameNode is the master node daemon which maintains, manages and operates all the slave data nodes. As a result NameNode acts as the recorder of metadata for all the data blocks stored within HDFS, consequently it contains all the block information such as size, location, source, and hierarchy, etc. It records all changes that happen to metadata within the HDFS so should any file get deleted in the HDFS, the NameNode will automatically record it in the EditLog.

NameNode listens for and maintains heartbeat information in order to determine the heath of each node in the cluster. It receives a heartbeat along with a block report from each of the data nodes in the cluster to ensure they are working and healthy.

DataNode:

The DataNode daemon is installed and runs on each slave machine. As the data nodes' act as a storage device the DataNode daemon takes responsibility to serve read and write request from the user.
DataNode also takes the responsibility of acting in accordance to the instructions of NameNode, which includes deleting blocks, adding blocks, and replacing blocks. In addition it is the DataNode daemon that is responsible for sending every three seconds the heartbeat reports to the NameNode.

YARN:

YARN (Yet Another Resource Negotiator) acts as the controller of the Hadoop ecosystem. It takes responsibility for providing all the resources needed for the application execution.
YARN consists of two essential components. They are Resource Manager and Node Manager, whereby Resource Manager works at the cluster level and takes responsibility of running the master machine. It stores the track of heartbeats from the Node manager.
It takes the job submissions and negotiates the first container for executing an application.
It consists of two components: Application manager and Scheduler.
Node manager:
Node Manager works on the node level component and runs on every slave machine.
It is responsible for monitoring resource utilization in each container and managing containers. It also keeps track of log management and node health. Further Node Manager also maintains continuous communication with a resource manager to give updates.

MapReduce

MapReduce is a software framework which enables the writing of applications that process large data sets using distributed and parallel algorithms. The parallel processing feature of MapReduce plays a crucial role in the Hadoop ecosystem. It also helps in performing Big data analysis by using multiple slave machines in the same cluster.

How does MapReduce work?

In the MapReduce program, there are two Functions; one is Map, and the other is Reduce.

The Map function converts the individual elements of the original input file into tuples. (Key/value pairs).

The Reduce function then takes the tuple data from the Map function as an input. Reduce function aggregates & summarizes the results produced by the Map function to produce the output.

Apache Spark:

Apache Spark is an essential product from the Apache software foundation, and it is considered to be in its own right a powerful data processing engine. Spark is a standalone product that does not need Hadoop to work and in many uses cases it is deployed as a direct replacement for Hadoop. This is because Spark handles real-time streaming data as well as batch processing, which is something that MapReduce is unable to handle. In addition Spark is believed to operate at speeds of up to 100 times faster than MapReduce. So the increased need for speed and the requirement for real-time analytics capability led to the invention and increasing deployment of Apache Spark.

Apache Spark Features:

Spark is a framework for real-time analytics in a distributed computing environment.

It processed data in-memory rather than on-disk which results in increased speed of data processing. This exceptional in-memory execution ability and other optimization features means that it can perform real-time data streaming processing.

Moreover, Spark is equipped with high-level libraries, which support R, Python, Scala, Java etc. These standard libraries make the data processing seamless and highly reliable. However, this doesn't mean that Spark is a replacement for Hadoop because although it can process enormous amounts of data with ease it is Hadoop that was designed to store the unstructured data which must be processed. Hence, when the two are combined we can get the best of both worlds.

Hive:

Apache Hive is the data warehouse component and open source software built on Apache Hadoop for performing data query and analysis. Hive mainly does three functions; data summarization, query, and analysis. Hive uses a language called HiveQL (HQL), which is similar to SQL. Hive QL works as a translator which translates the SQL queries into MapReduce Jobs, which will be executed on Hadoop.

Main components of Hive are:

Metastore - serves as a storage device for the metadata. This metadata holds the information of each table such as location and schema. Metadata keeps track of data and replicates it, and acts as a backup store in case of data loss.

Driver- this component receives the HiveQL instructions and acts as a Controller. It observes the progress and life cycle of various executions by creating sessions. Whenever, HiveQL executes a statement, driver stores the metadata generated out of that action.

Compiler- is allocated with the task of converting the HiveQL query into MapReduce input. A compiler is designed with the process to execute the steps and functions needed to enable the HiveQL output, as required by the MapReduce.

H Base:

Hbase is the NoSQL database that runs on top of Hadoop because it is scalable and distributed. Apache HBase is designed to store the structured data in table format which has millions of columns and billions of rows. HBase gives access to the real-time data to read or write on HDFS.

Apache H Base Architecture

HBase is an open source, NoSQL database based upon Google's Bigtable, which is considered to be a distributed storage system designed to handle big data sets.
H Base supports all types of data so it plays a crucial role in handling various types of data in Hadoop. The HBase is originally written in Java, and its applications can be written in Avro, REST, and Thrift APIs.

Components of HBase:

There are two main components in HBase. They are HBase master and regional server.
a) HBase master: It is not part of the actual data storage instead it manages load balancing activities across all Region Servers.
Therefore, it controls failovers as well as any administrative duties in addition to providing an interface for creating, updating and deleting tables. It also handles DDL operations while maintaining and monitoring the Hadoop cluster.
b) Regional server: It is a worker node. It reads, writes, and deletes request from Clients. Region server runs on every HDFS data node within the Hadoop cluster.

H Catalogue:

H Catalogue is a table and storage management tool for Hadoop. It exposes the tabular metadata stored in the hive to all other applications of Hadoop. H Catalogue accepts all kinds of components available in Hadoop such as Hive, Pig, and MapReduce to quickly read and write data from the cluster. H Catalogue is a crucial feature of Hive which allows users to store their data in any format and structure.

Benefits of H Catalogue:

It assists the integration with the other Hadoop tools and provides read data from a Hadoop cluster or write data into a Hadoop cluster. It allows notifications of data availability.
It enables APIs and web servers to access the metadata from hive metastore.
It gives visibility for data archiving and data cleaning tools.

Apache Pig:

Apache Pig is a high-level language platform for analysing and querying large data sets that are stored in HDFS. Pig works as an alternative language to Java programming for MapReduce and generates MapReduce functions automatically. Pig included with Pig Latin, which is a scripting language. Pig can translate the Pig Latin scripts into MapReduce which can run on YARN and process data in HDFS cluster.
Pig is best suitable for solving complex use cases that require multiple data operations. It is more like a processing language than a query language (Java, SQL). Pig is considered as a highly customized one because the users have a choice to write their functions by using their preferred scripting language.

How does Pig work?

We use 'load' command to load the data in the pig. Then, we can perform various functions such as grouping data, filtering, joining, sorting etc. At last, you can dump the data on a screen, or you can store the result back in HDFS according to your requirement.

Apache Sqoop:

Sqoop works as a front-end loader of Big Data. Sqoop is a front-end interface that enables in moving bulk data from Hadoop to relational databases and into variously structured data marts.

Sqoop replaces the function called 'developing scripts' to import and export data. It mainly helps in moving data from an enterprise database to Hadoop cluster to performing the ETL process.

Apache Sqoop undertakes the following tasks to integrate bulk data movement between Hadoop and structured databases:

- Sqoop fulfils the growing need to transfer data from the mainframe to HDFS.
- Sqoop helps in achieving improved compression and light-weight indexing for advanced query performance.
- It facilitates feature to transfer data in parallel for effective performance and optimal system utilization.
- Sqoop creates fast data copies from an external source into Hadoop.
- It acts as a load balancer by mitigating extra storage and processing loads to other devices.

Apache Oozie:

Apache Ooze is a tool in which all sort of programs can be pipelined in a required manner to work in Hadoop's distributed environment. Oozie works as a scheduler system to run and manage Hadoop jobs.

Oozie facilitates combining multiple complex jobs so that they can be run in a sequential order to achieve the desired output. It is strongly integrated with Hadoop stack supporting various jobs like Pig, Hive, Sqoop, and system-specific jobs like Java, and Shell. Oozie is an open source Java web application.

Oozie consists of two jobs:

1. Oozie workflow: It is a collection of actions arranged to perform the jobs one after another. It is just like a relay race where one has to start right after one finish, to complete the race.
2. Oozie Coordinator: It runs workflow jobs based on the availability of data and predefined schedules.

Apache Avro:

Apache Avro is a part of the Hadoop ecosystem, and it works as a data serialization system. It is an open source project which helps Hadoop in data serialization and data exchange. Avro assists in exchanging programs written in different languages as it serializes data into files or messages.
Avro Schema: The Avro Schema enables the serialization and deserialization processes without code generation. Avro needs a schema for data to read and write hence whenever data is stored in a file its schema is also stored along with it, with this schema the files may be processed later by any program.
Dynamic typing: it means serializing and de-serialising data without generating any code. It replaces the code generation process with its statistically typed language as an optional optimization.
Avro features:
- Avro makes Fast, compact, dynamic data formats.
- It has a container file in which it stores continuous data format.
- It helps in creating efficient data structures.

Apache Drill:

The primary purpose of Hadoop ecosystem is to process large sets of structured or unstructured data. To enable this Apache Drill is the low latency distributed query engine which is designed to measure several thousands of nodes and query petabytes of data. The drill has a specialized skill to eliminate cache data and releases space.
Features of Drill:

- It gives an extensible architecture at all layers.
- Drill provides data in a hierarchical format which is easy to process and understandable.
- The drill does not require centralized metadata, and the user doesn't need to create and manage tables in metadata to query data.

Apache Zookeeper:

Apache Zookeeper is an open source project designed to coordinate multiple services in the Hadoop ecosystem. Organizing and maintaining a service in a distributed environment is a complicated task. Zookeeper solves this problem with its simple APIs and architecture. Zookeeper allows developers to focus on core application instead of concentrating on a distributed environment of the application.

Features of Zookeeper:
- Zookeeper acts fast enough with workloads where reads to data are more common than writes.
- Zookeeper acts as a disciplined one because it maintains a record of all transactions.

Apache Flume:

Flume collects aggregates and moves large sets of data from the source and sends it back to HDFS. It works as a fault tolerant mechanism. It helps in transmitting data from a source into a Hadoop environment. Flume enables its users in getting the data from multiple servers immediately into Hadoop.

Apache Ambari:

Ambari is open source software from the Apache software foundation. It makes Hadoop manageable. It consists of software which is capable of provisioning, managing, and monitoring of Apache Hadoop clusters.
Hadoop cluster provisioning: Ambari guides us with a step-by-step procedure on how to install Hadoop services across many hosts. Ambari handles configuration of Hadoop services across all clusters.
Hadoop Cluster management: It acts as a central management system for starting, stopping and reconfiguring of Hadoop services across all clusters.
Hadoop cluster monitoring: Ambari provides us with a dashboard for monitoring health and status.
The Ambari framework acts as an alarming system to notify when anything goes wrong. For example, if a node goes down or low disk space on node etc., it lets us know through a notification.
Conclusion:
We have discussed all the components of the Hadoop Ecosystem in detail, and each element contributes its share of work in the smooth functioning of Hadoop. Every component of Hadoop is unique in its way and performs exceptional functions when their turn arrives. To become an expert in Hadoop, you must learn all the components of Hadoop and practice it well.

Chapter 11 –An introduction to Machine Learning

In this Chapter we will introduce machine learning and describe its relationship with Artificial Intelligence. As part of the discussion we will learn what Machine Learning is and how it differentiates from A.I. In the course of the Chapter we will learn about some features of Machine Learning and how some models such as deep neural networks are producing some profound discoveries and results across a variety of disciplines that not so long ago were thought to be beyond the realm of intelligent systems.

This is because the domain of learning has grown recently and has gained such importance that it has almost stopped being a sub-set of AI and has become its own discipline – the domain of Machine Learning (ML).

The consensus and general belief is that Machine learning is a subset of AI. That is, machine learning is AI, but not all AI is machine learning.

The AI Hierarchy of Needs

Monica Rogati's "The AI Hierarchy of Needs"

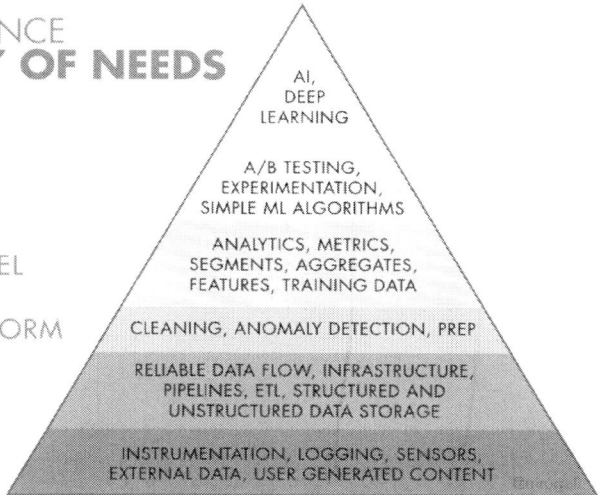

THE DATA SCIENCE
HIERARCHY OF NEEDS

AI,
DEEP
LEARNING

LEARN/OPTIMIZE

A/B TESTING,
EXPERIMENTATION,
SIMPLE ML ALGORITHMS

AGGREGATE/LABEL

ANALYTICS, METRICS,
SEGMENTS, AGGREGATES,
FEATURES, TRAINING DATA

EXPLORE/TRANSFORM

CLEANING, ANOMALY DETECTION, PREP

MOVE/STORE

RELIABLE DATA FLOW, INFRASTRUCTURE,
PIPELINES, ETL, STRUCTURED AND
UNSTRUCTURED DATA STORAGE

COLLECT

INSTRUMENTATION, LOGGING, SENSORS,
EXTERNAL DATA, USER GENERATED CONTENT

Monica Rogati's AI Hierarchy of needs can be considered to be analogous to Maslow's motivational theory in psychology – Hierarchy of Needs. In Maslow's hierarchy of needs for humans in their pursuit of self-fulfillness they begin their journey Maslow's theory suggests from a starting point of obtaining their basic needs of food and shelter. Then they strive for psychological wellness via building friendships and self-esteem before eventually aspiring to self-actualisation. In Rogati's AI Hierarchy of Needs the journey takes a similar path starting with the foundational skill of collecting, storing, aggregating and transforming the data before we can start to explore and analyse it to obtain insights. These after all are the fundamental skills required in any data analysis or business intelligence project. For a data engineer these are foundational skills that they must have as these are prerequisite when it comes to properly designing table schemas or constructing data pipelines.

Indeed most data engineers will spend a lot of their time maybe as much as 80% cleaning, preparing and planning the transformation of data. Hence these are not skills to be taken lightly as one old saying goes, garbage in – garbage out, well this is guaranteed when it comes to data analytics. After all we need clean relevant data in order to have a foundation for our optimization and learning techniques later on when we start to investing Machine Learning and AI.

Learning in Machine Learning

The "learning" part of machine learning relies heavily on negative feedback therefore ML algorithms attempt to optimize their performance through training and experience i.e. they usually try to minimize error or maximize the likelihood of their predictions being true. The ML agent works on the principle of a framework that manipulates inputs in order to guess as to the inputs' nature and their impact on the output. Different outputs being the results of various initial guesses are the product of the inputs and the algorithm. Usually, the initial guesses are way out of the ballpark, but if you are lucky enough to have ground-truth labels pertaining to the input, you can measure how wrong your guesses are by contrasting them with the truth table, and then use that error to modify your algorithm – this is negative feedback, the technique of using errors in the output to tune the input proportionately.

This is how neural networks work they keep on measuring the level of output error and correspondingly modifying their input parameters until they achieve a minimal error that is detected on the output that they are unable to reduce further and this is true Machine Learning.

However, what Machine Learning requires in the most typical and easiest scenario is to be trained with data that is labelled so that it can determine the level of error in the output. Therefore ML agents are an optimization algorithm and if they are trained with sufficient data to tune them accurately they will minimize their error by always working to bring the output closer to agreement with the reference goals.

In this Chapter we will study Machine Learning in practical terms by witnessing it in action. We will see the wide and diverse application of Machine Learning and understand its pervasiveness throughout most modern technologies. Some examples of these real world applications where Machine Learning is finding increasing success and progress are in the fields of:

Image Processing

Image processing problems basically have to analyse images to get data or do some transformations. Some examples are:

Automatic Machine Translation

This is a task where given words, a phrase or a sentence in one language AMT will automatically translate it into another language. However, automatic machine translation has been around for a long time, but powered by deep learning AMT is achieving increasingly higher results in two specific areas:

- Automatic Translation of Text.
- Automatic Translation of Images.

Text translation can be performed without any pre-processing of the sequence, allowing the algorithm to learn the dependencies between words and their mapping to a new language. Neural networks are used to identify images that have letters and where the letters are in the scene. Once identified, they can be turned into text, translated and the image recreated with the translated text. This is often called instant visual translation.

Object Classification and Detection in Photographs

This task requires the classification of objects that can be found within a photograph as being one of a set of previously known objects, for example a car or a desk. Very encouraging results have been achieved on benchmark examples of this problem using very large neural networks an example is the ImageNet project. ImageNet collected and labelled a training set of over one million images in their efforts to improve image classification. In a more complex variation of this task called object detection, which involves specifically identifying one or more objects within the scene of the photograph and drawing a box around them. ImageNet was able to detect with high confidence several diverse objects in a photograph and frame them, which is to draw a frame around each object, similar to the face recognition algorithms found in digital cameras. However, ImageNet has gone steps further by in addition to identifying and framing the object, for instance a white car, its DNN is also labelling the white car with its make, model and year – albeit this is a function of quality labelling in the initial training data.

Text Analysis

Text analysis is the process of extracting or classifying information from text, such as tweets, emails, chats, OCR and scanned documents, etc. Some popular examples are:
• Spam filtering, one of the most known and used text classification applications (assign a category to a text). Spam filters learn to classify an email as spam or ham depending on the content and the subject. Text classification can identify signature phrases or keywords in the spam but it can also learn over time what is likely to be spam or not based on the recipients behaviour.
• Antivirus, another tool that uses text analysis and by learning the virus's unique signature by text analysis during virus detection scans, again antivirus solutions using AI and ML can learn over time to improve performance.
• Sentiment Analysis, another application of text classification where an algorithm must learn to classify an opinion as positive, neutral or negative depending on the mood expressed by the writer.
• Information Extraction, the purpose is to extract samples from a text, and learn to extract a particular piece of information or data, for example, extracting addresses, entities, keywords, etc. This type of technology is used in scanning emails for sensitive keywords and is the technology used (reluctantly or otherwise) by the internet giants at the behest of the NSA and FBI.

Stock Trading

Financial, Stock and Futures exchanges utilize trading platforms to handle the extremely large data sets and they require a similar amount of analysis and computation to make recommendations. From a machine learning perspective, decisions are being made for you on whether to buy or sell a stock at the current price. Trading algorithms take into account the historical opening and closing prices and the buy and sell volumes of that stock.

Data Mining

Data mining is a whole field of applications on its own and is sometimes confused with AI and ML. The purpose of data mining though is to analyse large data sets such as entire databases, repositories or data lakes. The process requires that the algorithm discovers patterns, correlations or anomalies in the data as this can reveal insights that lead to predictions that improve decision making. Data mining is very useful in manufacturing and retail where operational and sales information can be interrogated for insights that can prove of value.
Data mining and ML have utility in many scenarios, for example:
• Anomaly detection: this is used to detect outliers – occurrences outside the norm - for example for credit card fraud detection, in this instance the algorithm could detect which transactions are outliers from the purchasing pattern of a user.
• Association rules: This is a common use case in retail as it is a prime way to uncover non-obvious correlations. For example, in a supermarket or e-commerce site, you can discover customer purchasing habits by looking at which products are bought together – Amazon is a good example of this where 'customers who bought this also bought ...' Information derived through association rules can be used for sales positioning or marketing purposes.

• Classification: for example, in a mortgage loan platform, potential customers can be classified or grouped by their credit history, spending behaviour or their profile.

• Predictions: predict a variable – a feature of interest - from the rest of the variables. For example, you could predict the credit score of new customers in a bank based by learning the profiles and credit score of current customers with similar profiles, such as postcode, salary, or gender.

Video Games & Robotics

Video games and robotics is a field where the reinforcement type of Machine Learning has been applied for a long time. Reinforcement learning requires no prior teaching cycle instead the agent learns to perform a task by learning from the reinforcement of the environment by trial and error. For example in robotics the reinforcement is negative if a robot hits an obstacle or positive if it gets to the objective.

In computer games there are two design options when deploying machine learning in games. One is learning at design-time, where the results of learning are applied before publishing the game; the other is learning at runtime, which enables learning the behaviour of a particular player.

Types of Machine Learning

Advancements in Machine Learning over the last decade have brought the capabilities to the masses as it is no longer the domain of the expert data scientist. This has come about through some of the A-list players in the field pursuing a policy of Machine Learning democratization. For example Google has released many of their AI and ML assets as open source or made them available via APIs. The latter approach means that you don't even need your own infrastructure you can simple send requests to a Google API, which will run on Google's infrastructure before returning you're the results. These serverless ML APIs are easily incorporated into your own applications as they come prebuild and pre-trained on Google's vast data sets.

However there is a second type of ML that is available where you run APIs on let's say GCP that have been pre-trained by Google but you can also train them using your own data. These solutions are called AutoML as they retain all the serverless and managed features but allow you to customize them through training on your specific data. The third type which is at the manual hands-on end of the spectrum is where you use platforms such as TensorFlow or Kubeflow to construct and run your own data models.

Introduction to Machine Learning algorithm

At this point we have to talk about the three general categories of Machine Learning algorithms: Supervised Learning, Unsupervised Learning and Reinforcement Learning algorithms. The main difference between the approaches is in the amount of training examples that are fed to the algorithm, how the algorithm uses them and the type of problems they solve.

Supervised Learning

In the case of supervised learning, as the name suggests the Machine Learning algorithm has to be supervised through a training cycle where it is fed training data to enable it to learn how to perform a task. Supervised learning can be viewed as a process that transforms a particular input to a desired output. The classic example of supervised learning is the use case of optical character recognition (OCR) as it is often used as the "Hello World" first learning step in Machine Learning.

With Supervised learning the Machine Learning process has to learn how to transform every possible input to the correct/desired output, so each training example has a specific input and the desired output. For example in the OCR scenario we could have many ambiguous handwritten examples of letters or numbers along with their correct definition. The more variations that the algorithm is exposed to of a handwritten letter or number the more thorough the training process.

Depending on the functionality of the algorithm, what task it is designed to perform, which is illustrated by the type of output, we have two subtypes of supervised learning:

Supervised Classification

When the output value belongs to a discrete and finite set, we're talking about a classification. The OCR scenario is a good example as it can be solved as a classification problem, the output is a finite set of options: A-Z and 0-9. In this case, our training examples will look like:

Supervised Regression

Not all tasks are classification orientated in some use cases the desired output value is a continuous number, for example, a probability, then it is a regression problem. The example of the credit rating for a loan request (example 3) is a case of regression learning as the result is a number between 0 and 1 that represents the probability that a person will repay the loan. In this case, our training examples will look like:

Supervised learning is the most popular category of Machine Learning algorithms but it does have a disadvantage. Using supervised learning is problematic in so much as that for every training example we have to provide a training set of data complete with the corresponding correct output. Of course most data does not come in this format and in many cases the data will need to be specially prepared. For example, in the case of image OCR categorization, we would need to construct a training set of images with each one correctly labelled so if we need 10,000 training examples (images), and that's a relatively small training set, we would have to tag each image of a character with the correct category (A-Z or 0-9 ...). This is a time consuming and tedious task, though for a common task like OCR, training sets are available online but gathering quality tagged training data for specialist task such as a company's sales projections, is a very common bottleneck for Machine Learning algorithm projects.

Another issue with supervised learning algorithms is in the inherent bias that we introduce into the training data. Often this is exactly what we want, for example in the OCR use case we want to influence the algorithms judgment as much as possible to enable it to learn and reduce instances of false categorization, for example we want it to differentiate between a 1 and a 7 as often as possible. On the other hand, if we are aiming to categorize images of people on a social media site we might not want to bias the outcome through influencing the training data set. In supervised learning this is one of the trade-offs required.

Unsupervised Learning

There's a second category of Machine Learning algorithms called unsupervised learning and in this case, the training examples only need to include the input to the algorithm, and not the desired output. The typical use case is to discover the hidden structure and relations between the training examples. A typical use case for unsupervised learning is the clustering algorithms, where the objective is to find groups of instances (clusters). For example, with Amazons retail website, it shows each visitor a custom view of product recommendations that is based upon their individual browsing and shopping history and Amazon will search and recommend similar products of interest. The purpose of unsupervised learning with the clustering algorithms like K-means is to "learn" to find similar instances by only looking at the input.

Reinforcement Learning

The third category of machine learning algorithms is reinforced learning and this group require no predetermined training data prior to beginning the task. Reinforcement Learning allows machines and software agents to automatically determine the ideal behaviour within a specific context, in order to maximize its performance. Simple reward feedback is required for the agent to learn its behaviour; this is known as the reinforcement signal.

There are many different algorithms that tackle this issue. As a matter of fact, Reinforcement Learning is defined by a specific type of problem, and all its solutions are classed as Reinforcement Learning algorithms. Within the context of the problem, an agent is supposed to decide the best action to select based on the current state.

The benefits of Reinforcement Learning are that it allows the machine to learn its own behaviour based on feedback from the environment through its own sensors. This autonomous behaviour can be learnt, once and for all, or be a continuous learning process adapting as time goes by. If the problem is modelled with care, some Reinforcement Learning algorithms can model their behaviour to maximize the reward; this is referred to as converging to the global optimum.

This method of automated learning has another significant attribute in so much as no training data is required, therefore no reliance on either input or output data. Consequently, less time will be spent designing a solution, since there is no need for hand-crafting complex training sets, or sets of rules as with Expert Systems. This implies that there is little need for a human expert who knows about the domain of application all that is required is someone familiar with Reinforcement Learning.

The possible applications of Reinforcement Learning are abundant, due to the generic nature of the algorithm specifications. Indeed a very large number of problems in Artificial Intelligence can be fundamentally mapped to a decision process. This is a distinct advantage, since the same theory can be applied to many different domain specific problems with little effort.

In practice, this ranges from controlling robotic arms to find the most efficient motor combination, to robot navigation where collision avoidance behaviour can be learnt by negative feedback from bumping into obstacles. Logic games are also well-suited to Reinforcement Learning, as they are traditionally defined as a sequence of decisions.

ML Families of algorithms

Algorithms are often grouped by similarity in terms of their function for instance the tasks that they can accomplish. They will often be classified as tree-based methods, neural networks, or Bayesian inspired methods. Of course when we classify algorithms towards function we naturally introduce some bias as the prevalence of problems in machine learning is heavily skewed towards solving problems in classification and regression. Additionally, the algorithms are listed in no particular order as there is no ranking. The reason for this, and this concerns all groups of functional algorithms, is that there is no best solution. It is part of the problem to figure out what the best algorithm is for the problem you're trying to model. Some algorithms may be very popular and they may tend to work better out of the box. However, that doesn't mean they cannot be outperformed by other (perhaps simpler) algorithms if you engineered the right features.

Regression Algorithms

Regression modelling concerns the relationship between variables that can be iteratively refined using a sample measure of error to improve the predictions.

The most popular regression algorithms are:

- Linear Regression
- Logistic Regression
- Stepwise Regression

Instance-based Algorithms

Instance-based learning models compare instances of data against their own examples of training data for similarity.

Instance-based algorithms build up a database of example data and compare new data to the database using a similarity function as a measure in order to find the best match and make a prediction. For this reason, instance-based methods are also called winner-take-all methods

or memory-based learning. Focus is put on the representation of the stored instances and similarity measures used between instances.
The most popular instance-based algorithms are:
- k-Nearest Neighbour (kNN)
- Learning Vector Quantization (LVQ)

Decision Tree Algorithms

Decision tree learning use a tree structure as a predictive model which maps observations about an item (represented in the branches) to conclusions about the item's target value (represented in the leaves). Decisions fork in tree structures until a prediction decision is made for a given record. Decision trees are trained on data for classification and regression problems based on actual values of attributes in the data
It is one of the most popular predictive modelling approaches used in machine learning. Tree models where the target variable can take a finite set of values are called classification trees; Decision trees where the target variable can take continuous values such as real numbers are called regression trees.
The most popular decision tree algorithms are:
- Classification and Regression Tree (CART)
- Iterative Dichotomiser 3 (ID3)
- C4.5 and C5.0 (different versions of a powerful approach)

Bayesian Algorithms

Bayesian logic is a branch of logic applied to decision making and inferential statistics that deals with probability inference: using the knowledge of prior events to predict future events. In machine learning Bayesian algorithms apply Bayes' Theorem for problems such as classification and regression.
The most popular Bayesian algorithms are:
- Naive Bayes

- Bayesian Network (BN)

Clustering Algorithms

Clustering is concerned with finding groups of similar type data within a larger set.
Clustering methods are typically determined by Euclidean or Manhattan distance from the data point to the cluster centroid, so are designed to best organize the data into groups of maximum commonality.
The most popular clustering algorithms are:
- k-Means
- k-Medians
- Expectation Maximisation (EM)

Association Rule Learning Algorithms

Association rule learning is a rules-based method for discovering interesting relations between variables in large data sets. Association rule learning methods extract rules that best explain observed relationships between variables in data such as a strong coherence or a strong anti-coherence.
Association rules can reveal many hidden relationships and associations between objects which are important and commercially useful in large multidimensional datasets.
The most popular association rule learning algorithms are:
- Apriori algorithm
- Eclat algorithm

Artificial Neural Network Algorithms

Artificial Neural Networks are models that are inspired by nature's biological neural networks. They are based very loosely on the brain's neuron network.

They are commonly used for regression and classification problems but are also used in variations for all manner of problem types.

The most popular artificial neural network algorithms are:

- Perceptron
- Back-Propagation

Deep Learning Algorithms

Deep Learning methods are a modern update to Artificial Neural Networks that exploit the cloud's abundance of cheap resources in compute, memory, storage and networks.

They are concerned with building much larger and more complex neural networks with much greater depth and are often applied to problems with semi-supervised learning working on large datasets contain very little labelled data.

The most popular deep learning algorithms are:

- Deep Boltzmann Machine (DBM)
- Deep Belief Networks (DBN)
- Convolutional Neural Network (CNN)
- Stacked Auto-Encoders

Ensemble Algorithms

Ensemble methods have become very popular lately as they have been found on many occasions to improve results over single pass algorithms. Ensemble models are composed of multiple weaker models that are independently trained and whose predictions are combined in some way to make the overall prediction more accurate. It is often described as 'the wisdom of a crowd of experts'.

- Boosting
- Bootstrapped Aggregation (Bagging)
- Random Forest

🔲

Deep Learning and Deep Neural Networks

Neural networks are a set of algorithms that are designed to recognize patterns and so they help us cluster and classify objects. They help to group unlabelled data according to similarities among the example inputs, and they classify data when they have a labelled dataset to train on. Those labels that could be applied to data: for example, spam or not_spam in an email filter teaches an algorithm the correlation between the labels and inputs.

Deep learning for example maps inputs to outputs to discover correlations. By having training data comprising correctly labelled examples of data the neural network can use negative feedback to refine its predictions from pure guess-work to learned predictions. A neural network is known as a "universal approximator", because it can learn to approximate an unknown function $f(x) = y$ between any input x and any output y. That of course assumes that there is some correlation or causation to begin with. Assuming they are related a neural network via the process of learning will find the right value of f, or the correct manner of transforming x into y, whether that be $f(x) = 3x + 12$ or $f(x) = 9x - 0.1$. Hence deep learning using neural networks has found many use cases, such as:

- Classification - All classification tasks depend upon labelled datasets so that the deep learning process can learn the correlation between labels and data. This is known as supervised learning. Any labels that humans can generate, any outcomes that you care about and which correlate to data, can be used to train a neural network.
- Clustering- the grouping or clustering of data points results in the detection of similarities between inputs. Deep learning does not

require labels to detect similarities. Learning without labels is called unsupervised learning.

- Anomaly detection - The reverse of detecting similarities is detecting anomalies between inputs. In many cases, unusual behaviour correlates highly with things you want to detect and prevent, such as fraud.
- Regressions – if exposed to enough of the right data, deep learning is able to establish correlations between present events and future events this is called Predictive Analytics. With Deep Learning we are becoming better at making prediction, and the better we predict the better we can prevent and pre-empt unwanted events from occurring.

Neural Network Elements

Deep learning is the name we use for a model of "stacked neural networks"; that is, networks of nodes arranged in several layers. The layers are made of nodes and these are just a place where some sort of computation occurs. A node combines an input from the data set we supply with a set of weights or biases, which either accentuates or attenuates that input. These weights therefore assign significance to inputs that are helpful in classifying data that the algorithm is trying to learn without error? These input-weight products are summed and then the sum is passed through a node's so-called activation function. This is where the algorithm determines whether the signal should progress further through the network and to what extent it may affect the ultimate outcome, say, and a classification. If the signals pass through, the neuron is said to have been "activated."

A node layer is a row of those neuron-like switches that turn on or off as the input is fed through the net. Each layer's output is simultaneously the subsequent layer's input, starting from an initial input layer receiving your data set.

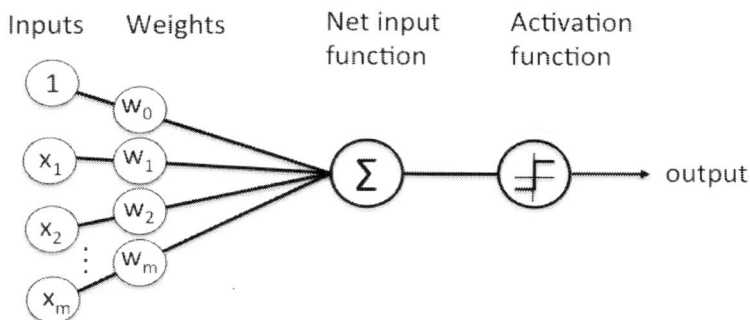

Inputs Weights Net input function Activation function

Pairing the model's adjustable weights with input features is how we assign significance to those features with regard to how the neural network classifies and clusters input.

Key Concepts of Deep Neural Networks

Deep-learning networks are distinguished from the more commonplace single-hidden-layer neural networks by their depth; that is, the number of node layers through which data must pass in a multistep process of pattern recognition. For example, typically more than three layers inclusive of the input and output layers will qualify as "deep" learning so a prerequisite for deep learning is more than one hidden layer.

In deep-learning networks, each layer of nodes trains on a distinct set of features based on the previous layer's output. The further you advance into the neural net, the more complex the features your nodes can recognize, since they aggregate and recombine features from the previous layer.

This is known as feature hierarchy, and it is because of this hierarchy of increasing complexity and abstraction, which makes deep-learning networks capable of handling very large, high-dimensional data sets with billions of parameters.

However, what is a highly valuable aspect of deep learning neural networks is that these neural nets are capable of discovering latent structures without labels using unstructured data, in unsupervised learning mode. Unstructured data is perhaps as much as 80% of data used in business, i.e. pictures, texts, video and audio recordings and one of the problems deep learning solves best is in processing and clustering unlabelled data. For example, deep learning might cluster raw text such as emails or news articles. Emails full of angry complaints might cluster in one corner of the vector space, while satisfied customers might cluster in another. Indeed, with time series, data might cluster around normal/healthy behaviour and cluster will occur around anomalous/dangerous behaviour. If the time series data is being generated by a fitness app on a user's smart phone, it may well provide insight into the users' health; if it is being generated by a machine part, it could indicate the need for some preventative maintenance to prevent a lost time breakdown.

In this section we will learn some of the basic principles behind algorithms and some of the important inherent constraints. We will discuss the concepts of Loss/Cost, the Bias-variance dilemma, the requirement for generalization, and our preference for simple over complex models. In addition we will introduce a commonly used term in Machine Learning, overfitting and we will learn the principle, how it occurs and why it is such an issue. We will also learn how we measure error accurately and suggest some trade-offs that improve performance.

Loss/Cost

Linear Regression is a Machine Learning algorithm that allows us to map numeric inputs to numeric outputs, fitting a line into the data points. Basically we plot our data-points on a graph and then draw a line that closely matches or best-fits their positions on the chart.
This simplistically allows us to model the relationship between one or more variables. From a Machine Learning perspective, this enables the model to predict outputs for inputs it has never seen before. Any data points that exactly match the line are said to have zero cost or loss. However any data points that the line does not pass through are deemed to have a loss that is proportionate to their distance from the line. The total loss for the model is calculated using a loss squared calculation that reflects the overall accuracy of the predictions by giving more weight to data points further from the line. Also, if we don't square the error, then positive and negative point will cancel out each other. The objective is to obtain a line that best fits all the data i.e. one where the total prediction error (all data points) is as small as possible. Error is the distance between the data point to the regression line. In our simplistic model we drew a

line that best fitted the data but the goal is to design a model that can create an equation by using training data that produces a regression line which will give minimum error. This linear equation is then used for any new data.

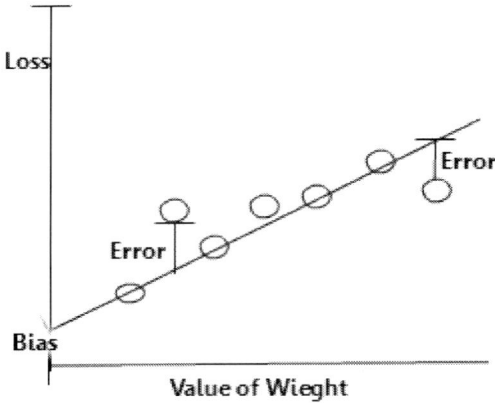

Reducing Error

A characteristic or regression problems is that they only one minimum; that is, only one place where the slope is exactly 0. That minimum is where the loss function converges.

Calculating the loss function for every conceivable value over the entire data set would be an inefficient way of finding the convergence point this is why we use a technique called gradient descent. When performing gradient descent, we generalize to tune all the model parameters simultaneously. Next, we modify the values based on their respective gradients. Then we repeat these steps until we reach minimum loss.

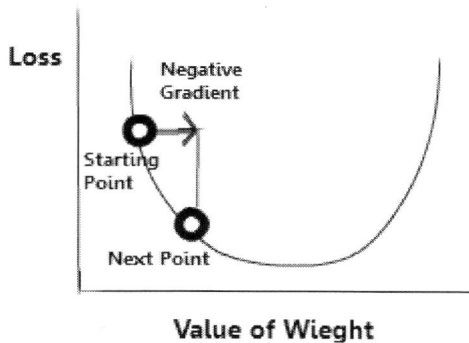

Value of Wieght

The gradient vector has both a direction and a magnitude so the algorithms multiply the gradient by a scalar known as the step size or learning rate to determine the next point. For example, if the gradient magnitude is 2.5 and the learning rate is 0.01, then the gradient descent algorithm will pick the next point 0.025 away from the previous point. Hence it is important that we determine an optimal learning rate or it will take forever for the algorithm to reach the point of convergence. On the other hand if we make the learning rate to big it might overshoot the point of minimal error and never converge.

The Bias-Variance dilemma

One major concept of machine learning is the principle of balancing bias and variance, which is commonly referred to as the bias-variance dilemma. Another common principle is that Machine Learning algorithms try to make generalizations, but that is a very desirable feature. That is, they try to explain something with the simplest theory, the one that makes fewest assumptions. Generalization is very important in enabling machines to learn in real world applications in so much as the machine doesn't require exact samples of training data it can generalize. Generally training data will consist of samples with varying amounts of bias and variance that is acceptable to the training hypothesis set. What we mean by these terms is that:

Hypothesis set – this term crops up occasionally and tends to leave some of us perplexed, so here is an explanation. A target function maps data to its target value; it is the engine within the algorithm. Generally the more specific the target function the simpler the model and higher the bias.

Bias – is a quality that is introduced to assist the machine to learn by tailoring the training data to make it easier for the learning function to distinguish between what is a target and what is not.

High Bias is when we make the training samples more specific perhaps by using several parameters that must be matched or by making one parameter highly specific. For example in the OCR example we could adjust the learning function to identify only specific computer font types, or make it even more specific by setting the target as only one font type, say Times Roman. This would be a case of high bias as our machine's target function would fail to recognize any handwritten characters or even any other diverse fonts.

Low Bias on the other hand would be if we trained the machine's learning/target function with a wide range of samples of say, computer and printed fonts and handwritten samples of characters, symbols and numbers. This would undoubtedly make it much more difficult for the target function to learn all the potential variations for each character but it would be far more effective when working on live data as it could generalize more.

Ultimately though we have to accept that there is no escaping the relationship between bias and variance in machine learning, the best we can do is a trade-off as;

- Increasing the bias will decrease the variance.
- Increasing the variance will decrease the bias.

Furthermore, in most cases we cannot calculate the real bias and variance error and this is mainly because we do not know the actual underlying target function within the algorithm. Nevertheless, the bias-variance relationship helps us to understand some of the performance constraints in machine learning algorithms, which are evident in predictive modelling.

Generalization error

Generalization is very important In Machine Learning as we need generalization to produce outputs for inputs not encountered during training. It provides the capability to produce results on unseen data that are as near to real outputs produced during training. In machine learning an algorithm is used to fit a model to data whether that is training, validation or live testing set. And in order to achieve this task our algorithm must first be trained.

During a training period the model is presented with examples of the target data. The training data, which should be a small random subset of the live working data, is fed to the algorithm and the model's target function (included in the hypothesis set). The target function tweaks its internal parameters to improve its performance to better understand the data samples over further iterations of training. Remember it can do this because the target function knows the correct answers due to training data being labelled.

Once the many training iterations are completed, the model is fed another small block of samples of new unseen data. The algorithm then uses what it has learned to map the new data and the output can be compared to its training performance to assess its effectiveness. This is what is called the validation period where the goal is to assess the models performance on unseen data.

Now here's where problems often arise, because often two issues arise. One is that the model that had previously performed well in training suddenly is hopeless on the validation or live data. This is due to the model having been over trained on the training samples. Over-training results in the model being able to identify 100% of the training data, as it has effectively tuned itself precisely to the exact examples in the training set. So now it will not understand the new data. We then say that the model is incapable of generalizing, or that it is overfitting the training data.

Naturally, any model is highly optimized for the data it was trained on. The expected error the model exhibits on new untested data will always be higher than that on the training data. Every Machine Learning algorithm, regardless of the paradigm it uses, will try to create the simplest hypothesis that explains most of the training examples.

Chapter 13 – Planning the ML Process

In this Chapter we come back to addressing the harsh practical reality of preparing a Machine Learning model. We will learn how to handle data, through acquisition, cleansing and preparation. We will also learn how to choose an approach, a method and an algorithm that suits our needs.

The ML Planning Process

Again, Machine Learning sounds like a magical concept, and by and large it is, but there are some processes involved that are not so automatic. In fact, many times the amount of manual steps that are required when designing the solution becomes apparent, this is where a lot of machine learning projects slip into oblivion. Nevertheless, these manual steps are some important prerequisites when dealing with Machine Learning that are of huge importance in order to obtain decent results. Some of those aspects are visible in planning for machine learning.

The Machine Learning planning process consists of several defined steps:

1)   Acquisition – collect the data (often not nearly as simply as it sounds)

2)   Prepare – clean and prepare the data (often this is a daunting task)

3)   Process – run machine algorithms and machine tools

4)   Report – present the results

Planning is an essential part of any project, for as the old maxim goes; if you don't have a plan then you are planning to fail. Therefore as every machine learning project starts with a question, we need to ask what it is we are hoping to achieve.

It is only after the answer to that fundamental question has been identified can you go on to making other project plans. Knowing the task and identifying the problem is the foundation of machine learning planning.

Once the project goals have been clearly defined we can start to look at other planning dimensions and the following are some common planning queries.

A common question when starting out on a ML project is which type of Machine Learning algorithm should I use?

Supervised or unsupervised?

The major criteria here involve the availability of sufficient quantities of clean tagged data. This is often the issue with ML projects in that there is often an abundance of data collected from many sources but it requires be collating, cleaning and categorizing before being checked for the required features. That is examples of the feature to be learned, the input with its corresponding desired output. If there are no issues with supplying a supervised learning algorithm with circa 10% of the source data for training purposes then supervised learning would in most cases be the best option. If not, then using untagged training data in an unsupervised algorithm can potentially solve the problem, though a lot depends on what you are trying to solve.

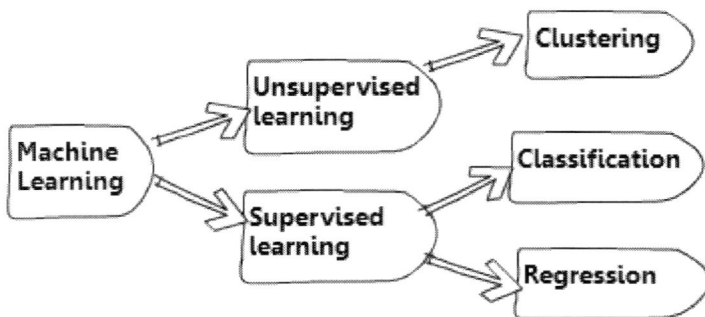

Classification, regression or clustering

Whether you choose to use classification, regression or clustering is dependent on what you're trying to solve as they are constructed for different purposes. If you want to categorize data (assign a tag within a discrete set of options) such as with the OCR example, classification will be the right option. If on the other hand, you need to assign a number, for example a score as in the credit score example, then regression may be the best option. Clustering is best for finding similarities between instances and discovering correlations within the raw data that might not be readily observable such as when Amazon recommends similar products to users depending on what they are currently viewing, so in that case clustering could be the best option.

Which algorithm is best?

There are many types or families of algorithm such as Deep Learning, SVM, Bayesian networks, Association rules, Decision Trees... so which one is best? There is no best algorithm, as a one size fits all solution due to the purpose, performance, scalability and success criteria are often so diverse. For example, decision trees are often treated with derision but if all that the algorithm requires is a structured nest of 'if .. then' statements then why over engineer a solution? SVM (Support Vector Machine) is a very popular model for a machine learning algorithm designed for classification, whereas Association Rules as its name suggests targets similarities and associations between data instances so is popular in retail and online e-commerce sites. Bayesian networks are in their element when dealing with uncertainty, probability and are particular useful in financial market forecasting and in sales and marketing analysis. Neural networks on the other hand have not had nearly the same success over the long term – the last few decades – but recently they have rose to prominence due to some astonishing work in the fields of deep learning. However, deep learning is still very much in the fields of research especially into the complexity of AGI (artificial general intelligence) whereas the others tend to fulfil the needs of machine learning in main stream applied AI.

Machine Learning Languages, Frameworks and Libraries

Machine learning and artificial intelligence-based projects differ from traditional software development due to differences in the technology stack so it needs a programming language that is stable, flexible, and has a wide variety of ML libraries and tools available. One language that fits that criterion is Python.

Python

The attributes that make Python a good fit for machine learning and AI-based projects include simplicity and consistency, access to great libraries and frameworks for AI and machine learning (ML), flexibility, platform independence, and a large thriving community of ML developers. These benefits add to the overall popularity of the language.

Simple and consistent

Python offers concise and readable code. While complex algorithms and versatile workflows typically stand behind machine learning and AI, it is Python's simplicity, which allows developers to write reliable code. Hence, developers are able to put all their effort into solving an ML problem instead of focusing on the technical nuances of the coding language. Additionally, Python is appealing to many developers as it's easy to learn. Python code is understandable and readable by humans, which makes it easier to build and share models for machine learning. Due to these qualities it's generally accepted that Python is suitable for collaborative implementation when multiple developers are involved.
Many programmers say that Python is more intuitive than other programming languages. Others point out the many frameworks, libraries, and extensions that simplify the implementation of different functionalities. Since Python is a general-purpose language that can also accomplish complex machine learning tasks this combination enables you to build and test your ML prototypes quickly.

Extensive selection of libraries and frameworks

Implementing AI and ML algorithms can be tricky and requires a lot of time. It's vital to have a well-structured and well-tested environment to enable developers to come up with the best coding solutions.

To reduce development time, programmers turn to a number of Python frameworks and libraries. A software library is pre-written code that developers use to solve common programming tasks. Python, with its rich technology stack, has an extensive set of libraries for artificial intelligence and machine learning. Here are some of them:

- Keras, TensorFlow, and Scikit-learn for machine learning
- NumPy for high-performance scientific computing and data analysis
- SciPy for advanced computing
- Pandas for general-purpose data analysis
- Seaborn for data visualization
- Scikit-learn features various classification, regression, and clustering algorithms, including support vector machines, random forests, gradient boosting, k-means, and DBSCAN, and is designed to work with the Python numerical and scientific libraries NumPy and SciPy.

With these solutions, you can develop your product faster. Your development team won't have to reinvent the wheel and can use an existing library to implement necessary features.

What is Python good for?

Here's a table of typical AI use cases and technologies that are best suited for each purpose:

Data analysis and visualization	NumPy, SciPy, Pandas, Seaborn
Machine learning	TensorFlow, Keras, Scikit-learn
Computer vision	OpenCV

| Natural language processing | NLTK, spaCy |

Platform independence

Platform independence refers to an attribute of a programming language or framework, which permits developers to implement code on one machine and reuse the code on another machine without any (or with only minimal) changes. One key to Python's popularity is that it's a platform independent language. Python is supported by many platforms including Linux, Windows, and MacOS. In addition, Python code can be used to create standalone executable programs for most common operating systems, which means that Python software can be easily distributed and used on those operating systems without a Python interpreter.

What's more, developers usually use cloud services such as Google or Amazon for their computing needs. However, you can often find companies and data scientists who use their own machines with powerful Graphics Processing Units (GPUs) to train their ML models. And the fact that Python is platform independent makes this training a lot cheaper and easier.

Jupyter Notebook

Jupyter Notebook is a lightweight IDE that is a favourite among data engineers. In most cases, the installation package for Python already includes Jupyter Notebook. In Google Cloud Platform you have an enhanced version of Jupyter Notebooks called AI Platform Notebooks, which is based upon the enhanced JupyterLab. Jupyter Notebooks allows you to build, test applications and train ML models locally before you deploy them to the on-premise or cloud systems.

Some other Python libraries you will need are:

NumPy

NumPy, is shortened from Numerical Python, it is the most universal and versatile library both for pros and beginners. Using this tool you are able to operate with multi-dimensional arrays and matrices with ease and comfort. Such functions like linear algebra operations and numerical conversions are also available.

Pandas

Pandas, is a high-performance tool for handling and presenting data frames. Using it you can load data from almost any source, calculate various functions and create new parameters, build queries to data using aggregate functions akin to SQL. What is more, there are various matrix transformation functions, a sliding window method and other methods for obtaining information from data. So it's totally an indispensable thing in the arsenal of a good specialist.

Matplotlib

Matplotlib is a flexible library for creating graphs and visualization. It is powerful but somewhat heavy-weight. At this point, you can skip Matplotlib and use Seaborn to get started

Scikit-Learn

Scikit-Learn is a Python ML library that hosts a wide-range of machine-learning algorithms that are easy to plug into actual applications. There is an array of ML functions in-built that you can use such as; regression, clustering, model selection, pre-processing, classification and more.

Keras

Keras is an open-source neural-network library written in Python. It is capable of running on top of TensorFlow. It is designed to enable fast experimentation with deep neural networks as it focuses on being user-friendly, modular, and extensible. GCP has integrated Keras APIs into its ML TensorFlow framework to make them easier to work with.

TensorFlow

TensorFlow – originally developed by Google - is an open source library for large-scale machine learning and computation. TensorFlow is a comprehensive ML framework that bundles together a collection of machine learning and deep learning models and algorithms. It works with both Python and R to provide a convenient front-end API for building applications. However TensorFlow relies on high-performance C++ for execution and computation.

TensorFlow can train and run deep neural networks (deep learning) for a vast array of use-cases such as; handwritten numbers and letters classification, image recognition, natural language processing, and sequence-to-sequence models used in automated machine translation. TensorFlow was originally said to be complex and difficult to work with but the latest version TensorFlow 2.0 goes a long way to address that issue. Now TensorFlow supports Keras APIs, which greatly eases the burden. But one thing TensorFlow has always been acclaimed for remains and that is its ability to handle production prediction at very-large scale, using the same models deployed in training.

How TensorFlow works

The TensorFlow framework enables developers to create dataflow graphs— these graphs are multi-dimensional structures that describe how data moves through a series of processing nodes. Each node in the graph represents a mathematical operation, and each connection between the processing nodes represents a multidimensional data array, or tensor. TensorFlow handles all of this for the developer via the Python or R languages. Python is typically more commonly used as it is easy to learn and work with. In TensorFlow the nodes and tensors are Python objects, which provides a high=level abstraction for how they are coupled together. However, to take advantage of superior speed the actual math operations are written as high-performance C++ binaries.

TensorFlow applications are platform independent and can be run on almost any system for example: a local Jupyter Notebook, a cluster in the cloud, or on mobile iOS and Android devices. Furthermore, they can run on multiple CPUs or GPUs or you can use Google's own custom TensorFlow Processing Unit (TPU) for even better performance.

TensorFlow 2.0 is the latest improved version of the framework based on the relatively simple Keras APIs for model training. However, it is not fully backwards compatible so code written for earlier versions of TensorFlow will most likely require to be rewritten if you want to take advantage of the new TensorFlow 2.0 features.

TensorFlow benefits

The single biggest benefit TensorFlow provides for machine learning development is its high-level abstraction of the interfacing of Nodes and Tensors. Hence, instead of you having to figure out the proper ways to interconnect nodes and connect the output of one function to the input of another when implementing a new algorithm the developer can focus on the overall logic of the application. TensorFlow will handle all of the connectivity and implementation details for you.

In addition to being easier to deploy there are many other benefits with TensorFlow, such as; there is the TensorBoard visualization suite, which allows you to inspect and profile the way graphs run via an interactive, web-based dashboard. This can be very useful in debugging as you can watch each individual graph running on a node in isolation. There is also an online hub (marketplace) for sharing TensorFlow ML models; there are in-browser and mobile-friendly installations of the framework; and much more.

PyTorch

PyTorch is a Python-based scientific computing package that uses the power of graphics processing units. It is also one of the preferred deep learning research platforms built to provide maximum flexibility and speed. It is known for providing two of the most high-level features; namely, tensor computations with strong GPU acceleration support and building deep neural networks on tape-based autograd systems.

There are many existing Python libraries which have the potential to change how deep learning and artificial intelligence are performed, and this is one such library. One of the key reasons behind PyTorch's success is it is completely Pythonic and one can build neural network models effortlessly.

PyTorch creators envisioned this library to be highly imperative which can allow them to run all the numerical computations quickly. This is an ideal methodology which fits perfectly with the Python programming style. It has allowed deep learning scientists, machine learning developers, and neural network debuggers to run and test part of the code in real time. Thus they don't have to wait for the entire code to be executed to check whether it works or not.

You can always use your favourite Python packages such as NumPy, SciPy, and Cython to extend PyTorch functionalities and services when required. Some of the key highlights of PyTorch include:

- Simple Interface: It offers easy to use API, thus it is very simple to operate and run like Python.
- Pythonic in nature: PyTorch functionalities are built as Python classes hence all its code can seamlessly integrate with Python packages and modules.
- Dynamic Computational graphs: PyTorch provides dynamic computational graphs unlike TensorFlow's static graphs thus you can interact and alter them during runtime. This is highly useful when you have no idea how much memory will be required for creating a neural network model.

Python-Approach

PyTorch provides a complete end-to-end ML framework with the most common building blocks required for every day deep learning research. It allows chaining of high-level neural network modules as it supports Keras-like APIs.

Part II – Google Cloud Platform Fundamentals

Chapter 14 - An Introduction to the Google Cloud Platform
In the following chapters we will build upon this subject by introducing the four main categories of cloud services: compute, storage, Big Data and machine learning. However, we must not forget cloud security and networking as these are the essential glue that holds everything together in a robust and low latency manner.
Moreover, we will explain how GCP is flexible enough to provide you options for computing and hosting where you can choose a platform to:

- Work in a serverless environment – Function Engine or Cloud Run
- Use a managed application platform – Apps Engine
- Leverage container technologies to gain lots of flexibility – Kubernetes Engine or Cloud Run on GKE
- Build your own cloud-based infrastructure to have the most control and flexibility – Compute Engine

When you consider what technologies constitute Google Cloud Platform you should also contemplate the areas of shared responsibility. You can imagine a spectrum where, at one end you have most of the responsibilities for resource management, which is Compute Engine. At the other end of the spectrum is Cloud Function Engine and Cloud Run, where Google retains most of those responsibilities as they are fully managed services often called a serverless environment. Regardless, the GCP gives you options for both hands on managing of resources or to take advantage of Google's managed services, it's up to you.
Figure-1

Operational Responsibility

User ← ops ═══════════ no-ops → Google Cloud Platform

VM Infrastructure	Container cluster management	Managed Apps Platform	Serverless environment
IaaS	hybrid	PaaS	SaaS
Compute Engine	Kubernetes Engine	App Engine	Cloud Functions

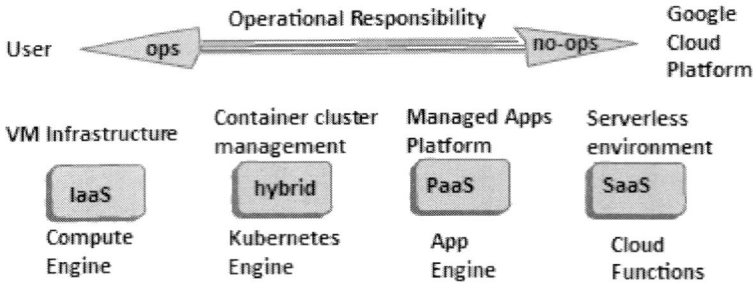

In this chapter we will start by focusing on the VM infrastructure within the compute and storage services together with the topic of networking. Networking is important to us as we cannot effectively use any of the cloud's resources without using the Cloud Networking services. However cloud networking is often the least understood component of cloud computing as it differs in several ways from the traditional on-premises networking that you may already be familiar with.

As a result we will through the course of this book build upon the overview we present in this chapter by providing deeper and wider discussions on cloud networking in subsequent chapters. The same can be said of security. Similarly we will first introduce some basic security concepts that pertain to the cloud before going into greater detail later in the book. But for now let us start with some basic concepts on cloud computing.

Cloud Computing Concepts

Cloud computing is about the seamless delivery of computing services— including infrastructure such as virtual servers, large scale storage, databases, and networking, as well as platforms for Big Data, advanced analytics, and artificial intelligence— all over the Internet ("the cloud"). These services provide you with the means for faster innovation through flexible infrastructure and rapid deployment of resources, with the benefits of economies of scale. You typically will pay only for cloud services you use; this helps you lower your capital expenditure, run your infrastructure and operations more cost efficiently, as well as the capability to scale to meet your business requirements.

Cloud computing platforms have become very popular over the last decade due to some fundamental principles:

- First, the cloud is a very cost-effective and highly efficient place to rapidly develop, deploy, run your applications and store your app data. This is mainly because it reduces any upfront capital investments in servers and other infrastructure but also because it greatly reduces the operational burden if not the overall cost because it means you are no longer burdened with many time consuming tasks such as provisioning servers, then having to maintain them or even backing them up so it frees you from a lot of housekeeping chores.

- Secondly, scale, Cloud services scale dynamically both growing and shrinking resource consumption as required. This type of dynamic or elastic scaling of resources can result in reasonably priced access to high performance and almost infinite infrastructure resources.

- Thirdly, performance, cloud computing provides truly global access which enables the delivery of your services and products closer to your customers across the cloud provider's own global-scale infrastructure. This vast network inherently provides global load balancing and the distribution of content closest to the customer resulting in lower latency and economy of scale.

- Fourthly, reliability, Cloud computing makes data backup, disaster recovery, and business continuity easier and less expensive because data can be mirrored at multiple redundant sites on the cloud provider's network at a fraction of the cost of an on-premise solution.

- Last, but not least, productivity, as on-premises data centres typically require a lot of manual installation of hardware, application and stack provisioning on top of hardware configuration, software and security patching, and many other support duties. Cloud computing removes the need for many of these tasks, so IT teams can spend time on achieving more innovative and business orientated goals.

Those are the main features and benefits of cloud computing in general but how is Google's Platform organized and what differentiates it from the competition?

Google Cloud Platform

As we have just seen, the five drivers behind cloud computing that enthuse customers to migrate their IT systems to remote service providers, relates to cheaper and more efficient availability of resources. This also provides for disaster recovery and business continuity solutions that come at a fraction of the cost of redundant data centres. However, although this explains the attraction for companies with limited budgets, technical resources, little in-house IT skills, or only a local presence, it doesn't address the needs of SME or larger organizations where IT skills are in abundance and where there are multiple locations for business continuity. Furthermore, with these large enterprises it is control, security and management that are the key concerns. Indeed for many large organisations the actual cost saving that are so apparent to the smaller organisation and the startup are possibly going to prove neutral or even negative. This is simply because the cloud financial model shifts the burden away from one-time capital expenditure (CapEx) onto operational recurring costs (OpEx). Consequently, a large organisation with thousands of applications and servers may find that the cloud is not the cost effective nirvana they have been led to believe.

Framing the ROI

Consequently when framing any questions regards return on investment for moving to the cloud for all but the smallest of companies or startup we should avoid stressing the cost saving benefits. The reason for this is two-fold, one it may not actually be true for larger or well established organizations. Two, it is better to concentrate on composite ROI whereby you take a three tier approach. The lower tier would be regards the infrastructure Total-Cost-of Ownership (TCO) and capital investments in modernisation. For a startup the value generated at this tier could be significant but for most larger organizations the CapEx and OpEx ratio will typically be neutral or even negative over 3-5 years. Then we should consider the second tier which concerns Human Resources (HR) with regards to the operations and maintenance and this is where organisations can make some positive ROI due to offshoring much of the operations, management and maintenance burden and thus reducing staffing, training and administration requirements. However, even at this HR tier the ROI is typically only around 5%. It is at the third tier, which measures business value that we will typically see significant return on investment. Indeed when we consider business benefits in the ROI this is where we start to see ROI in excess of 50%.

Therefore, when considering ROI for moving to the cloud you should take a holistic approach by considering infrastructure, HR and business value to reach a composite value. This will require involving the business-teams in technology decision making as well as elevating IT to become a business function with responsibilities to create business value. After all this is what digital transformation is all about.

Spoilt for Choice

So switching perspective we can now view the benefits from a SME or start up point-of-view. Thus we are now seeing more enterprises moving their IT operations to the cloud, but the old question persists, to what cloud? The question is difficult to answer as it depends on circumstances. As we discussed earlier if you are heavily dependent on a particular technology say Oracle, IBM or VMware then it makes sense to lift-and-shift your operations straight up to the respective vendors cloud. However, for the vast number of Microsoft business clients it makes more sense to deploy to Microsoft Azure cloud. This is simply due to the respective vendors knowing their products better than anyone else. For SMBs and SMEs with more general requirements and open source solutions then Amazon AWS is by far the most popular and largest cloud environment. AWS has the largest global reach and number of points-of-presence; it also has by far the largest portfolio of cloud services. So, why would an SMB, SME or large enterprise want to move their operations to specifically the Google Cloud Platform?

The Google Cloud Platform

Google has built one of the largest fibre optic networks in the world and they have invested billions of dollars over the years to build the network to meet their own vast global requirements. As a result, the network has been designed to deliver the highest throughput with the lowest possible latencies for their internet based applications. To meet their own specifications required that Google designed an SDN network unlike any vendor's roadmap at the time.
Google's cloud network's global scope may not be as large as AWS but Google is investing heavily and catching up quickly. For example, the global scale of the network requires interconnects at more than 90 Internet exchanges, which ensures fast efficient connection with low latency. What is more Google has more than 100 points of presence worldwide that are geographically and strategically placed. This global distribution of PoPs ensures redundancy and high availability. Thus, if an Internet user sends traffic to a Google resource that is temporarily unavailable, Google will detect the request and will respond via the closest edge network location. This method provides the lowest latency and provides the best customer experience.

In addition, Google's Edge-caching network also provides geographical caching of content so that it always delivers content closest to the end user. A distributed cache will minimize latency and increase customer experience by reducing connection and download times as well as provide a measure of business continuity.

 Although Google may be considered to have been slow of the mark to benefit from sharing their global network they have tried over the last few years to catch up with Amazon's AWS cloud platform. Consequently, they have invested billions of dollars building their own cloud platform and global network fibre links to ensure its networks are low latency, resilient and highly efficient.

Today, Google strives to make their cloud platform attractive, affordable and available to their customers. This change in strategy appears to come about as Google has come to believe like Amazon, that presently and in the future data is and will be integral to all businesses, regardless of size or industry. This was not always the case, as even quite recently IT was often considered to be a service function of a business. After all manufacturing or product development, sales, marketing and finance were the core profit generating business units. IT was simply a service department that generated no new money or profit. But as technology has become integrated and almost inseparable with all these traditional business functions cloud providers have come to realize that the way a company will differentiate itself from its competitors will be through leveraging cost effective advanced IT technology in order to create new business value from its data. Google's belief is that future companies will largely deal in data, through advanced analytics, Artificial Intelligence and its subset of machine learning.

 Hence, Google's focus is on providing cloud services for businesses that focus on data and analytics, but also for companies that need to reimaging there data centres in the cloud to extend their scale and global reach. As, in the future, companies must have the ability to service customers around the globe. Hence, customers that build on-premises solutions will be at a severe disadvantage as the cost are simply prohibitive. What is worse it is crucial capital that is wasted as it should be spent on core business functions that generate profit.

Thus, Google believes that every company will have a need to rely on data analytics as well as have a global presence and this will require a global partner that can provide them the infrastructure to scale to their ambitions. Ultimately, this strategy will allow them to release their cash and energy to be spent on developing digital processes that permeates the entire organisation and its value and supply chains. It is by following this road-map that places an emphasis on pursuing affordable, scalable, global and highly-advanced technology that will enable organisations to differentiate themselves and become digital leaders and the creators of innovative business value.

Cloud Native Architecture

Google's network is designed to support its eight key web-based products which each have in excess of one billion subscribers so it must be designed to be robust, scalable and efficient. But how does it differ from traditional network design?
At a high level, we can consider cloud-native architecture to mean a design that adapts to take advantage of the many new possibilities—but also the very different set of architectural constraints—offered by the cloud compared to traditional on-premises infrastructure. If we look to some of the high level elements such as:

- The functional requirements of a system
- The non-functional requirements
- The architectural constraints

What we actually will find is that the cloud is not much different from the on-premises data centre. This is simply because the cloud is made of the same fabric of servers, disks and networks that makes up traditional infrastructure. This means that almost all of the principles of good architectural design still apply for cloud-native architecture.

While many of the functional aspects remain the same regardless as to on-premises or cloud the latter is often more challenging when it comes to the non-functional aspects. These do often result in design constraints. Indeed, some of the fundamental assumptions about how the infrastructure fabric performs do change when you're in the cloud. The differences are in speed and flexibility. For instance, provisioning a replacement server can take weeks in traditional environments, even in VM environments it still takes a day, whereas in the cloud, it takes seconds. Hence in the cloud it's much easier to provision a full application stack with fully automated scaling and fail-over scenarios than on-premises. However in order to take advantage of these properties it is a requirement that the cloud provider has many application and vendor partners. To this end Google Cloud Platform support a very large partner network, which allows you to provision both proprietary and open source solutions with a single click via the Cloud Launcher service.

Google's SDN network facilitates a cloud-native design, which also tends to focus on key metrics such as resilience, horizontal scaling, distributed processing, and automation. So we need to take these characteristics into account when you are evaluating other cloud-native architectures that are not based on Google's own SDN cloud network.

Google Software Defined Network

The Google Cloud Platform is organized as a software defined network, now that might sound confusing but it's not really and we will consider the architecture later in some detail. But for now all you need to know is that Google's global network is defined by segments and its smallest entity is a Zone, which can be defined as a deployment area for Google Cloud Platform Resources. It could be simplified to mean a data centre but that is not always the case as a zone could have several points of presence within a local zone. However a zone works as one large switch operating within a common subnet so entities within a zone communicate at layer-2 or the Ethernet data layer – which we will cover later – but it means latency is minimal and configuration negligible.

When you launch a virtual machine for example, in a GCP zone using Compute Engine, you will be prompted to select a local zone. This is the local area where you wish the application or service to run. Hence you would select the closest zone to where you want the application or service to run. This will ensure that the associated compute, storage and network resources are local and close to the area they serve to deliver low latency and high performance. However zones, as we have seen, can be large geographical areas that contain several data centres which are many kilometres apart and this allows for a measure of redundancy and business continuity planning. For instance you could mirror your infrastructure across two zones perhaps 100 km apart to give you a measure of mitigation for disaster recovery or business continuity should one zone's data centre suffer a natural catastrophe.

Zones are grouped into regions

As we have seen zones are segments in larger independent geographic areas called regions. This means that you can select what zone and region you're GCP resources reside in. Importantly, all the zones within a region have very fast and very low latency interconnected network connectivity among them as they operate much like an Ethernet switch at layer-2 in the data communications protocol stack. Intercommunication between Zones within a region will typically have round trip network latencies of under-five milliseconds, which is very fast when you consider the devices may be 100 km apart or more.

What this means is that zones within a region can be considered to be from a data network perspective both a single broadcast domain as well as a single failure domain. This is important when you contemplate building a fault tolerant application, as you can easily spread the application's resources across multiple zones within a region. This is because they share a common subnet so the fail-over from one server to another will be seamless. Sharing a common layer-2 domain helps protect against unexpected failures as well as greatly assist in real-time synchronization or replication of data between cluster peers or master/slave models despite the fact they may be 100s of miles apart.

Furthermore, you can run synchronised or mirrored resources in different regions if you want greater security against natural disasters. However it is not just for business continuity or disaster recovery that you may want to mirror infrastructure across regions as many organizations choose to do this in order to deliver content to customers' at the most convenient point of presence. Thus you may choose to use regions to deliver content closer to your customer base. For example this is how Google brings their applications closer to their users wherever they may be in the world. Diversifying across regions also protects against the loss of an entire region, say, due to a submarine fibre cable being severed or some natural disaster.

Sometimes you will find that some Google Cloud platform services do support placing resources in what we call a Multi-Regional configuration. Currently the GCP is configured to support 15 regions. What this means is that data may well be stored across regions within the parent region. For example data may be redundantly stored across several geographically diverse locations within the US Multi-Region. In practice this means that there is a copy of the data stored in at least two geographic locations, separated by at least 160 kilometres within the US. You may want to look into this if you are located in Europe or Asia for example as some nations despite being in the same broad geographical region may not wish or be allowed to store data out with their own borders. If that is the case then you can easily stipulate the regions and zones you wish your data to be backed-up that meet your nation's regulatory compliance.

Sustainable Cloud Networks

In the era of the new green deal and the awakening of public awareness that demands a future based upon sustainable and carbon neutral industry, enterprise data centres have come under the spotlight. It is hardly surprising as computer networks consume vast quantities of energy and produce equal amounts of wasted energy in the form of heat. Indeed, the internet is built on physical infrastructure, and all those servers consume vast amounts of energy and produce heat as a by-product that has to be controlled or dissipated. Around the world today data centres consume around two percent of the world's electricity supply; hence there is a responsibility for the major data centre providers to provide sustainable and eco-friendly energy plans. To this end Google strives to make their internet-scale data centres run as energy efficiently as possible.

As a result of their efforts Google's data centres were the first cloud providers to achieve ISO 14001 certification, which is the gold standard for improving resource efficiency and reducing waste. In order to achieve this certification Google is one of the world's largest corporate purchasers of wind and solar energy, which means that Google has been 100 percent carbon neutral since 2007, and will shortly reach a 100 percent renewable energy sources for its data centres.

Today many of Google's customers pursue environmental goals as part of their mission statements, for sustainable and green business practices and they can responsibly live up to those ideals by running their workloads in GCP.

Cloud Efficiency Model

The most commonly used list of benefits for adopting cloud computing is the one created by the US National Institute of Standards and Technology. In their definition, cloud computing is considered to be a model for efficiency in remotely hosting and running I.T. services, which have typically five equally important components.

First, Google Cloud Platform provides you with access to online remote computing resources; these are delivered as an on-demand and self-service model. Hence, GCP is ideal for small medium business (SME), small medium enterprises (SME) or for those matter companies of any size. This is because all you have to do is to use a simple interface to access all the processing power, storage, and network resources that you require. Importantly though you can have access to all the infrastructure, services and resources without the need for any of your own infrastructure or in-house skills as access to most GCP managed services requires no human intervention at all.

Second, because GCP resources are distributed around the globe and accessible on the internet you access these resources over the net from anywhere you have an internet connection. Furthermore, your customers can also access your applications or services from anywhere in the world with low latency and high availability. As a result you or your customers don't need to know or care about the exact physical location of those resources. What this means is that you can mirror your IT environments not only across zones but also regions and even continents to ensure business continuity in the case of a local or regional disruption of service. Previously, that would have required vast expense establishing multiple data centres and moreover in keeping them synchronised.

 Third, Google has their own internet-scale network infrastructure, which provides a vast pool of resources that are allocated dynamically to their clients on a pay-as-you-use basis. That model allows Google to dynamically service their customer with only the resources they require at any given moment so Google can get vast efficiencies by balancing their pool of resources across their demand driven network of customers. The elastic nature of the allocation of resources means that should you quickly need more resources such as CPU, memory, network bandwidth or storage you will get allocated them seamlessly and rapidly without any human intervention being required. However, if the demand were to fall you can then scale back. The consequences of this are that you only pay what you use or reserve so if you no longer use a resource, you will no longer be charged for it.

Fourth, Security, Google supports a wide array of vendor software and hardware but they also use their own securely built servers. These secure servers have Google's own Titan security chips and secure-boot processes, which makes Google's cloud infrastructure highly secure.

Fifth, Google like other internet-scale providers takes advantage of economies of scale by buying and building infrastructure, licenses and services in bulk and then passing the savings on to the customers. However, Google has the largest partner network, which manifests itself through a wide array of open-source and proprietary software, which is pre-provisioned and available at a click. Thus, the considerable ease-of-use advantages when provisioning servers and application stacks or environments. What is more each will have the correct versions, dependencies and libraries installed automatically doing away with a lot of the troublesome tasks when deploying stacks. For example, a LAMP (Linux, Apache, MySQL, and PHP) stack can be provisioned in just a click of a button and the same is true of other environments such as Java. In addition networking becomes easier as it is configured automatically in most cases meaning the requirement for in-house expert-level networking skills is no longer a requirement.

GCP Charging Model

A key reason for migrating IT to the Google Cloud Platform is to reduce costs and typically GCP offers several ways to reduce operational spending and overall costs. For start-ups and Greenfield companies cloud computing greatly reduces the capital expenditure required as there are no upfront investments in servers and network equipment. Established businesses however can also benefit by reducing maintenance, administration and operational costs of running a data room/centre. This is primarily due to clouds typical pay-as-you-use model, rapid provisioning of servers, and reduced time to profit in product/service development, which translates to tremendous saving if managed correctly.
Indeed, all cloud providers follow this pay-as-you-use model but it was Google that first introduced billing by the second rather than rounding up to the minute for the virtual machines that you configure as part of the Compute Engine service.
Initiatives such as charging by the second can have a large impact on monthly billing if you are running thousands of VM instances. However, the per second model for billing is not restricted to the use of virtual machines through the Compute Engine as it is also available for several other services as well such as;

- Kubernetes Engine, which is GCP's container managed Infrastructure as a Service,
- Cloud Dataproc. which is GCP's open source Big Data system Hadoop as a service, and
- App Engine Flexible Environment which is GCP's platform as a service.
- Cloud Spanner, which is GCPs vastly scalable SQL relational database

Moreover GCP has several other cost reducing or cost management initiatives that you should be aware of and take into consideration when planning deployments of services. For example, Compute Engine offers you discounts based upon consistent use of a VM resource. These discounts are automatically applied to reward sustained usage, i.e. these are automatic discounts for running a virtual machine for more than 25% of the billing month.

This discount translates to a significant saving for every incremental minute you use it over the 25% threshold.

 Savings can also be made through diligent sizing of the VM that you create. This is because when you initially provision a VM you will select among other things, the memory size and how many virtual CPUs you require. In most cases customers will pick a reconfigured VM from a drop down menu but you can customize your VM. Because Compute Engine allows you to select the required memory or virtual CPUs when provisioning the VM this enables you to fine-tune the VM to tailor the pricing to match your workloads.

Moreover, if you are in development you might want to take advantage of the micro VMs that GCP offers within Compute Engine. These are minimal VMs that are ideal for building prototypes or proof-of-concept models. By using micro VMs in development you can reduce the cost significantly. Another way is to use pre-emptive VMs to reduce costs. A pre-emptive VM is one that Google can reclaim at any time so they are only suitable for certain applications but the pricing is significantly reduced.

Avoiding Vendor Lock-In

Earlier in this chapter we highlighted some of the reasons why customers are moving their IT operations to the cloud and to Google Cloud in particular. However not every IT customer was initially enamoured with the prospect of potentially losing control of their data's security and integrity. That was the major factor amongst customers for not migrating operations to the cloud but there was another common reason and that was the fear of vendor lock-in.

Many companies were concerned that if they were to move their workloads to the cloud they might become so dependent on the providers service that they became effectively locked into a particular vendor. This is a common concern amongst IT leaders.

Google recognizes this concern and provides customers with the ability to run their applications elsewhere should the GCP no longer be the most suitable service provider.

For examples of how GCP allows customers to avoid being locked in Google has designed the GCP services to be compatible with open source products.

For example, if we consider GCP's Cloud Bigtable, which is a massive database, which we'll discuss later in detail. But for now what is important is that Cloud Bigtable uses the same interface as the open source database Apache HBase, which gives customers the benefit of code portability. Another example is GCP's Cloud Dataproc, which offers the same open source Big Data environment Hadoop, as a managed service.

In addition Google is committed to the open source community and projects and regularly publishes key elements of technology using open source licenses. By doing so Google participates in creating and supporting open source ecosystems. These open source communities and systems provide customers with options other than Google.

For example, TensorFlow, which is an open source software library for machine learning was originally developed inside Google, but is now a robust open source ecosystem.

In addition to Google's commitment to the open source paradigm they are making efforts to integrate open source projects into GCP in order to provide maximum interoperability.

For example, Kubernetes provides GCP customers with the tools to mix and match microservices running on-premises or even on other clouds. There is also Google Stackdriver, which is GCP's monitoring and management application, which is a collection of open source tools that allows customers to monitor workloads across multiple cloud providers, such as Amazon's AWS.

Summary

In this chapter – An Introduction to the Google Cloud Platform we described the benefits of cloud computing in general and then specifically the GCP, We were introduced to some of the GCP core service offerings which can be broadly categorized as compute, storage, Big Data, machine learning, networking, security, operations and tools.
Hence, GCP's services can be leveraged to utilise computing, storage, Big Data, machine learning and application services and functionality for your web, mobile, analytics and backend solutions.
We also demonstrated that GCP is an internet-scale solution, that has global reach, high availability and reliability yet it is still cost effective, Furthermore GCP is open source friendly and it's designed for business continuity and security in mind.
In the next chapter we will take a deeper dive into each of the compute services and the storage services, how these services and how customers can best use them. Also because Google has itself seven major cloud services supporting over a billion users then this makes security in the GCP paramount and ensures that the GCP is designed with security in mind.

Use Case: 1

A start up business ABC Technology, has sent you an RFC for a proposal for architectural change to accommodate growth, business continuity and disaster recovery for the business, their applications, and data. Their entire operation is presently dependent on on-premises hardware that supports a three-tier web application consisting of webserver, application server and a database. They have three set-ups one for production and another for development and testing and another for data storage/archive. They are looking for a cost effective and high performance solution. What can you propose when answering the RFC. Solution

As a first stage you could propose that the client mirrors their on-premises architecture to Google Cloud Platform by using VMs in Compute Engine. This is readily achievable and can be quickly prototyped for demonstration. All that would be required is for you to reproduce their current architecture to GCP using VMs and lift and shift the code and data. By mirroring and then replicating the databases to the cloud you will have solved their business continuity and disaster recovery requirements with an easy to implement solution but is it a cost effective solution? To address the cost effectiveness we would need to ascertain the desired level of continuity requirement. For example how much down-time and data loss can the business accept? If the client can be flexible regards the recovery time objectives (RTO) then it would be possible to build and test a warm DR cloud environment. In this case we would build the cloud infrastructure replicate the databases and leave them active but tear down everything else after copying the configuration into a deployment manager template. This would mean that you could rapidly recreate the environment on demand. If however the RTO is zero then we would need to build and run the entire cloud architecture 24/7 but that would have not insignificant financial consequences. However you still have to address the issue with accommodating growth and scale. In order to do this you might suggest that after the first stage is complete and the client is happy that they switch over to using the cloud infrastructure and only use the on-premises as the backup site for local storage and archiving of data. As the GCP is elastic and highly scalable this would provide the automatic scalability of the hardware needed for the forecasted growth. You could also detail a third stage whereby they later retire the on-premises data centre altogether and replicate everything in the cloud and mirror the infrastructure and storage across two zones or regions. This solution would meet all of their objectives for handling growth, business continuity and disaster recovery in an efficient and cost effective manner.

GCP – Security by Design

Security or rather the opaqueness of the security controls in place in the cloud was a major inhibitor to cloud adoption a decade or so ago. However cloud providers have gone to great lengths to address this issue so you will find that security is both pervasive and transparent throughout the infrastructure that the GCP and Google services run-on. In this chapter we will introduce some of the high-level security features build-in to GCP. However, a deeper dive into security will be covered in detail later in the book. But for now we just want to introduce some basics. So let's consider some of the approaches Google takes to protect the privacy and integrity of their customers' data.

Google's Bottom-Up Approach to Security

When contemplating an overview of the key security controls and functions inherent in the GCP it is helpful to start at the bottom of the security stack and work up. At the lowest layer in the stack are the data centre buildings that houses Google's infrastructure. Google designs and builds its own data centres and they protect physical access to these buildings by deploying multiple layers of physical security protections. This layered approach has increased levels of security controls applied at each layer as we work our way from the perimeter gates into the core of the data centre. For example at the perimeter gates access will only be given to data centre staff or pre-booked visitors however at the data centre server room access there is via an air lock door. These security doors only allows one person to pass at a time as sensors in the floor detect the presence of more than one person so this prevents tail-gating. In addition, the air locks can only be enabled through biometric sensors such as an iris scan, which also mitigates an authorized employee scanning in an unauthorised guest. Also access to these data centres is limited to only a very small fraction of Google employees on a work requirement basis. In short if you don't have a specific work requirement and an authorised permit to work you will not get access. But the physical security doesn't stop there as within the server rooms the entire hardware infrastructure in Google data centres, such as the server boards and the networking equipment, are custom designed by Google. These are not off-the-shelf commodity servers they are custom designed and built with security in mind during the design process. In addition, Google also designs many of its own custom chips, which includes a hardware security chip called Titan, which is baked into each server. This custom designed security chip is currently being deployed on both servers and network equipment and peripherals. But this is not just security by obscurity as Google goes much further to protect their infrastructure.

Secure Infrastructure

When we consider the security by design approach we can see that Google takes the integrity of their server machines very seriously. The servers use their custom Titan chips to instigate a secure boot process whereby the servers use cryptographic signatures to verify the software, drivers and firmware at every stage of the boot process this makes sure they are booting only clean authenticated and verified software. Also to minimize the threat-footprint Google servers are hardened to remove any potential software vulnerabilities and developers are supplied with secure libraries that are free of commonly known bugs or vulnerabilities.

In addition to Google's servers' secure boot and their proprietary Titan security hardware Google's infrastructure is also protected by cryptographic privacy and integrity at the data and network layers. This layer of security is for the protection of software remote procedure calls (RPC), which is called data-on-the-network. This is the way that networks allow sharing of files, data, and other types of information. Google services communicate securely with each other using RPC but the infrastructure automatically encrypts data traffic in transit between applications, servers and data centres as data is encrypted by default at rest and in flight.

Identity and Access Management (IAM)

Google Cloud Platform also has robust identity and access management functions (IAM), which provides the central identity service. IAM controls authentication, access permission and authorization. In simplistic terms this can be seen by end users as the Google log in page, but it reality it goes well beyond simply asking for a username and password. The IAM service will intelligently challenge users for additional information based on risk factors such as whether they have logged in from a known device or from a similar location in the past. Identity and Access Management will be discussed in detail later.

However, an authentication control you are probably familiar with is 2-factor authentication as this is when Google prompts the users of its services such as Gmail to use a registered mobile phone when signing in. This can be any registered phone but this can include other devices which are based on universal second factor standard (U2F).

Encryption at rest and in flight

Most applications access physical storage indirectly via storage services so GCP has encryption built into those services. Google also enables native encryption support in hard drives and SSDs. That's how Google manages to encrypted all of the customers' data at rest. On the other hand when data is in flight data is also encrypted using TLS or HTTPS. Google services that want to make themselves available on the Internet have to register with an infrastructure service called the Google frontend (GFE). The GFE is responsible for checking all incoming network connections for correct SSL/TLS certificates and adherence to security best practices.
In addition the GFE applies mitigation techniques against denial of service attacks. These are common brute force attacks typically deployed by an attacker attempting to swamp the available open TCP connections by repeatedly attempting to open a connection but never completely the process, which results in tens of thousands of incomplete sessions. Once the server runs out of available TCP sessions no one can connect to it hence the term, denial of service.
However the internet-scale of Google's infrastructure enables their network to simply absorb even the most determined of the distributed denial-of-service (DDOS) attacks. But even still, behind the GFEs there are additional multi-tier denial-of-service fortifications that mitigate any denial of service impact.

AI and Incident Response

Inside Google's infrastructure, machine intelligence and rule-based algorithms analyse at wire speed any traffic and warn of possible incidents. To ensure both proactive and reactive response Google conducts Red Team exercises that simulated network attacks in order to improve the defences and the effectiveness of the security operation centres responses. Hence the security NOC will monitor servers and network infrastructure 24/7 and in addition Google aggressively limits and actively monitors the activities of employees who have been granted administrative access to the infrastructure.
Some other notable security procedures Google has in place are:
- To guard against phishing attacks against Google employees their accounts are protected by and require use of U2F compatible security keys.

- To help ensure that code is as secure as possible Google stores its source code centrally and requires two party review of new code.
- Google also gives its developers secure libraries that keep them from introducing certain classes of security bugs.
- Google also runs a vulnerability rewards program, where they will pay a bounty to anyone who is able to discover bugs in the infrastructure or their applications.

Security Trust Model

Google's security philosophy is based upon the premise of building the most trusted cloud available. To that purpose Google is striving to provide security on the cloud by building a robust and secure infrastructure on which customers can host and run their cloud applications and services. Also they are striving to take the next step by addressing security built in the cloud, which addresses security for applications, data and services. Last but not least they are provisioning security services which customers can use to deploy security tools and functions across their on-premises or other clouds.

In their pursuit of building the most trusted cloud Google look to establish several key factors:
- Establish a verifiable secure platform
- Deliver unparalleled visibility and transparency into operations
- Verification through trusted third-parties
- Simplify security controls
- Continuous improvement and investment

The GCP approach is to minimise the potential attack service and thus increase the customer trust surface. The way they increase trust is based upon increased transparency as to how the GCP works. Hence Google's desire to not only deliver a secure verified platform but to create the trust for a shared security model by providing the transparency, knowledge, and tools that the customers need to secure their applications that run on top of the GCP.

To understand Google's motivations in developing a shared security model we have to recognise that Google considers that a) the data belongs to the customer, b) that Google respects the customers data privacy, c) Google will not use customer data for advertising/marketing purposes or allow access to a third party, d) Google will provide the user with visibility and transparency into its security controls and methods.

Visibility and Transparency

Data integrity, which is today a major concern for customers due to compliance and privacy regulations, is ensured by encryption at rest and in travel. This ensures customers data is protected to the highest standard at all times. Google manages visibility and transparency which we see as being the core elements underpinning trust in five key ways:

1. Operations – Google make available to customers white papers and documentation as to how security controls are applied throughout the GCP operations everything is open and available for the customer or third party security vendor to scrutinize

2. Request and Reporting – Google provides documentation for legal and regulatory use to ensure compliance with national laws. Google was also the first to produce a transparency report that details how many requests for access to customer data they have had from government or regulators and the actions taken

3. Contractual Commitments – Google doesn't just claim to be transparent they are contractually obliged to do so. Google makes themselves legally obliged to provide operational and security processes and procedures they commit through contract with you

4. Privacy – Google will provide detailed reports as to who in Google has access to your data, what they did, and why they did it.

5. Regulatory Compliancy –Google is audited by third parties for regulatory compliancy for relevant international standards such as those in force in the Americas, Europe/Middle East and Asia

Regulatory Compliancy

Google Cloud Platform takes regulatory compliance very seriously and the platform regularly undergoes independent verification of their security, privacy, and regulatory compliance controls. Furthermore they undertake and achieve international certifications, attestations of compliance, as well as independent audit reports against regulatory standards around the globe. But Google goes further by making their knowledge of regulatory compliance around the world available to their users by making available resource documents and mappings against frameworks and laws. They can also provide information where formal certifications or attestations may not be required or applied.

In addition GCP presents their compliancy documentation by Region, Category or Industry to make it easier for you to find the area you are interested in. By filtering by Region you can see what laws or regulations you need to be concerned about, currently the regions are: Asia Pacific, USA, EMEA, Canada and Latin America. The categories are: Certifications/Attestations/Reports; Laws/Regulations; and Alignments/Frameworks. With the filter for Industries providing focus on several key industries where regulatory compliance tends to be heavy, such as: Finance Services, Health Care and Life Science, as well As Government and Public sector but GCP also caters for Media and Entertainment, Education and the automotive industry. This hierarchy of compliance documentation and services makes it much easier to navigate all the regional and industrial compliance issues that can affect any global business today.

Introduction to the GCP Hierarchy

In the previous section when we introduced security within the GCP we took a bottom-up approach as it was easier to visualise the placement of the different controls. So now when we introduce the GCP structure and hierarchy we will take that same approach as understanding the hierarchy is crucial in you playing your part in securing the CGP – remember Google's shared security model means that you also have a responsibility in securing your data.

Therefore we feel that may find it easiest to understand the close bonds between security and the GCP resource hierarchy if we consider them consistently from the bottom up.

Projects and Folders

When you start to build your GCP virtual cloud infrastructure you will start off creating a project. Projects are essential as they are the administrative and billing domains for all of the resources you use. Every resource you use will be stored and billed against that project - whether they're virtual machines, cloud storage buckets, SQL tables or anything else in GCP they must reside in a billable project.

There are some CGP basic rules concerning projects:

- All of the Google Cloud platform resources that you deploy must belong to a single project.
- Projects are the mechanism for enabling and using the GCP services like managing APIs, enabling billing and adding and removing collaborators and enabling other Google services.
- Each project is a separate compartment and each resource belongs to exactly one.
- Projects can have different owners and users, they're built separately and they're managed separately.
- Each GCP project has a name and a project ID that you assign. The project ID is a permanent unchangeable identifier and it has to be unique across GCP.

Project IDs are used in several contexts within GCP to enable it to support multi-tenancy as the project ID establishes unambiguously which project you are working in. For example when using storage buckets for your data you will create a bucket with a unique global identifier, which for convenience is typically based upon your project ID. The unique ID then provides complete segregation of the projects data from any other project. Project IDs are assigned by CGP at project creation and cannot be changed. Also project IDs are made to be human readable strings and you'll use them frequently to refer to your projects. On the other hand, project names are simply for your administrative convenience they have no deeper system relevance so you can assign and change them to something meaningful yourself.

GCP also assigns each of your projects a unique project number and you'll see that displayed to you in various contexts. Project numbers are like project IDs as they cannot be changed by the user.

Now you could have a different GCP project for each department or IT project undertaken, for example, an application development initiative, a digital transformation initiative or an IoT deployment initiative. This is fine for a small start-up company with flat organisational structures and fluid roles. However, for larger organisations with many departments and strict hierarchal policy control then managing individual projects which may eventually run into the thousands is unsustainable.

Another secure approach would be to assign projects to a single administrative unit called a folder. One caveat is though, is that to use folders you will need to have an organization node at the top of the hierarchy but we will come to that later.

Now you can organize projects into folders although you don't have to it is just easier to administer and manage. Nonetheless, folders are simply an elegant way of segregating projects it can be thought of as an organisational tool that CGP provides to make your life easier. For example, you can create a folder to represent each functional department to provide separation, let's say HR, Finance, IT, and as they are also hierarchal this means other nested folders can be made for their own individual teams, applications or development environments, within the parent's department folder.

The advantage of using folders is that permission and access controls can be applied to the folder. This means when you place the appropriate projects into the parent folder the project will automatically be segregated from other folders but not its own sub-folders and they will inherit the folders permissions policy. As I'm sure you can image this can save a lot of tedious and repetitive work should changes be required in policy across many projects. But with folders the change will only need to be done at the highest hierarchal folder level instead of on every individual project or sub-folder. For example, a big advantage of having folders is maintainability as it provides departments and project teams with a level of autonomy to delegate administrative rights or determine their own access policy within their own projects that over-rides organisational policy. As the resources in a folder inherit IAM policies from the parent folder then if several projects are administered by the same team, you can put IAM policies into the parent folder instead of on the individual projects or resources. Trying to accomplish this without folders would require putting duplicate copies of the policy on each project and resource in turn, which would be very tedious and error prone.

The Organizational Node

Most organizations will want to use an organisational node to bring diverse projects and folders under one single administrative umbrella that provides full visibility and a place for centralised policy control over the entire organizations cloud infrastructure domain. This is not always the case when companies start investigating moving to the cloud. However it soon becomes obvious that recreating the organisations structure in the cloud is the most rapid path to migration. Therefore it is a good idea to organize all those diverse and autonomous projects and sprawling folders in your company under a single hierarchal structure. This can be considered the organization node as it provides the starting place to locate the domain administration, which allows you to apply policy centrally as it sits at the very top of the hierarchy.

To understand the benefits of reproducing the organizational node based hierarchy in the cloud we need to consider some of the features that it brings you. An organizational node has some special roles, for example, you can designate an organization policy administrator. Having centralized administration can enforce company administrative policy such as Identity and Access Management (IAM) across the organisation i.e. the policy can establish default behaviour across all folders and projects. It also ensures that only people with organisational administrative privileges can change company-wide policies.

You can also assign a project creator role, this allows the organisational administrator to delegate responsibility to an individual project manager, which is a great way to allow them autonomy and to manage the resources they consume and control the money they spend.

However, if you have an organizational node, with a hierarchy of folders and projects below then you need to understand the flow of policy and permissions. For example there are some GCP resources such as data storage buckets, which let you apply access policies at the individual resource level. Therefore, we must understand how policies are inherited and how some seemingly conflicting policies are resolved.

The first key point is that the organization unit is at the top of the hierarchy and the place for central administration of policies. Importantly these centralized policies are inherited downwards in the hierarchy. Therefore, setting policies at the organizational unit level will automatically be inherited by all the hierarchy – the underlying folders, projects and resources. But that doesn't mean they are definitive in fact it is far from it. Indeed, policies applied at the lower folders or even at the resources level may take precedence. To understand why this happens we need to take a closer look at the hierarchy starting with the organisational node.

So how do you get an organization node?

If you are an existing G Suite customer then you will have a G Suite domain and as such an organizational node therefore any GCP projects will automatically belong to your organization node. But if you are not a G-Suite customer then you can use Google cloud identity to create one. However once you get your new organization node, the default operation is to allow anyone in the domain to be able to create projects and billing accounts. This is necessary to prevent disruption during a transition so everyone retains the same rights as before.

Thus the first step must be to apply the organizational administrative policy to the new organization node.

Once you have an organization node, you can create folders underneath it and put in projects.

Here's an example of how you might organize all your GCP resources:
Figure-2

GCP Resource Management

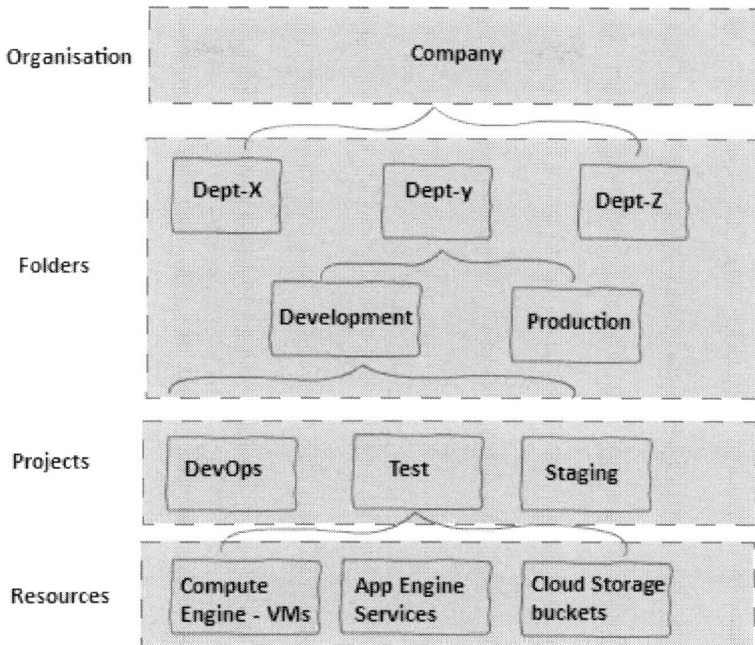

There are three folders directly beneath the organisational node labelled Company they are; "Dept-X", "Dept-Y", and "Dept-Z". In this example, if we consider the folder for "Dept-Y" we can see that it has been separated into two folders, Development and Production. Each folder contains their own projects or other child folders, and within the Development folder, there are three projects, DevOps, Test, and Staging and each will contain the resources needed for the specific project. Thus we can see that the Test project contains the resources; Compute Engine-VMs, App Engine Services and Cloud Storage buckets. What is crucial to remember here is that folders are just like any other resources in that they inherit the policies of their parent.

For instance, if you set a policy at the organization level, it will automatically be inherited by all its children folders as well as their folders and projects and ultimately the projects own resources. This means that the inheritance is transitive and that is one important rule to keep in mind.

However, that is great for applying general organizational policy across the board but many departments may need autonomous control of their access policies on their own projects and resources. This means that they could potentially provide access to resources that contradict the organizational unit's access policy. Therefore we need to understand which rules take precedence. In CGP the policies implemented at a higher level in this hierarchy can't take away access that's granted at a lower level.

For example, suppose that a policy applied on the Test GCP project gives a user the right to modify a cloud storage bucket, but an inherited policy at the organization level says that the user can only view cloud storage buckets and not change them. Then there will be a clear conflict. Therefore the second rule to understand and remember is that the more generous policy is the one that takes effect. In this example the user will have access to modify the cloud storage bucket despite this grant being applied lower down the hierarchy it is the more generous policy.

Identity and Access Management (IAM)

Many enterprises and large companies today deploy their own on-premise Identity and Access Management solutions in order to assist them in applying robust and coherent identity and access polices across the entire organization's infrastructure. Moving all or part of their operations to the cloud will require that they have the same consistent policies across the virtual parts of their business. Google Cloud Identity & Access Management (Cloud IAM) thus lets administrators apply the same granular polices so that they can authorize who can take action on what resources. In short Cloud IAM gives you all the granular control and visibility to manage cloud resources.

Cloud IAM is designed to scale to meet the requirements of even large enterprises with complex organizational structures, hundreds of workgroups, and potentially thousands of projects. Cloud IAM provides a central and unified view into applying security policy across your entire organization, with additional auditing capabilities to ease compliance processes.

Cloud IAM is the service that administrators use to authorize who can take action on specific resources within the GCP. An IAM policy whether on-premises or in the cloud typical has two parts. One part determines and identifies the user, which is the identity function in so much as it is responsible for the identification and authentication of the user. There is then the access part, and this determines what the user is authorized to do and on what resource.

The identity part of IAM will name the user or users you're addressing in the policy rules and in Cloud IAM policy this can be defined by a Google account, a Google group, a Service account, an entire G Suite, or a Cloud Identity domain.

The access policy which is what rights and permissions that the user has been given is defined by an IAM role. Thus a Cloud IAM policy will define by a Google account or ID combined with a Role.

The Purpose of an IAM Role

If you have ever considered applying access permissions in windows or Linux at the file system levels you will undoubtedly recognise that to do any meaningful work you need to apply a combination of permissions. This is no different in IAM.

For example, to manage instances in a project, you will need to have the permissions to create, delete, start, stop, and change an instance. Of course other users may need to have only read access, others read, write and modify, while managers and administrators would require full access across many of the resources within the project. However, that is only manageable on a per user basis in very small organizations.

The typical way around this conundrum is to group the permissions that are typically needed for a job function all together into a role. This then makes IAM much easier to manage and much less error prone.

Cloud IAM Role Types

There are three kinds of roles in Google's Cloud IAM service, which you can use depending on your requirements. The categories of role types are primitive roles, predefined roles and custom role types.

Primitive Roles

The first type is what is known as the Primitive roles as these are very broadly defined. You apply them to a GCP project and they affect all resources in that project. The broad roles are; the Owner, Editor, and the Viewer.

Thus, If you're designated the role of a viewer on a given resource, you can examine it but not change its state.

On the other hand If you're designated the role of an editor, you can do everything that a viewer can do, plus change its state.

Finally, if you are privileged to have an owner role, you can do everything an editor can do, plus they can manage rolls and permissions on the resource. Moreover, the owner role on a project also let you do one more very important task and that is to set up billing. However that might not be compatible with your company's internal policy.

The reason that the owner is also given the billing task is that they are typically in charge of the resources and responsible for the budgets. But in many organizations there are strict rules governing finance and spending. Therefore, a new role is created that of the Billing Admin role, which allows the administrator to delegate the authorisation for billing for a project to a user without giving them the right to change the resources in the project. In this way we can separate the owner's access permissions from the billing permissions. For example, you may want to grant someone other than the owner the billing administrator role, such as the project manager or a finance employee.

A word of warning though about primitive roles as they may be too coarsely defined and not granular enough to provide the separation of duties required in most teams. This is especially true if you have several people working together on a project that contains sensitive data. In that scenario, primitive roles are probably too course to be fit for purpose.

Predefined Roles

In order to address this shortfall, GCP Cloud IAM provides a finer grained version of role types that cover many more job types and task scenarios. These refined GCP services offer their own sets of predefined roles and they define where those roles can be applied.

For example, Compute Engine, which offers virtual machines as a service offers a set of predefined roles. You are then able to apply these refined roles to Compute Engine resources in a specific project, a folder, or across an entire organizational unit.

By applying refined roles for example those provided for the Compute Engines VMs such as the InstanceAdmin Role lets you pass the required permissions to anyone designated that role to perform a certain set of actions on virtual machines. Thus they will be able to list all VMs within that project, read and modify their configurations, as well as change their state by starting and stopping them.

Custom Roles

However, as we have seen if you designate a user to be in the InstantAdmin role for VMs that will apply to all instances of VMs within that project. In many cases this may still be too broad and you may need something even finer-grained. To address the requirements for highly specific and fine grained roles Cloud IAM introduces custom roles. The requirement for custom roles is driven by many companies adhering to a least privileged access model in which each person in the organization has the minimum amount of privilege needed to do his or her job. So, for example, maybe you will need to define a Role that has the inherent permissions to allow a user to start and stop Compute Engine and virtual machines, but not be allowed to reconfigure them. This would be a suitable case for an InstanceOperator role.

Because of this requirement Cloud IAM allows us to make custom roles, which allow you to customise a similar role by adding or removing some permission as we just saw when changing InstanceAdmin to the more restrictive InstanceOperator role.

There is however a couple of caveats we need to be aware of when using custom roles. First, if you decide to use custom roles you will need to manage their permissions manually. This is very like the manual granting of individual permissions to a group or resource as the interaction between permissions can be complex and unpredictable. This can make custom roles error prone and even security risks.

As a result, some companies require any custom roles to be thoroughly audited by a third party or a peer review before being assigned. Others have simply decided they'd rather stick with the predefined roles than accept the risk.

Another thing to be aware of is that custom roles can only be used at the project or organization levels, which rules them out at the folder level.

Service Accounts

So far in our discussion regards the Cloud IAM we have been addressing the situation where a user or a group of users require identification, authentication and then given access to a resource to perform tasks compatible with their role. However, there is also the very common scenario where one resource needs to interact and communicate with another resource. For example you may need to give permissions to a Compute Engine virtual machine, rather than to a person, in order to automate a process.
The way this is done is by the use of a service account.
For instance, you may have an application running in a virtual machine, such as a web server, that needs to communicate with another VM, which runs the business logic for the application. This VM in turn needs to store data in Google Cloud Storage, but you have to lock down the access so that only that virtual machine can directly access the data. In this scenario, you would create a service account to authenticate your VM webserver to the VM application and then only the VM application to the cloud storage.
The way that Service accounts work is that they are set up with an identity that corresponds to an email address. That is pretty straightforward but the authentication is less so as a VM cannot enter a password as we certainly do not want to be hard coding a password. Therefore, instead of hard coded passwords, the service accounts use cryptographic keys to access resources.
A simple example is if you consider that you have created a service account, which you have granted the InstanceAdmin Role. By having this role the service account could effectively be used to permit an application running in a VM to create, modify, and/or delete other instances. But the interesting thing about Service accounts are they are more than just identities as they are also resources so they can have their own IAM policies attached to it.

This is very handy because service accounts also need to be managed. An example, is maybe Alice needs to manage what can use a given service account, while Bob just needs to be able to view them. Thus, you can give Alice an editor role in a service account and Bob can have the viewer role. This is just like granting roles for any other GCP resource.

However another thing to be aware of is that you can grant different groups of VMs in your project with different identities by creating different service accounts for each distinct group of VMs. Another convenience is that you can also change the permissions of the service accounts without having to recreate the member VMs.

If we consider a more complex example we can see this principle in action. So let us say that we have a very common design whereby we have an application that's implemented across a group of Compute Engine virtual machines.

However the design criteria demands that one component of your application needs to have an editor role on another project, but the other components must not have access.

In this case it is possible to manage both design criteria by creating two different service accounts, one for each subgroup of virtual machines. Only the first service account will be granted privilege on the other project and this reduces the potential impact of a miscoded application or a compromised virtual machine affecting the other project.

Blended Security

In practice security is applied across the GCP through the blending of resource management, organisational policy and IAM rules. It is by combining strategically the policy, rules and privileges at those different tactical levels that we can obtain the fine grained policies that deliver the security principles of separation, maintainability and simplicity.

Cloud Security Principles

Many companies that move to the cloud are concerned by the lack of transparent security controls and they wish to see a clear methodology that adheres to the basic cloud security principles of separation, maintainability and simplicity. However, what does that mean in real terms?

Ideally the principle addresses the security in the cloud where there may be issues with separation of data in multi-tenant environments. It might also raise security concerns due to its obscurity, which makes it difficult for administrators to maintain and reproduce a coherently policy that can be applied consistently without errors. Finally, there are concerns that simplicity in the cloud amounts to an incomprehensible web of security controls.

The way that GCP addresses security is through blended controls that deliver on separation through the use of IAM, folders, projects and firewall ACLs to segregate multi-tenant data. Also it uses the strengths and flexibility of IAM to provide granular permissions tied to roles for users and groups to access or be denied access to resources. Finally, the blending of these GCP security controls demonstrates the simplicity of administration and in applying RBAC, firewall rules, subnets and user authentication constraints at granular level across the organisation to fine tune the access policy.

For an example of blended security control let us take a brief look at a common use case where we could apply these important security principles;

A business wishes to move to the cloud but they have concerns due to their business model, which demands collaborating with partners and supply chain democratisation. They want to open up some of their resources to their partners but not all. They also want to be confident that the partners can only access what they grant them and no more. However, the issue is that some individuals need further access to other departments such as IT for posting project documentation as well as HR to post their timesheets.

The way the company could address this is through a blend of security controls. Initially they could contain the shared project within its own folder that would provide separation from other business units in both directions. Then they could provide IAM access rights to that folder and assign them to a specific group that had specific access only to the project folder and no others. The problem comes when some employees need cross reference access across projects but for only one purpose. In this case we could create a GCP IAM group that had access to read/write to their home project but also access to post to a specific resource for the timesheet repository as well as to the IT code repository but with no access to any other resource. We could do this in other ways, which we will learn later but for now this is an elegant solution.

Study Use Case -2

The client ABC returns to you with a request for more details on your proposal; 1) to provide cloud based business continuity and disaster recovery solution. This time they are concerned more about the security of the GCP cloud and how they could convince their management and stakeholders that the data was secure and stored under conditions compliant with regulatory best practices. Point 2), they are also looking at automation and how the solution could work autonomously rather than having IT copying data across from the production servers to the storage/archive servers. Point 3), how can they ensure the principles of separation, maintenance and simplicity with regards security in their cloud environment? How can you answer their concerns and also provide a workable solution for an automated hands free solution to data archiving.

Solution

There are a number of security controls that you can address to reassure the client regards the security of data stored in the cloud such as data by default is encrypted within GCP at rest and in flight. Hence data is encrypted when in the database and archived storage and also when traversing the network. Moreover a secure VPN is used to encrypt and provide for privacy when traversing the internet. These controls ensure the integrity of the data at all times. Should the client still have concerns you could suggest that they encrypt their data before sending to the cloud or bring their own encryption keys but that's not really advisable unless they have experience in key management.

The second concern regarding automation can be fulfilled using service accounts to manage the archiving of data using IAM. A service account allows a VM instance to be granted privileges and so its application can then perform autonomous actions such as handling a data archive process without any user intervention.

When addressing point 3, you could stress the importance of taking a blended view towards security controls such as merging hierarchy controls such as folders with IAM. You could explain how together they could control the separation, authentication and authorization of users while enforcing the access permission they are entitled too and no more. You could also explain about how projects and folders enforce separation by default. But also how you can relax that separation by allowing restricted privileges and access for employees. This can be accomplished by placing them in an IAM group, which has access to both the Production and Development environments despite them being in different projects or folders. This can be demonstrated quite readily through a prototype in GCP.

Chapter 16 - Interacting with Google Cloud Platform

Introduction

There are perhaps four ways you can interact with Google Cloud Platform, some are easier than others and you will be introduced to each in turn but we will in this book tend to stress the shell code method. These diverse methods of interaction are led by specifically the Console, this is the most interactive way for someone to control and configure the Cloud infrastructure. The problem is that as a web interface it requires the user to understand the steps required in order to configure a resource as well as to find their way about the GUI, which can be slow and time consuming.

On the other hand the SDK and Cloud Shell provides a way to configure the GCP through using command line scripts and this means that you can develop a library of scripts that can be easily customized to create any resource you require. Once you have such a library of configuration scripts you can provision infrastructure in seconds.

In addition there is the Mobile App, which is simply another device orientated method for utilising the web or script methods of configuration. The final method is far more interesting as it uses APIs to provide the software templates that are required to input the crucial operational data that is required to trigger the Application Programmable Interfaces (APIs). An interesting point is regardless of whether you are using the console, cloud shell or the mobile app you are ultimately interacting with GCP cloud through the APIs.

The GCP Console

The GCP Console is a web-based administrative interface and dashboard, which provides an administrator with a graphical user interface with an easy point and click action. The console is designed for administrative use only, so if you build an application in GCP, you'll most likely use the console or at least at first, but the end users of your applications do not have access to it. This is because the console lets you as the administrator view and manage all your projects and all the resources they use. It also lets you enable, disable and explore the APIs of GCP services. Also from the console GUI you can conveniently access Cloud Shell.

Cloud Shell

The Cloud Shell is a command-line interface to GCP that's easily accessed from your browser. From Cloud Shell, you can use the tools provided by the Google Cloud Software Development kit (SDK) without having to first install them somewhere. Whereas the console is a great graphical interface for creating and modifying resources as it is based upon check boxes and drop down menus to assist you in configuration options. However, it can be slow and tedious if you have to configure or modify many resources. This is where the Cloud Shell command line excels as it can run shell scripts. This means you can execute a customised shell script to create resources such as several VMs very quickly and automatically. Unfortunately many administrators that are new to GCP work through the console but conversely you will find that experienced professionals work almost exclusively using Cloud Shell. This is not them showing off, it's just once you have built up a library of basic functional scripts say for creating VMs or storage buckets, its far quicker, less tedious and a much more efficient way of working. In this book we will concentrate primarily on Cloud Shell running the SDK commands because once you understand and become familiar with customising scripts and handling the configuration options then reverting back to using the console GUI becomes highly intuitive. Also explaining scripts doesn't require hundreds of screenshots.

The GCP Software Development Kit

The Google Cloud SDK is a set of command line tools that you can use to manage your resources and your applications on GCP. The easiest way to get to the SDK commands is to click the Cloud Shell button on a GCP Console.

The SDK includes the gcloud tool, which provides all the main command line interface commands for Google Cloud Platform products and services. These are all the functional commands you will use when creating and administering VMs and containers. In addition there is also the gsutil set of commands, which is for Google Cloud Storage and there is another specialized bq command set, which is for BigQuery.

The SDK is stand-alone software that you can download and install anywhere, such as on your laptop or on-premises server or even in another cloud, it doesn't matter. The SDK is also available as a docker image, which makes it really easy to download and install in a VM. The most convenient way is to access it via the command line in your console web browser on a virtual machine with all these commands already installed.

Using APIs

The important thing to understand is that the services that make up GCP provide application programming interfaces (APIs) so that the code you write can access and control them. Hence, when you write scripts and execute them in the Cloud Shell you are directly interfacing and consuming the APIs of the relevant GCP services.

These APIs that the services offer are what are called RESTful, which means they adhere to the representational state transfer model. For now all we need to know about RESTful APIs are that they are the standard way of passing information between an API and a client, which simply means that your code will consume Google services using the same methods that web browsers talk to web servers i.e. through URLs. Therefore we find that because they are based on RESTful the GCP APIs will reference the resources and GCP services using URLs. This is a convenient way to connect and pass your code and any information to GCP.

The APIs present or offer preconfigured services that you write your code to interact with. But although this is programming and its code that you are writing you cannot just pass them anything for the code must adhere to a strict form, which is much like a template. This makes customizing templates very easy even for non-coders as it just requires the substitution of key parameters. What is more is that the APIs use JSON which is very readable for humans so it is a popular way of passing textual information over the web.

As the SDK is very powerful you will need to secure access to it and there's an open system for user log in and access control. You can also conveniently browse through the library of available APIs within the console browser and this is where you can turn on and off any APIs. By default many APIs will be switched off as many are associated with quotas and limits.

By having the APIs deactivated by default protects you from inadvertently using resources. Therefore, it is a best practice to enable only those APIs you need and then you can request increases in quotas if or when you need more resources. However you must be careful when using APIs for managing quotas and system resources as they can be quite tricky to predict. For example, if you're writing an application that needs to control GCP resources, you'll first need to experiment with the correct APIs to ensure you get the adjustments just right. Fortunately GCP has a tool for this and it's called the APIs Explorer.

Using the API Explorer

The GCP hosts many APIs and as we have just seen some of these are used to control limits and quotas so need careful planning. However the GCP console includes a tool called the APIs Explorer that enables you to interactively try out the APIs and learn about their use even with just basic user authentication. API Explorer also lets you see what APIs are available and in what versions. But as we saw earlier APIs expect parameters and some will be required while other may be optional so to understand the APIs functionality and whether it is appropriate for our use we need access to the documentation. Fortunately, all the GCP API documentation is built in and accessible through the explorer.

API Client Libraries

If we consider the scenario that you have explored GCP for a suitable API and you are confident that you can provide it with its required parameters so now you're ready to build an application that uses it. Now the great thing about APIs is that you can build applications using APIs and some glue code so you don't have to start coding the application from scratch. Indeed to make life even easier for non-coders Google provides client libraries that take a lot of the skill out of the task of calling GCP services via the APIs from your code.

The GCP contains two kinds of libraries. Google clouds latest and recommended libraries for the GCP hosted APIs are called the Cloud Client Libraries and they adopt the native styles and idioms of each language.

On the other hand, the Google API Client Library is available for your desired language if for some reason a Cloud Client Library doesn't support the newest services and features.

Regardless of which you use you will find that these libraries are designed for generality and completeness. You will also find that utilising these libraries to bring GCP APIs into your code will take a lot of the drudgery out of coding your application.

Finally, to return back to administration there is one more tool that is of interest in today's mobile world, the mobile App for Android and iOS. This mobile application lets you view and manage the resources you're using at GCP by allowing you to build your own custom dashboards so that you can get all the information you need at a glance.

Google Cloud Launcher

A key advantage to cloud over on-premises is the time it takes to provision an application server. After all it might take all day to build a real server with the OS and the environment and software stack. But with cloud many application servers can be provisioned in minutes. Hence, if you would like to try out Google Cloud Platform and a quick way to get started with GCP, with minimal effort is to use the Cloud Launcher tool.

The Google Cloud Launcher enables you to get started quickly by deploying functional software packages on Google Cloud platforms. Everything is provisioned automatically; including the software stack, the optimal environment settings and all dependencies so there's no need to manually configure the software, virtual machine instances, and storage or network settings. Although, you can still do that by modifying many of the settings before you launch if you have specific custom requirements. Moreover, not only do these application packages come preconfigured with the latest versions and security patches. Many of the latest software packages in Cloud Launcher are provided at no additional fee so long as they are open source. However, there will be some proprietary software packages within Cloud Launcher and they do charge user's

fees, particularly those published by vendors who require a commercial license for their software. However, before you provision the software the Cloud Launcher will show you estimates of the monthly charges, so make sure you are comfortable with the fees before you launch the software image.

Moreover, you should be aware that these estimates are for the software it doesn't take into account network usage as that depends a lot on how you use the application which cannot be determined prelaunch.

In addition, GCP will continuously manage updates and security patches to the base images for the software packages to fix critical issues and vulnerabilities. However, it does not update the software after it's been deployed this is necessary to prevent any disruption or breakage of a deployed and working application.

Therefore you may need to check that your application works on the latest version and update level before you deploy any upgrade.

Despite those caveats however using Cloud Launcher is a way to expedite the provisioning of applications and to ensure a consistent stack throughout your environment.

Use case -3

Things are going well with your proposal to ABC and you have been asked in again to answer some awkward questions such as how do we as the client organisational administrators allow other departments to have autonomy over their respective projects so that they can interact with their own GCP project infrastructure? Now you have to answer a serious question as to how you give project administrators and developers the same rights and privileges that are inherent in their on-premise environments but also restrict the access rights of other team members. The problem being is that as a startup company employees multitask and have several job functions dependent on the project or task. Therefore it is not easy to identify a specific role and then delegate a role to an individual so they need something more flexible as job roles are fluid. There is also the problem of how do they directly interface with the Cloud Infrastructure as there are several potential solutions and they are not sure which the best way is.

Solution

One approach you could take is to propose the company deploys IAM using custom roles. In this way you could assign each employee the actual base privileges that they need to do their job but still restrict them access to all other areas. For example, you could grant permissions for custom access to roles then apply these to specific groups that have will have access to both the Production and Development environments but deny these groups access to HR and Finance. Although creating custom roles and groups per individual is not recommended as it soon becomes unsustainable in large organization. However, in a startup company with few employees it can be the preferred method of deploying IAM. Creating custom roles for each employee that performs multi-roles within the business is the best way to provide the access required while still maintaining the principle of least privilege.

With regards interacting with the GCP you could inform them of the benefits of each of the methods; the console, Cloud Shell, which is the command line using the SDK, APIs for programming, and templates and scripts for automating tasks or for running batch tasks using Cloud Shell.

Chapter 17 - Compute Engine and Virtual Machines

Introduction

The way that most organisations migrate their applications to the cloud is by using a lift and shift methodology. By doing so the architects are trying to replicate the on-premise environment in the cloud by using virtual machines to mimic real world servers. This is the most common way to run workloads in the cloud. Indeed this is the most intuitive way as Compute Engine lets you replicate your data centre configuration and then run your applications within virtual machines on Google's global infrastructure. In this chapter, we'll learn how Google Compute Engine works with a focus on Google virtual networking.

Now for those of you that are new to virtual computing the best thing about virtual machines is that they have the power in generality of a full-fledged server with an operating system running in each instance. This is how in on-premise servers you could run several VMs with each one running a different OS, such as Windows Server, Ubuntu, Linux Red Hat, etc. and all share the common hardware resources such as CPU, I/O bus, network, memory, disk, etc.

We saw previously that a quick and clean method for getting started with GCP is to use Cloud Launcher to provision applications and a proprietary software stack as a package along with the underlying virtual infrastructure that they need to run. In the cloud this is how Google uses the same technique of virtualisation to make the most efficient use of shared hardware through multi-tenancy models whereby many diverse customers may be hosted on the same physical server.

Hence, you will configure a virtual machine much like you build out a dedicated physical server by specifying its amounts of CPU power and memory, along with the desired amounts and types of storage and its operating system. You can flexibly reconfigure them, however, and a VM running on Google's cloud has then got global network connectivity.

Virtual Private Cloud (VPC)

Cloud Launcher has its uses but the other way a lot of people get started with GCP is to define their own Virtual Private Cloud (VPC). In this context we consider a VPC as being your own cloud virtual network. It is an on-demand configurable pool of shared computing resources allocated within the GCP environment. This shared pool does however provide a certain level of isolation between the different organizations using the resources.

Figure-

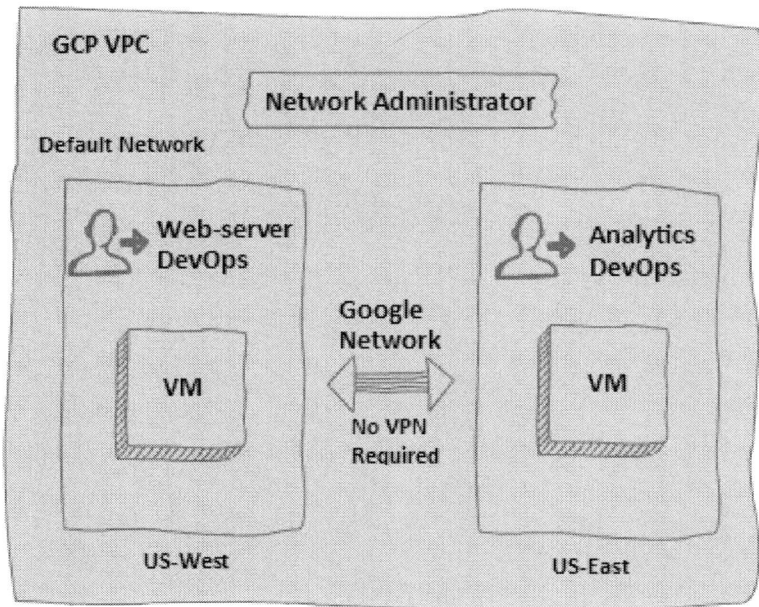

Another important component of a VPC is it provides the critical internetworking between resources, such as VMs. It does this in a global and flexible way to ensure that all your cloud based resources and services can interact with one another. Thus a popular way to get started in GCP is through creating a VPC.

When you start out you can create the PVC inside your first GCP project, or you can simply choose the default VPC and use that. Regardless, your VPC provides the networking capabilities and services to connect your Google Cloud platform resources to each other and to the internet.

Basic Cloud Networking

Google's GCP provides you with the concept of the VPC which to all intent and purposes resembles your own private network. It also provides the underlying networking required to connect your cloud resources to each other and the internet. This networking service is typically automated and requires no intervention from you. However if you like you can do many of the network tasks that you perform on your on-premises network such as you can segment your networks, use firewall rules to restrict access to instances, and create static routes to forward traffic to specific destinations.

However there is a key difference between your on-premise networking and Google GCP networks. Google's GCP is built upon a Software Defined Network which can be considered to be one vast layer-2 network with global reach. Thus the Virtual Private Cloud networks that you define will have global scope. This means that they can have subnets in any GCP region worldwide and importantly the subnets can span the zones that make up a region.

This architecture makes it easy for you to build redundancy into your design as there will be very low latency between resources in different zones as they are on the same subnet and communicating at layer-2 much like they were connected to the same switch. This is perfect for business continuity as a failure in one zone can be addressed seamlessly by the resources in another zone. Moreover the SDN architecture makes it easy to define your own network layout with a global scope as in addition to supporting resources in different zones on the same subnet, you can dynamically increase the size of a subnet in a custom network by expanding the range of IP addresses allocated to it without affecting the already configured VMs.

In this example, your VPC has one network.

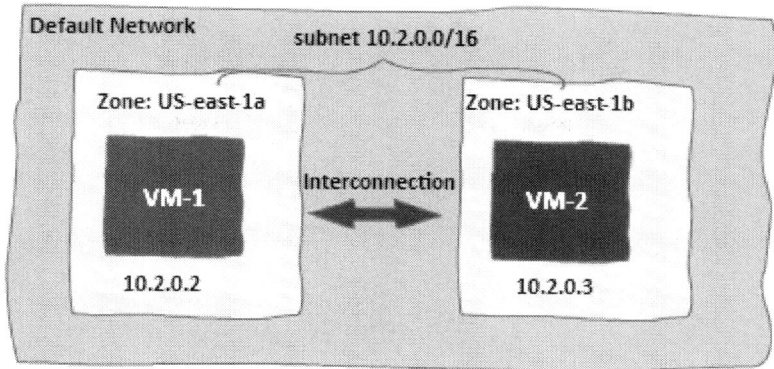

Figure -4

So far, it has one subnet defined in GCP us-east1 region. Notice that it has two Compute Engine VMs attached to it.

They are neighbours on the same subnet even though they are in different zones.

You can use this capability to build solutions that are resilient but still have simple network layouts.

The Fundamentals of Compute Engine and VMs

Compute Engine is the GCP service that allows you to create and run virtual machines on Google infrastructure. In contrast to on-premises servers there are no upfront investments and you can provision and run thousands of virtual CPUs on a system. Moreover the systems are designed to be fast and to offer consistent performance.

You can create a virtual machine instance by using the Google cloud platform console or the gcloud command line tool and you can run Linux and Windows Server images that are provided by Google or use your own customized versions of these images. For example you can even import your corporate custom server images from your physical servers.

Creating a VM

CPU

When you create a VM, the first decision is to pick a machine type which determines how much memory and how many virtual CPUs it has. These selectable choices range in size from micro to behemoth but if you can't find a suitable predefined type that meets your needs perfectly, you can always make a custom VM.

Speaking of using custom processing power, if you have workloads like machine learning and heavy data processing that can take advantage of GPUs and even TPUs, then you should be aware that GCP provides GPUs as well as Google's own TPUs (Tensor Processing Units) and these are also available for you to use.

The Google developed TPU is their custom application-specific integrated circuit (ASIC) tailored for machine learning workloads on TensorFlow it was developed as a cloud based rival to Nvidia's GPU for handling heavy machine learning workloads.

Storage

The next decision is what type of storage you want your VM to use. VM are like physical computers they need disks to store persistent data. You can choose two kinds of persistent storage, standard or SSD.

The importance of the term persistent is that it lets us know that the data will survive the termination or deletion of the host VM. For example, a persistent drive is actually an external storage area which we can separate from the VM itself. For example we can elect to delete a VM but to retain its data i.e. the persistent disk.

However there is another type of disk storage that is very fast and should you have a requirement in your application for very high performance scratch space, you may want to attach a local SSD. However, a local SSD is part of the VM so be sure to store data of any permanent value somewhere else because local SSD's content doesn't survive when the VM terminates. Because of this you cannot separate a VM and a local SSD disk as you can with a persistent disk. Anyway, most people will begin with using the standard persistent disks and that's the default.

Another convenient aspect of VM is taking backups. Once your VMs are running it is easy to take a durable snapshot of their disks. These are useful as backups but they also are required when you need to move a VM to another region.

The Boot Image

The next step is that you choose a boot image. As we have discussed already GCP offers a wide selection of Linux and Windows versions that are pre-configured but if you want you can import your own images. Indeed, a common request made by GCP customers is that they want their VMs to always boot with a specific configuration, such as installing specific updates or packages at boot time.
Therefore it is common for people to use GCP VM start-up scripts that will control the start process by following the commands in the script. But you can via the scripts also pass into the VM other kinds of metadata.

Pre-emptive

Another factor you might want to consider is if you want to make your VM pre-emptible. You can save a lot of money if you choose to use pre-emptible VMs where they are appropriate. However pre-emptible VM are only suitable in certain use-cases as they behave differently from ordinary VMs. The difference is that with a pre-emptive VM you are effectively agreeing to allow the Compute Engine to terminate the VM should its resources be needed elsewhere and you will only get around 30 seconds warning. Furthermore a pre-emptive VM is guaranteed to be terminated after 24 hours if it hasn't already been pre-empted. However, if deployed wisely you can save a lot of money - around 80% discount - using pre-emptible VMs in the right scenarios, but be sure to make sure that your workloads are able to be stopped and restarted gracefully.

Auto-scaling

Auto-scaling is another factor to consider because despite the fact you can create huge VMs - the maximum number of virtual CPUs in the VM is 96 and the maximum memory size in beta is at 624 gigabytes – and these huge VMs are great for workloads like in-memory databases and CPU intensive analytics but you may not want to start off at that size.

For example, most GCP customers start off by scaling out, not scaling up. What that means is they add more standard sized VMs to loadbalance across, this is called horizontal scaling, rather than increasing the size of their existing VMs, which is known as vertical scaling.

When it comes to horizontal scaling VMs Compute Engine has a feature called auto scaling that lets you add and take away VMs from your application based on load metrics.

However to get that to work effectively there is a need for a robust load balancing function that can handle the intelligent balancing of the incoming traffic across the group of VMs. To help with this Google VPC supports several different kinds of load balancing, which we will cover in detail later.

Cloud Networking Revisited

Much like physical networks, VPCs have their own routing tables that are populated with the shortest routing information that we will use to forward traffic from one instance to another instance within the same network, across sub-networks and even between GCP zones without requiring any external IP addresses. By using private RFC1918 addresses rather than routing external IP addresses to communicate between VPCs ensures lower latency.

VPCs routing tables are built in to the VPC so you don't have to provision or manage a router. Moreover, with GCP you don't have to provision or manage a firewall instance as a VPC comes with a global distributed firewall. However even though you do not manage a firewall instance you can still control or restrict access to instances for both incoming and outgoing traffic. The way that this is done is by defining firewall rules or you can use metadata tags on Compute Engine instances, whichever you find is more convenient.

For example, you can tag all your web servers with a tag, web, and then write a firewall rule, which states that all traffic arriving on ports 80 or 443 with the tag, web, is allowed into all VMs, no matter what the source or destination IP address happens to be.

Something that may cause some initial confusion is that VPCs belong to specific GCP projects. That is fine if your company only has one project or if projects are required to be strictly segregated but more often a company will have many GCP projects and the VPCs do need to communicate.

If that is the scenario then you may simply want to establish a peering relationship between two VPCs so that they can exchange their routing information – subnets by default – so that they can then exchange traffic, that's what VPC peering does.

On the other hand, if you want to have finer control such as you want to utilise IAM to control who and what in one project can interact with a VPC in another project then that's what a shared VPC is for.

A shared VPC allows an organization to connect resources from multiple projects to a common VPC network. The goal is to allow the VPCs to communicate with each other securely and efficiently using internal IP addresses. If or when this happens you use what is known as a shared VPC. In this case you designate one project (VPC) as the host project and then attach one or several other service projects to it in order to share resources. A shared VPC also allows the organization administrator to delegate responsibilities, such as creating and managing instances to the service project admins, while maintaining centralized control of the network.

Load Balancing

Earlier when we discussed VMs and how VMs could auto scale under fluctuating loads by scaling sideways by increasing the number of available VMs we didn't address how do your customers get to your application. The issue is that with horizontal scaling the number of available VMs will change so it might be provided by four VMS one moment and 40 VMS at another? We briefly explained that it would require intelligent load balancing but what it really requires is Cloud Load Balancing.

Cloud Load Balancing

Cloud Load Balancing is fully distributed software and a defined managed service for all your traffic. Because the load balancers are a managed service and they don't run in the VMs that you have to manage, you don't have to worry about scaling or managing them.

Therefore you can place Cloud Load Balancing in front of all your traffic, HTTP and HTTPS, other TCP and SSL traffic, and UDP traffic too.

With Cloud Load Balancing, a single 'anycast' IP front ends all your backend instances in regions around the world. The Load Balancers in the region closest to the traffic source will receive the traffic as its using anycast and this also provides the cross-region load balancing, including automatic multi-region failover.

In addition to its anycast functions Cloud Load Balancing reacts quickly to changes in users, traffic, backend health, and many network conditions, which will result in traffic being gently moved in small fractions if the backends start to become unhealthy.

Although you do not have to manage or administer the load balancing as it is a managed service you do need to select the correct type of load balancer to match your traffic. For example if you want a cross-regional load balancing for a web application, then you would want to use HTTPS load balancing.

However, there are several types of global load balancers available so you would want to use the global SSL proxy load balancer for Secure Sockets Layer traffic that is not HTTP.

Or if its TCP traffic that does not use Secure Sockets Layer, then you would want to use the global TCP proxy load balancer. But those two proxy services only work for specific port numbers, and they only work for TCP.

So if you want to load balance UDP traffic or traffic on any port number, you can still load balance across a GCP region with the regional load balancer.

Additionally, all those versions of the load balancing services are intended for traffic coming into the Google network from the internet. Therefore if you are looking to load balance traffic within the GCP such as between the presentation layer and the business logic layer of your application then you would need to use another type called the internal load balancer.

The internal load balancer will accept traffic on a GCP internal IP address and load balance it across Compute Engine VMs. We will discuss how to deploy and use the internal load balancer later.

Google DNS Service

A good example of Google's cloud infrastructures reliability and global reach is demonstrated via the Google DNS service on IP address 8.8.8.8 which provides a public domain name service to the world.

Google's global DNS is the public network service that translates the internet host names used in URLs to public IP addresses. It does this by looking up the registry for the public IP addresses that the network needs to be able to establish communications.

DNS is one of those unsung heroes of the internet because without it everything just stops working. Despite this DNS has been rather neglected over the years but came to more widespread attention when several of the main DNS providers came under denial of service attacks rendering large portions of the internet unreachable.

Google has a highly developed DNS infrastructure that by its global scale protects it against denial of service attacks. Google makes 8.8.8.8 a freely available managed service so that everybody can take advantage of it and Google is so confident in this service that it is the only one that they provide with a 100% SLA.

DNS servers resolve registered hostnames to public IP addresses so this begs the question as to how will the internet host names and addresses of applications you build in GCP be registered if the IP addresses are register to Google but assigned to you.

This why GCP offers the Cloud DNS service, it is to help the world find your applications and services. Cloud DNS is another managed DNS service running on the same infrastructure as Google so it has the same global reach, low latency and high availability making it a cost effective way to make your applications and services available to your users. The way it works is that although the Cloud DNS is a managed service it is also programmable. This enables you to publish and manage millions of DNS zones and records using the GCP console, the command line interface or the API. The DNS information you publish will be served from Google's data centre locations around the world.

Content Delivery

Google has infrastructure and network locations in regions and zone around the globe and this gives it a global system of geographically diverse edge caches. You can use these edge caches to accelerate content delivery in your application using Google Cloud CDN. What this means is that if your services are built in a US zone then customers in another region such as Asia will need to traverse the globe to reach your content in the US. However as Google have data centres in many zones in Asia or any region for that matter, it can host your content in a cache close to the customer. By presenting your content closer to them means your customers will experience lower network latency.

Furthermore, your original content services will experience reduced load as requests are now offloaded to the regional caches and so you can save money on network charges too.

Also it's another managed service which means it is easy to deploy as all you have to do is set up the HTTPS load balancing and then simply enable Cloud CDN with a single checkbox.

You may already be using CDN from a third party provider as there are lots of other CDNs out there. But that should not be a problem as Google runs the CDN interconnect partner program so if your CDN provider is a member then you can continue to use it.

Connecting to the GCP

One attraction of the cloud is that you can spin up VMs quickly and cheaply and that allows you to build a development infrastructure that is segregated from your production network. This is the reason that many organisations start with cloud deployments as it gives the development or project teams their own space to experiment and try out proof of concept or build prototypes cost effectively. However, eventually you may want to create a production environment and many GCP customers want to do that. The problem of course is that you will eventually need to interconnect your on-premises or other cloud networks to the Google VPCs.

This causes a significant issue as when you first build the PVC you can operate and test it out using just an internet connection. However, when you want to move to production you will need to be able to replicate your on-premises infrastructure in the cloud. This will mean constructing cost-effective communication channels between your network and Goggles cloud. After all you may need to transfer 100's of gigabytes of date from an on-premises data base to cloud storage.

In order to meet the requirements of organisations GCP offers a selection of technology choices. For many customers the starting point will be through a web browser with the GCP environment segregated from the company's internal network. Running a development network in the PVC and accessing it via a browser is fine. However when you shift to production you will often find the need to upgrade to a Virtual Private Network (VPN) secure connection that runs over the internet using the IPSEC protocol. This will not only secure the connections but it will allow you to transport data, administer resources and interconnect as if the cloud is an extension of your own on-premises network.

A basic SSL browser connection is a very good starting solution when using Goggle cloud as it allows you to work in a development area that is segregated from your on-premises network. If you do wish to interconnect then all you have to do is install some static routes that point towards the subnets used in either network. For small deployments using static routing this is very desirable as it removes all of the complexity of dynamic routing protocols. After all it only requires one static route in each direction to direct traffic to a given network. The problem is that if you start to go to production then you may need many static routes installed that are continually changing.

To make the routing updates dynamic, then you have to use a router and a routing protocol and GCP uses a feature called cloud router. The managed service that is cloud router will analyse traffic and using algorithms learn and work out the best paths from your network to other connected networks. It will do this automatically and update your Google VPC exchange route information with any newly learned networks over the VPN using the Border Gateway Protocol (BGP).

BGP is however an external routing protocol that is only really required for internet scale networks. For instance, if you add a new subnet to your Google VPC, your on-premises network will automatically exchange routes with it and vice versa. This may or may not be what you want as some customers don't want to use the internet, either because of security concerns in so much as they do not wish to advertise their networks or because they feel they need more reliable and secure bandwidth.

If you do not want to use a VPN or a Cloud Router then you can consider peering with Google via a direct peering arrangement. PVC peering relates to collocation where you put your own router in the same public data center as a Google point of presence and then directly connect, share routes and exchange traffic. In order to facilitate this Google has more than 100 points of presence around the world, there are also many Internet Exchanges such as in London, New York and Frankfurt amongst many others that provide the same interconnect services.

However, for the many customers who are not located close to a point of presence there is still the possibility that they can contract with a partner in the carrier peering program to get connected. This would mean again collocating but at a closer and more convenient geographical zone.

A caveat of peering though is that it isn't covered by a Google service level agreement.

For customers who require five 9's reliability and availability for their interconnection with Google then they should consider using a dedicated interconnect in which customers get a direct private connections to Google.

The advantage here is that if these connections have topologies that meet Google's specifications, they can be covered by up to a 99.99 percent SLA. These connections can be backed up by a VPN for even greater reliability to provide a strong measure of business continuity.

Use case - 4

The client ABC returns with a request for more details on how they can give access to their different development sub-teams to the main Development project. These teams typically work autonomously on a single function or topic so are deployed within independent projects but they obviously need access to the main Development project that hosts the application.

Solution

The proposed solution that you could present is based upon using a shared-VPC for the main development project and allowing the other projects to share its resources. In this way their main Development project that hosts the app will be designated as the host project. The other projects that are configured to share those resources will be designated as service projects.

Figure -5

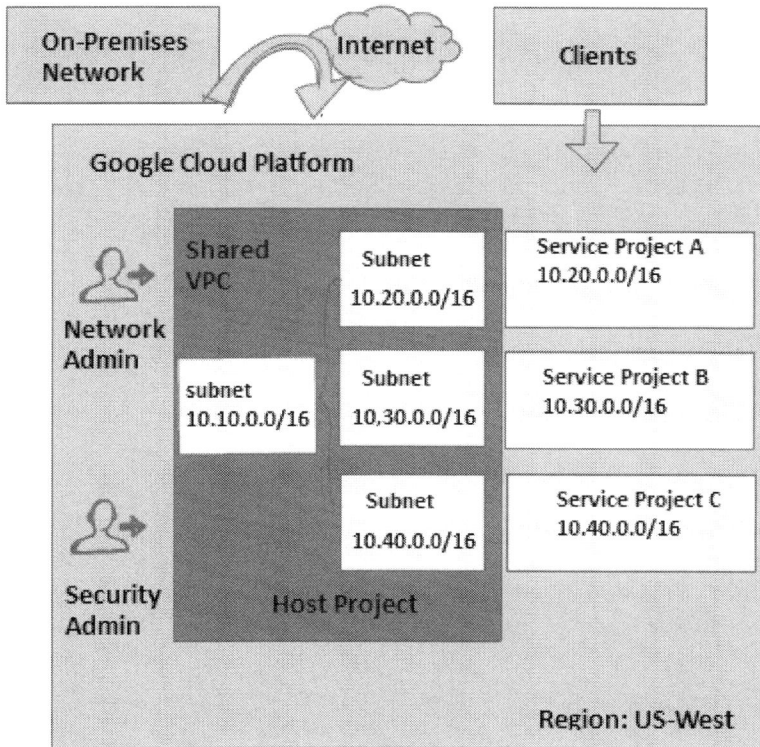

There are several caveats that you need to consider such as making sure that all projects are within the same folder – if you are using folders – you will also need to create a central administrator to manage all the projects. This means creating a central administrator role and giving them permissions to create new service projects as well as having the instant.admin role in each service project so that they can configure the networking.

To secure this environment you should recommend disabling the service projects external access so they can only access and be accessed by internal resources.

Chapter 18 – Cloud Data Storage

Application will almost always need to store some data, whether that be media to be streamed or sensor data from devices or customer account balances, or maybe simply the fact that they need to maintain session information via cookies. Moreover, we can see that different applications and workloads will often require diverse storage quotas, limits and solutions.

However in the cloud the available data storage options are quite diverse and you need to be specific about the type you select. You already know from earlier that you can store data on your VM's persistent disk or on SSD local disks.

But, Google Cloud Platform has other storage options to meet your needs as not all data is the same. Indeed data can be categorized into several groups; structured, semi-structured, unstructured, transactional, and relational data and they are best stored in a different format.

Cloud Storage Options

In this section we will discuss the core the diverse GCP storage options that have come about to address modern needs, these are: Cloud Storage, Cloud SQL, Cloud Spanner, Cloud Data Store and Google Big Table.

Why do we have different storage types you may ask? Simply it is because each storage type is best suited to the type and quantity of the data. This is due to data having some basic characteristic such as being structured or unstructured.

Figure -6

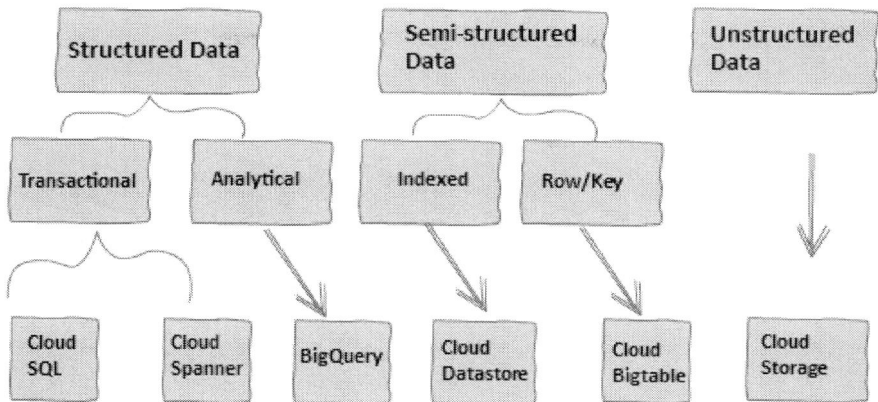

Structured Data

Structured data fits a predefined schema, which makes it possible for search engines to search, organize, and display your content. Structured data is representable, is in a standard format so is understandable and can communicate to search engines what your data means.
Examples of structured data include numbers, dates, and groups of words and numbers called strings that fit a predefined record. Structured data accounts for about 20 percent of the data that we handle and is the data you're probably used to dealing with. It's usually stored in a relational database.

Unstructured Data

Unstructured data is defined as being information that does not have either a pre-defined data structure or is not organized in a pre-prepared manner. Unstructured information is typically of an undetermined size; it can be text-heavy but may also contain data such as dates, numbers, and facts as well.

Examples of Unstructured Data often include text and multimedia content, such as e-mail messages, news articles, videos, photos, audio files, presentations, webpages and many other kinds of business documents of an undetermined size. As these data types size are typically unpredictable they are stored as data objects or rather as data blobs. Whereas structured data is stored in predefined fields and records in an orderly database schema, unstructured data, due to its unpredictability is stored as an object, a lump of data, in a region of storage. In this case each data object can be accessed using its unique identifier or a more complex expression through attached metadata that refers to the object. In addition, each object has a unique data type.

As we will see each type of Google storage is designed for a specific purpose to store a type of data and perform a function that depends on your applications requirements. Therefore, you might want to use one or several of these services in combination to meet the storage requirements that best suits your data.

Google Cloud Storage

This is GCP's object file storage which means that instead of storing data in a schema or a file system it stores your data as an arbitrary bunch of bytes – a blob - and the storage system lets you address it with a unique key. Typically these unique keys are in the form of URL's which means object storage interacts nicely with Web technologies.

This is how Google's Cloud Storage works and as it is a form of object storage you don't have to provision capacity or develop a schema before you use it. What this means is that you simply make objects and the service stores them with high durability and high availability and references them via a URL.

Cloud Storage is suitable for many types of data storage requirements such as when serving website content, storing data for archival and even for storing data for disaster recovery.

Cloud Storage as we have seen is very web friendly as each of your objects in Cloud Storage has a URL this makes it an ideal method for making available to your end users large data objects via web download.

Google's Cloud Storage is a managed service and it stores your data for you in storage areas called buckets. You will initially create and configure your unique storage bucket then use it to hold your storage objects. The storage objects stored within a bucket are actually immutable, which means that you cannot edit them in place but instead you create new versions. In addition Cloud Storage always encrypts your data on the server side before it is written to disk and you don't pay extra for that. Furthermore, in a Cloud storage bucket encryption is applied by default at rest and when data is in-transit using HTTPS. This makes it a convenient and secure way to initially move data from your on-premises servers or your computer into GCP. In this way Cloud Storage acts as an ideal landing post for your data before you move it onwards to other GCP storage services.

This is a good way to upload data into GCP as your Cloud Storage objects will be securely stored and organized into buckets. When you create a bucket, you give it a globally unique name and you specify a geographic location where the bucket and its contents are to be stored and you choose a default storage class.

Therefore, you need to consider a few things before you go ahead and pick a location as ideally you will want a location close to your customer base that will minimizes latency for your application and your end users. In other words, if most of your users are in Europe, you probably want to pick a European location. There are also in some countries legal restriction about where your customers' data can be stored so for example in the European Union you must store their data within the EU unless you have their explicit permission to store it outside the EU. Therefore, it's best if you operate in Europe or have a large European user base to store your data in a region and zone in Europe.

Securing your Data

Your objects will be stored as encrypted data when it is at rest or in-flight but there will usually be others that need to access the data. Therefore, GCP provides several ways to control access to your objects and buckets. The preferred way to control access and assign user permissions is to use Cloud IAM. When you deploy IAM to authenticate and authorize users the most efficient way is for you to assign roles and the permission attached to each of the roles is inherited from project to bucket to object.

In some case you feel that you need finer control, in that case you can create access control lists (ACLs) that offer greater granularity for specific users. Typically you will use ACLs to define who has access to your buckets and objects and then what they are authorised to do. Hence, each ACL you configure will consists of a scope which defines who can perform the specified actions and this can be a specific user or group of users and a permission which defines what actions can be performed. For example, read or write.

However when data is stored in a bucket then that Cloud Storage object becomes immutable so if you do need to change the object you have to create a new version. To help you keep track of the versions you can turn on object versioning on your buckets. If you do activate versioning, then Cloud Storage keeps a history of modifications. You can list the archived versions of an object, restore an object to an older state or permanently delete a version as needed. If you don't turn on object versioning, a new version always overrides an older version.

However with versioning there is the risk of junk accumulating so Cloud Storage also offers life-cycle management policies. In this case you could instruct Cloud Storage to keep only the three most recent versions of each object in a bucket that has versioning enabled. But the polies can be flexible so you could also delete objects older than 365 days or you could create a policy that will delete objects created before a certain date.

Cloud Storage Classes

Another important consideration when using Cloud storage is that you must choose the type of storage class that best suits your needs. There are four different types of storage classes: regional, multi-regional, nearline, and coldline. All of the storage classes are accessed in comparable ways using the cloud storage API and they all offer millisecond access types. However that's where the similarity ends. Multi regional and regional are high performance object storage designed for frequent access, whereas nearline and coldline are designed for infrequent access for backup and archival storage and as we will learn they are priced accordingly.

You must be clear on the storage classes or you could pay over the odds for the wrong service class.

Regional vs. Multi Regional

Regional storage allows you to create your bucket and store your data in a specific GCP region for example, in US Central one, Europe West one or Asia East one. It's cheaper than multi regional storage but it offers less redundancy.

Multi regional storage on the other hand, is more expensive but it provides geographical redundancy. That means that when you pick multi-regional storage you select from a broad geographical location like the United States, the European Union, or Asia and cloud storage will then store your bucket and data in at least two geographic locations separated by at least 160 kilometres.

You would tend to want to use Multi regional storage for frequently accessed data such as for, website content, interactive workloads, or data that's part of mobile and gaming applications.

Regional storage on the other hand is best for storing data that requires frequent access with high performance and low latency for data intensive computations. This make regional storage that is located close to their application running on their Compute Engine virtual machines a better option.

Nearline vs. Coldline

In GCP Cloud Storage there are two much cheaper options for storing infrequently accessed data. The options are Nearline and Coldline.
  Nearline storage can be considered to be a low cost, highly durable service for storing infrequently accessed data. Remember in all classes there is low latency access so lower performance is not an issue. The differences are in cost, which is based upon frequency of access i.e. data base read.

The Nearline storage class is a better approach to either multi regional storage or regional storage in scenarios where you plan to read or modify your data once a month or less.

A typical use case for Nearline storage class is when you want to run monthly analytics against a batch of data. In this scenario you can continuously add log files to your cloud storage bucket on a daily bases as there is no restrictions on adding data – restrictions apply to egress or read access - and then access the aggregated data once a month for analysis.

On the other hand, we have Coldline storage, which is a very low cost, highly durable service for data archiving, online backup, and disaster recovery. You can consider Coldline to be the best choice for data that you plan to access (egress/read) very rarely, less than once a year at most.

However Coldline has some caveats you must contemplate such as it has slightly lower availability, 90-day minimum storage duration, higher costs for data egress access, and higher networking costs for egress accessing of your data.

These additional costs are there to deter Coldline being used much like Nearline for monthly access as the additional egress access and data transport network costs would negate any cost benefit.

However when used correctly Coldline is a very low cost option as the addition access and network charges are insignificant when incurred annually. This makes Coldline storage ideal if you want to archive data but still have rapid access to it in case of a disaster recovery event.

Availability of these storage classes varies with multi regional having the highest availability of 99.95 percent followed by regional with 99.9 percent and then Nearline and Coldline with 99 percent.

As for pricing, all storage classes incur a cost per gigabyte of data stored per month, with multi regional having the highest storage price and Coldline the lowest storage price.

Egress and data transfer charges may also apply.

In addition to those charges, Nearline storage also incurs an access fee per gigabyte of data read and Coldline storage incurs a higher fee per gigabyte of data read.

Data Transfer into Cloud Storage

The availability, flexibility, cost effectiveness and scale of Google cloud storage offers the potential to solve a wide range of enterprise technical challenges. But not all on-premise infrastructure will be easy to integrate into cloud technology. It is very attractive to first use GCP for development and proof of concept but eventually we will want to take advantage of the financial and operational benefits and shift production systems into the cloud but how do we do that without major upheaval?

Shifting production to the cloud requires careful planning as not all areas of IT are so easily accomplished when moving operations to the cloud. There are obvious candidates such as backups and real time replication of databases for business continuity, which makes sense. But there are others such as large scale monolithic applications or mainframes that simply are not suited to a cloud environment. Nonetheless, there are areas in a modern IT environment where cloud is hugely beneficial and we can examine some of them now.

Where cloud data deployment is beneficial

Many of our applications need to be delivered with speed, at scale and while reducing costs and these are the common challenges many of us face in our enterprise when deploying new systems. These operational criteria are often difficult to achieve with more traditional approaches, but this is where cloud excels as it has vast scale, geographical reach, agility and flexibility – so how can we utilise the GCP to meet enterprise demands, such as low latency, high performance and security?

Why Cloud Native?

While our existing enterprise on-premises technology maybe restrictive, it is deeply ingrained into in the way we operate. Enterprise IT are typically expert in developing and running applications on-premises and operations teams are skilled in running their data centres at highly efficient levels. IT is also skilled in running their networks in order to optimise service delivery.
However when we contemplate shifting to native cloud services – those designed and built to run in the cloud – it is not a trivial task. Indeed reimagining applications and services may require the rewrite of applications, workflows and retraining of staff. This is not a trivial pursuit as all of these efforts will cost time and money, and have the potential to introduce risk.
However, integrating cloud technology with familiar enterprise technologies can help simplify use of the cloud, and allow us to more easily and widely adopt it. We will discuss cloud native design later.

Designing Cloud Tiers

The ever-increasing amounts of data we hold has become a real challenge as it is not just for historical records or analytics it is also due to regulatory demands. However, as well as production and regulatory compliance data, there are also archives, backups and other "cold", infrequently-accessed data. What is more, we will often need to keep a mirror image of all our operational data for business continuity so that we can switch over operations at a flick of a switch to another diverse geographical region in case of a local catastrophic failure. All of this cold storage data will need to be archived but accessed quickly in the case of a disaster recovery scenario.

Where to store different classes of data, so that it is held on the most cost-efficient tier – including on-premise or in the cloud – presents a real technical and business issue. We have already considered the GCP options of Nearline and Coldline but the question still remains, how do we size our data storage requirements accurately and easily grow our capacity on demand? How do we manage our data so that backups and infrequently used data are placed in cold storage so that they do not consume expensive frequent access storage but still remain accessible? Fortunately, Google's cloud storage options with its scalability and attractive pay-as-you-use model has created the almost perfect long-term repository. However, this technology as compelling as it is, is not without its challenges. Cloud storage cost are not the only expense as we need to consider the issues of retrieving data from a cloud repository, as there are always network charges but the benefit that a cloud storage tier delivers make it worthy of consideration.

Data protection in the cloud

One of the single most stubborn obstacles that enterprises state as preventing them from adopting a cloud deployment is that they will lose control over their data security and the data integrity. In this scenario enterprises feel that their responsibility for data protection is a high priority that cannot be readily compromised. Hence in many enterprises today they see this as a challenge as they feel responsible for protecting much more data and for even longer lifespans. They also have to meet ever more stringent regulatory compliance legislation and all of this puts a huge strain on their existing data protection infrastructure.

Data protection suppliers have seen how large-scale, relatively low-cost repositories such as Google Cloud Storage can help lessen some of these problems with the scale and flexibility that the GCP data protection provides for your data. Such cloud based functionality allows for data to be moved to a cloud location based on policies defined to meet the needs of the enterprise and do it as part of your standard backup operations. A caveat however is that you should be aware the limitations of this approach. Associated cloud costs such as network data transfer costs, and egress read access to data, need to be taken into consideration when pricing the service. Similarly you must consider the impact on your recovery capability of restoring large amounts of data from a public cloud.

Geographic data sharing

One of the longest-standing issues many organisations face is finding an effective way to share data across multiple locations in order to minimise latency and provide high customer levels of experience.
The challenge is complex with on-premises as it involves synchronising transactions as well as potentially moving large amounts of data while maintaining file integrity. Traditionally, this issue of synchronicity has been accomplished via a distributed file system, which typically relied on the replication of databases across a network. This however has its own problems as there may be replication lag if a database is overwhelmed. It also comes with management issues like maintaining a single source of truth or ensuring the security and integrity of the data through global file locking. But spreading and replicating data over large geographic areas is a staple capability of cloud. But the problem still persists how do we get those large data sets to the cloud?

Importing Data into the Cloud

Regardless of which storage class you choose, whether that is regional, multi-regional, Nearline or Coldline, there are issues that you need to overcome. The most significant is how you import all the relevant data into the cloud storage. With GCP there are several ways to bring data into cloud storage. The most commonly used way especially for operations with smaller data sets is simply to use gsutil, which is the cloud storage command from the GCP Cloud SDK.

However, you can also move data in with a drag and drop in the GCP console, if you use the Google Chrome browser but that only works for small data sets. But what can you do if you have to upload terabytes or even petabytes of data?

If you have to move vast quantities of data then Google Cloud platform offers the online storage transfer service and the offline transfer appliance to help. In the case of the online storage transfer service it lets you schedule and manage batch transfers to cloud storage from another cloud provider from a different cloud storage region or from an HTTP(S) end point.

On the other hand if you need on-premises data transfer then the transfer appliance is a physical and rack mounted device, which is a high capacity storage server that you lease from Google Cloud. You simply connect it to your network, load it with data and then ship it to an upload facility where the data is uploaded to cloud storage. This may seem primitive but it is still probably the fastest and cheapest way to upload vast amounts of data into the cloud. Using this service enables you to securely transfer up to a petabyte of data on a single appliance.

There are other ways of getting your data into cloud storage as this storage option is tightly integrated with many of the Google cloud platform products and services. For example, you can import and export tables from and to BigQuery as well as Cloud SQL. You can also store App Engine logs, Cloud Datastore's backups, and objects used by App Engine applications like images. Cloud storage can also store instant start-up scripts, Compute Engine images, and objects used by Compute Engine applications.

In summary, cloud storage is often the ingestion point for data being moved into the cloud from on-premises or other cloud locations and because of this it is frequently the long term storage location for most user data. Consider using Cloud Storage if you need to store Immutable blobs that is larger than 10 megabytes such as large images or movies.

This storage service scales up to petabytes of capacity with an upper limit of five terabytes per object.

Cloud Bigtable

Cloud Bigtable is Google's NoSQL, Big Data database service. What the term NoSQL with regards database technology means is that it is 'Not Only SQL' and the difference between NoSQL and the traditional SQL relational database is that the former is better suited to today's application data loads and development lifecycles.

Relational databases require that schemas be defined before you can add data. A schema is a collection of relational tables that consist of records and fields. For example, you might want to store data in a customer record that hold data in fields, such as phone numbers, first and last name, address, city and postcode. Hence, an SQL database needs tables, records and fields in a DB schema to be preconfigured in advance in order to store the data into the relevant customer record.

However, this pre-configuration and planning of the database schema fits poorly with modern agile development approaches, because each time you complete new features, the schema of your database often needs to change. If the database is large or reiterations frequent, this can involve significant downtime. Also it is unlikely that, using a relational database, you would be able to effectively accommodate data that's completely unstructured or unable to fit a pre-defined schema.

The modern approach is to use NoSQL databases, which are built to allow the insertion of data without any predefined schema. That makes it easy to make significant application changes in real-time, without worrying about service interruptions – which means development is faster, code integration is more reliable, and less database administrator time is needed.

Despite this SQL and relational databases do excel in certain areas such as in transactional processes as an enforced schema is a big help for some applications but it is also a big hindrance for others. This is simply because many modern apps require a much more flexible approach, hence the move towards the NoSQL schema.

These applications do not need all the rows to have the same columns. And in fact, the database might be designed to take advantage of that by sparsely populating the rows.

That's part of what makes your NoSQL database in Bigtable what it is as its tables are sparsely populated so that they can scale to billions of rows and thousands of columns allowing you to store petabytes of data.

Fortunately Google GCP offers Cloud Bigtable as a fully managed service so much of the technology complexity and data schema is transparent to you, so you don't have to worry about configuring and tuning it. Therefore you can just look upon it as being an ideal place for storing large amounts of data with very low latency. As such it is also perfect for storing data that has a single lookup key and it also supports high throughput, both read and write, so it's a great choice for both operational and analytical applications including Internet of Things, user analytics and financial data analysis.

Cloud Bigtable is offered through the same open source API as HBase, which is the native database for the Apache Hadoop project. Having the same API enables the portability of applications between HBase and Bigtable.

However Cloud Bigtable has a few advantages most notably with regards scalability. For if you have worked with and managed your own Hbase installation, you will know that once you hit a certain rate of queries per second scaling gets difficult. But scaling with Cloud Bigtable is easy as you can just increase your machine count which doesn't even require downtime.

Also, Cloud Bigtable handles administration tasks like upgrades and restarts transparently.

Furthermore, security and privacy in Cloud Bigtable is robust and inbuilt as all data is encrypted by default both in-flight and at rest. Also to control authentication and authorisation to access the data you can use IAM permissions to control who has access to your Bigtable data.

As Cloud Bigtable is part of the GCP ecosystem, it can interact with other GCP services and third-party clients. Thus, from an application API perspective, data can be read from and written to Cloud Bigtable through a data service layer like managed VMs, the HBase rest server or a Java server using the HBase client to serve data to applications, dashboards and data services.

Data can also be streamed in through a variety of popular stream processing frameworks, like Cloud Dataflow Streaming, Spark Streaming and Storm.

However, if you prefer to do batch processing rather than streaming then data can also be read from and written to Cloud Bigtable through batch processes like Hadoop map reduce, Dataflow or Spark. Often summarized or newly calculated data is written back to Cloud Bigtable or to a downstream database.

Finally, should you remain unconvinced here is a stellar reference to its ability as Cloud Bigtable is actually the same database that Google uses to host many of its core services including search, analytics, maps and Gmail.

Consider using Cloud Bigtable if you need to store a large amount of structured objects.

Cloud Bigtable does not support SQL's queries nor does it support multi-row transactions.

This storage service provides petabytes of capacity with a maximum unit size of 10 megabytes per cell and 100 megabytes per row.

Relational Databases

In the previous section we covered NoSQL databases but there is still a demand for traditional relational database services. Remember, relational database services use a predesigned database schema laid out in tables in order to help your application keep your data consistent, and correct. This makes relational database services great for handling transactions. Without database transactions, your online bank wouldn't be able to offer you the ability to move money from one account to another. Typically, relational databases require an expert to design, configure, maintain, manage, and administer.

However if you want the transactional power along with the protections of a relational database, then you can use GCP's Cloud SQL.

Cloud SQL offers you the choice of database engine such as, MySQL, PostgreSQL and SQL Server as a fully managed service, which again decouples a lot of the complexity associated with setting up and managing these types of databases.

But you don't have to use Cloud SQL as you could always run your own database server instance inside a Compute Engine virtual machine which a lot of GCP customers do but CloudSQL offers MySQL, SQL Server and PostgreSQL databases that are capable of handling terabytes of storage. There are some other notable benefits of using the CloudSQL managed service instead of managing your own database instance within a VM.

- Firstly, CloudSQL provide several replica services like read, failover, and external replicas. This means that if an outage occurs, CloudSQL can replicate data between multiple zones with automatic failover.

- Secondly, CloudSQL helps you backup your data with either On-Demand or scheduled backups.
- Thirdly, CloudSQL can scale both vertically by changing the machine type, and horizontally via read replicas.

Moreover, if we consider Cloud SQL from a security perspective, you will get as part of the managed service, network firewalls, encrypted data on Google's internal networks, and when stored in database tables, temporary files, and backups.

Another benefit of CloudSQL instances is they are readily accessible by other GCP services and even external services. This means you can easily authorize Compute Engine instances to access CloudSQL instances and configure the CloudSQL instance to be in the same zone as your virtual machine for low latency and high performance.

Finally when it comes to administration you can manage CloudSQL just like on-premises database as it supports other applications and tools like SQL Workbench, Toad, and other external applications that use standard MySQL drivers.

Cloud Spanner

If CloudSQL does not fit your requirements because you need a horizontal scale capability, then consider using Cloud Spanner as it can provide petabytes of capacity. In addition to its scale Spanner can also offer transactional consistency at a global scale, it also supports relational schemas, SQL, and even synchronous replication for high availability.

You might want to consider using Cloud Spanner as opposed to Cloud SQL if you have outgrown your present relational database, or require sharding your databases in order to scale horizontally, have a demand for higher throughput and higher performance, or need transactional consistency at a global scale and strong consistency, or just want to consolidate your databases.

Natural use cases for Cloud Spanner include financial applications, and inventory applications. You would be well advised to consider using Cloud SQL for relational database support especially if you use MySQL or PostgreSQL or if you require vast scale then try Cloud Spanner. If you need full SQL support for an online transaction processing system then Cloud SQL provides terabytes of capacity, while Cloud Spanner provides petabytes of capacity. If Cloud SQL does not fit your requirements because you need horizontal scalability not just through the replicas, consider using Cloud Spanner.

Cloud Datastore

Google Cloud Platform also supports another data storage service, Cloud Datastore, which is a highly scalable NoSQL database and its primary use cases is to store structured data from App Engine apps. You can also utilise Cloud Datastore as the integration point when you build solutions that span App Engine and Compute Engine VMs.
As you would expect from a fully managed service, Google handles all Cloud Datastore administration as it is designed to shard and replicate, providing you with a highly available and durable database that scales automatically to handle your workload.
Unlike Cloud Bigtable, it also offers transactions that can affect multiple database rows, and it lets you do SQL-like queries.
To get you started, Cloud Datastore has a free daily quota that provides storage, reads, writes deletes and small operations at no charge. Consider using Cloud Datastore if you need to store unstructured objects or if you require support for transactions and SQL like queries. This storage services provides terabytes of capacity with a maximum unit size of one megabyte per entity.
There is another type of storage called BigQuery, which it sits on the edge between data storage and data processing, and it is used predominantly in Big Data and Machine Learning in the Cloud.
The usual reason to store data in BigQuery is to use its Big Data analysis and interactive query capabilities. You would not want to use BigQuery for example as the backend store for an online application.
Considering the technical differentiators of the different storage services does help some people decide which storage service to choose. Others like to consider use cases. In which case:

- Cloud Datastore is the best for semi-structured application data that is used in App Engines applications.
- Bigtable is best for analytical data with heavy read write events like AdTech, Financial or IoT data.
- Cloud Storage is best for structured and unstructured, binary or object data like images, large media files and backups.
- SQL is best for web frameworks and in existing applications like storing user credentials and customer orders.
- Cloud Spanner is best for large scale database applications that are larger than two terabytes, for example, for financial trading and e-commerce use cases.

But it may well be that depending on your application requirements that you use several of these services to get the job done.

Use case – 5

Now that they have committed to a cloud infrastructure solution it only remains for them to choose suitable cloud storage. They would also like to know whether to stick with MySQL residing on VMs or to migrate to CloudSQL to derive many of the benefits of the cloud. What solutions can you propose that is simple to implement and cost effective?
Solution
You have proposed in the original design that the backup/archived data be stored in Cloud Storage as Coldline as this will be cheaper and easier to manage due to versioning and other management tools. This is still the preferred option if they insist on archiving their data in the cloud. However they should be aware that this will take a lot of time to recover and restore the data over the internet and bear costs and significant network charges when they retrieve the data. It will also use up a lot of internet bandwidth so you will need a dedicated channel just for this data migration. It might therefore be better to leave the backup/archived data where it is and continue with their existing backup and offsite storage method. Once they have switched over and the cloud infrastructure is active then they can start using the Cloud Storage coldline storage as that will no longer require internet transfer as it will all be handled across Google's network.

Before making a cloud storage decision, be sure to answer the following questions:

- What are your workload performance characteristics?
- What type of cloud media is appropriate to meet those performance demands?
- What levels of resilience are needed?
- How often do you need to access the data?
- What would be the cost of moving data out of the cloud?
- Do you fully understand the public cloud cost model?

Moving to CloudSQL will be relatively straightforward as it is itself MySQL so it will be a like for like swap. This makes transferring the schema and data straightforward as a simple sqldump that is uploaded into Cloud Storage is all that is required. Cloud SQL can then build the schema and data using the sqldump object in the Cloud Storage bucket. There might be an issue with down time or service disruption but replicating the on-premises master to the CloudSQL MySQL instance will keep the two synchronised without the need for any service disruption.

Chapter 19 - Containers and Kubernetes Engine

In this chapter we will shift the focus away from GCP storage portfolio to containers and the Google Kubernetes engine. We will describe in this chapter why you want to use containers,
what their benefits are and how to manage them in Kubernetes engine.

An introduction to Containers and Kubernetes

In an earlier chapter we introduced you to the Compute Engine, which is GCP's Infrastructure as the Service offering (IaaS), with access to servers, file systems, and networking through the deployment of VMs. We will also discuss the App Engine service, which is GCP's Platform as a Service (PaaS) offering in the next chapter. However for now, it is time to introduce you to containers and Kubernetes engine, which is a hybrid service that conceptually sits between the Compute Engine and App Engine, and as you will see provides benefits from both of the services. Compute Engine and its functions that deliver automation and elasticity introduce the model of programmable infrastructure. Indeed using IaaS or PaaS such as App Engine makes your applications self-aware and allows them to scale-out and scale-in dynamically.
Nonetheless, technology doesn't stand still and a new wave of technological innovation has arrived in the form of immutable infrastructure and micro-services. At the forefront of this change is a popular Linux-based technology called containers, this is where a single kernel has the ability to run multiple instances of a VM upon a single underlying operating system.

When we use Compute Engine VMs we are utilizing the benefits of Infrastructure as a Service, which allows you to share compute resources with other developers by virtualizing the hardware using virtual machines. In this case, each developer can deploy their own application environment. Thus they can build their applications in their own self-contained environment with access to an operating system, RAM, file systems, networking interfaces, and so on. This is one of the several benefits of using virtual machines as they provide you with a self-contained environment where you can install your favourite applications, run-times, tools, web server, database, middleware, and so on. Also in addition to being able to custom configure the operating environment you are also able to configure the underlying system resources such as disk space, disk IO, and networking.

But that isolation and flexibility comes at a cost as the smallest unit of compute is an app with its VM. Remember that a VM is a virtualised server that will contain its own guest OS and that will be large; perhaps gigabytes in size, and also it may take several minutes to boot the OS. That may not be a problem when you are starting out and perhaps building a development location in GCP but as you move to production and the application grows you will need to scale horizontally by adding replica VMs to meet the demand.

However, this is where some issues arise, because as demand for your application increases, you will have to copy an entire VM, and boot the guest OS for each instance of your app, which can be slow, costly and inefficient.

However, one way around this was to use the App Engine services, as you get access to programming services. Hence, all you had to do was use those services to write your code and your self-contained workloads including any dependent libraries. This meant that when demand for your app increased, the platform would scale your app seamlessly and independently by workload and infrastructure. This solution scales rapidly, but you sacrifice the benefit of being able to fine tune the underlying architecture to save cost but that is where containers come in to play.

What are Containers?

The idea of a container is to give you the independent scalability of workloads, but with an abstraction layer of the OS and hardware. Therefore what you effectively get is a VM without a dedicated guest OS. Indeed the container acts just like its name suggests as a box around your code and its dependencies. However the container also comes with limited access to your own partition of the file system and hardware. This means it doesn't require its own guest OS so It only requires a few system calls to create and start, which means it doesn't have to boot an OS so it can be up and running as quickly as a process.

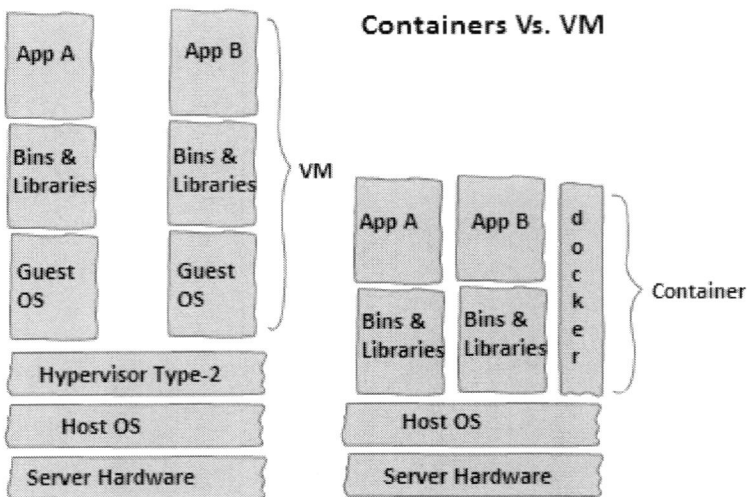

Figure -7

To run your application in a container all you need on each host is an OS kernel that supports containers, and a container runtime. In essence, you're virtualizing the OS; it scales well and also gives you nearly the same flexibility as IaaS.

However a huge benefit with containers is that through this abstraction of the underlying OS, your code is now highly portable, so you can deploy it readily on any OS or hardware. This means you no longer have to make different versions of your app to support different OS, which means you can rapidly and continuous deploy your application. Thus you will go from development, to staging, to production, and deployment to the cloud without reconfiguring or rebuilding the application. This is a tremendous boon for rapid and continuous deployment in DevOps environment but it gets even better.

Containers scale well horizontally so if for example you were running a web server, you can scale your application in seconds and as many containers as you need, depending on the size of your workload, on a single host. Nonetheless, that's not the best way to go about it.

With containers you'll want to shift away from running an application on a single container as you will benefit more by building your application using lots of containers each performing their own function like microservices. If you take this approach to building your app using single function microservices or micro-apps and deploying them in containers connected via the network this will make them modular, easy and quick to deploy, and they will scale independently across a group of hosts.

Building Containers

The first thing you will need to know is how to build a container and then run it and the most common way us to use an open source tool called Docker or you could use Google Container Builder. These tools define a format for bundling your application, its dependencies, and machine specific settings into a container.

When you use the docker build command to build the container it builds and stores the container locally as a runnable image. You can save and upload the image into a container registry service, and share or download it from there. Then, you will use the docker run command to run the image.

Nonetheless, the tasks involved in building and packaging applications into containers is only a small part, the vast majority of the work is associated with application configuration, service discovery, managing updates, monitoring and orchestration.

Potentially when you use containers a host can scale up or down and start and stop the containers on-demand as demand for your application changes, or if a host fails. But you will need tools to orchestrate and control the provisioning process and that is where Kubernetes comes in.

The Role of Kubernetes

Kubernetes acts as the orchestrator managing many containers deployed on many hosts and scaling them as microservices. Kubernetes also plays an important role in automatic provisioning and deploying rollouts and rollbacks.

To understand how and why we need Kubernetes as an orchestrator we have to comprehend that deploying and managing containers manually is not really feasible. This is due to fact that there is a lot more too just building and running containers there are the other tasks associated with service discovery, managing updates, monitoring, and provisioning, which are the essential components of an automated, reliable, scalable, distributed system.

To assist us in automating the management and provisioning of our container base we can use Kubernetes, which is an open source orchestrator that abstracts containers at a higher level so you can better manage and scale your applications.

Kubernetes can be thought of as a set of APIs that you can use to deploy and manage containers. The Kubernetes system is organised as a set of master components that run as a control plane, and a set of nodes that run containers. In Kubernetes, a node represents a computing instance like a virtual machine. Specifically in Google Cloud, Kubernetes nodes are virtual machines running in the Compute Engine.

At a very high level of operations, you describe a set of applications and how they should interact with each other, and Kubernetes figures how to make that happen.

Nodes, Pods and Clusters

Kubernetes uses the concept of a cluster which is basically a set of containers. Hence once you have built your container, the first thing you will need to do is deploy it into a cluster.

However, Kubernetes clusters can be configured with many options and add-ons, which can be complex and time consuming so instead, you can use the Kubernetes Engine, or GKE.

GKE is hosted Kubernetes by Google. Within GKE clusters can be customized, they can support different machine types, numbers of nodes, and network settings. Kubernetes is also able to launch containers in existing VMs or to provision new VMs and place the containers within them. Kubernetes goes well beyond simply booting containers as it also provides the tools to monitor and managing them. With Kubernetes, administrators can create Pods; these are logical groups of similar or tightly coupled containers that are related to an application. Pods are duly provisioned within the Compute Engine VMs.

When using Kubernetes Engine, it will deploy containers on Compute Engine VMs using a wrapper around one or more related containers called a pod. This is the smallest unit in Kubernetes that you can create or deploy. Logically a pod will represent a running process on your cluster. It can be either a component of your application, or the entire application. Typically, you only would place one container per pod, but if you have multiple containers with a hard dependency, you can package them into a single pod, and share networking and storage. The pod provides a unique network IP and the containers inside a pod can communicate with one another using the 'localhost' interface and the ports will remain fixed as they are started and stopped on different nodes.

Starting a Deployment

One way to run a container in a pod in Kubernetes is to use the 'kubectl' run command. This starts a deployment of a container running in a pod. A deployment represents a group of replicas of the same pod and keeps your pod running even when nodes they run on fail.

It could represent a component of an application or an entire app. By default, pods in a deployment are only accessible inside your GKE cluster.

Exposing a Deployment

To make them publicly available, you can connect a Load Balancer to your deployment by running the 'kubectl' exposed command.

In GKE, the Load Balancer is created as a network Load Balancer and Kubernetes creates a service with a fixed IP for your pods. Any client that hits that IP address will be routed to a pod behind the service.

The Kubernetes service defines a logical set of pods and a policy by which to access them. It is an abstraction that enables you to separate the deployments - to create and destroy pods, allow them to get their own IP address, - from the complexity of individual administration. However, those addresses don't remain stable over time. To get around this issue we use service groups.

Service Groups

A service group is set of pods, which provides a stable endpoint or fixed IP for them.

For example, if you create two sets of pods called front-end and back-end, and you put them behind their own services, back-end pods IP addresses may change over time but the front-end pods are not aware of this, nor do they care, as they simply refer to the back-end service by name rather than by IP addresses.

Scaling a Deployment

To scale a deployment, run the 'kubectl' scale command. In this case, three pods are created in your deployment, and they're placed behind the service and they will share one fixed IP.

So far you have learned to run imperative commands like run, expose and scale. This works well to learn and test Kubernetes step by step. But the real strength of Kubernetes comes when you work in a declarative way. Instead of issuing commands, you provide a configuration file that tells Kubernetes what you want your desired state to look like, and Kubernetes figures out how to do it.

Use Case -6

A client has come to you requesting your advice on whether they should build their apps using containers. They explain they are keen to take advantage of container technology as they want to embrace a continuous improvement and rapid deployment culture. The problem is that their current infrastructure isn't very flexible and they are not sure how to manage the change, would a cloud development environment be fit for purpose?

Solution

There are actually two parts to this question, first there is the issue of building apps using containers and secondly whether to build a development environment in the cloud. If we address the second point first we can propose that creating the development environment in the cloud would be a highly flexible and agile solution. This is because developers can spin-up VMs and other resources in seconds without any capital outlay or provisioning delays. This makes development fast and flexible. Moving the development to the cloud also lessens the internal burden on networks and IT as they no longer will need to be involved every time a developer wants to spin up an instance. So long as it is managed and audited frequently to ensure there is no proliferation of zombie VMs around it can be a cost effective solution.

Regards the point about containers, we need to take a few things into consideration. One of the points is whether the development team has the required skills or any experience in creating and managing containers. That of course is not for us to say so we can only advice on which platform they could use that supports containers. Here they have a choice of App Engine Flexible Environment, Compute Engine or of course the specialist platform Kubernetes Engine. Each has their place but if they are serious about containers then Kubernetes is the optimal platform for handling and managing containers at scale.

Chapter 20 - App Engine

So far we have discussed two GCP products that provide the compute infrastructure for applications: virtual machines for Compute Engine and containers for Kubernetes Engine.

But perhaps you just want a Platform as a Service so that you can focus on your application code and not have to concern yourself with infrastructure. Well that is why there is Google's PaaS, the Cloud App Engine.

App Engine is what is known as a platform as a service. In GCP, the App Engine platform manages the hardware and networking infrastructure required to run your code. What this means is that when you want to deploy an application on App Engine, you just handle the application's code and the App Engine service will give you access to the platform runtime and libraries of your choice and provision and manage the infrastructure on your behalf.

To accomplish this, App Engine provides you with the built-in services that many web applications require by default, such as a NoSQL database, in-memory caching, load balancing, health checks, logging and a way to authenticate users. But there are no servers for you to provision or maintain as everything is handled transparently within App Engine.

The concept behind App Engine is that you code your application to take advantage of these services and App Engine will provide them for you. Moreover, App Engine will automatically scale your application's resources in response to the demand and amount of traffic but you will only pay for those resources that you use. The billing model and the automated and elastic scaling is why App Engine is especially suited for variable workloads or unpredictable applications such as web and mobile backends.

App Engine offers two choices of environments, standard and flexible. Of the two App Engine Environments, Standard is the simpler. It offers a simpler deployment experience than the Flexible environment. However the most notable difference is that with the Standard Environment your low utilization applications might be able to run at no charge as it offers a free daily usage quota for the use of some services.

In order to assist in the deployment of code to the cloud App Engine Google provides an App Engine SDK. These are available in several languages and provide you with simple commands for deployment and an environment for testing your application locally before you upload it to the GCP's App Engine service.

Now, what often intrigues people is the question of what does the application code actually run on?

App Engine Standard Environment

The short answer to that is it runs in App Engine on an executable binary called a runtime.

In App Engine Standard Environment, you use a runtime provided by Google. Also the Standard Environment provides runtimes for specific versions of Java, Python, PHP and Go. As well as the libraries that supports all the App Engine APIs.

For many applications, the App Engine Standard Environment runtimes and libraries may maybe all you need. But, if you code your application in another language then the Standard Environment is not the right choice so you will need to use the Flexible Environment.

The Standard Environment also has some other caveats that you may need to contemplate such as it runs in a Sandbox. That is a software and security construct that enforces independence of the hardware, operating system, file system or physical location of the server it runs on and it also enforces the segregation and isolation of the code.

Running your code in a sandbox is not necessarily an issue as one of the reasons why App Engine Standard Environment can scale so effectively and manage your application in a very fine grained way is because of the sandbox. They are also very secure as the code is isolated from the OS, other applications, and the file system.

Nonetheless, sandboxes can and do impose some constraints such as your application can't write to the local file system. Therefore, your application will have to use a database service if it needs to store data persistently. As a result, Cloud Datastore is tightly coupled with App Engine standard edition to provide that service.

Also, all the requests your application receives will have a 60-second timeout, and because code is segregated by design you can't install arbitrary third party software in a sandbox.

If these constraints will adversely affect your development then that would be another pointer towards using the Flexible Environment. Here's a brief roadmap of how you'll use App Engine Standard Environment in practice;

- First you develop your application and run a test version of it locally using the App Engine SDK.
- Then you use the SDK commands to deploy it.
- Each App Engine application runs in a GCP project.
- App Engine automatically provisions server instances and scales and load balances them.
- Your application can make calls to a variety of services using dedicated APIs.

App Engine Flexible Environment

If you find the constraints of the App Engine standard environments sandbox model is just too restrictive or you need to code in another language not supported in the standard environment, then you may want to consider the Flexible Environment version.

A notable difference is that instead of using a sandbox, App Engine flexible environment lets you run your application inside Docker containers on Google Compute Engine Virtual Machines, VMs. In addition it lets you specify the container your App Engine runs in and the App Engine manages these Compute Engine virtual machines for you. Furthermore, the VMs are monitored, health checked, healed as necessary, and you select the geographical region that you want them to run in. Another feature of the flexible Environment is that App Engine will apply automatically any critical backward compatible updates to their operating systems. All this works transparently so that you can just focus on your code.

App Engine apps use standard run times that can access App Engine services such as data store, memcached, task queues, and so on. The simpler standard environment starts up instances of your application faster, but because of the sandbox you get less access to the infrastructure in which your application runs.

Flexible environment, however, lets you SSH into the virtual machines on which your application runs. It lets you use local disk for scratch base, and it lets you install third-party software. Flexible Environment also lets your application make calls to the network without going through App Engine. On the other hand, the standard environment can save you a lot of money as the billing can drop to zero for any idle applications. This is very attractive in a DevOps environment.

An interesting thing is that in the Flexible Environment the App Engine uses Docker containers instead of a sandbox. So how does App Engine flexible environment compare to Kubernetes Engine?

Here's a quick comparison of use-cases for App Engine with Kubernetes Engine.

- App Engine Standard Environment is for people who want the service to take maximum control of their applications deployment and scaling.
- Kubernetes Engine gives the application owner the full flexibility of Kubernetes orchestration.
- App Engine flexible edition is somewhere in between.
- App Engine Flexible Environment treats containers as a means to an end, but for Kubernetes Engine, containers are the fundamental organizing principle.

A common use case for App Engine is to host API services. This is because they can be quickly uploaded to App Engine and it will manage any scaling and authentication issues. API's are a very common way of opening an application up to the outside but in a strictly limited way. Indeed all our interaction with the GCP so far whether that was via the console or the SDK has been ultimately via the APIs that Google expose for your use.

Application Programming Interfaces, APIs

We have mentioned Application Programming Interfaces, APIs, several times already as a method for connecting to a service. However, let us now give them a description and definition that is more precise.

The problem that persists in software services implementation is that they can require precise interfaces that become complex and they are frequently changeable.

The issue is that integrating services requires connecting other pieces of software and that requires knowledge of the code and also the internal details about how they work. This would make local integration with in-house applications very difficult but integration with third parties nigh on impossible.

Nonetheless, integrations with third parties, even banks do go ahead, as instead application developers write software that abstracts away all the needless internal details to provide templates for the delivery of necessary parameters. This presents a clean, well-defined interface. Then they document that interface as an API.

API Management

Now that we know what an API is we can consider how Google Cloud Platform manages their library of APIs. A feature of the API concept is that the underlying implementation can change as long as the interface remains working. Thus, other pieces of software that use the API don't have to change anything.

However, sometimes you will have to change an API to add or deprecate a feature. In this case then the clients or other software that use that API will have to know about the changes. Therefore, developers need to version and track their APIs.

In order to manage and make this transition as clean as possible developers need to document the changes so that client and other developers know that an API has been depreciated or functionally upgraded. In the latter case the developers should document that version two of an API contains additional functional calls that version one does not.

This means that applications that consume the API can specify the API version that they want to use in their calls.

Managing and supporting an API is very important task and Google Cloud platform provides two API management tools. The first approach is related to issues where you're developing a software service and using one of GCP's backends. The criteria you would like to meet are that you'd like to make it easy to expose this API but you'd like to make sure it's only consumed by other developers whom you trust. Thus you'd like for the API to know which end user is making the service call. In addition you would like the API to be monitored and the usage logged.

Cloud Endpoints

In this scenario you would use Cloud Endpoints as it implements these capabilities and more using a proxy that is easy to deploy in front of your backend services. It also provides you with an API console to wrap up those capabilities in an easy to manage interface. Cloud Endpoints supports applications running in GCPs compute platforms in your choice of languages and your choice of client technologies.

Apigee Edge is also a platform for developing and managing API proxies but it has a different approach as it is primarily focused on business problem such as rate limiting, setting quotas, and providing analytics. However, because the backend services for Apigee Edge need not be in GCP, engineers often use it when decomposing a legacy application into microservices or micro-apps.

It is advantageous and a less risky way to move a monolith application into the cloud. By doing it this way you avoid replacing the entire application in one risky move. Instead they can use Apigee Edge to peel off its services one by one, standing up micro services to implement each in turn until the legacy application can be finally retired.

Use Case – 7

The client likes the idea of building a development environment in the cloud but they would like to know which platform to use App Engine or Kubernetes?

Solution

The issue here is that both Google Kubernetes Engine (GKE), which is a cluster manager and orchestration system for running your Docker containers and Google App Engine (GAE), which is a Google managed container service can be the right choice it depends on the degree of control that you need.

They will both provide you with the same benefits such as scalability, redundancy, rollouts, rollbacks, etc. However, the difference between them is in their management. This is because GKE gives you the fine grained control over everything about your cluster. On the other hand GAE manages the containers on your behalf with as little configuration or management as possible. Of course this also restricts your control.

So if you choose GKE then you will have more fine control, but also more work for you to do. For example, you may need to configure the network, security, software updates etc. On the other hand with GAE most of this is done for you leaving the developers to focus on their app.

However GKE does provide you with more freedom as you can change cloud providers easier than if you are using GAE so there is less risk of vendor lock-in.

Chapter 21 – Serverless Compute with Cloud Functions and Cloud Run

In the previous chapter we discussed App Engine and how as a PaaS it was designed for application development environments. The object was to abstract the underlying infrastructure for the application code, thereby allowing developers to focus solely on their code. App Engine either ran application code and typically API services in a runtime or within a container depending on the version of App Engine being used. However, some applications use even smaller segments of code for micro-applications, which are typically one function apps, much like microservices. For this type of development you can further abstract the underlying infrastructure and applications and utilise Google's serverless platform, Cloud Functions.

Many applications contain event-driven components that are triggered by some criteria being met, for example, maybe you have an application that lets users upload videos.

Whenever that happens, you need to know so that you can process that video. An event can trigger the application to process the user's uploaded video and perform a transcription of the video into various text files, and then store each file in a repository.

You could always integrate this function into your application, but then you have to worry about capacity planning and providing all the compute resources necessary to meet the demand. The issue with a new application is you don't know whether user uploads will happen once a day, once an hour or once a millisecond.

But, what if you could just ignore the tedious task of capacity planning and forecasting and simply make that provisioning problem irrelevant? What would be required is a single purpose function that could perform, in this example, all the necessary video transcription and storage tasks. Then you would only need it to be triggered to run automatically whenever a user uploads a new video.

And that is exactly what cloud functions lets you do.

Introducing Cloud Functions

The beauty of cloud functions is that you just pay whenever your functions run in 100 millisecond intervals. Also you don't have to worry about servers or runtime binaries. You just write your code in JavaScript in a Node.js environment that GCP provides and then you configure it to be triggered by an event. Cloud functions can trigger on events in cloud storage, Cloud Pub/Sub, or in an HTTP call. We will introduce Pub/Sub to you in detail later.

However, you only get billed when your event triggers your function and only then for the duration that it runs. Therefore, you no longer need to be concerned – from a capacity planning perspective - whether it runs once a day, once an hour or once a millisecond as GCP is responsible for managing and providing the required resources.

The way that you can deploy cloud functions is quite simple as you start by setting up a cloud function and choose which events that you wish to acts as triggers. For each event type, you declare to the cloud functions that this is the event that they react to.

Then comes the difficult part as you will need to write and attach your applications JavaScript functions to your triggers. This ensures that should an event of interest trigger your function that it will subsequently be executed.

After you have set up your applications functions with corresponding events and suitable triggers, your functions will run whenever the event occurs.

Some applications, especially those that are based upon microservices architecture can be implemented entirely in cloud functions, which make it very cost effective. This makes deploying cloud functions a very efficient and easy to deploy application. Specifically when you are seeking to enhance an existing application, which may have variable demand as it removes the worry about scaling.

Why Cloud Functions?

If we cast our memory back to the first chapter we mentioned the design issue whereby at one end of the scale there is managed infrastructure and at the other end an extreme dynamic infrastructure. However, you will often come to the conclusion that you can choose where you want to be along that line. For example, you may choose to be further towards the Compute Engine if you want full control to deploy and manage your application in virtual machines that run on Google's infrastructure. Similarly, if you need control but want to use containers then you can use the Kubernetes Engine as these clusters define a measure of control. On the other hand you may well choose to relinquish much of the control and management burden and select to use the App Engine service as it is ideal if you just want to focus on your code and leave infrastructure provisioning and management to Google. Conversely, standard environment may be too restrictive as you may want to retain some control of your custom runtime environment and that is what the App Engine flexible environment lets you do. Of course to relieve yourself from the chore of managing infrastructure, capacity planning and to build or extend your application, then you can use Cloud Functions.

When you deploy applications through Cloud Functions, you only need to supply chunks of code for business logic, you set the event triggers and attach the code and it will get spun up on demand in response to specific events to create functions.

Microservices and Service Mesh

Adopting microservices architecture in order to decompose large monolithic applications can bring many benefits, including increased flexibility, independence and modularity. However these benefits often come at the expense of added complexity as the process of decoupling a single-tier monolithic application into many smaller service modules introduces many design hurdles. For example, when you decompose a monolith down to 1000s of autonomous microservices how do you know what's running? Indeed, if you don't have visibility into what microservices are running how do you monitor, update or secure your microservices?

To address to these significant challenges, you can always deploy a service mesh. This is a software solution that helps you discover and make sense of all those thousands of interconnections between services. A service mesh also helps you with orchestration, security, and in collecting telemetry data across distributed microservices and containers.

The way that a service mesh works is that it decouples your applications dependency from the network. Thus it can monitor all traffic for your application, typically through a set of network proxies or sidecars that sit alongside each microservice. These sidecar proxies provide for individual policy implementation and even language independence at the microservices level. This in turn, allows local and remote development teams to work independently and be language agnostic.

Google Cloud Platform has its own GCSM which is a fully managed service that is built on the high-performance Envoy sidecar proxy and the open source Istio service mesh provides the overlay on your microservices running in Kubernetes for container API support. The Google Cloud Service Mesh supports end-to-end encryption between services using mTLS (mutual TLS), as well as a granular traffic control, routing, and authorization policy. It also integrates with Stackdriver to monitor and alert on key metrics. Further, this is all achieved with no change to your application code.

Istio on GKE provides a managed, mature service mesh that you can deploy that spans both the Cloud and on-premise networks with just one click. However the real utility of the Istio service mesh is in the context of the cloud-native ecosystem as it provides a path towards infrastructure abstraction and process automation in a cloud or a hybrid cloud environment.

Automation

Organizations are increasingly moving toward automation as it delivers efficiencies, velocity and quality in the development process. Today many organisations strive for continuous improvement and rapid deployment to deliver their products. Hence development has become a pipeline-based approach for automating application upgrades and rapid deployment.

Google Cloud Service Mesh based on Istio integrates seamlessly with continuous delivery systems and the deployment pipelines. For example, you can configure your pipeline to deploy Istio VirtualServices in order to manage granular traffic management or even in-flight A-B testing without any manual intervention. Istio can also work with modern GitOps workflows due to its declarative configuration model. In this scenario it is the source control that serves as the central source of truth for both your application and infrastructure configuration.

Traffic Director

Traffic Director is GCP's fully managed traffic control plane for service mesh. It is an abstraction that's used to deliver microservices and modern applications. The service mesh data plane, is deployed through service proxies like Envoy and it controls the flow of traffic and the control plane enforces policy, configuration, and intelligence. With Traffic Director, it is easy to configure traffic control policies. You can also use Traffic Director to deploy simple load balancing as well as deploy it across multiple regions as VMs or containers and use Traffic Director to deliver global load balancing with automatic cross-region overflow and failover. Some advanced features like request routing and percentage-based traffic splitting enables seamless scalability within Compute Engine and Kubernetes Engine environments.

Serverless, with Service Mesh

Today, serverless computing transforms your source code into workloads that are executed only when called or triggered by an event. Organizations are adopting the serverless approach as it decouples code from infrastructure, which in turn reduces infrastructure costs, increases efficiency while simultaneously allowing developers to focus on writing code that delivers more business value.
However, today most organisations are typically running heterogeneous development environment so are not solely running serverless workloads. Indeed they are also likely to have stateful applications, including microservices apps within containers on Kubernetes infrastructure. Therefore, the GCSM allows Kubernetes users to deploy container applications and serverless functions onto the same cluster.

Further, the ability to work with serverless functionsin the same way that you work with your traditional containers helps you to provide a uniformed standard methodology between your serverless and Kubernetes environments. This means that you can use the same Istio traffic rules, certificate issuance, authorization policies, and metrics uniformly across all your workload pipelines.

Portability

Organisations are increasingly adopting more complex cluster configurations as they reap the benefits of code portability. But this requires lower latency, security, and the need for tools that span both cloud and on-premise. Hence, Google's Cloud Services Platform is there to provide the interoperable environment, which can combine complementary solutions that include Google Kubernetes Engine, GKE On-Premise, and Istio. The goal is to move towards creating a seamless Kubernetes experience across hybrid development environments.

Introducing Cloud Run

A newly released service is Cloud Run, which is a serverless compute platform for running your stateless applications in an http accessible container. Being serverless means that it abstracts away the entire infrastructure concerns leaving you to simply build and deploy your HTTP applications.

No longer do you have to be caught in the dilemma of running your code in a limited server environment or in a complex container platform such as GKE so that you can get control over the language or environment you can have the best of both worlds. Previously, running container or a VM meant that you could effectively choose your own language, with any framework or libraries but it did mean that you had to configure the environment, the networking and all of the infrastructure and this could mean a lot of additional work. On the other hand if you chose to go the serverless root you had none of those worries as your invisible infrastructure was provisioned for you and it scaled up and down in sympathy with the load. In addition there was no need to over provision or worry about billing as you paid for only the resources that you used. So what you lose in flexibility you gained in productivity and efficiency. However, now with the release of Cloud Run you no longer have to choose as you can have flexibility as well as productivity – you get the best of both worlds.

Cloud run provides the following benefits of simplicity and flexibility:

- Invisible infrastructure
- Automatic scaling
- Pay-per-use

Plus

- Any programming language
- Any libraries
- Any Frameworks

There are two versions of Cloud Run, the first runs HTTP stateless applications on a serverless compute platform. The second version runs on top of Kubernetes Engine and it is called Cloud Run on GKE. As we know GKE is a powerful platform for supporting containers but some developers are put off by the complexity it introduces. As a result Google has developed Cloud Run to sit on top of the powerful GKE platform. Both have a lot in common as they provide the same advantages:

- They both provide a simpler developer environment
- They both run HTTP apps and services
- They are both program language, frameworks and library agnostic
- They both handle autoscaling
- Both are based on standard container technology

- Both are integrated with Stackdriver monitoring and logging
- And both are Knative compatible

The differences between Cloud Run and Cloud Run on GKE are:
- Cloud Run is on a pay-as-you-use basis whereas Cloud run on GKE is dependent on the Kubernetes cluster deployed
- Cloud Run provides a default memory configuration whereas Cloud Run on GKE allows you to reconfigure memory, CPU, GPU and networking
- Cloud Run automatically provides you with URLs and SSL certificates on the other hand Cloud Run on GKE may require that you get your own SSL certificates
- Finally, Cloud Run is isolated from the other resources in your private network whereas Cloud Run on GKE can access your out network resources.

Use Case - 8

The client ABC is looking over your proposal with interest but they are becoming confused when they do their own research into GCP as they cannot differentiate between the services and how they are used. They request that you provide a high-level summary of each with perhaps some use-cases?
Solution
In order to meet the clients request you can summarise the difference between the services in a brief summary. Such as the one below:

Summary of Platform Properties
App Engine Standard

PROS

- This is a cost effective way to host development apps or for production platforms for APIs or low throughput apps.

- This is a low maintenance platform as App Engine manages the infrastructure for you
- App Engine also handles auto scaling on your behalf and it is fast and lightweight as it is based upon instance classes
- Additional functions such as version management and traffic splitting are built into App Engine standard and flexible environments
- Native access to Datastore as it has co-location with App Engine Standard environment
- There is also built-in access to Memcache
- Standard environment runs in a secure sandbox. This is inherently more secure way of working compared to Compute Engine where you need to do your own security controls.

CONS

- The secure sandbox prevents interact with the file systems and persistent storage and there are other constraints such as the instances are kept smaller so they can benefit from the fast autoscaling.
- There is no networking with the standard edition's sandbox so there is no support for Cloud Load Balancer
- Limited to supported runtimes: Python 2.7, Java 7 and 8, Go 1.6-1.9, and PHP 5.5.

App Engine Flex

PROS

- Not limited to the standard runtimes as it can support custom runtimes
- Integration with GCE networking
- In built version and traffic management
- larger instance sizes makes it more appropriate for large applications or Java applications that consume a lot of memory

Cons

- No internal load balancers or support for shared VPCs
- No native integration with Memcache

Google Kubernetes Engine

PROS

- Natively integrates with containers, which allows for custom runtimes
- Tight coupling with containers for better management and cluster configuration
- Enforces best practices for virtual machines,
- Provides for easy roll back of VMs too previous versions
- Containers provide a flexible and platform neutral deployment framework
- Open source Kubernetes, provides a method for portability between on-premises and the cloud
- Private Clusters, now in beta, eliminate the need to expose public IP addresses
- Version management through Google Container Registry

CONS

- There is no native traffic management
- There is some management overhead
- Not really intuitive so there is a learning curve due to many new concepts such as pods, deployments, services, ingress, and namespaces
- Public IPs need to be exposed to locations where you want to run 'kubectl' commands
- Monitoring tool integration is limited
- No L7 internal load balancing so you have to use third party solutions

Compute Engine

PROS

- Intuitive and will little learning curve this is what makes Compute Engine the most popular method
- You have almost total management and administrative control so you can load whatever tools or third party add-ons that you want
- No need for public IPs
- You can run docker containers using the container-Optimized OS

CONS

- As you have total control it can be complex to manage and control as you have to do most things yourself
- More management overhead
- Autoscaling is slower than App Engine
- Installing software on custom GCE instances can be difficult to maintain

Google Cloud Development Tools

There are many popular third-party tools for development, deployment and monitoring that will work natively in GCP. However, apart from the myriad of open source tools that work out of the box you also have the option of using the in-built tools that are tightly-integrated with GCP. In development and DevOps environments that are utilizing the Cloud App Engine there is a requirement for managing code, libraries and repositories. This will often require many tools to assist in managing code versioning, libraries, and source code trees. To do this many GCP customers use the well-known repository Git to store, distribute and manage their code. What that entails is them running their own Git instances or using a hosted Git provider.

Cloud Source Repositories

Running your own Git instance is a great way of managing a code repository because you have total control. On the other hand using a hosted Git provider may mean some loss of control but it is a lot less work. A potential solution to this dilemma is that GCP provides its own way to keep code private to a GCP project. Further, it can also use IAM permissions to protect access to it. But the good part is that you do not have to maintain the Git instance yourself.
That's what Cloud Source repositories is all about. When you use the Cloud Source Repository the managed service provides Git version control to support your development of any application or service that are running on App Engine, but it can also be used on Compute Engine and Kubernetes Engine.

In addition, Cloud Source Repositories, lets you handle any number of private Git repositories, which allows you the freedom to organize and manage your code as you see fit. Further, the Cloud Source Repository also contains a source viewer so that you can browse and view repository files from within the GCP console.

Initially setting up your environment in GCP can entail many steps, such as configuring the compute network and storage resources, as well as keeping track of their configurations.

This is considered an imperative method as you issue direct commands. You can do it all by hand if you want to but if you want to clone your environment, you have to replicate all those commands again. A better way is to take a declarative approach and proactively work out the commands you need to set up your environment and then make a template as this is more efficient.

 This is good if you already have a strong idea of how you wish the environment to be and later should you want to change your environment, you can readily reconfigure it. However this does mean you have an idea of what the environment should look like but not necessarily know how you want the environment to be configured so it's declarative rather than imperative.

GCP provides Deployment Manager to let you do just that.

Deployment Manager

Deployment manager is an Infrastructure Management Service that automates the creation and management of your Google Cloud Platform resources for you based upon a template.

To use deployment manager, you will create a template file using either the YAML markup language or Python that will describe what you want the components of your environment to look like. You don't need to imperatively state the commands just what you want it to finally represent.

Then, you give the template to Deployment Manager which figures out how it can achieve your design and then does the actions needed to create the environment your template describes.

If you need to change your environment, edit your template and then tell Deployment Manager to update the environment to match the change.

Here's a tip, you can also store and version control your Deployment Manager templates in Cloud Source Repositories.

Stackdriver

There is little doubt that in order to run an application reliably and with any stability you need to have robust monitoring.
Managing is only possible with diligent monitoring of the application as it passes you the information about how the system is working and handling demand and traffic fluctuations and provides early warnings as to potential flaws. It also indicates where potential changes may be required to mitigate issues and then subsequently whether the changes you made are working or not. Monitoring of an application also lets you respond to issues through informed decisions rather than with guesswork or in blind panic mode.
Stackdriver is the built-in GCP tool for monitoring, logging and diagnostics and it provides the low level tools, which gives you access to many different kinds of signals from your Infrastructure platforms, virtual machines, containers, middleware and application tier, logs, metrics and traces. By providing access to this system level signals it also gives insight into your application's health, performance and availability. So if issues occur, you can fix them before a condition escalates to a serious problem. The core components of Stackdriver consist of components responsible for detecting the Monitoring, Logging, Trace, Error Reporting and debugging.
Stackdriver monitoring checks the endpoints of Web applications. This also occurs with other Internet accessible services, such as those running on your cloud environment. Using Stackdriver you are able to configure uptime checks, which you can link to particular URLs, groups or specific resources that you wish to monitor such as specific VM instances or load balancers. In addition Stackdriver allows you to configure alerts on interesting criteria, like when health check fail or up-time checks fall to levels that need immediate action. Furthermore you can combine Stackdriver to work with a lot of popular notification tools so you can create dashboards to help you visualize the state of your application. Stackdriver logging lets you view logs from your applications and filter and search on them.

Logging also lets you define metrics, based on log contents that are incorporated into custom dashboards and alerts. You can also export logs to BigQuery, Cloud Storage and Cloud Pub/Sub.

By incorporating Stackdriver into your existing network management system or Network Operation Centre software you can leverage its in-depth error reporting to notify you when new errors are detected. It can also track, group and categorise error in your applications.

But you can also use Stackdriver trace to proactively sample the latency of App Engine applications and report on per-URL statistics so you can be notified ahead of time of a gradual degradation in a specific service.

How about when tasked with the dreaded debugging of code? A tedious method in debugging code in an application is to go back into it code and enter lots of logging statements.

Stackdriver debugger reduces a lot of this drudgery by debugging code and logging errors in a different way. It does this by connecting your applications production data to your source code. In this way it allows you to inspect the state of your application at any code location in production. That means you can view the application state without adding logging statements.

Stackdriver Debugger works best when your application source code is available, such as in Cloud Source repositories, although it can also work if your code is held in other repositories too.

Anthos

Anthos is an application management platform that provides a consistent development, operations and security experience for use on both cloud and on-premises environments. Anthos is different from other public cloud services. It's not just a product but a fully software based umbrella for multiple services aligned with the themes of application modernization, cloud migration, hybrid cloud, and multi-cloud management.

Anthos is a collection of complementary services, which helps manage containers in either cloud or on-premises environments. Anthos brings benefits to all areas of the business. From a developers perspective we can consider Anthos as supplying a Kubernetes container management platform. It enables developers to deploy containers and microservices based architectures. It does this though providing Git-compliant management and CI/CD workflows for configuration. It also provides the code for deploying Anthos Configuration Management as well as code-free protection of services via mTLS and instrumentation using Istio and Stackdriver. However it has also got inbuilt support for GCP Marketplace so that a developer can easily drop off-the-shelf products into clusters. Now when we consider Operations then Anthos provides centralized, efficient, and deployment templates as well as the management of clusters. The benefit to operators is that Anthos enables them to use single command deployment of new clusters with GKE and GKE On-Prem (gkectl). It also provides a platform for the centralized configuration management and compliance as well as simplified deployment and roll back via Anthos Config Management and Git check-ins. As a result Anthos provides operators with a single pane of glass visibility across all clusters from infrastructure through to application performance and topology with Stackdriver.

From a security perspective, we can consider Anthos to enforce security standards on clusters, deployed applications, and even the configuration management. Anthos provides a central point for audit and a secured workflow via Git compliant repositories. It also provides for compliance enforcement of cluster configurations using namespaces and labels as well as inherited configurations and the securing of microservices via Istio and in-cluster mTLS certificates.

Furthermore with Anthos Migrate you can now let Anthos auto-migrate your VMs from on-premises, or other clouds, directly into containers in GKE. This new migration technology lets you easily and quickly migrate your infrastructure without modifications to the original VMs or applications. This frees-up operations from managing housekeeping tasks like VM maintenance and OS patching, so it can focus on managing and developing applications.

Istio

Istio is an open source service mesh that reduces the complexity of microservice deployments. A service mesh is often necessary to describe and manage the network of connections that proliferate when applications use microservices. A service mesh is therefore a centralised interconnect a patch panel for services that handles all the interactions between modules and applications. As a service mesh grows in size it grows exponentially in complexity, so it becomes much harder to understand and manage. Developers and administrators thus need methods that enable microservice discovery, load balancing, failure recovery, metrics, and monitoring. Istio provides this visibility and connectivity by layering transparently onto your existing distributed applications. It is also a platform with its own range of APIs so it integrates into any logging platform, or telemetry or policy system. Istio enables you to operate a distributed microservice architecture, which provides you with a uniform way to secure, connect, and monitor microservices. However what makes Istio so popular in cloud environments is it makes it easy to create a network of deployed services and container clusters with load balancing, service-to-service authentication, monitoring, and even canary testing, with few or no code changes in service code. You simply add Istio support to services by deploying a special sidecar proxy throughout your environment. The sidecar (Envoy) intercepts all network communication between the associated microservices or clusters, which then allows you to configure and manage the services using Istio. Some of Istio's functionality includes:

- Automatic load balancing for HTTP, gRPC, WebSocket, and TCP traffic.
- Fine-grained traffic control with routing rules, retries, failovers, and recovery.
- A policy and configuration API supporting access controls, rate limits and quotas.
- Support for metrics, logs, and traces for all traffic within a cluster, including cluster ingress and egress.
- Secure service-to-service communication in a cluster with strong identity-based authentication and authorization.

Istio is essential for traffic management, security and observability in cloud and hybrid environments when using microservices or containers via Istio Connect, Istio Secure and Istio Monitoring respectively.

In GCP Istio is integrated with GKE and you simply have to install Istio on Kubernetes Engine with the Istio on GKE add-on. You can also integrate Compute Engine VMs into an Istio mesh deployed on Kubernetes Engine. Furthermore, Istio can be used with Google Cloud Endpoints service.

Use Case -9

The client ABC has raised concerns regards how their in-house support teams can monitor the new cloud environment. They need to be able to configure alerts and notifications as well and build dashboards that provide data on performance KPIs for reporting purposes. In addition they want to explore ways for moving their existing virtualisation environment consisting of VMs to the cloud container platform GKE.

Solution

The obvious solution for this proposal is to configure Stackdriver for uptime, application and system monitoring. To achieve this you can configure uptime checks using HTTP, HTTPS, UDP or TCP on URLs, applications, load balancers and most resources. In addition to simple uptime checks you can also delve deeper using application level monitoring. In this case you are interested in alerts about the health of the application rather than the VM. If you are using App Engine you can even get latency checks performed. Then there are the system checks whereby you configure alerts for such things as CPU and memory usage, network traffic utilisation or open TCP connections. However you can also configure for processes such as to audit which processes are running, sleeping or are zombies.

Stackdriver also provided a method for logging, which support teams will require when troubleshooting. Logging is inbuilt into Stackdriver and App Engine and it can capture some GKE events. However for Compute Engine you will have to install the agent. Stackdriver Logging UI supports several methods for searching such as by time interval, response code, log level, log source amongst other things. However, if the standard search capabilities of the Logging UI are not enough, you can export your logs to Google BigQuery, which can quickly query, aggregate or filter several terabytes of data.

With regards migrating or managing containers on-premises then Athos is something you might want to consider. Although a relatively new product it is designed for hybrid environments as well as multi-cloud ones so would be a good fit for the clients' purpose. Indeed the Anthos' hybrid functionality is available both on Google Cloud Platform (GCP) with Google Kubernetes Engine (GKE), and there is now a data center edition with GKE On-Prem. This software solution also lets you manage workloads running on third-party clouds like AWS and Azure, so you can deploy, run and manage your applications on the cloud or premises that you want. Anthos will give the client a unified management view of their hybrid deployment and a consistent platform to run their workloads. However if you are deploying on GKE and using clusters or microservices then you would want to look at deploying Istio for GKE as it can provide the necessary discovery, connectivity, monitoring and traffic control you will need in that environment.

Chapter 23 - Cloud Big Data Solutions

Google believes that in the future every company will be a data driven company and making the best use of information will be a critical competitive advantage. To that end Google Cloud provides a way for every business to take advantage of Google's investments in infrastructure and data processing innovation. By doing so, they have abstracted the complexity of building and maintaining data and analytics systems from the inherent constraints of expertise and financial restrictions.

In this chapter we will learn how to leverage Google's technologies for the fastest and most cost effective way to deliver competitive advantage by using the GCP Big Data services.

Whether the business initiative is to strive for real time analytics or pursue machine learning these Big Data tools are intended to be simple and practical to use. Google has designed them for you to readily embed in your applications so that you can get those business critical insights faster.

Google's Cloud Big Data solutions help you transform your business and user experiences with meaningful data insights without you having to have multi-million dollar on-premises infrastructure or a team of in-house data scientists.

Big Data Solutions

Google likes to describe Big Data Solutions as an Integrated Serverless Platform. Where a Serverless platform means you don't have to worry about provisioning compute instances to run your jobs. As with App Engine and Service Functions this is a fully managed service, so it provisions the required infrastructure and resources seamlessly and transparently when needed and you pay only for the resources you consume.

The platform is integrated, so that GCP data services work together to help you create custom solutions.

Big Data Solutions is built around and compatible with Apache Hadoop, which is an open source framework for Big Data. You may often hear the term Hadoop used informally to mean the Apache Hadoop and all its associated services such as Spark, Pig, and Hive.

Regardless, Hadoop is built on the MapReduce programming model which Google invented and subsequently published. The concept behind the MapReduce model is that it works on two functions. The first function is called the Map function, which runs in parallel with a massive dataset to produce an intermediate set of results. Then a second function called the reduce function will use the intermediate set of results as a source from which to build a final result set.

Cloud Dataproc

Cloud Dataproc is a managed service that enables you to use the open source data tools for tasks such as batch processing in batch and streaming modes, querying and machine learning.

Cloud Dataproc is a fast, easy, and managed way to run Hadoop, Spark, Hive, and Pig on Google Cloud Platform. All you have to do is request a Hadoop cluster. It will be built for you in 90 seconds or less on top of Compute Engine virtual machines whose number and type you may control. If you need more or less processing power while your cluster is running, you can scale it up or down at will.

You can use the default configuration for the Hadoop software in your cluster or you can customize it. Also you can monitor your cluster using Stackdriver. However a significant attraction to running Big Data and Dataproc is that when running Hadoop on-premises it will require a major capital hardware investment and considerable operational costs. On the other hand running these Hadoop jobs in Cloud Dataproc, allows you to only pay for hardware resources used during the life of the cluster you create so there is no capital investment (CapEx) and little in comparison to on-premises operation expenditure (OpEx) as Dataproc is a managed service. This makes it very efficient and cost effective.

Although the rate for pricing is based on the hour, Cloud Dataproc is built by the second.

GCP's Cloud Dataproc clusters are built in one second clock time increments and subject to a one minute minimum billing. So, remember when you're finished using your cluster, you should delete it as then the billing stops. This is a much more agile use of resources than on-premise hardware assets.

You can also save money, by telling Cloud Dataproc to use pre-emptible Compute Engine instances for your batch processing. However you must make sure that your jobs can be restarted cleanly if they're terminated.

But if they can be stopped gracefully restarted then you can get a significant discount in the cost of running the VM instances - around 80 percent cheaper.

Be aware though that the cost of the Compute Engine instances isn't the only component of the cost of a Dataproc cluster, but it's a significant one.

Once your data is in a cluster, you can use Spark and Spark SQL to do data mining.

And you can use MLib, which are Apache Spark's machine learning libraries to discover patterns through machine learning.

Cloud Dataproc is great when you have a data set of known size or when you want to manage your cluster size yourself. But what if your data shows up in real time or its arrival is of unpredictable size or rate?

That's where Cloud Dataflow is a particularly good choice.

Cloud Dataflow

The GCP service Cloud Dataflow is a fully-managed ETL (Extract, Transform and Load) service that is equally capable of handling streaming data in real time and/or historical data in batch mode. Cloud Dataflow is serverless, which means there is no need for resource provisioning and management, Google handles all this for you. However, with Dataflow you still have access to almost infinite capacity to leverage against your toughest data processing and analysis challenges.

You can use Dataflow to build data pipelines via expressive SQL, Java, and Python APIs in the Apache Beam SDK, and these pipelines work for both batch and streaming data with equal reliability. There's no need to spin up a cluster or to size instances as Cloud Dataflow will fully automate the management of whatever processing resources are required.

Cloud Dataflow frees you from operational tasks like resource management and performance optimization.

You use Dataflow to build really expressive pipelines where each step in the pipeline is elastically scaled. Some of those transforms you see are considered to be map operations and some are considered to be a reduce operations. Furthermore, there is no need to launch and manage a cluster as the service provides all resources on demand.

People use Dataflow in a variety of use cases as it's a data pipeline as well as a general purpose ETL tool. Hence it has use case as a data analysis engine, which comes in handy in things like fraud detection in financial services, IoT analytics in manufacturing, healthcare and logistics as well as click stream, point of sale and segmentation analysis in retail.

And because those pipelines can orchestrate multiple services even external services it can be used in real time applications such as personalizing gaming user experiences.

Nonetheless, what if instead of a dynamic pipeline, your data needs to be analysed more in the way of searching by trawling through a vast ocean of data. For example you want to make ad-hoc SQL queries against a massive data set – well then the GCP has a solution for that and it is called, BigQuery.

BigQuery

This is Google's fully manage petabyte scale, low cost analytics data warehouse.

Because there's no infrastructure to manage, so you can focus on analysing data using the popular and commonly understood SQL command syntax to find meaningful insights.

It is also easy to get your data into BigQuery as you can load it direct from cloud storage or cloud data store, or stream it into Big Query at up to 100,000 rows per second.

Once the data has been loaded, you can run SQL queries against multiple terabytes of data in seconds making queries run super-fast. In addition to running SQL queries, you can also easily perform read and write in BigQuery via GCP's ETL service called Cloud Dataflow, or even use the Big Data open source Hadoop, or Spark.

BigQuery is built upon and uses the processing power of Google's infrastructure to deliver its high performance and vast scale so it can be used by all types of organizations from startup to Fortune 500 companies. Indeed, smaller organizations will often take advantage of Big Query's free monthly quotas, while larger organizations like its seamless scale, capacity, SQl queries and it's available of 99.9 percent service level agreement.

Google's infrastructure is global and so is BigQuery, which lets you specify the region where your data will be kept. This can be an important decision based upon technical criteria such as latency and network traffic or by regulatory compliance such as GDPR.

So, for example, if you want or are required to keep data only in Europe, you don't have to go set-up a cluster in Europe. Just specify the EU location where you create your data set. The US and Asia locations are also available.

Regardless of where you store your data you still retain full control over who has access to the data stored in BigQuery. This includes sharing data sets with people in different projects. Moreover, if you do share your data sets with other projects that won't impact your cost or performance, people you share with pay for their own queries, not you.

On another billing topic, because BigQuery separates storage and computation, you pay for your data storage separately from queries. That means you pay for queries only when they are actually running.

In addition there is long term storage pricing, which is an automatic discount for data residing in BigQuery for extended periods of time. So for example if your data exceeds a storage time of 90 days in BigQuery, then Google will automatically apply a discount to the price of the storage.

As BigQuery is a data analytics warehouse its natural use cases are applications such as real-time inventory systems, large-scale events and log analytics, IoT, predictive maintenance, digital marketing and data distribution with large scale commercial or public data sets.

Pub/Sub Messaging Service

For modern applications that require the analytics of data streams from many distributed sources such as the IoT, especially if these are event-driven processes working in real time, it is necessary in order to scale to have a messaging service.

The GCP uses the Cloud Pub/Sub service as its messaging service and this model is designed on the publish/subscribe pattern that is commonly found in software and networking design.

The concept of the Pub/Sub messaging service is that it designates entities as being a publisher of a message and others as explicit subscribers –this means that a publisher will only send a message to an entity that has subscribed to the message - this makes it an efficient, simple, reliable, scalable foundation for stream analytics.

Moreover, the Pub/Sub service allows you to interconnect independent applications you build or interface with to efficiently send and receive messages but importantly they remain decoupled so that they are able to scale independently.

The way the Pub/Sub works is that an application can publish messages in Pub/Sub and one or more subscribers will subscribe for those specific messages in order to receive them.

However, sending and receiving messages doesn't have to be synchronous and it's designed to provide at least once delivery at low latency, which makes Pub/Sub great for decoupling systems.

However when we say at-least-once delivery, we mean that there is a small chance some messages might be delivered more than once. This is very important to understand when you write your application. For example, you don't want double or triple transactions to go through in a financial or trading application.

You can configure your subscribers to receive messages on a push or pull basis. In other words, subscribers can get notified when new messages arrive for them or they can check for new messages at intervals.

Cloud Pub/Sub builds on the same technology, which Google uses within its own global products for messaging and in event-driven applications. It is an important building block for applications that handle ingress data traffic that arrives at high or unpredictable rates like Internet of Things systems. Cloud Pub/Sub offers on demand scalability to one million messages per second and beyond but you simply choose the quota you are comfortable with.

If you're in the business of analysing streaming data, Cloud Dataflow as a streaming pipeline is a natural pairing with Pub/Sub. Applications built on GCP's Compute Engine platform are also good candidates for and easily interfaced using Pub/Sub.

We will revisit Pub/Sub later in more detail in subsequent chapters as it is such an important component in Cloud architecture.

Cloud Datalab

Scientists have long used lab notebooks to organize their thoughts and explore their data.

For data scientists they also use web-based applications called notebooks because it is a natural way to aggregate their data analysis with their comments about their results in one accessible place.

A popular environment for hosting those is Project Jupyter as it lets you create and maintain web-based notebooks containing Python code and you can run that code interactively and view the results. In GCP the Cloud Datalab service addresses this need and it also takes the management work out of maintaining lab notebooks.

Datalab runs in a Compute Engine virtual machine, so to get started, you simply specify the virtual machine type you want and what GCP region it should run in. When it launches, it presents an interactive Python environment that's ready to use. As it is tightly integrated with BigQuery, Compute Engine, and Cloud Storage, you will find that accessing your data doesn't run into authentication issues. Moreover, Datalab also orchestrates multiple GCP services automatically, so you can focus on exploring your data.

Once you have Datalab up and running, you can visualize your data with Google charts or map plot line. Also if you want tips or learn more there is an interactive Python community, which publish their notebooks. There are also many existing packages for statistics, machine learning, and so on. With Datalab, you will only pay for the resources you use so there is no additional charge for Datalab itself.

Use Case -10

A client has an API hosted on GKE and they wish to log the events into a database for later analysis. They don't require any transformation just straight insertion as-is so they have considered; option 1, inserting the events directly into BigQuery using its API, or option 2, using Pub Sub to stream events into Dataflow for insertion into BigQuery. What would you propose?

Solution

Option 1 may be the simplest solution as you don't need to transform the data but they must be aware that it won't scale and they won't be able to handle errors properly i.e. back-off-and-retry. Therefore the recommended method is to use the following configuration: App -> Pub Sub -> Dataflow (streaming) -> BigQuery.

That's the way to get the solution to scale and handle errors correctly and it is the most fault-tolerant and scalable solution.

Chapter 24 - Machine Learning

Machine learning is an exciting branch of the field of artificial intelligence that has really caught the imagination over the last decade though it has been around for much longer than that.

Machine Learning has huge potential in business and industry as it is a way of solving problems without explicitly coding the solution or even knowing the solution beforehand. Instead, human coders build machine learning systems using algorithms that are designed to be highly iterative and self-learning so they can improve themselves over time through repeated exposure to sample data which we call training data.

One of the issues with machine learning is that it requires vast amounts of data and the corresponding infrastructure to handle it. That doesn't just mean storage but also the networks, processing power, software and servers to operate at the required scale. This constraint meant many SMEs felt that machine learning at any serious scale was beyond them. However, the Google Machine Learning Platform is now available as a cloud service so that you can add innovative capabilities to your own applications without having to build your own infrastructure and applications.

Indeed, Google applications that rely on machine learning such as YouTube, Photos, Google mobile App and Google translate have shown what machine learning can achieve when using Google's internet-scale infrastructure.

In addition the Google Machine Learning Platform gives you the necessary tools to run machine learning exercises using pre-trained models or to generate your own custom models.

As with other GCP products, there's a range of services that stretches from the highly general and pre-configured to the highly specialized and pre-customized in order to suit all needs.

Google not only provides the internet scale infrastructure and services that will enable you to run machine learning it also provides the applications, algorithms and libraries. TensorFlow is Google's own open source software library that's exceptionally well suited for machine learning applications like neural networks. TensorFlow was developed for Google's internal use and then made available to the open source community. As a result you can use TensorFlow wherever you like but GCP is an ideal place for it because machine learning models need lots of on-demand compute resources and lots of training data.

Moreover when it comes to machine learning you start to move into the realms of huge processing power and the need for GPUs. However Google has developed a processor especially designed for TensorFlow. These TPU's, Tensor Processing Units, which are hardware devices designed to accelerate, machine learning workloads with TensorFlow can be thought of as cloud based rivals to the GPU.

GCP makes the TPU available in the cloud with Compute Engine virtual machines and each cloud TPU provides up to 180 teraflops of performance.

But, because you pay for only what you use, there's no upfront capital investment required in order to get your hands on the potentially infinite resources you may require for your machine learning adventure.

Nonetheless, machine learning is not for the faint-hearted and even with all the Google resource on-tap many business want a more managed service. Hence, Google Cloud Machine Learning Engine will let you construct machine learning models that will work on any type or any size of data set. Also, the Machine Learning Engine can take any TensorFlow model and perform large scale training on a managed cluster.

Moreover, if you want access to add various machine learning capabilities to your applications then Google Cloud also offers a range of machine learning APIs suited to specific purposes. This provides you with access to machine learning functions and services without you having to concern yourself with the details of how they are provided.

Organizations in all sorts of fields use the Cloud Machine Learning Platform for lots of diverse applications. But they can almost always fall into two categories depending on whether the data they work on is structured or unstructured.

Based on structured data, you can use ML for various kinds of classification and regression tasks like customer churn analysis, product diagnostics and forecasting.

It can be the heart of our recommendation engine for content personalization and cross-sells and up-sells.

You can use ML to detect anomalies as in fraud detection, sensor diagnostics or log metrics.

On the other hand if your machine learning is based on unstructured data, you can use ML for image analytics and many popular use cases in commerce and industry, such as, for identifying substandard components on a conveyor belt, identifying damaged shipments, or for automated inventory and stock control.

But you can also do text analytics too, which opens up opportunities for automating processes such as validating forms, blog analysis, language identification, topic classification and even advanced sentiment analysis. You will likely find that beneath the hood of many innovative applications are machine learning systems that contain several of these kinds of applications working together. The Google Cloud machine Learning Platform makes that kind of interactivity well within your grasp.

GCP Managed Services

In the last few chapters, we have focused on how to create, use and manage cloud infrastructure in GCP. However there is an alternative to creating, running and managing infrastructure in the first place and that is to integrate an existing solution into your application design. If you would rather spend your time working on the development of your applications rather than on building the architecture that they run on, then you should consider GCP's built-in managed service.

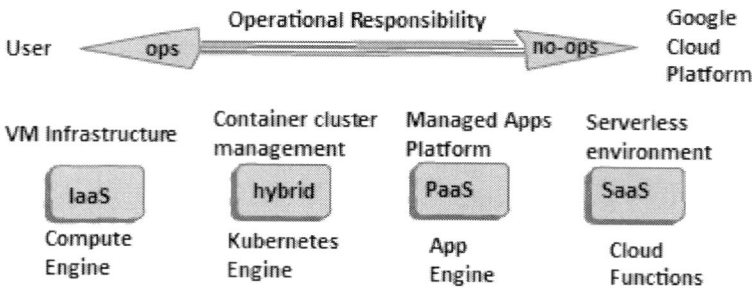

Figure -8

In short, if we consider Compute Engine to be at the hands on IaaS end of the spectrum then we can consider managed services to be at the Serverless end of the spectrum as it is typically a partial or complete zero-touch range of managed solutions offered as a service.

However not all managed services are completely serverless so in practice they actually exist on a continuum between platform as a service and software as a service, which is

Determined by how much of the internal methods and control are actually exposed to the user. Generally though, if you choose to deploy a managed service you are in effect outsourcing the provisioning, running and lifecycle management of the service and all its dependencies to Google. For a lot of companies whose core businesses is something other than network design, management and support this approach makes a lot of sense. Focusing on the core business releases a lot of precious resources and passed the administrative and maintenance burden to Google.

If this sound likes a match with your business model then instead of setting up an infrastructure to support specific types of workloads, you may want to take advantage of some of the many services that Google have to offer on GCP as managed services.

In this chapter we will be covering some fully managed services such as Dataproc, Dataflow, BigQuery, and some other managed services of interest. Most of these are Big Data, machine learning and data analytics orientated, which is really where most small to medium businesses lack skills but where Google excels, especially on their own cloud infrastructure.

Let's take a look at the continuum of solution options.

On-premises	IaaS	PaaS	SaaS
Application	Application	Application	Application
Data	Data	Data	Data
Runtime	Runtime	Runtime	Runtime
Middleware	Middleware	Middleware	Middleware
OS	OS	OS	OS
Virtualisation	Virtualisation	Virtualisation	Virtualisation
Servers	Servers	Servers	Servers
Storage	Storage	Storage	Storage
Networking	Networking	Networking	Networking

In the table above you the user are responsible for looking after the blue coloured functions and Google is responsible for the orange functions. As you can see with IaaS you can pretty much build everything you want by building your own infrastructure using the console, cloud shell, and virtual machines. We'll also learn a little bit later about automating our infrastructure using Cloud API in programmatic deployments using Deployment Manager. However, when you start to deploy managed services you begin to move from Infrastructure as a Service towards Platform as a Service and then eventually to Serverless Computing, so you don't have to worry about programmatically automating processes. Compute Engine and Deployment Manager provide you with the means to actively control and architect your environment and allows you to hands-on build your infrastructure. However when you move to adopting managed services such as Dataproc and Dataflow you are now well into Platform as a Service territory. What this means is that you have less control but also less administrative burden. When you move further towards BigQuery, which is GCP's vast data warehouse, it is a fully embracing managed service more akin to Software as a Service.

There is a continuum of services and platform options available in GCP. Several can perform a similar function but you should consider all options in a particular context. Now, contemplating the diagram, we can see that the solutions to the left offer greater outsourcing of management and administrative overhead, but with a loss of control. On the other hand, the solutions to the right offer greater hands-on control but with increased responsibility and management overhead.

We can look to three of the managed services we discussed earlier to see how this works in practice. For example, if we look at the data processing managed services we can see that they comprise three core services. The first one is Dataproc, which is a managed service which lets you spin up a Spark Hadoop cluster quickly and cost effectively with both Hive and Pig in-built capabilities. Now, what you have to consider is just how long and at what expense would it take to accomplish that on-premises? But in GCP you can spin up this environment that utilizing a preconfigured deployment manager process we call Dataproc in a matter of minutes.

The second data processing managed service is Dataflow and it is of interest as it is GCP's ETL batch and streaming processing pipeline. Dataflow is based on the Apache Beam open SDK framework. This means it is compatible with Apache Beam and so you can create your own ETL jobs. You can submit them yourselves on your own platform, or you can push them to Google Cloud's Dataflow. In this case Dataflow will handle all that automatic scaling and realtime streaming, in order to speed up the ETL processing.

Finally, the third service is Google's BigQuery. Now as we know BigQuery is a fully managed data analytic service that can scale to the petabyte scale. Further, BigQuery is also a fully -fledged Software as a Service. However to better understand each of these data processing components we need to learn a little bit more about each of them in turn.

DataProc

Cloud Dataproc, is a managed Spark and Hadoop service that lets you take advantage of open source data for batch processing, querying streaming and machine learning. Indeed as a managed cloud service DataProc has a number of interesting features probably the most notable is it is very affordable. This is due to GCP having automated the deployment process and by utilizing Google's vast compute network and infrastructure to derive cost at scale. These benefits also include per second billing, sustained use discounts, the ability to use pre-emptible virtual machines, amongst several other discounts.

Nonetheless, DataProc is also outstanding with regards to its technical features. Despite these high technical capabilities DataProc is actual very quick and easy to deploy. Further it is easier to provision and maintain these resources because Google is responsible for most of the maintenance burden.

Another compelling feature with regards DataProc is that GCP supports all of the major third party ETL data analytics software packages whether they be open source or proprietary. This means they are likely to support the packages that you may already be utilizing on-premises or feel that you might want to utilize in the cloud.

GCP also integrates as you would expect very tightly with a number of other related Google products, including Google Cloud Storage, Bigtable and BigQuery. Indeed, you can output or even ingest data directly from Bigtable because it's using a compatible HBase API.

With reference to performance DataProc is notably faster when data processing workflows because less time is wasted having to wait for clusters to provision and start executing applications. To connect to your Dataproc cluster, you can use the web-based user interface to submit jobs. You can also use the YARN Web UI, HDFS web user interface, as well as SSH through a SOCKS proxy.

When it comes to starting a cluster, DataProc doesn't just spin up a bunch of VMs using its own logic, though it can do if that is what you want. Instead DataProc remains controllable, so by using the G-Cloud tool and the Cloud Dataproc API you can interact and control clusters in a programmatic fashion.

Moreover, if you are looking for more granular control you can always deploy and configure Stackdriver to assist in the management, notification, alerting and monitoring of DataProc.

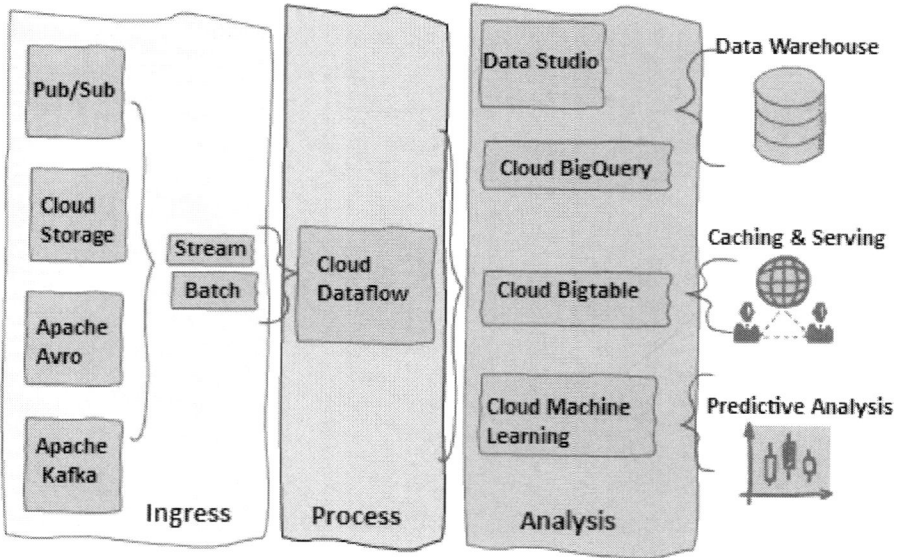

Figure - 9
Dataflow

Dataflow is GCP's online batch and stream ETL processing service. It is based on the open source based Apache Beam SDK. The data process of Extract, Transform, and Load (ETL) are the three key functions that are applied to data being extracted from one source, transformed into a new format and then loaded into another sink database, typically a data warehouse.

ETL thus is the process that acts as an interface and translator facilitating the conversion and separation of data. It is simply part of the data processing function and hence, Dataflow helps retrieve, order, and format the data as its being streamed in to the data processing environment. Indeed, you may input data from many different sources both on-premises or from other clouds. Typically though it would be from Cloud Datastore but you could output the reorganised data or input it directly into cloud storage such as BigQuery, Bigtable or Cloud Datastore.
The way that this works is that Dataflow creates Pipelines, PCollections, Transforms, and I/O Sources and Sinks.

- Pipelines are a series of computations that accepts data and transforms it, outputting to an external or to an internal Sink. The input source and output Sink can be the same in a Pipeline, as this allows for data format conversion.
- PCollections are a specialized container of nearly unlimited size that represents a set of data in the Pipeline.
- Transforms incoming data to a format suitable for an outgoing process such as our data processing operation.
- I/O Sources and Sinks are different data storage formats. Cloud Storage, BigQuery, Tables, and more, as well as custom data source/sinks.

The following examples give you a sense of the processing capabilities of Dataflow. In this simple model Pipeline data is input from a source into a PCollection, transformed and then output.
In diagram 9 we can see each of the components that make up a pipeline of data processing jobs from multiple sources.
Figure -10

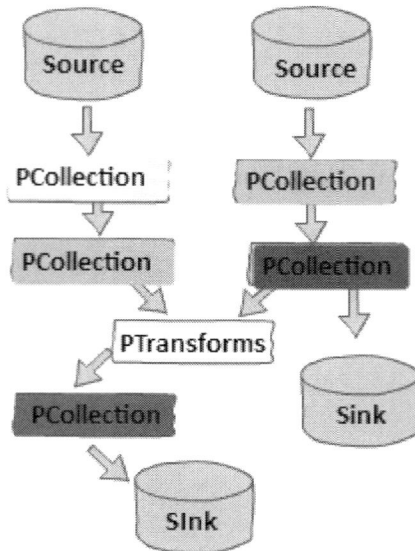

Pipelines: these are data processing job that is made up of a series of computations including input, processing and output.

PCollections: These are bounded (or unbounded) data sets which represent the input, intermediate and output in pipelines.

PTransforms: These are when data processing steps merge in a pipeline and one or more PCollections serve as both an input and output.

I/O Sources and Sinks: APIs for reading and writing data which can be considered to be the roots and endpoints of the pipeline.

In the multiple transform pipelines, data is read from BigQuery then filtered into two collections based on the initial character of the name.

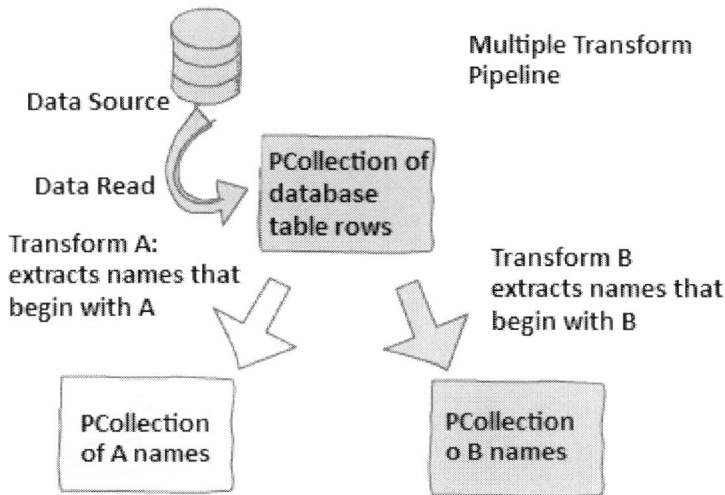

Figure-11

In the merge pipeline example, the purpose is to collect all sorts of data that maybe you've ingested from BigQuery or another data source. We can transform those different names as well, so we can split everything back, and then flatten those out.

In the multiple input pipeline you're doing joins from different data sources. There are different ways to connect the pieces, but Dataflow's job is to ingest the data in parallel as fast as possible, scale out and then of course output an ETL that's friendly for whatever the normal source it's going to.

BigQuery

BigQuery is a powerful Big Data analytics platform used by all types of organisations. BigQuery is Google's fully managed enterprise scale data warehouse for analytics. BigQuery is low cost, serverless and considered to be Software as a Service (SaaS). Therefore, with BigQuery there is no infrastructure to manage and you don't need a database administrator. So you can focus on preparing and analysing the data to find meaningful insights using familiar techniques and processes.

BigQuery allows you to analyse all your batch and streaming data by creating a logical data warehouse over managed columnar storage. BigQuery has in-built Business Intelligence (BI), and Machine Learning (ML) capabilities that let carry out geospatial analysis on gigabytes to petabytes of data using simple SQL to produce analysis dashboards, spreadsheets, datasets and reports. On performance, BigQuery is very powerful streaming ingestion captures and analysing data in real time, ensuring insights are always current.

Nonetheless, probably BigQuery's biggest selling point is that it can be setup in minutes and then scale seamlessly across its serverless architecture without you having to provision any environment resources or invest in on-premises hardware. BigQuery is a fully managed service so it eliminates the entire operational and maintenance burden by automatically replicating your data for redundancy and to guarantee business continuity. Also, for those wanting to try their hand at Big Data analysis or machine learning you can analyse up to 1 TB of data and store 10 GB of data for free each month.

If you are planning venturing into machine learning or advanced analytics then you may want to look to some other GCP managed services that are available. Cloud Datalab is a managed service for data analysts and data scientists that runs on iPython Notebooks, and it combines both a Python library, in which you can write Python code, with real time visualization. If you're writing Python code to run queries from BigQuery, then you can output those visualizations directly within the Cloud Datalab interface. Because these are Jupyter Python notebooks you can actually save these notebooks and share them with colleagues.

Cloud Datalab doesn't just support Python; it also supports interactive SQL and JavaScript.

When we consider data visualisation we mustn't overlook another managed service for data scientists, Data Studio, which lets you create dynamic, visually compelling reports, and dashboards.

With Data Studio, you can easily connect to a variety of data sources, visualize your data through attractive, dynamic, and interactive reports and dashboards, and share and collaborate with others, just as you can in Google Drive.

Cloud Vision

Following on from image detection there is the Cloud Vision API which enables developers to understand the content of an image. This API classifies images into thousands of categories, bus, car, traffic lights, sailboat, cat, and so on. It is designed to detect and identify individual objects within images, which is difficult for machines but easy for humans. Nonetheless, it is now advanced enough to also be able to find and read printed words contained within images.

The Cloud Vision API encapsulates powerful machine learning models behind an easy to use API. Therefore, you can use it in your applications to build Meta data on your image catalogue, moderate offensive content or even do image sentiment analysis.

Cloud Speech API

Many of the use cases for Image API can also work with the cloud speech API as it too enables developers to convert audio to text. This can have high utility in business and commerce as the internet brings an increasingly global user base.

Some natural use cases are, transcribing the audio to text in videos, enable command and control through voice command in smart devices, or more mundanely transcribing dictated audio files.

Leading on from the Cloud Speech API we have a natural progression from transcribing audio to text to actual language translation.

Cloud Natural Language API

This service offers a variety of natural language understanding technologies to developers. The API recognizes over 80 languages and variants and it can do a lot of great things such as; syntax analysis, by breaking down sentences supplied by our users into tokens, identify the nouns, verbs, adjectives, and other parts of speech and figure out the relationships among the words.

It can also do entity recognition whereby it can parse text and flag mentions of people, organizations, locations, events, products, and media.

Another function is that it can understand the overall sentiment expressed in a block of text. This is becoming a popular use case in call centre use of sentiment analysis on, email, web blogs and text messages.

Furthermore it can perform these capabilities in multiple languages, including English, Spanish, and Japanese.

Cloud translation API

This API provides a simple, programmatic interface for translating an arbitrary string into a supported language. Google translate is an example of machine learning and natural language APIs working in tandem to learn and improve. This is clearly demonstrated by the huge leaps in accuracy and quality in the translation service over just the last few years. It still isn't perfect but it's continuously improving and what's more if you don't know the source language, the API can automatically detect it for you.

Cloud Video Intelligence

The Cloud Video Intelligence API lets you annotate videos in a variety of formats.
It helps you identify key entities that are nouns within your video and when they occur.
You can use it to make video content searchable and discoverable within search engines such as Google.

Dialogflow

The service Dialogflow is considered to be a development suite that you can use when creating conversational interfaces for websites, mobile applications, popular messaging platforms, and IoT devices. Dialogflow is an end-to-end service based upon a build-once deploy-everywhere use case to create UI interfaces such as chatbots and conversational IVR that enable you to build a natural and rich interaction between interactive users and your business infrastructure. Dialogflow is what is known as a Knowledge Connector, which allows you to aggregate large volumes of data from your enterprise to your agent, such as when building FAQs and knowledge-based resources. Dialogflow

AutoML

Cloud AutoML is a suite of machine learning products that enables developers with limited machine learning expertise to use their own labelled data to expand Google's own pre-trained ML models, which makes them specific to their specific use-case. The way it works is that a developer can use one of Google's pre-trained ML models such as AutoML Vision to add ML capabilities to their applications. However, although AutoML Vision has been trained to identify 1,000 of categories of images it may not recognise specific images. In that case the developer can train AutoML Vision with their own images to classify them according to their own defined labels. All that is required is that you do the following:

- Copy a set of images into Google Cloud Storage.
- Create a CSV listing the images and their labels.
- Use AutoML Vision to create your dataset, and train and deploy your model.

Furthermore you can use several other Google AutoML models such as:

- AutoML Translation - Automatically detect and translate between languages
- AutoML Natural Language – Reveal the structure and meaning of text through ML
- AutoML Video Intelligence – Enable powerful content discovery and engaging video experiences
- AutoML Tables – Automatically build and deploy state-of-the-art machine learning models on structured data.

To demonstrate the ease with which you can work with Cloud AutoML consider the following example where we train a Natural Language model in AutoML.
In the GCP Console, on the project selector page, select or create a GCP project and make sure that billing is enabled and the Cloud AutoML and Storage APIs are activated.

Create a dataset

The first step is to open the AutoML Natural Language Entity Extraction UI and select your project from the drop-down list in the title bar. The second step is to train your custom model, using a dataset that you provide that has representative samples of the type of texts you want to analyse. The dataset must be annotated with labels that identify the types of entities you want AutoML Natural Language Entity Extraction to identify within the text. You need to supply between 50 and 100,000 text items to use for training your custom model. Then you use between one and 100 unique labels to annotate the entities you want the model to learn to extract. Each annotation is a span of text with an associated label. Label names can be between 2 and 30 characters, and can be used to annotate between one and 10 words. We recommend using each label at least 200 times in your training data set. Once you have prepared the CSV dataset file you can save in into Cloud Storage.

- Click the New Dataset button in the title bar.
- On the Create dataset page, enter a name for the dataset then click Create dataset.
- Enter the location of the training data to import.

In the Select a CSV file on Cloud Storage text box, enter the path for the sample CSV file:

cloud-ml-data/NL-entity/dataset.csv

Note: gs:// prefix will be automatically added to the cloud-ml-data/NL-entity/dataset.csv
After adding the data source → Click Import
When your training data has been successfully imported, the Status column says 'Success:importing' data and the UI shows the generated ID for the dataset (used when making AutoML API calls) as well as the number of items imported.

Train your model

- From the Datasets listing page, click the dataset name.
- Click Start Training.
- Enter a name for your custom model or accept the default name.

- Click the 'Deploy model after training finishes' check box to deploy your model automatically when training is complete.
- Click Start Training.

Training a model can take a long time perhaps several hours to complete. After the model is successfully trained, you will receive a message at the email address you used to sign up for the program.

Evaluate the custom model

After training a model, AutoML Natural Language Entity Extraction evaluates the quality and accuracy of the new model. To see the evaluation metrics for your model:
- Open the AutoML Natural Language Entity Extraction UI and click the Models tab in the left-side navigation bar.
- Click the name of the model you want to evaluate.

If training has been completed for the model, AutoML Natural Language Entity Extraction shows its evaluation metrics on the evaluation page. Here it provides information on the precision and recall scores for the model as a whole and for each extracted entity (a label in the UI). Precision and recall measure indicates how well the model is capturing information, and how much it's missing:
- Precision indicates, from all the items identified as a particular entity (label), how many actually were correctly identified.
- Recall indicates, from all the items that should have been identified as a particular entity (label), how many were actually identified.

You can use the information on the evaluation page to determine whether the model is ready or whether it requires additional training cycles. However, be careful as although low precision or recall scores may indicate that your model needs additional training data a high or perfect precision and recall indicators can indicate that the data is too easy and the model will not generalize well when subjected to real-world data.

Part III – Data Engineering on the Google Cloud Platform

Chapter 25 – Working with Data Storage

Data is often characterised by the 3Vs; variety, which refers to its structural variability as to how similar or different the data can be; velocity, which is essentially how fast the data arrives; and finally, volatility, which refers to how long the data retains value and therefore how long it needs to be stored and made accessible. There is a 4V, which is veracity a measure of the correctness and integrity of the data but that isn't relevant to our topic regarding cloud data storage methods. Nonetheless, when we contemplate the various data storage techniques it doesn't really matter from an application's point of view whether the storage technology is a database or an object store. What is important, from the application perspective is that the technology behaves like a service, which provides the efficient and reliable storing and retrieving of the data.

When you take a look at GCP's service offerings for data storage, there are a lot of services to choose from. In previous chapters we discussed all of these at a high functional level and compared their individual suitability for specific tasks. In this chapter we will take a deeper dive into the workings of each of them; Cloud storage, Cloud SQL, Cloud Spanner, Cloud Datastore/Filestore, and Cloud Bigtable.

Cloud Storage

Cloud storage is designed for storing unstructured data at scale - petabytes and even exabytes of capacity. There are four classes of Cloud Storage; regional, multi-region, nearline and Coldline. We have discussed all these types earlier along with their specific properties, characteristics and usability. Nonetheless in this chapter we want to look under the bonnet so to speak to see how they store and access data in their own specific ways. We will also see how we can control individual, group, or service accounts to protect the data and control the authorised access that they may require via IAM.

Cloud storage is perfect for unstructured data because conceptually it is simply a big bucket and you're going to store objects, which are unstructured blobs of variable size and type of data, in that bucket. This makes it the perfect staging point for ingress data into GCP. As a result when you upload data to GCP you will typically initially upload it into a cloud storage bucket before it is sent to its final storage destination, such as Cloud SQL for example.

This is because the concept of an unstructured data bucket where you simply dump your diverse data makes it very flexible and intuitive to use. Indeed you don't have to worry about schemas or the like you just dump the data as it is and Cloud storage provides you with a URL to access it. Conceptually it is just a lump of data – a blob - so it can be anything from raw text such as log files to video files it doesn't matter to cloud storage. There is no easy way to index all of these files like you would in a file system as all you have is a specific URL to access each object in the bucket. You can create directories but that is just another object that points to the various objects in the bucket so it kind of defeats the purpose.

So let's look at how cloud storage works and to do so we have to break it down into a couple of different components. First, there are buckets, which are required to have a globally unique name, and they cannot be nested. The data that you point to in those buckets are objects that inherit the storage class of the bucket, and those objects could be text files, doc files, video files, etc. There's no minimum size to those objects, and you can scale this as much as you want as long as your code allows it.

To access the data, you can use the SDK tool commands in the console, or either the JSON or XML API's. We will look at how to access objects later in the chapter.

For now, let's consider that once you've created a bucket, you might want to change the storage class of that bucket. There are several caveats here that you should be aware of;

- The first is that you can change the default storage classes of a bucket, but you can't change a regional bucket to a multi-regional and vice-versa.
- Second, a regional or a multi-regional can be changed to coldline and nearline storage classes.
- Third, you are able to move objects from one bucket to another using the GCP console.
- However, moving objects to buckets of different storage classes, requires using the gsutil command-line tool in the console.

Securing the Data

Dumping your data objects into a bucket might sound convenient but security and convenience are rarely good bed partners, so how secure is it? To understand how the GCP provides convenience while preserving the object's security and privacy we need to consider how GCP controls access to your objects and buckets.

When you create a Cloud storage bucket it automatically becomes just like any other resource in a project. Therefore we can use the Cloud IAM service to apply a policy for access control. Using the IAM service enables us to explicitly dictate what individual user, group or service account can access the bucket. Furthermore we can determine who can see the bucket, list the objects in the bucket, view the names of the objects in the bucket, or create new buckets.

IAM Cloud Storage Roles

You can grant roles at either the project level or at the bucket level. However, granting roles at the lower more specific bucket level does not affect any existing roles that you have already granted at the project level, and vice versa. Thus, this gives you some flexibility in the way that you can use these two levels of granularity to tailor your permissions. For example you might use a general set of permissions at the project level say to view all buckets and all their objects but only grant the permission to create objects to a specific bucket. Moreover, there are some roles that can be used at both the project level and the bucket level. In this case, to avoid conflict if the role is used at the project level, the permissions they contain apply to all buckets and objects in the project. When used at the bucket level, the permissions only apply to a specific bucket and the objects within it. Examples of IAM Cloud Storage roles that can be applied at both project and bucket level are; roles/storage.admin, roles/storage.objectViewer, and roles/storage.objectCreator. On the other hand there are also some roles that can only be applied at one level. For example, you can only apply the Viewer role only at the project level, while you can only apply only at the bucket level the roles/storage.legacyObjectOwner.

Deploying IAM as the method for access control for objects and buckets will for most purposes be sufficient as the IAM roles are inherited from project, to bucket, to object.

However there are more granular access controls techniques that you may wish to implement. One of these is an access control list or ACL and this offers even finer control. Project and Bucket level roles work sympathetically with ACLs in so much as they both work independently from the ACL. This provides a way to create more granular policies. For example you could grant permissions at the bucket level to grant access to all objects then at the ACL level block access to specific objects.

However, if you need even more detailed control, you can use signed URLs, which provide a cryptographic key, which gives the key holder highly-restricted access to a bucket or object. Finally, a signed access policy document further refines the control, by determining what kind of file can be uploaded by someone with a signed URL.

Access Control Lists

An ACL is a simple mechanism or technique that you can use to define who has access to your buckets and objects, as well as state what level of access they have.
An ACL consists of one or more entries hence the term list, and these entries consist of two pieces of information; a scope, and a permission. The scope defines who can perform the specified actions such as a specific user, group or service account. The permission stipulates what actions can be performed, for example, view or modify.

Signed URLs

Access lists are fine generally but for some applications there is a need to enforce time-based access control criteria. For example, if you are making available for anonymous download a video file for a predefined time then is will be easier and more efficient to grant limited time access tokens. Access tokens can also be used by any user, instead of using account based authentication for controlling resource access. For example, if you wished to allow visitors to your site free access to a download or when you don't require users to have a registered account. If those are the criteria than instead of access lists you can use signed URLs, which lets you do this for anonymous access to cloud storage.
Signed URLs are also simple to set up and all you have to do is first create a URL that will grant a permission such as read or write access to a specific cloud storage resource.
Then you can optionally specify when the access permissions will expire. The URL is then signed using a private key associated with a service account.
When the request is received, cloud storage will verify that the signed access granting URL was issued by a trusted service account as it delegates its trust of that account to the holder of the URL.

However there are some security concerns you should be aware of because once you give out the signed URL, it is out of your control. So, you want the signed URL to expire after some reasonable amount of time. An example of a signed URL is shown below:

```
https://storage.googleapis.com/example-bucket/car.jpeg?X-Goog-
Algorithm=GOOG4-RSA-SHA256&X-Goog-
Credential=example%40example-
project.iam.gserviceaccount.com%2F20181026%2Fus-central-
1%2Fstorage%2Fgoog4_request&X-Goog-Date=20181026T181309Z&X-
Goog-Expires=900&X-Goog-SignedHeaders=host&X-Goog-Signature=
```

This signed URL provided access to read the object car.jpeg in the bucket example-bucket. Your applications could call it, or you could make the URL available to individuals for download.

The query parameters that make this a signed URL are:

- X-Goog-Algorithm: The algorithm used to sign the URL.
- X-Goog-Credential: Information about the credentials used to create the signed URL.
- X-Goog-Date: The date and time the signed URL became usable, in the ISO 8601 basic format YYYYMMDD'T'HHMMSS'Z'.
- X-Goog-Expires: The length of time the signed URL remained valid, measured in seconds from the value in X-Goog-Date.
- X-Goog-SignedHeaders: Headers that had to be included as part of any request that used the signed URL.
- X-Goog-Signature: The authentication string that allowed requests using this signed URL to access car.jpeg.

Signed URLS are good way to ensure a predetermined expiration to the access of a file. This means you do not have to rely on life cycle management to delete older files. However, there are some considerations you should be aware of:

- Always transmit the link to your users using HTTPS
- When specifying credentials, identify your service account by using its email address; however, the use of the service account ID is also supported.

Cloud Storage Features

There are a variety of different object management features that come with Cloud Storage. For example you can use your own encryption keys, instead of the Google-managed keys which are available for Cloud Storage.

Cloud Storage also provides Object-Lifecycle Management, which lets you automatically delete or archive objects after a specified time period. Another feature is Object Versioning which allows you to maintain multiple versions of objects in your bucket.

There are other features such as Object Change Notification, Data Import and Strong Consistency, but we will discuss these in more detail after discussing Object Versioning and Object Lifecycle Management.

Object Versioning

To provide a measure of protection for objects from being deleted or overwritten while in Cloud Storage, Google offers the Object Versioning feature. You can help with the retrieval of objects that have been accidently over-written by enabling Object Versioning for a bucket.

The way that Object Versioning works is that once it is enabled, Cloud Storage will track objects within a bucket. Now objects are immutable so they cannot be modified while in a Cloud Storage bucket but they can be over-written and deleted. To prevent accidental loss and to help in the subsequent retrieval of a deleted or over-written object the Object Versioning feature creates an archived version of an object each time the live version of the object is overwritten or deleted.

The archived version retains the name of the object, but is uniquely identified by a generation number, such as g1. However, you should be aware that this is considered from a billing perspective to be an additional object so you will be charged for the storage of the versions in the archives accordingly.

Nonetheless, once Object Versioning is enabled, you will be able to list archived versions of an object, restore the version of an object from an older state, or permanently delete an archived version as needed. You can turn versioning on or off for a bucket at any time. Turning versioning off leaves the existing object versions in place. However, it does stop any further versions being created so the bucket will stop accumulating new archived object versions.

Object Lifecycle Management

To support some of the use cases that are common place in the enterprise such as setting a time to live for objects, archiving older versions of objects, or migrating objects to longer term cold storage classes to help manage costs, Cloud Storage offers Object Lifecycle Management.
The way that lifecycle management works is that you assign a set of rules to a bucket. The rules will apply to all the objects in the bucket. So when an object meets the criteria of one of those rules, Cloud Storage automatically performs a specified action on the object.
Here are some use cases where you could use lifecycle management to your benefit;

- You could set a time to live for downloadable objects that you wish to make available during a promotion
- you could downgrade the storage class of objects older than two years to Coldline Storage
- You can archive or delete objects created before a specific date for example January the 1st 2018
- If you have versioning enabled, you could decide to keep only the three most recent versions of an object and archive/delete the others

When you change the lifecycle configuration it doesn't take effect immediately and it may take up to 24 hours to come into effect. So be aware that when you change your lifecycle configuration, the Object Lifecycle Management service may still perform actions based on the old configuration for up to 24 hours.

Object Change Notification

Object Change Notification can be used to notify an application when an object is updated or added to a bucket through a watch request. Completing a watch request creates a new notification channel. This is the channel over which a notification message is sent to an application watching a bucket.
After a notification channel is initiated, Cloud Storage will send a notification to the application any time an object is added, updated, or removed from the bucket.

Storage Transfer

The GCP Cloud Storage browser allows you to conveniently upload individual files to your bucket. However, in real world scenarios you may have to upload terabytes or even petabytes of data so you are going to need a more robust transfer mechanism.

The GCP provides three services that address this issue; Storage Transfer Service, Google Transfer Appliance, and Offline Media Import.

The Storage Transfer Service enables high performance imports of online data. That data source can be another Cloud Storage Bucket, an Amazon S3 Bucket or an HTTP or HTTPS location.

Transfer Appliance on the other hand, is a specialist solution consisting of a high capacity storage server that you lease from Google. However it is not available in all regions. If you are lucky enough to be in a region that does offer this service then all you have to do is simply connect it to your network. Then load it with data and ship it to an upload facility where the data is uploaded to Cloud Storage. This service enables you to securely transfer up to petabytes of data on a single appliance.

Finally, Offline Media Import is a third party service where physical media such as storage arrays, hard disk drives, tapes and USB flash drives is sent to a provider who uploads the data.

When you upload an object to Cloud Storage and you receive a success response, the object is immediately available for download and operations from any location where Google offer the service. This is true whether you create a new object or override an existing object. This is because when you perform an upload the data will be now strongly consistent, so you will never be likely to receive a '404 Not Found' response. Moreover you are also unlikely to experience stale data after a Read-after-write or Read-after-meditate-update operation.

Strong global consistency also extends to deleting objects. If a deletion request succeeds, an immediate attempt to download the object or its metadata will result in a 404 Not Found status code. You get the 404 error because the object no longer exists after the delete operation succeeds.

Also Bucket listing is strongly consistent. For example, if you create a Bucket, then you immediately perform a list Bucket's operation; the new Bucket appears in the return list of Buckets without any lag or delay.

Finally, object listing is also strongly consistent. For example, if you upload an object to a bucket and then immediately perform a list object's operation, the new object appears in the returned list of objects again without delay.

Structured data services

In the previous section we dealt only with unstructured data in the Cloud Storage core service. But many transactional type operations do need to store data within a structured schema or a relational data storage service.

Cloud SQL

If you do need a structured data storage service then there are several options. From a customer experience and convenience perspective Cloud SQL is a fully managed, no ops, database service. This makes it easy for you to implement as Google will set up, maintain, manage, and administer your relational databases on the Google Cloud Platform.

Alternatively, if you want you could install your own SQL database application image, such as MySQL on a VM using Compute Engine. In this case you would have to build the schema, set up, maintain, manage and administer the database yourself. This method gives you all the freedom and flexibility to run your own database as you perhaps are used to doing on-premises. But there are certain benefits to be had when using Cloud SQL as a managed service instead of running your own instance of a database engine.

For example, Cloud SQL can scale to a high capacity database, which is capable of handling terabytes of storage. Accessing and using the databases will be exactly the same as they are relational, which means that you can simply run SQL type queries such as SELECT statements to read a field's data or INSERT statements to write a field's data.

In addition since Cloud SQL is a fully managed service, you can choose either MySQL, SQL Server or PostgreSQL database engines, the security patches and updates are automatically applied for you.

Now, if we consider MySQL as an example we can see that Cloud SQL is not a simulation it is a real MySQL instance. This means that there will be no compatibility issues and you should be able to easily lift and shift the on-premise to the cloud without any issues. After that Google will manage the MySQL cloud instance for you. However, you will still have to administer the database users but you can also do this through the native authentication tools that come with these databases.

However, Cloud SQL also supports other applications and tools that you might be familiar with, such as, SQL Workbench, Toad, and other external applications that use the standard SQL drivers.

Cloud SQL is available in two different generations. It is recommended to use the second generation unless you have some legacy constraints because it provides up to seven times the throughput and 20 times the storage capacity of the first generation. As a result the 2nd Generation provides up to 208 gigabytes of RAM and 10 terabytes of data storage.

Also, the 2nd generation version works with either MySQL 5.6 or 5.7, but be aware that it will only supports InnoDB as the storage engine.

On the other hand, the 1st generation version provides considerably lower memory and storage capacity and only works with MySQL 5.5. However, this generation does support the MyISAM storage engine as well as connections over both IPv4 and IPv6 addresses. In addition it also supports the on-demand activation policy.

On-premises MySQL vs. Cloud SQL

Regardless of the generation, the MySQL functionality provided by a Cloud SQL Instance is exactly the same as the functionality provided by a locally hosted MySQL Instance.

However, there are a few differences between a Standard MySQL Instance and a Cloud SQL Instance. For example, user-defined functions are not supported in Cloud SQL and some additional services that are required to be enabled and configured in standard MySQL are automatically provided by Cloud SQL as part of the managed service.

For example, The MySQL replication feature, which requires considerable thought to the design and configuration in an on-premise standard MySQL deployment, can be enabled as part of the Cloud SQL managed service by just ticking a few checkboxes. The replication service will replicate data between multiple zones and provide automatic failover without loss of service if a service outage should occur in one of the regions.

In a similar vein Cloud SQL also provides automated and on demand backups with point in time recovery.

Just as you can with an on-premises MySQL instance you can easily import and export databases using MySQL dump or import and export CSV files. However, another feature of Cloud SQL that is difficult to reproduce on-premises is its ability to scale up, albeit it does require a machine restart, or scale out by using read replicas.

Essentially, choosing between a standard MySQL instance and Cloud SQL managed service comes down to a few basic questions. If you have specific OS requirements, custom database configuration requirements, or special backup requirements. If that is the case then you perhaps want to consider hosting your own database on a VM using Compute Engine. Otherwise, it is strongly recommended to use Cloud SQL as a fully managed service for your relational databases.

SQL IAM

You can control permissions and access to Cloud SQL resources via primitive roles (owner, editor, and viewer) or through the predefined roles. The difference between them is down to the level of granularity that is available when working with the predefined roles. You can of course also create your own custom IAM roles.

Primitive Roles:

- roles/owner - Full access and control for all Google Cloud Platform resources; manage user access
- roles/writer – (Editor) Read-write access to all Google Cloud Platform and Cloud SQL resources (full control except for the ability to modify permissions)
- roles/reader – (Viewer) Read-only access to all Google Cloud Platform resources, including Cloud SQL resources

Predefined Roles:

- roles/cloudsql.admin - Full control for all Cloud SQL resources.
- roles/cloudsql.editor - Manage specific instances. No ability to neither see or modify permissions, nor modify users or SSL Certs. No ability to import data or restore from a backup, nor clone, delete, or promote instances. No ability to start or stop replicas. No ability to delete databases, replicas, or backups.
- roles/cloudsql.viewer - Read-only access to all Cloud SQL resources.
- roles/cloudsql.client - Connectivity access to Cloud SQL instances from App Engine and the Cloud SQL Proxy. Not required for accessing an instance using IP addresses.

Cloud SQL Connections

When it comes to configuring connections between applications and the database there are a couple of options you should be aware off. A very popular method of connection favoured in development environments uses a basic connection. This is where you simply grant any application access to a Cloud SQL instance by authorizing the applications host IP address.

This is the fastest, easiest, but least secure method to make a connection, hence its popularity in non-production development environments but it is certainly not recommended for production instances.

Instead, for a more secure access, but only suitable for temporarily access you can use whitelist IP addresses to easily connect from the GCP Console. These are fast and secure enough for quick administration tasks requiring the MySQL command line tool. But for regular client connections you should configure SSL certificate management for a Cloud SQL Instance and connect to the MySQL client using TLS/SSL.

Cloud SQL also provides instance level access to authorize access to your Cloud SQL Instance from an application or client that could be running on Google App Engine or on another GCP service such as Compute Engine or even running externally.

Cloud SQL Proxy

For production or robust development environments there is an alternative method of connecting a MySQL client to your Google Cloud SQL instances over IP and that is using the Cloud SQL Proxy.
The Cloud SQL Proxy provides you with a method for secure access to your Cloud SQL second generation instances without having to whitelist IP addresses or having to configure TLS/SSL. Cloud SQL Proxy works by having a local client called eth-proxy running in the local environment. Your application will directly communicate with the SQL proxy not through IP but by using the standard database protocol that is used by your database. To accomplish this task the Proxy will establish and use a secure tunnel to communicate with its companion process running on the server.

Cloud Spanner

If Cloud SQL does not fit your capacity criteria because you need large scale horizontal scalability, then you might consider using Cloud Spanner. This is the specialist fully-managed storage service built by Google to scale for the Cloud. Cloud Spanner is designed specifically to combine the benefits of relational database structures with non-relational horizontal scale. This means that the Spanner SQL service can provide petabytes of capacity, support over 4,000 concurrent connections and offer transactional consistency at global scale. Just like Cloud SQL it supports schemas, SQL, as well as automatic synchronous replication for high availability and business continuity.
In addition to its design-criteria for scalability the Cloud Spanner service is also designed to deliver strong consistency including strongly consistent secondary indexes. It also natively provides SQL support with alter statements for schema changes. Moreover, Cloud Spanner also offers managed instances with inherent high availability through transparent synchronous built-in data replication. These features make large transactional intensive operations such as financial trading systems and inventory management applications traditionally served by a relational database technology the most suitable use cases for Cloud Spanner.

Cloud Spanner use cases

In order to better understand the concept behind Cloud Spanner and how we can benefit from its vast scale yet high consistency it is often beneficial to compare it with both relational and non-relational databases. After all Cloud Spanner is designed to be like a relational database, as it has schema, SQL and strong data consistency. But, it is designed to resemble a non-relational database as Cloud Spanner offers high availability, horizontal scalability and configurable replication. Cloud Spanner is essentially a hybrid that offers the best features of the relational and non-relational worlds. These features deliver the performance that match mission critical use cases, such as building consistent systems for financial trading, ecommerce transactions and inventory management in the financial services and retail industries. Cloud Spanner supports many open standards. It also supports many workloads like transactional workloads where companies that have outgrown their single instance relational database management system and have already moved to a NoSQL solution but need transactional consistency or are looking to move to a scalable solution.

Cloud Spanner also allows for database consolidation where companies that store their business data in multiple database products with variable maintenance overheads and capabilities need consolidation of their data. To a better understand how all of this works, let's look at the architecture of Cloud Spanner.

Cloud Spanner Architecture

A Cloud Spanner instance will replicate data in 'n' cloud zones which can be contained within one region or spread across several regions. This feature of configurable database placement means you can not only choose which region to put your database in for performance, politics or legal constraints. You can also use this choice of placement to design an architecture, which allows for high-performance, high-availability and global reachability.

This is due to the high-speed replication of data being synchronized across zones over Google's global fibre network. This high speed, SDN network uses atomic clocks that ensure atomicity when you're updating your data. This ensures the high levels of data consistency demanded by large global transactional systems.

IAM Roles

Cloud Spanner has its own set of IAM access roles. This allows you to have the same security mechanisms without having to create something separate for your database. These IAM permissions can be granted to a database, instance or GCP project.

The predefined roles that you will use at either a project or database level are:

- roles/spanner.admin – This is recommended at the project level and it provides for; Grant and revoke permissions to other principals for all Cloud Spanner resources in the project; Allocate and delete chargeable Cloud Spanner resources; Issue get/list/modify operations on Cloud Spanner resources; Read from and write to all Cloud Spanner databases in the project; Fetch project metadata.

- roles/spanner.databaseAdmin - This is recommended at the project level and it provides for; Get/list all Cloud Spanner instances in project; Create/list/drop databases in the instance on which it is granted; Grant/revoke access to databases in the project; Read from and write to all Cloud Spanner databases in the project.

- roles/spanner.databaseReader – This is a machine role so it is applied at the database level. It provides for; Read from the Cloud Spanner database; Execute SQL queries on the database; View schema for the database.

- roles/spanner.viewer – This is a person role applied at the project level and provides for; View all Cloud Spanner instances (but cannot modify instances); View all Cloud Spanner databases (but cannot modify databases and cannot read from databases).

Like all predefined roles in IAM you can combine roles for added flexibility. For example you could combine the roles/spanner.viewer so that they can have view only access to all instances and databases with the roles/spanner.databaseUser to grant a user access to a specific database.

Additional features in Cloud Spanner

Cloud Spanner offers many features such as tables, primary and secondary keys, database splits, transactions and timestamp bounds. However to understand what features are essential to you and under what circumstances you would use Cloud Spanner, you need to consider a few salient points.
 If you have outgrown your existing relational database or are sharding your databases for high performance throughput. Then you are probably looking for transactional consolidation for global data with strong consistency in your databases, then you should consider using Cloud Spanner.
If you however you feel that these features are not essential and you don't need many of these relational focused capabilities, consider a NoSQL server such as Cloud Datastore which we will cover next.

Cloud Datastore

If you're looking for a highly scalable database, but do not need relational properties then a NoSQL database might be the answer. A NoSQL database will allow you to store structured data for your web and mobile applications if these are your typical use cases then you should consider using Cloud Datastore. A key benefit of using the Cloud Datastore service is its ability to scale seamlessly as your application's data storage needs grow. This allows you to concentrate on developing your applications rather than concerning yourself with capacity planning and trying to forecast for anticipated loads.
Another key feature is that Datastore is schema-less, which provides you with a much more flexible data structure. This is also important as it again means that you can concentrate on writing the application rather than struggling with modelling the database schema.

Furthermore, you can think of Cloud Datastore as a persistent hash map that can scale to terabytes of capacity. Cloud Datastore is a managed service and that means it handles all regional and multi-regional replication and sharding on your behalf, while maintaining a good balance of strong and eventual consistency. This is because Cloud Datastore will strive to find the entities that match the lookup key and in the case of ancestor queries they will always receive strongly consistent data. All other queries are deemed to be eventually consistent. This consistency model facilitates the delivery of strong query consistency while handling large amounts of multi-regional data and a global user base.

Yet this is a simple and flexible database, which is easy to provision and integrate making it a perfect point of connection for web and mobile apps that span across App Engine and Compute Engine.

Datastore use cases

Indeed, one of Cloud Datastore's original purpose and its main use cases is to store structured data from App Engine apps. You can think of Cloud Datastore as a persistent hash map that can scale to terabytes of capacity yet it can perform at the highest levels despite its scale. A hash map can be thought of as a collection of key and value pairs where each key maps to a value. Cloud Datastore's performance though comes about because it is paired with a Memcache service to increase performance for repeatedly read data. Typically in development, the App Engine application will try Memcache first, and then on a cache miss, access Cloud Datastore. This strategy radically improves performance and reduces costs.

In addition, Cloud Datastore provides a myriad of capabilities, such as ACID transactions, SQL-like queries, indexes, and much more.

Datastore structure

Despite the Cloud Datastore interface sharing many of the same features as a traditional database it is actually a No-SQL database. As such it differs from traditional relational databases in the way that it describes relationships between data objects. We can see this in this table;

In Cloud Datastore, a category of object is known as a kind, an object is an entity, individual data for an object is a property, and a unique ID for an object is a key, whereas in a relational database these would be table, row, field, and primary key respectively.

Also, built-in to Datastore is synchronous replication over a wide geographic area. When you first create a Cloud Datastore you must choose a location where the projects data is stored. To reduce latency and increase availability store your data close to the users and services that need it.

GQL

Cloud Datastore does not use SQL as there is no concept of tables, rows and columns. However, it does have a way to make similar type queries and that is by using an API called GQL.

Here is an example of a GQL query:

// List Google companies with less than 400 employees.

var companies = query.filter('name =', 'Google').filter('size <', 400);

Cloud Datastore actually originated from Google's internal-use database, Megastore, and it is believed to be going to be superseded by Google Firestore, which is part of the Google mobile platform suite.

IAM Roles

With IAM, every API method in Datastore mode requires that the account making the API request has the appropriate permissions to use the resource. Permissions are granted by setting policies that grant roles to a user, group, or service account. In addition to the primitive roles, owner, editor, and viewer, you can grant Datastore mode roles to the users of your project. The following list shows the Datastore mode IAM roles:

- roles/datastore.owner with roles/appengine.appAdmin – Gives full Datastore admin
- roles/datastore.owner without roles/appengine.appAdmin - Full access to Datastore mode except the user, group, or service account cannot: enable Admin access; see if Datastore mode Admin is enabled; disable Datastore mode writes; see if Datastore mode writes are disabled

- roles/datastore.user - Read/write access to data in a Datastore mode database. Intended for application developers and service accounts.
- roles/datastore.viewer - Read access to all Datastore mode resources.
- roles/datastore.importExportAdmin - Full access to manage imports and exports.
- roles/datastore.indexAdmin - Full access to manage index definitions.

You can grant multiple roles to a user, group, or service account. However something that you should be aware of is that an entity that is assigned the App Engine owner, editor, and viewer primitive roles and the App Engine Admin predefined role have complete access to the Datastore mode Admin page.

Geographical Database Placement

There are two types of geographical placement where you can store data using Cloud Datastore, multi-regional locations and regional locations. Both of these options have trade-offs you will need to consider when evaluating the best placement for your apps. Multi-regional locations provide multi-region redundancy with higher availability. On the other hand Regional locations provide lower write latency and the opportunity to co-locate within the same region/zone as your other GCP resources that your application may use.
Both of these options provide high availability but with slightly different SLAs for monthly uptime percentage.

Cloud Firestore

Cloud Firestore is a cloud-native database, which has been introduced as an upgrade to Cloud Datastore to deliver a more scalable solution. Indeed Firestore is built from the ground up to take advantage of Google Cloud Platform's powerful infrastructure. It is designed to provide a great developer experience and simplify app development with live synchronization, offline support, and ACID transactions across hundreds of documents and collections. Cloud Firestore is integrated with both Google Cloud Platform (GCP) and Firebase, Google's mobile development platform.

Cloud Firestore is a flexible, NoSQL, scalable database for mobile, web, and server development on the Google Cloud Platform. Firestore is the successor or next generation of Cloud Datastore as it has a few key advantages. Although for backwards compatibility Cloud Firestore can operate in Datastore mode, making it fully compatible with Cloud Datastore. To do this you can create a Cloud Firestore database in Datastore mode, which makes it compatible so that you can access Cloud Firestore's improved storage layer while also maintaining your business logic and query behaviour. Cloud Firestore in Datastore mode removes the following Cloud Datastore limitations:

• Queries are no longer eventually consistent; instead, they are all strongly consistent.

• Transactions are no longer limited to 25 entity groups.

• Writes to an entity group are no longer limited to 1 per second. Datastore and Firestore are both NoSQL databases but they are designed for different purposes, with the latter targeted at web and mobile applications. Both Datastore and Firestore scale from zero upwards but, if you require NoSQL flexibility and efficiency but also need vast scale but importantly, you don't require transactional consistency, you might want to consider Cloud Bigtable.

Cloud Bigtable

Cloud Bigtable is Google's NoSQL Big Data database service. Cloud Bigtable is a sparsely populated table that can scale to billions of rows and thousands of columns allowing you to store terabytes or even petabytes of data.

Cloud Bigtable is ideal for storing very large amounts of single key data with very low latency. A single value in each row is indexed and this value is known as the row key.

Cloud Bigtable also supports higher read and write throughput at low latency, which makes it suitable for both operational and analytical applications including IoT, user analytics and financial data analysis.

Cloud Bigtable is actually the same database that powers many of Google's core services including search, analytics, maps, and Gmail. Nonetheless, despite its pedigree Cloud Bigtable is simple to deploy and use as it is a fully managed NoSQL database with petabyte-scale and very low latency. Further, Bigtable can seamlessly scale for throughput and it also learns to adjust for specific access patterns.

There are different ways for applications to interact with Cloud Bigtable such as through multiple client libraries including a supported extension to Apache HBase library. Also, Cloud Bigtable also excels as a storage engine for batch Map Reduce operations, steam processing/analytics, and machine learning applications.

Cloud Bigtable's powerful backend servers offer several key advantages over a self-managed HBase installation. From a scalability perspective, a self-managed HBase installation has a design bottleneck that limits the performance after a certain query per second rate is reached. Cloud Bigtable does not have this bottleneck and so you can scale your cluster up to handle more queries by increasing your machine count.

Also, Cloud Bigtable handles administration tasks like upgrades and restarts transparently and can resize clusters without downtime.

Cloud Bigtable Structure

Cloud Bigtable stores data in massively scalable tables each of which is a sorted key value map. The table is composed of rows, each of which typically describes a single entity, and columns, which contain individual values for each row.

Each row is indexed by a single row key and columns that are related to one another are typically grouped together into a column family. Also, the tables within Cloud Bigtable are sparse, as every cell does not need to contain any data, hence it does not take up any space.

What is interesting about the Bigtable architecture is that processing is done through a front end server pool consisting of nodes, but this is handled separately from the storage. A table is sliced into a shard of blocks of contiguous rows called tablets which helps to balance the workload of queries. Tablets are stored on Colossus, which is Google's file system in SS table format. An SS table provides a persistent ordered immutable map from keys to values where both keys and values are arbitrary byte strings.

As mentioned earlier, Cloud Bigtable learns to adjust to specific access patterns. If a certain big table node is frequently accessing a certain subset of data, Cloud Bigtable will update the indexes so that the other nodes can distribute that workload more evenly. That throughput scales linearly. So, for every single node that you add, you're going to see a linear scale of throughput performance up to hundreds of nodes.

Cloud Bigtable use cases

In short, if you need to store more than one terabyte of structured data, have very high volumes of writes, need read-write latency of less than 10 milliseconds along with strong consistency, or need a storage service that is compatible with the HBase API, then you should consider using Cloud Bigtable.

However, the smallest Cloud Bigtable cluster you can create has three nodes and can handle 30,000 operations per second, but do you need that scale? Keep in mind that you pay for those nodes while they are operational whether your application is using them or not.

If you don't need any of these and are looking for a simple to use starter service that scales both up and down well, then consider using Cloud Datastore.

IAM Roles

Cloud Bigtable uses Google Cloud Identity and Access Management (IAM) for access control. However when using IAM for controlling access to Cloud Bigtable, you can configure access control at the project level and the instance level. You can use primitive roles (owner, editor and viewer) or predefined roles such as:

- roles/Bigtable.admin - Administers all instances within a project, including the data stored within tables. Can create new instances. Intended for project administrators.
- roles/Bigtable.user - Provides read-write access to the data stored within tables. Intended for application developers or service accounts.
- roles/Bigtable.reader - Provides read-only access to the data stored within tables. Intended for data scientists, dashboard generators, and other data-analysis scenarios.
- roles/Bigtable.viewer - Provides no data access. Intended as a minimal set of permissions to access the GCP Console for Cloud Bigtable.

If these predefined roles are not sufficient even in combination you can roll your own custom roles.

Comparing Data Storage Options

The problem that having a wide spectrum for data storage options is it can be confusing as to which option is the best choice. For example, Cloud data storage options on GCP range from the unstructured Cloud Storage to the structured relational options like Cloud SQL, to NoSQL Cloud Datastore, and then to options such as Cloud Bigtable, Cloud BigQuery, and Google Spanner. The last three however, as their names suggest, are focused on scalability and handling large volumes of data.

Use Case Summary
Cloud SQL

To summarise what we covered earlier Cloud SQL is a relational database that supports customized table views, stored procedures, tons of indexes and ACID compliance. If this is what you need then Cloud SQL is definitely your choice. However, it is not quite that simple as Google Cloud SQL database service supports three popular types of databases: MySQL , SQL Server and PostgreSQL. Both these options support High Availability (HA) and Pay per Use without Lock-in. In addition Cloud SQL can scale up to 32 processor cores and more than 200GB RAM. This option is popular as it does make moving your data from on-premises to the cloud easier. However you do miss out on some of the key advantages of the cloud as it does have all the limitations inbuilt in MySQL, SQL Server and PostgreSQL that they do not scale well for huge data volume.

Cloud Datastore

Google Cloud Datastore is the GCP NoSQL database for web and mobile applications. It is a scalable NoSQL database as it automates sharding and replication but interestingly it also supports ACID transaction, SQL-like queries and REST API. Datastore is optimized for smaller set of data, which for most general purposes this is what you will be looking for rather than its sibling, Bigtable. Although Cloud Datastore is a NoSQL data storage so there is no need to define a schema before storing data, it actually uses more capacity when having to do ad-hoc storage of structured data.

Cloud Firestore

Essentially, Cloud Firestore's is GCP's next generation NoSQL database but with Cloud Firestore you store data in structures called documents, which contain fields mapping to values. These documents are then stored in collections, which are containers for your documents, which are used to organize your data and make it easier to build queries. Documents support many different data types, from simple strings and numbers, to complex, nested objects and you can create sub-collections within documents and build hierarchical data structures that scale as your database grows. Additionally, the way that you make a query in Cloud Firestore is efficient and flexible as you can create queries to retrieve data targeted at the document level. This means you do not need to retrieve the entire collection, or for that matter any nested sub-collections. Furthermore you can also add sorting, filtering, and limits to your queries to make them more expressive and to paginate the results. The Cloud Firestore data model supports whatever data structure works best for your app and to keep data in your apps current, without retrieving your entire database each time an update happens, you can also add realtime listeners. This feature also keeps your data in sync across client apps, which makes it popular for mobile apps and offers offline support for mobile and web so you can build responsive apps that work regardless of network latency or Internet connectivity. Finally, we can consider that Cloud Firestore also offers you the opportunity for seamless integration with other Firebase Platform and Google Cloud Platform products.
Pricing
When you use Cloud Firestore, you are charged for the following:

- The number of reads, writes, and deletes that you perform.
- The amount of storage that your database uses, including overhead for metadata and indexes.
- The amount of network bandwidth that you use.
- Storage and bandwidth usage are calculated in gigabytes (GiB), where 1 GiB = 230 bytes. All charges accrue daily.

However you get 1GB of free storage per month and 50,000 document reads per day as well as 20,000 document writes and deletes per day. After that quota has been exceeded the price is $0.06 per read, $0.18 per write and $0.02 per delete. Storage is charged at $0.18 per Gigabyte per month.

Bigtable

Google Bigtable is Google's cloud storage solution for high-performance and low latency data access. It is widely used in many Google's core services like Google Search, Google Maps, and Gmail. Big Table, like Cloud Datastore is designed in NoSQL architecture, but it can still use row-based data format. Where Big Table comes into its own is in throughput as it can handle data read/write under 10 milliseconds, which means it is perfect for those applications that have frequent and large amounts of data ingestion. Furthermore, unlike Datastore, which is similar in purpose, it is designed to scale to hundreds of petabytes and handle millions of operations per second (IOPS).

What makes Bigtable popular is its compatibility with HBase 1.0 API via extensions as this simplifies any migration from HBase. Bigtable, like Cloud Datastore, has no SQL interface and you can only use the API to use Put/Get/Delete commands on individual rows or run scan operations. Bigtable can also be readily integrated with other GCP tools, like Cloud Dataflow and Dataproc.

Pricing

Unlike other cloud providers, GCP prices the compute and storage separately therefore you will need to consider the following three billable items when calculating the overall cost.

1. The type of Cloud instance, and the number of nodes in the instance.
2. The total amount of storage you use.
3. The amount of network bandwidth used by egress traffic.

The problem here is that although it is good that you are billed only for active instances and you pay only for the storage used it is not easy to forecast if you have a large datasets. Moreover, the compute cost becomes less important as it is the same no matter if you choose an SSD or an HDD storage type. For example the difference in performance between SSD and HDD are not comparable. For example, although the timing to perform writes is the same for both cases, the timing for reads is about 20 times faster with SSD. Of course there is a case for going with HDD as scans for HDD lags behind SSD by just 20%. Hence, if you know your access pattern is mostly going to be scans, then HDD option might be a good option as HDD storage is only 15% of the cost of SSD.

BigQuery

Finally we will address BigQuery as it is Google's Cloud-based version of a data warehouse. But, unlike Bigtable, it targets data as a big picture and can run a query against vast volumes of data in a short time. This is because in BigQuery the data is stored in columnar data format so it is much faster in scanning large amounts of data compared with Bigtable. In addition, BigQuery allows you to scale to petabyte and is targeted at the enterprise data warehouse for analytics market space. BigQuery is serverless, which means it is a fully managed service. Serverless computing also benefits from seamless scalability as computing resource can be spun up on-demand without involving administrators managing any infrastructure. As a result of this transparent scalability BigQuery can scan Terabytes of data in seconds and Petabytes of data in minutes. On the other hand with regards data ingestion, BigQuery integrates to load or stream data from/to Google Cloud Storage, or Google Cloud Datastore. However, we must remember that BigQuery is designed as a data warehouse so is best for analytical (OLAP) type of query and scanning large amount of data and is not designed for transaction type queries (OLTP). For example, for small read/writes, it takes about 2 seconds while Bigtable takes about 9 milliseconds for the same amount of data. Bigtable is much better off for OLTP type of queries. Although BigQuery support atomic single-row operations, it lacks cross-row transaction support.
For pricing, there are two major components in the cost of using BigQuery: Storage Cost and Query Cost.
For storage cost, it is $0.02 per GB/month. However, Google has a long term storage pricing, which is 50% off to $0.01 per GB/month. The definition that Google uses is that long term storage is defined as a table that is not edited for 90 days. Each partition in the table is considered separate storage. So you could have standard pricing for some recent partitions while have long term storage pricing for some historical partitions. Even the data is in long term storage, there is no degradation of performance, durability and availability.

For query cost, the first 1 TB of data processed in a month is free, and then it is $5 per TB. No charge for cached queries. As BigQuery is stored in columnar data format, the query cost is based on the columns selected. For enterprise with large amount of data and tons of applications, although the bill for data storage is predictable, the bill for query cost is not. The good news is that Google does offer a flat rate monthly cost model instead of on-demand pricing. For example, you could decide to pay $5,000 for 100 BigQuery Slots and then BigQuery will automatically manage the quota.

Cloud Spanner

Cloud Spanner is a globally distributed database and it is a versioned key-value store. From this perspective, it is similar to Bigtable. However, it supports general-purpose transactions and also provides SQL-based query language.

Two stands out features of Cloud Spanner are:

1. Replication Configuration

Data replication is handled automatically and transparently. But user application can control the way how data is stored. For example, if user data has the requirement to stay in USA only, you could specify to store data in US data centres only. If you want to improve the read performance and availability, you could increase the number of replicas used and geographic placement of replicas to make the data is close to the users as much as possible. If you want to have fast write throughput, you could decide how far replicas are from each other.

2. A globally-distributed database does allow consistent reads and writes. This feature is critical if you want to have a consistent backup, or have consistent reads at global scale. The implementation of this feature is using Google's TrueTime. Instead of using only one source for the time reference, TrueTime is based on the time references from both GPS and atomic clocks. Google indicates the reason to use two different kinds of time reference because they have different failure models. The use of atomic clocks is essential as you need precision as standard clocks can fail over long periods of time or drift significantly.

Spanner is organized in a set of zones. Each zone has one zone master and 100 to 1000 spanserver. Each table is split into multiple tablets. A table's state is stored in set of B-tree like structure files and Write-Ahead Log on a file system called Colossus. Colossus is a global distributed file system and the successor to Google File System (GFS). Spanner's data model is a hybrid so not relational instead it can be considered to be semi-relational. Each row must have a unique name, and each table must have an ordered set of one or more primary-key columns. Google publishes a Best Practice for Spanner Schema Design.

The following shows the option to create a Spanner instance with 10 nodes.

The storage cost is $0.30 per GB/month and $9 per hour per node. Each Spanner node can provide up to 10,000 QPS of reads or 2000 QPS of writes (writing single rows at 1KB data per row), and 2 TB disk storage. Google also recommend provision more spanner nodes to keep CPU utilization below 75%.

Among these five database storage options in GCP, deciding the best option can be problematic so Google has provided a decision tree to help you to determine the best option for you.

Figure 15

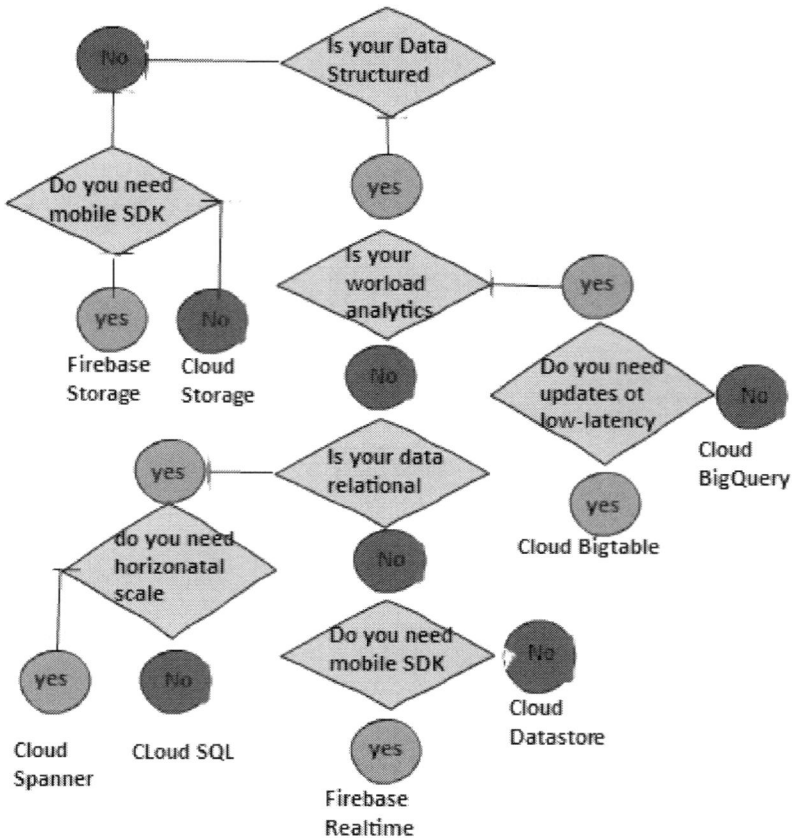

Summary

In this chapter, we covered the different data storage services that GCP offers. Specifically, you learned about cloud storage, a fully managed object store. Cloud SQL, which is a fully managed MySQL, SQL Server or PostgreSQL database service. Cloud spanner, which is also a relational database service with transactional consistency, global scale, and high availability features. Also we considered Cloud Datastore, a fully managed NoSQL document database, and introduced its successor in many ways, Cloud Firestore. Finally, we contemplated Cloud Bigtable, which is a fully managed NoSQL wide column database.

From an infrastructure perspective, the goal was to understand what services are available, and how they're used in different circumstances.

Use Case – 15

You are required to accomplish the following tasks, 1) transfer data from Cloud Storage in project A into project B. 2) transfer data from Cloud Storage to BigQuery, How can you go about this?
Solution
Moving data between projects involves the following steps:

1. Create a Cloud Storage bucket to hold the data from your source project A.
2. Export the data from your source project to the bucket you have just created.
3. Give your destination project B the required permissions to read from the new bucket.
4. Import the data from the new bucket into your destination project B.

With regards the transfer of data from Cloud Storage to BigQuery you must provide the Cloud Storage URI. The Cloud Storage URI comprises your bucket name and your object (filename). For example, if the Cloud Storage bucket is named projectabucket and the data file is named projecta.csv, the bucket URI would be gs://proctectabucket/projecta.csv. You can also use a wildcard in the URI if you a multiple objects.

1. Browse the list of buckets and objects using the 'gsutil ls', command to view all the buckets and objects.
2. Compose the URI, by replacing the URL parameters, i.e. gs://bucket/file with the appropriate path, for example, gs://projectabucket/projecta.json. Where the bucket is the Cloud Storage bucket name and file is the name of the object (file) containing the data.
3. To import the data into BigQuery you will have to have the relevant permission these roles have them; bigquery.dataEditor, bigquery.dataOwner, bigquery.admin

4. You can then use the console or the bq load command to update a table and load the data in a single step.

Part III – Data Engineering on GCP

Chapter 25 – Data Lifecycle from a GCP Perspective

The Google Cloud Platform (GCP) has a catalogue of services designed to manage data throughout its entire lifecycle, from initial acquisition to final visualization. In this part of the book you will learn about the features and functionality of each service that relate to data engineering so that you can make informed decisions about which services and infrastructures will best fit your workload and budget.

GCP Data Lifecycle

When we contemplate data from the perspective of data engineering we discover that the data lifecycle has four distinct stages.
- **Ingest**: The initial stage in the data life-cycle is when we collect and ingest raw data, this can be through triggered events, messaging services or streaming data from devices.
- **Store**: After the data has been collected, the data will need to be stored somewhere that is durable and in a format that can be easily accessed.
- **Process and analyse**: When it comes to processing the data it will need to be transformed from its original raw format into some sort of actionable information.
- **Explore and visualize**: The final stage is to produce the output of the transformation into presentable results in a format that is easy to analyse and enable users to draw insights.

Let's look at each stage from the perspective of GCP in more detail:

Ingest

When we contemplate how to collect and ingest raw data into our systems there are a number of approaches available and these are typically determined based on the data's size, source, and tolerance of latency. For example:

- **Apps**: Data that is generated from app events, such as log files or user events is typically collected from the app using a push model. This is where the app calls an API to send or 'push' the data to a storage area.
- **Streaming**: In this case the data consists of a continuous stream of small, asynchronous messages with unbounded limits so it can be considered infinite in size and duration.
- **Batch**: This is where we handle large but bounded amounts of data – with a distinct start and finish - these are stored in a set of files that are transferred to storage in bulk.

The following chart shows how GCP services map to app, streaming, and batch workloads.

Application	Streaming	Batch
Stackdriver Logging	Cloud Pub/Sub	Cloud Storage
Cloud Pub/Sub	Cloud Dataflow	Cloud Transfer Service
Cloud SQL		Cloud Appliance

Cloud Datastore	Cloud Dataproc
Cloud Bigtable	
Cloud Firestore	
Cloud Spanner	

The data transfer model you choose depends on your workload, and each model has different infrastructure requirements.

Ingesting app data

Whether hosted on-premises or in the cloud apps generate a significant amount of data that can be further analysed to reveal user trends and provide valuable business insights.

However it is when you move the apps and services to GCP that you get the full benefit of having a variety of integrated services you can use to host apps such as:

- Virtual machines in Compute Engine,
- the managed platform of App Engine,
- the container management of Google Kubernetes Engine (GKE) or
- The serverless platform of Function Engine or
- The serverless platform for stateless HTTP containers deployed in Cloud Run or Cloud Run on GKE

These services are highly integrated with all the GCP tools and processes for data management so they enable us to build tightly-coupled architectures for data processing.

For example:

- **Writing data to a file**: An app can output batch CSV files directly to Cloud Storage, which in turn triggers an event, which allows the import function of BigQuery to pull the data from Cloud Storage into BigQuery for analysis.

- **Writing data to a database**: A more typical solution is where an app writes data directly to the managed MySQL of Cloud SQL or the NoSQL databases such as Cloud Datastore or Cloud Bigtable.
- **Streaming data as messages**: In this scenario an app streams data into the real-time messaging service Cloud Pub/Sub. A second app, can then subscribe to the messages within a specific topic, and subsequently transfer the data either to storage or it may process it immediately in situations such as in an IoT control process.

Nonetheless, there are plenty of other benefits to be had when hosting your apps and services on the Google Cloud Platform, such as:

Stackdriver Logging: Centralized log management

When your apps are hosted on GCP you can easily collect the logs via integrated Stackdriver logging and then store them using built-in tools that send the data to Cloud Storage, Cloud Pub/Sub, and BigQuery.
In addition you can use the Logging service to stream log data from common third-party apps and system software to Stackdriver Logging using the fluentd agent. The agent runs on a VM in GCE or on a container cluster managed by GKE.

Ingesting streaming data

When it comes to ingesting data from the IoT or for telemetry you will often be required to handle streaming data. Streaming data comes with its own challenges as you have to manage the delivery of many small messages that are sent asynchronously, without expecting a reply. Streaming data can be used for firing event triggers, performing real-time analysis, as well as being used as an input for machine learning tasks.

Cloud Pub/Sub: Real-time messaging

When dealing with streaming asynchronous data streams between apps there needs to be some intermediary service that can act as a messenger service. In GCP that messenger is the Cloud Pub/Sub service, which allows you to send and receive messages between apps in real-time.

As streaming data is often generated by users or systems distributed across the globe Cloud Pub/Sub has global endpoints that leverages Google's global front-end load balancer to support data ingestion across all GCP regions, with minimal latency. In addition, Cloud Pub/Sub scales quickly and automatically to meet demand, without requiring the developer to pre-provision the system infrastructure or resources.

Cloud Pub/Sub doesn't provide guarantees about the order of message delivery. However, strict message ordering can be achieved with buffering or using Cloud Dataflow.

A reason to deploy Cloud Pub/Sub is to reliably move streaming data from an app or service into Cloud Dataflow for real-time processing. When processed, the output can be collected by a subscriber app or delivered to a persistent storage service, such as Cloud Datastore and BigQuery, which support queries ordered by app timestamps.

Kafka on GCP (Confluent Cloud on GCP)

GCP now offers a managed version of Apache Kafka through a partnership with Confluent as Kafka has become a leading open-source solution for event streaming. When it comes to stream ingestion, Google Cloud Pub/Sub is GCP's inbuilt messaging service but sometimes the open source Kafka can make more sense. For example customers migrating to the cloud may not want to rewrite their on-premises systems to GCP-native services such as Pub/Sub. Others may have adopted an event sourcing model that is uniquely dependent on Kafka's log data structure.

Confluent Cloud on GCP is a fully-managed streaming service based on Apache Kafka, which provides enterprises with a real-time streaming platform built on a reliable, scalable ecosystem. Furthermore, Kafka offers a broad range of connectors, plug-ins, monitoring tools, and configuration tools as well as a thriving developer community. Confluent on GCP integrates this Kafka ecosystem with GCP's big data and machine learning services, and provides a managed service for Kafka, which abstracts the underlying cluster infrastructure and removes the provisioning maintenance burden for developers looking to build streaming applications.

Confluent Cloud on GCP complements GCP's own stream analytics and data warehousing services. For example, Cloud Dataflow service and BigQuery integrate natively with Kafka as do Google's other analytics, machine learning, and serverless compute services.

Ingesting bulk data

Advanced analytics and Machine Learning is not just about handling streaming data as there is also the issue of dealing with bulk or typically historical data. This consists of handling large datasets where ingestion requires that you have high aggregate bandwidth between a small number of sources and the target. This requires a different set of tools as the data could be stored in diverse systems or formats. Furthermore, the source data could be located on-premises or on other cloud platforms. Efficiently transporting this quantity of data raises another set of technical issues.

Storage Transfer Service: Managed file transfer

To be able to transport bulk - data volumes greater than 1 TB - requires specialist services such as GCP's Storage Transfer Service, which manages the transfer of data to a Cloud Storage bucket. The data source can be an AWS S3 bucket, a web-accessible URL, or another Cloud Storage bucket.

Or you can move data between Cloud Storage buckets, such as archiving data from a Multi-Regional Storage bucket to a Nearline Storage bucket to lower storage costs.

Transfer Appliance: Shippable, high-capacity storage server

For really large bulk transfers – 60 TB - you may need to do this offline by using the Transfer Appliance, which is a high-capacity storage server that you lease from Google. You connect it to your network, load it with data, and ship it to an upload facility where the data is uploaded to Cloud Storage.

Cloud Storage gsutil: Command-line interface

Cloud Storage provides gsutil, a command-line utility that you can use to move file-based data from any existing file system into Cloud Storage. The utility gsutil is written in Python so it runs on Linux, MacOS and Windows systems.

Cloud Storage Offline Media Import / Export

Offline Media Import / Export is a third party solution you can use to load data into Cloud Storage by sending your physical media, such as hard disk drives, tapes, and USB flash drives, to a third party service provider who uploads data on your behalf. Offline Media Import / Export can be helpful if you're limited to a slow, unreliable, or expensive internet connection.

Database migration tools

If your source data is stored in an on-premise database or hosted by another cloud provider, there are several third-party apps you can use to move your data into GCP. These apps are often co-located in the same environment as the source systems and provide both one-time and on-going transfers. For example, apps such as Talend and Informatica provide extract-transform-load (ETL) capabilities with built-in support for GCP. GCP has several target databases suitable for migrating data from external databases.

*   **Relational databases**: Data stored in a relational database management system (RDBMS) can be migrated to Cloud SQL and Cloud Spanner.
*   **Data warehouses**: Data stored in a data warehouse can be moved to BigQuery.
*   **NoSQL databases**—Data stored in a column-oriented NoSQL database, such as HBase or Cassandra, can be migrated to Cloud Bigtable. Data stored in a JSON-oriented NoSQL database, such as Couchbase or MongoDB, can also be migrated to a Cloud Datastore instance.

Store

Data comes in many different shapes and sizes, and its structure is wholly dependent on the sources from which it was generated and the subsequent downstream use cases. For data and analytics workloads, ingested data can be stored in a variety of formats or locations.

Storing object data

Files are a common format for storing data, especially bulk data. With GCP you can upload your file data to Cloud Storage, which makes that data available to a variety of other services.

Cloud Storage: Managed object storage

Cloud Storage offers durable and highly-available object storage, which means it can store both structured and unstructured data. Files in Cloud Storage are organized by project into individual buckets. You control access to these storage buckets via IAM permissions or through custom access control lists (ACLs).

Because of Cloud Storage's versatility it is used as a staging post for uploading data into the GCP. Cloud Storage acts as a distributed storage layer, accessible by apps and services as well as through other channels such as Stackdriver Logging or Monitoring.

Cloud SQL: Managed MySQL, SQL Server and PostgreSQL engines

Cloud SQL is a fully managed, cloud-native RDBMS that offers MySQL, SQL Server and PostgreSQL engines with built-in support for replication. It's useful for low-latency, transactional, relational database workloads. Because it's based on MySQL, SQL Server and PostgreSQL, Cloud SQL supports standard APIs for connectivity. Cloud SQL offers built-in backup and restoration, high availability, and read replicas.

Cloud SQL supports RDBMS workloads up to 10 TB for MySQL, SQL Server and PostgreSQL. Cloud SQL is accessible from apps running on App Engine, GKE, or Compute Engine.

However, Cloud SQL is not an appropriate storage system for online analytical processing (OLAP) workloads or data that requires dynamic schemas on a per-object basis. If your workload requires dynamic schemas, consider Cloud Datastore. For OLAP workloads, consider BigQuery. If your workload requires wide-column schemas, consider Cloud Bigtable.

For downstream processing and analytical use cases, data in Cloud SQL can be accessed from multiple platform tools. You can use Cloud Dataflow or Cloud Dataproc to create ETL jobs that pull data from Cloud SQL and insert it into other storage systems.

Cloud Bigtable: Managed wide-column NoSQL

Cloud Bigtable is a managed, high-performance NoSQL database service designed for terabyte- to petabyte-scale workloads. Cloud Bigtable is built on Google's internal Cloud Bigtable database infrastructure that powers Google Search, Google Analytics, Google Maps, and Gmail. The service provides consistent, low-latency, and high-throughput storage for large-scale NoSQL data. Cloud Bigtable is built for real-time app serving workloads, as well as large-scale analytical workloads.

Cloud Bigtable schemas use a single-indexed row key associated with a series of columns; schemas are usually structured either as TALL or WIDE and queries are based on row key. The style of schema is dependent on the downstream use cases and it's important to consider data locality and distribution of reads and writes to maximize performance. TALL schemas are often used for storing time-series events, data that is keyed in some portion by a timestamp, with relatively fewer columns per row. WIDE schemas follow the opposite approach, a simplistic identifier as the row key along with a large number of columns. Cloud Bigtable can also be used as a drop-in replacement for systems built using Apache HBase, an open source database based on the original Cloud Bigtable paper authored by Google. Cloud Bigtable is compliant with the HBase 1.x APIs so it can be integrated into many existing big-data systems. Apache Cassandra uses a data model based on the one found in the Cloud

Bigtable paper, meaning Cloud Bigtable can also support several workloads that leverage a wide-column-oriented schema and structure. While Cloud Bigtable is considered an OLTP system, it doesn't support multi-row transactions, SQL queries or joins. For those use cases, consider either Cloud SQL or Cloud Datastore.

BigQuery: Managed data warehouse

For ingested data that will be ultimately analysed in BigQuery, you can store data directly in BigQuery, bypassing other storage mediums. BigQuery supports loading data through the web interface, command line tools, and REST API calls.

For streaming data, you can use Cloud Pub/Sub and Cloud Dataflow in combination to process incoming streams and store the resulting data in BigQuery. In some workloads, however, it might be appropriate to stream data directly into BigQuery without additional processing.

Process and Analyse

In order to derive business value and insights from data, you must first transform and then analyse it. This requires a processing framework that can either analyse the data directly or prepare the data for downstream analysis. You will also need tools to analyse and understand the processed results.

- **Processing**: During this process the data ingested from source systems is cleansed, normalized, and processed across multiple machines, and then passed to the analytical systems.
- **Analysis**: Processed data is stored in the analytical systems this allows for ad-hoc querying and exploration.

- **Understanding**: Based on the analytical results, data can then be used to train and test automated machine-learning models.

GCP provides services to process large-scale data, to analyse and query big data, and to understand data through machine learning.

Processing large-scale data

Large-scale data processing typically involves reading data from source systems such as Cloud Storage, Cloud Bigtable, or Cloud SQL, and then conducting complex normalizations or aggregations of that data. In many cases, the data is too large to fit on a single machine so frameworks are used to manage distributed compute clusters.

Cloud Dataproc: Managed Apache Hadoop and Apache Spark

The capability to deal with extremely large datasets has evolved since Google first published the MapReduce paper in 2004. Many organizations now load and store data in Hadoop Distributed File System (HDFS) and run periodic aggregations, reports or transformations using traditional batch-oriented tools, such as Hive or Pig. Hadoop has a large ecosystem to support activities such as machine learning using Mahout, log ingestion using Flume, and statistics using R, amongst others. The results of this Hadoop-based data processing are often business critical so it is a non-trivial exercise to migrate them to a new framework.

Recently, Spark has gained popularity as an alternative to Hadoop MapReduce. This is due to Spark's performance, which is generally considerably faster than Hadoop MapReduce. Spark achieves this by distributing datasets and computation in memory across a cluster whereas MapReduce is optimised for disk access. In addition to the speed increases, Spark's distribution method provides the ability to deal with streaming data via Spark Streaming as well as handling the traditional batch analytics, transformations and aggregations using Spark SQL and a simple API. The Spark community is also very active and supports several popular libraries including MLlib, which is used for machine learning tasks. Nonetheless, when running either Spark or Hadoop at an ever-growing scale creates operational complexity and overhead as well as continuously growing costs. Even if an on-premise cluster is only needed at discrete intervals, you still end up paying the cost of a persistent cluster. However, these costs can be reduced by moving the cluster to the cloud. For example, with Cloud Dataproc, you can move your existing Hadoop or Spark deployments to a fully-managed service that automates cluster creation, simplifies configuration and management of your cluster, has built-in monitoring and utilization reports, and can be shut down when not in use.

Starting a new Cloud Dataproc cluster takes 90 seconds on average, which makes it easy to create a 10-node cluster or even a 1000-node cluster on demand. This reduces the operational and cost overhead of managing a Spark or Hadoop deployment, while still providing the familiarity and consistency of either framework. Cloud Dataproc provides the ease and flexibility to spin up Spark or Hadoop clusters on demand when they are needed, and to terminate clusters when they are no longer needed. Consider the following use cases.

- **Log processing**: With minimal modification, you can process large amounts of text log data once per day from several sources using existing MapReduce.
- **Reporting**: Aggregate data into reports and store the data in BigQuery. Then you can push the aggregate data to apps that power dashboards and conduct analysis.
- **On-demand Spark clusters**: Quickly launch ad-hoc clusters to analyse data stored in blob storage using Spark (Spark SQL, PySpark, Spark shell).
- **Machine learning**: Use the Spark Machine Learning Libraries (MLlib), which are preinstalled on the cluster, to customize and run classification algorithms.

Cloud Dataproc also simplifies operational activities such as installing software or resizing a cluster. With Cloud Dataproc, you can natively read data and write results in Cloud Storage, Cloud Bigtable, or BigQuery, or the accompanying HDFS storage provided by the cluster. With Cloud Storage, Cloud Dataproc benefits from faster access to data and the ability to have many clusters seamlessly operate on datasets with no data movement, as well as removing the need to focus on data replication. This ability to store and checkpoint data externally makes it possible for you to treat Cloud Dataproc clusters as ephemeral resources with external persistence, which can be launched, consumed, and terminated as required.

Cloud Dataflow: Serverless, fully managed batch and stream processing

Having the capability to analyse streaming real-time data has transformed the way organizations manage automation. However, having to maintain different processing frameworks to deal with batch and streaming analytics does increase the complexity as you need to support two different pipelines. This means spending time optimizing cluster utilization and resources for Spark and Hadoop jobs, which distracts from the basic objective of processing your data.
Fortunately, Cloud Dataflow has been designed for both streaming and batch workloads by merging the programming and execution model. Therefore, instead of you having to specify a cluster size and then managing capacity, Cloud Dataflow does this for you as it is a managed service where resources are created, autoscaled, and parallelized on-demand. Further, as a true ZERO-OPS service, Cloud Dataflow is constantly monitoring, identifying, and rescheduling work, including splits, to idle workers across the cluster - if needs be workers are added or removed based on the demands of the job.
Consider the following use-cases.

- **MapReduce replacement**: Process parallel workloads where non-MapReduce processing paradigms have led to operational complexity or frustration.
- **User analytics**: Analyse high-volume user-behaviour data, such as in-game events, click stream data, and retail sales data.
- **Data science**: Process large amounts of data to make scientific discoveries and predictions, such as genomics, weather, and financial data.
- **ETL**: Ingest, transform, and load data into a data warehouse, such as BigQuery.
- **Log processing**: Process continuous event-log data processing to build real-time dashboards, app metrics, and alerts.

The Cloud Dataflow SDK is perhaps better known as the open source project Apache Beam. Cloud Dataflow is an ideal place to run your Apache Beam workflows due essentially to its autoscaling and ease of deployment.

Cloud Dataprep: Visual data exploration, cleaning, and processing

Cloud Dataprep is a code-free service you can deploy for visually exploring, cleaning, and preparing data for analysis. Cloud Dataprep is accessible via a browser and it automatically deploys and manages any transformational resources it requires on demand.

With Cloud Dataprep, you can transform data of any size stored in CSV, JSON, or relational-table formats. Cloud Dataprep is integrated with Cloud Dataflow, which it uses to scale automatically to handle terabyte of data. Because Cloud Dataprep is fully integrated with GCP, you can process data in Cloud Storage, in BigQuery, or on-premises servers. Furthermore, you can output the clean and prepared data directly to BigQuery. Also, you can manage user access and data security with Cloud IAM.

Here are some common use cases for Cloud Dataprep:

- **Machine Learning**: You can clean training data for fine-tuning ML models.
- **Analytics**: You can transform raw data so that it can be ingested into data warehousing tools such as BigQuery.

Access and Query data

After data is ingested, stored, and processed, it needs to end up in a format that lets it be easily accessed and queried.

BigQuery: Managed data warehouse

BigQuery is a fully-managed data warehouse, which you can use to store, organise, analyse, and understand data. It uses standard SQL queries, business intelligence and visualization tools, so it provides a familiar interface.

Understanding data with machine learning

Machine learning has become a critical component of the analysis phase of the data lifecycle. It can be used to augment processed results, suggest data-collection optimizations, and predict outcomes in data sets. Consider the following use cases.

- **Product recommendations**: You can build a model that recommends products based on previous purchases and site navigation.
- **Prediction**: Use machine learning to predict the performance of complex systems, such as financial markets.

- **Automated assistants**: Build automated assistants that understand and answer questions asked by users.
- **Sentiment analysis**: Determine the underlying sentiment of user comments on product reviews and news stories.

There are a number of options for leveraging machine learning in GCP.

- **Task-specific machine learning APIs**: GCP provides turn-key, managed, machine-learning services with pre-trained models for vision, speech, natural language, and text translation. These APIs are built from the same technologies that power apps such as Google Photos, the Google mobile app, Google Translate, and Inbox smart replies. These pre-trained models require no user code you simply add the API to your app.
- **Custom machine learning**: AI Platform is a hosted, managed service that runs custom models at scale. In addition, Cloud Dataproc can also execute machine learning models built with Mahout or Spark MLlib.

Explore and Visualize

The final step in the data lifecycle is in-depth data exploration and visualization to better understand the results of the processing and analysis.

Fully exploring and understanding these data sets often involves the services of data scientists and business analysts, people trained in probability, statistics, and understanding business value. However the GCP has several services and tools that can assist you in gaining insights from your analysis.

Cloud Datalab: Interactive data insights

Cloud Datalab is an interactive web-based tool that you can use to explore, analyse and visualize data. It is built on top of Jupyter notebooks, which was formerly known as IPython. Using Cloud Datalab, you can, with a single click, launch an interactive web-based notebook where you can write and execute Python programs to process and visualize data. Out of the box, Cloud Datalab includes support for many popular data-science toolkits, including pandas, numpy, and scikit-learn, and common visualization packages, such as matplotlib. Cloud Datalab also includes support for TensorFlow and Cloud Dataflow. Using these libraries and cloud services, a data scientist can load and cleanse data, build and verify models, and then visualize the results using matplotlib. This works both for data that fits on a single machine or for data that requires a cluster to store and process it.

Visualizing business intelligence results

During the analysis phase, you might find it useful to generate complex data visualizations, dashboards, and reports to explain the results of the data processing to a broader audience. To make this easier, GCP integrates with a number of reporting and dash boarding tools.
Google Data Studio provides a drag-and-drop report builder that you can use to visualize data into reports and dashboards that can then share with others. The charts and graphs in the reports are backed by live data that can then be shared and updated. Reports can contain interactive controls allowing collaborators to adjust the dimensions used to generate visualizations.
With Data Studio, you can create reports and dashboards from existing data files, Google Sheets, Cloud SQL, and BigQuery. By combining Data Studio with BigQuery, you can leverage the full computing and storage

capacity of BigQuery without having to manually import data into Data Studio or create custom integrations.

If you prefer to visualize data in a spreadsheet, you can use Google Sheets, which integrates directly with BigQuery. Using Google Apps Script, you can embed BigQuery queries and data directly inside Google Sheets. You can also export BigQuery query results into CSV files and open them in Google Sheets or another spreadsheet. This is useful to create smaller datasets for sharing or analysis. You can also do the reverse, use BigQuery to query across distributed data sets stored in Google Sheets or files stored in Google Drive.

BigQuery also supports a range of third-party business intelligence tools and integrations, ranging from SaaS to desktop apps.

Orchestration

Incorporating all of the elements of the data lifecycle into a set of connected and cohesive operations requires some form of orchestration. Orchestration layers are typically used to coordinate starting tasks, stopping tasks, copying files, and providing a dashboard to monitor data processing jobs. For example, a workflow could include copying files into Cloud Storage, starting a Cloud Dataproc processing job, and then sending notifications when processing results are stored in BigQuery.

Orchestration workflows can range from simple to complex, depending on the processing tasks, and often use a centralized scheduling mechanism to run workflows automatically. There are several open-source orchestration tools that support GCP, such as Luigi and Airflow. For custom orchestration apps, you can create an App Engine app that uses built-in scheduled tasks functionality to create and run workflows.

Chapter 26 - Working with Cloud DataProc

Cloud Dataproc is a managed Spark and Hadoop service for batch processing, querying, streaming, and machine learning. Cloud Dataproc automation helps you spin-up and spin-down clusters on-demand, meaning you can save money by running clusters on a per job basis and turning them off when you don't need them.

Why use Cloud Dataproc?

The Hadoop Ecosystem is generally considered as a platform or a framework which is used to resolve Big Data analytical issues. However, establishing an on-premises cluster that meets everyone's requirements can be costly to set up and manage. You may boost the performance of workloads, including machine learning and data processing, by attaching graphics processing units (GPUs) to master and worker Compute Engine nodes in a Cloud Dataproc cluster. Also the job queuing for processing time on the cluster, which is often a feature with on-premise clusters no longer exists with Cloud DataProc. Indeed if you consider the options you might find that Cloud Dataproc has a number of unique advantages over on-premise solutions for clusters of three or even up to hundreds of nodes:

- Using unsupervised learning to aggregate your data into clusters and identify natural groupings is very helpful. The k-means algorithm has been used for everything from understanding customer segmentation to computer vision and astronomy.
- Dataproc automatically checks our agent for errors during training. This means you can access and choose to ignore or correct the errors to manage the quality and performance of your agent.
- Low cost — Cloud Dataproc is priced at only 1 cent per virtual CPU in your cluster per hour but this is on top of the other Cloud Platform resources you use. In addition you can create Cloud Dataproc clusters that include pre-emptible instances and this

further reduces your costs. Further, Cloud Dataproc charges you for resources used using second-by-second billing and a low, one-minute-minimum billing period.

- Fast provisioning —Cloud Dataproc clusters are easy and very quick to start, scale, and shutdown, each taking typically around 90 seconds or less. This makes it feasible to create a cluster per job i.e. create on-demand.

- Hence you can spend less time matching entities that require an exact match.

- Integrated — Cloud Dataproc has tight integration with other Google Cloud Platform services. This means it is inherently integrated with Cloud Storage, Cloud Bigtable, BigQuery, Stackdriver Logging, and Stackdriver Monitoring. This methodology means that you can build a complete data processing platform as opposed to having a stand-alone Hadoop/Spark cluster. For example, you can use Cloud Dataproc for an ETL pipeline that can handle the import of terabytes of raw log data directly into BigQuery without you having to understand the business reporting or writing any code.

- Managed — Cloud DataProc is a zero-ops system so you are free from any administrative burden. This means that you can interact with your clusters and jobs through the Google Cloud Platform Console, the Google Cloud SDK, or the Cloud Dataproc REST API. The real benefit though is that once your job finishes you can simply turn the cluster off, so you don't spend money or waste time administering or maintaining an idle cluster.

- Simple and familiar — You can use Spark and Hadoop clusters without the assistance of an administrator or special software as you don't need to learn new tools or APIs to use Cloud Dataproc. This makes it easy to move existing projects into Cloud Dataproc without redevelopment. Furthermore, Google handles software updates and as Spark, Hadoop, Pig, and Hive are frequently updated, this can save you a lot of time and effort.

Building a Demo Hadoop cluster on GCP

The easiest way to demonstrate how you can take advantage of the short term cluster per job model is to show the basic steps required to spin up a Hadoop cluster. You can do this using either the tradition method to build a Hadoop cluster, which is to create a group of VM instances and then manually install Hadoop cluster on these VM instances. This is the tried and tested method used both on-premises and in the cloud. However with Cloud DataProc there is a much quicker method. The caveat here is that with this method we are going to use Cloud Storage as the file system to replace HDFS. We can do this because Hadoop is actually only loosely coupled to HDFS so we can easily replace it with a Cloud Storage bucket. The followings show the steps to create a Hadoop Cluster using the browser and submit a spark job to the cluster.

1. Click Dataproc -> Clusters
2. Then click Enable API
3. Cloud Dataproc screen shows up -> Click Create cluster
4. Input the following parameters:

   - Name : cluster-test1
   - Region : Choose use-central1 (Global region is the default)
   - Zone : Choose us-central1-c

Then we have to create and configure the cluster;

1. Master Node
- Machine Type: The default is n1-standard-4, but I choose n1-standard-1 just for simple testing purpose.
- Cluster Mode: There are 3 modes here. Single Mode (1 master, 0 worker), Standard Mode (1 master, N worker), and High Mode (3 masters, N workers). Choose Standard Mode.
- Primary Disk Size: 10GB is sufficient for testing
2. Worker Nodes
   - Machine Type: The default is n1-standard-4, but I choose n1-standard-1 just for simple testing purpose.
   - Primary Disk Size: 15GB is sufficient for testing

You might notice that there is option to use local SSD storage. You can attach up to 8 local SSD devices to the VM instance. Each disk is 375 GB in size and you can not specify 10GB disk size here. The local SSDs are physically attached to the host server and offer higher performance and lower latency storage than Google's persistent disk storage. The local SSDs are used for temporary data like shuffling data in MapReduce. The data on the local SSD storage is not persistent.

Click Create, and the Hadoop cluster will be created in around 90 seconds.
To submit a Spark Job;
Click Cloud Dataproc -> Jobs.
It is as simple as that with the Cloud DataProc managed Hadoop and Spark service.

Building a Working Hadoop Environment in GCP

The only real difference here is that you will initially have to set up a dedicated project and billing – if that is an internal company requirement – and a VPC network.

You can create a Cloud Dataproc cluster using the Cloud SDK gcloud command-line tool in a local terminal window or in Cloud Shell, or from the Google Cloud Platform Console.

In the previous example, the required Compute Engine Virtual Machine instances (VMs) that were made for us for use in the Cloud Dataproc cluster, consisting of master and worker VMs. These VMs need to communicate directly with one another so they require full internal IP networking access. The Cloud DataProc cluster is normally constructed using the default network, which allows all intra-cluster traffic sourced from the 10.128.0.0/9 subnet, which ensures this access. However, when you are building your permanent Hadoop area you might want to create your own network in which to locate your Cloud Dataproc cluster(s). In this scenario you would need to create an appropriate firewall rule that reflected your own IP subnet range that allowed access to the 'udp:0-65535;tcp:0-65535;icmp' ports.

It is worth mentioning that if you have the default firewall rule allowing TCP traffic without any source tags or subnets listed such as:

```
gcloud compute firewall-rules create my-subnet-firewall-rule --allow tcp
```

Then the default subnet will allows ALL TCP traffic from ANY source, which is a huge security vulnerability. Therefore you should create a more specific rule such as:

```
gcloud compute firewall-rules create "tcp-rule" --allow tcp:80 \
    --source-ranges="10.0.0.0/22,10.0.0.0/14" \
    --description="Narrowing TCP traffic"
```

This rule allows traffic only from the local subnet to destination hosts on port 80.

Creating a VPC for Cloud DataProc

The other thing that you might want to do is provide greater segregation through specifying your own Virtual Private Cloud (VPC) network when you create a Cloud Dataproc cluster. To do this it is important to follow the correct order of task; first, you must first create a PVC network only then can you configure the associated firewall rules. Then, when you create the cluster, you can associate your network and its firewall rules with the cluster.

Something to note is that you have the choice of configuring an auto-mode PVC network or a custom-mode PVC. The difference is that with the auto-mode PVC everything is managed for you and IP addresses are assigned by default. On the other hand with the custom-mode PVC you will need to assign your own subnets and firewall rules. Hence, when you chose a custom-mode PVC you must specify the region and private IP address range for each subnetwork. To enable full internal access among VMs in the network, you can specify an IP address range of 10.128.0.0/16. You can use the Cloud SDK - gcloud dataproc clusters create - command with the --network or --subnet flag to create a cluster that will use an auto or custom subnetwork.

You can use the --network flag to create a cluster that will use a subnetwork with the same name as the network in the region where the cluster will be created.

```
gcloud dataproc clusters create my-cluster \
    --network network-name \
    ... other args ...
```

For example, since auto networks are created with subnets in each region with the same name as the auto network, you can pass the auto network name to the --network flag (--network auto-net-name) to create a cluster that will use the auto subnetwork in the cluster's region.

You can use the --subnet flag to create a cluster that will use an auto or custom subnetwork in the region where the cluster will be created. You must pass the --subnet flag the full resource path of the subnet your cluster will use.

```
gcloud dataproc clusters create cluster-name \
   --subnet projects/project-id/regions/region/subnetworks/subnetwork-name
   ... other args ...
```

Shared PVC

Another common network configuration for Cloud DataProc clusters is to set the host PVC as shared PVC that other authorised projects/users can participate in. This is called a Shared PVC or a Service Project. A Cloud Dataproc cluster can use a Shared VPC network by participating as a service project. With Shared VPC, the Shared VPC network is defined in a different project, which is called the host project. The host project is made available for use by IAM members in attached service projects.
To configure this setup an IAM member who is a Shared VPC Admin must perform the following tasks in order.

1. Configure and enable the Shared PVC
2. Connect the Cloud DataProc project to the host project
3. Configure either or both of the following service accounts to have the Network User role for the host project. Cloud Dataproc will attempt to use the first service account, falling back to the Google APIs service account if required: service-[project-number]@dataproc-accounts.iam.gserviceaccount.com
   Or you can use the Google APIs service account, [project-number]@cloudservices.gserviceaccount.com
4. Navigate to the IAM tab on the IAM & admin page.
5. Use the project drop-down list at the top of the page to select the host project.
6. Click ADD. Repeat these steps to add both service accounts:

7. Add the service account to the Members field.
8. From the Roles menu, select Compute Engine > Compute Network User.
9. Click Add.

Once you have the Cloud DataProc project and PVC network configured and the cluster built you will now we ready to run a job.
To run a job requires that you submit a job via either the console/browser, SDK or Cloud Shell. The following is an example of the submit command via Cloud Shell:

```
gcloud dataproc jobs submit job-command \

   --cluster cluster-name --region region \

   other dataproc-flags \

   -- job-args
```

Alternatively you can test the new Cloud DataProc cluster out using the inbuilt sample job that is preinstalled on the master node.
Spark job submit example:

```
//Run the SparkPi example pre-installed on the

//Cloud Dataproc cluster's master node

   gcloud dataproc jobs submit spark \

      --cluster cluster-name --region region \

      --class org.apache.spark.examples.SparkPi \
```

```
            --jars file:///usr/lib/spark/examples/jars/spark-
examples.jar \


            -- 1000
```

Terminal output:

Job [54825071-ae28-4c5b-85a5-58fae6a597d6] submitted.

Waiting for job output...

...

Pi is roughly 3.14177148

...

Job finished successfully.

Logging & Monitoring using Stackdriver

When a job runs in Cloud DataProc it outputs its status messages and details via the job driver. You can access Cloud Dataproc job driver output using the GCP Console, the gcloud command-line tool, or Cloud Storage. The output of the job driver is displayed on the console and you can see the output stream on another computer or a different window by passing the jobs ID to the 'gcloud dataproc jobs wait command' as shown below:

```
gcloud dataproc jobs wait 5c1754a5-34f7-4553-b667-8a1199cb9cab \

--project my-project-id --region my-cluster-region
```

Migration to the GCP

So how do customers migrate Hadoop clusters into the Google Cloud Platform and why?
The advantages are many so let's look at some:

- Pay for use – you can map your infrastructure to real world usage
- Scale as needed – and updated with the latest patches and security updates
- Flexible job execution – you can run a job per cluster and schedule jobs per cluster
- Job efficiency – by spinning up clusters per job allows schedulers to relay jobs as they are submitted
- Flexible job scheduling – although Cloud DataProc is a managed service it still allows you to have many controls that allow you to fine-tune the execution of a job
- Make HDFS data available – by using Cloud Storage as a source and destination it allows you to access and integrate with the data that would normally be siloed in HDFS storage.

Cloud DataProc	Google Cloud Platforms fully managed Apache Spark and Hadoop service
	Rapid cluster creation
	Ephemeral clusters on-demand
	Tightly integrated with other big data services on GCP
	Customizable machine-types
	Familiar open-source tools
	Integration with Stackdriver for logging

Hadoop Ecosystem in GCP

Dataproc for Hadoop:

Dataproc is considered as being the managed Hadoop service for the cloud. By using Dataproc in GCP, we can run Apache Spark and Apache Hadoop clusters on Google Cloud Platform in a powerful and cost-effective way. Dataproc is a fully managed Spark and Hadoop service that allows the user to create clusters quickly, and then hand off the cluster management to the service. Cloud Dataproc is best for environments which depend on specific components of the Apache big data ecosystem like tools/packages, pipelines, and skill sets of existing resources.

Dataflow for Hadoop

There is another service provided by Google for Hadoop, which is Cloud Dataflow. Dataflow is generally used when the user wants to perform Stream processing (ETL) and Batch processing (ELT). In Dataproc, we can only perform Batch processing. Also, Dataflow is used when the user wants a pre-processed workload for machine learning with Cloud ML Engine.

Dataflow uses Apache Beam and supports pipeline portability across Cloud Dataflow, Apache Spark, and Apache Flink as runtimes. To decide whether to use DataProc or Dataflow you can use the decision-tree below:

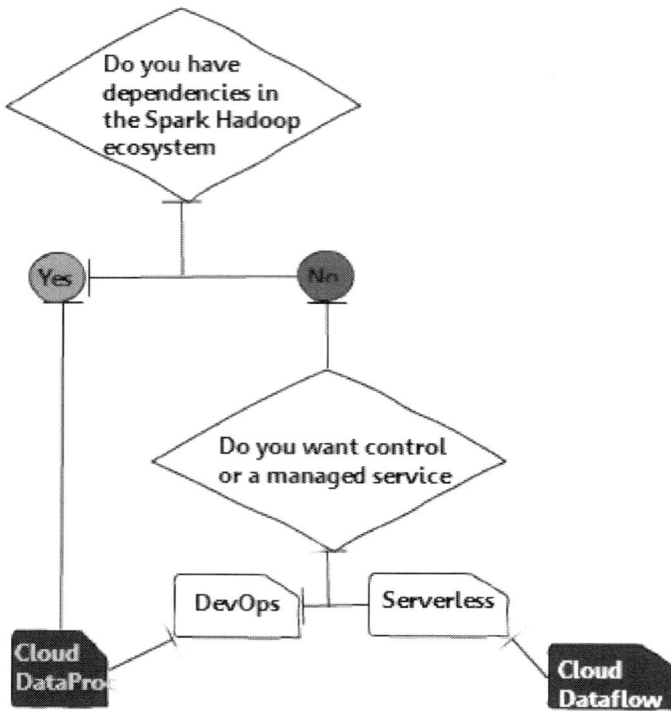

Do you have dependencies in the Spark Hadoop ecosystem

Yes / No

Do you want control or a managed service

DevOps — Serverless

Cloud DataProc — Cloud Dataflow

Cost effective way of using GCP for Hadoop

As, in GCP, we can use Google Cloud Storage instead of HDFS (Hadoop Distributed File System), there is no need to keep the clusters activated after the job is completed. We can delete the clusters once the job of the cluster is completed; so by doing that, we can save a huge amount of expense on the clusters.

In GCP, we can use a type of VM instance known as preemptible VM instance, which we can use to create the worker nodes of the cluster which will run for a maximum of 24 hours and will automatically be deleted. As a result of the fault tolerance feature, the Dataproc will introduce another preemptible instance of similar feature and machine type. So since the preemptible instances are very cheap, we, as a user, can save loads of money.

Advantages of migrating Hadoop to GCP

Built-in tools for Hadoop:
GCP's Cloud Dataproc is a managed environment for Hadoop and Spark. Users can use Cloud Dataproc to run most of their existing jobs with minimal changes, so the users don't need to alter all of the Hadoop tools they already know.

Automatically managed hardware and configuration:
When a user runs Hadoop on GCP, all the worries related to physical hardware are handled by the GCP. The user just needs to specify the configuration of the cluster, and Cloud Dataproc allocates resources required. Later on, the user can scale the cluster at any point of time.

Version simplification management:
One of the most complex parts of managing a Hadoop cluster is keeping the open source tools up to date and working together. When users use Cloud Dataproc, much of that is managed and handled for them by Cloud Dataproc versioning. So it saves their time and extra efforts.

Flexible job configuration:
In a typical Hadoop setup, many purposes are served by a single cluster. But after moving to GCP, users can focus on individual tasks, creating as many clusters as they need. This removes the complexity of maintaining a single cluster with growing dependencies and software configuration interactions.

Monitoring the process:
Users can use Stackdriver Monitoring to understand the performance and health of their Cloud Dataproc clusters and examine HDFS, YARN, and Cloud Dataproc job and operation metrics.
Cloud Dataproc Cluster resource metrics are automatically enabled on the clusters and the users can use this monitoring resource to see these metrics.

Planning of migration from an on-premise Hadoop solution to GCP

Migrating from an on-premises Hadoop solution to GCP needs a shift in approach. Generally, the on-premises Hadoop system contains a monolithic cluster which supports many workloads across multiple business areas because of which the system becomes more complex with time and will require administrators to make everything work, in the monolithic cluster. When users move their Hadoop system to GCP, they will be able to reduce the complexity of the administration. But to get the most efficient processing in GCP with the minimal cost, the users have to give emphasis on the structure of their data and jobs.

So the simplest solution for the users will be to use a persistent Cloud Dataproc cluster to replicate their on-premises setup. However, there are some limitations to this approach:

- It is recommended by Google to store the data in Cloud Storage instead of keeping the data in a persistent HDFS cluster using Cloud Dataproc, as it is more expensive.
- Also, keeping data in HDFS cluster limits the ability of users to use their data with other GCP products.
- For particular use cases, it is more efficient and economical to replace some of the open-source-based tools with the related GCP services.
- It is easier to manage the targeted clusters that serve individual jobs or job areas than using a single persistent Cloud Dataproc cluster for the jobs.

From the above discussion, we can conclude that shifting the on-premise Hadoop Ecosystem to Google Cloud Platform can save money, time, and reduce the complexity of the platform. Also Cloud Dataproc easily integrates with 3rd party Hadoop tools and with other Google Cloud Platform (GCP) services, providing users with a powerful integrated platform for data processing, analytics, and machine learning.

Cloud Dataflow and Apache Spark

A tangible benefit of running Beam pipelines on the Cloud Dataflow service is autoscaling.

This feature is hugely advantageous as users typically spend a lot of time preparing and tuning their jobs. This task often included having to guess the number of workers they would need to use to run their job/cluster. To complicate matters a set number of workers per cluster is never ideal as demand for worker nodes grows and shrinks dynamically throughout the jobs lifetime.

The autoscaling capability of Google Cloud Dataflow provides a dynamic, zero-ops method where you no longer need to proactively specify worker counts as the algorithm will duly optimize the worker count over time, using algorithms developed based on Google's experience running Hadoop/Spark cluster systems internally.

Cloud Dataflow's autoscaling is automatic and highly integrated with other GCP data-processing-specific services.

The need for dynamic scaling

The issue that autoscaling addresses is that with traditional workloads provisioning involved predetermining the optimum number of workers and subsequently the correct number of data partitions based on the selected worker count or data size. The issue was that when using a fixed set of workers for a specific job it is very likely that the cluster will be over or under provisioned at some time during the lifetime of the job. Hence, we have the requirement and operational burden of continually having to tune the cluster per job.

The problem is further exacerbated when we are using unbounded data sources such as real-time streaming as we need to respond re-actively to variations in the input rate. Previously there was no solution to this dilemma, and users had to try and guess a happy medium between conflicting operational requirements: over-provision and pay more for wasted resources or under-provision and risk high latency and slow running times or even degradation of correctness in their data pipelines.

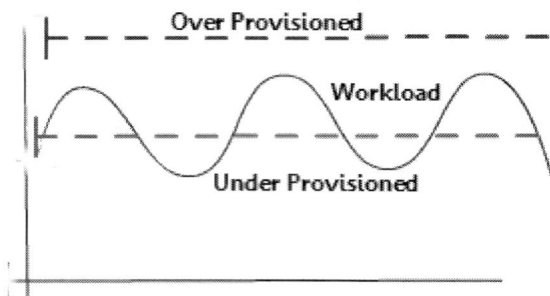

FIXED-SIZE PROVISIONING

The problem associated with fixed size provision is not confined to streaming sources with variable inputs as batch bounded source are just as problematic. This is due to batch or bounded data is best processed in stages where each stage may have scale limitations. For example, the same job pipeline may be used to process datasets of different input sizes (e.g., daily, monthly, jobs), that require different tuning.

Moreover, in addition to configuring the number of workers, another related problem is configuring the number of partitions per datasets. If the number of partitions is fixed the user has to either specify it, or the system has to guess the "right" number based on the cluster size, data size or profiles from previous runs of the same pipeline. The problem being if you use too few partitions then the system won't be able to utilize all the available workers. Also, user's guesses are often inaccurate, forcing them to specify manual overrides.

Scaling Options

Spark also has methods to automatically provision resources for a job, but it takes a different approach. With Spark, users still deploy a cluster and then they deploy a job on the cluster. This however creates two boundaries for users to scale and makes autoscaling tricky. Spark uses a technique called Dynamic Resource Allocation, which allocates available workers in a cluster to a job however it is unable to resize the cluster so users must still do this through scripts. Cloud Dataflow, on the other hand, is only concerned with deploying jobs. Google Cloud Platform manages your autoscaled cluster by deploying the required number of workers for your job just in time to execute a job and then tears them down when they are no longer needed.

Upscaling the cluster allows more jobs or bigger jobs to run but even if we had a way to autoscale a Spark cluster, the jobs running in it wouldn't necessarily benefit unless enough tasks/partitions were already specified. Cloud Dataflow, on the other hand, was designed to autoscale in the cloud so autoscaling not only dynamically adjusts the number of workers for a given job - it also adjusts the number of tasks to keep the workers busy.

Autoscaling relies on several signals to make decisions. Most of these assess how busy and/or behind workers are, including CPU utilization, throughput and the amount of work remaining (or backlog). Workers are added as CPU utilization and backlog increase and are removed as these metrics fall. For example, a workload with regular variation would resize several times as work increased (or decreased) and then maintain size through a peak or trough before repeating in the opposite direction (see Figure 3).

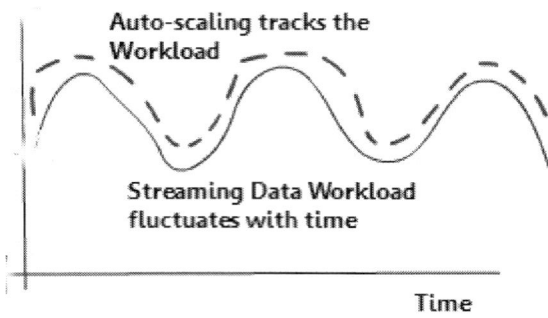

Auto-scaling tracks the Workload

Streaming Data Workload fluctuates with time

Time

Chapter 27 - Stream Analytics and Real-Time Insights

A highly integrated stream analytic platform can be built on GCP utilising the autoscaling properties of its core infrastructure components—Cloud Pub/Sub, Cloud Dataflow, and BigQuery— as the GCP reduces the complexity by handling the provisioning and integration on your behalf. GCP will provision and integrate the exact resources needed to ingest, process, and analyse fluctuating volumes of real-time data. With the provisioning and integration complexity abstracted, Google Cloud makes stream analytics accessible to both data analysts and data engineers through simple and familiar tools.
Google Cloud's streaming infrastructure autoscales to match the exact needs of your job, even if you're not sure what those needs are. That means you can offload the challenges of variable data volumes, performance tuning, resource provisioning, and more to Google, while you focus on the real-time analysis and gaining of insights. Hence, there is no need to plan ahead or to overprovision the infrastructure, and so no need to waste or overpay for unused resources.

Adopt simple ingestion for complex events

When it comes to handling the ingress of complex events then Cloud Pub/Sub, Google Cloud's stream ingestion service, can ingest and deliver hundreds of millions of events each second. With Cloud Pub/Sub, once an event is published to a topic, any number of data pipelines can subscribe and then receive it. Global topics make ingestion seamless across your choice of geographies, either directly from servers or from connected devices through IoT Core. However, Pub/Sub is not the only way to ingest streaming data as you can also use BigQuery's streaming API. This provides direct stream ingestion into the data warehouse for SQL-based ELT use cases. There is also connectors for Apache Kafka users, from Confluent a Google Cloud partner, which can deliver Kafka as a native service.

Stream ingestion service

Typically businesses want to be able to unify their stream and batch processing operations without any vendor lock-in. To that end Cloud Dataflow is designed to handle real-life streaming, where the data comes in either batch or stream modes. However as it is highly compatible with Apache Beam this enables engineers to export/import and reuse code. As a result of this Apache Beam provides pipeline portability for hybrid or multi-cloud environments. It also provides some language flexibility as the SDK includes Python, SQL, and Java. Moreover, Dataflow automatically handles resource management and also ensures exactly once processing, which makes your streaming pipelines more reliable, accurate and consistent.

Real-life streaming and batch processing

When you contemplate how to handle streaming and batch processing in the GCP. You are probably already handling these processes on-premises or on another cloud platform so are keen to keep your current tools wherever possible.
Typically, users will have their existing on-premises and cloud streaming architectures built on Apache Kafka, Apache Spark or Apache Flink. Fortunately, Google Cloud Platform can interact with these via Cloud Dataproc or host managed versions such as with Cloud Confluent. Further when these services combine with Cloud Data Fusion's GUI, you can then build streaming pipelines that are accessible to other Google AI products that can speed up and deepen your streaming analysis.
Dataflow features support for both batch and streaming processing and it is typically deployed under the following circumstances:
- Event-driven Applications
- Data Analytics Applications
- Data Pipeline Applications

Event-driven Application

An event-driven application can be considered to be a stateful application that ingests events from one or more event streams. Typically the application reacts to the incoming events by triggering an external action, state updates, or some type of computation.

Event-driven applications differ from the traditional application design which has separated compute and data storage tiers and applications read data from and save data to a remote transactional database. On the other hand, event-driven applications are stateful stream processing applications, which mean that the data is stored locally in-memory or disk. Fault-tolerance and data persistence is achieved by the application periodically writing checkpoints to remote data storage. Because event-driven application use local storage instead of remote this increases the performance but the limits of event-driven applications are defined by how well a stream processor can handle time and state. The figure below depicts the difference between the traditional application architecture and event-driven applications

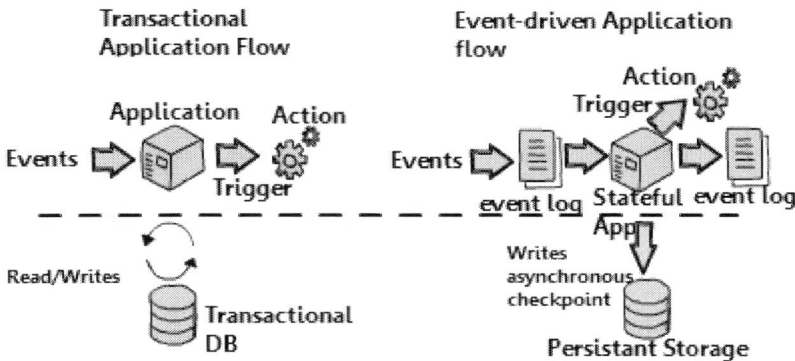

Typical use-cases for event-driven applications are:
- Fraud detection
- Anomaly detection
- Business Process monitoring
- Social media monitoring

Data Analytics Applications

Data engineers run analytical jobs to extract information and business insights from raw data. Traditionally, analytics were performed as batch queries on historical data available as bounded data sets. In order to incorporate the latest data into the result of the analysis the query or application is rerun. The results are typically output to a storage system or as reports.

However, with a stream processing engine, analytics can be performed in a real-time. Therefore, instead of reading bounded historical data sets, application can now ingest real-time event streams. This means they can continuously produce and update results. The results are either written to an external database or maintained as internal state. Dashboard application can read the latest results from the external database or directly query the internal state of the application.

Dataflow supports streaming as well as batch analytical applications as shown in the figure below.

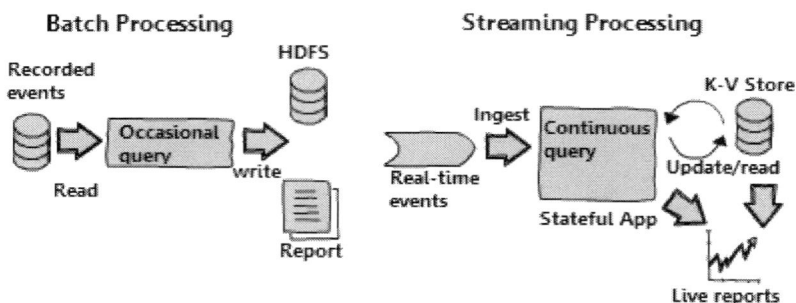

Data Pipeline Applications

A data pipeline can be considered as a chain of transformations required to ingest data at a source and then write it to a data sink in the correct format at the finish. An example of a data pipeline is the common Extract-transform-load (ETL) process to convert and move data between storage systems. Often ETL jobs are periodically triggered to copy data from a transactional database to an analytical database.

Hence, data pipelines transform data so that it can be moved from one storage system to another. However, they are required to operate in a continuous streaming mode instead of being periodically triggered.

Hence, they are able to read records from sources that continuously produce data and move it with low latency to their destination.

The figure below depicts the difference between periodic ETL jobs and continuous data pipelines.

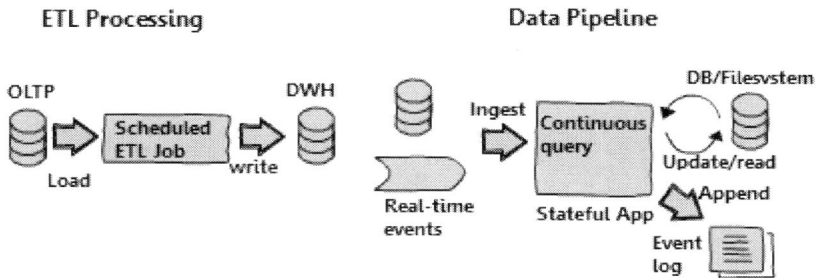

The obvious advantage of continuous data pipelines over periodic ETL jobs is the reduced latency of moving data to its destination. Moreover, data pipelines are more versatile and can be employed for real-time processing in more use cases because they are able to continuously input and output data. Examples of Dataflow use cases for data pipelines are:
- Real-time search index building in e-commerce
- Continuous ETL in data warehouses

Streaming Architecture for event-driven apps

As we have seen you can use Google Cloud Platform to build the elastic and scalable infrastructure that you need to be able to execute business rules when importing vast amounts of data or processing complex events. However, any architecture designed to handle complex event processing (CEP) must have the following attributes; it must have the inherent capability to import data from multiple, heterogeneous sources; it must also be able to apply complex business rules; and finally to reliably and consistently drive outbound actions.

The following architecture diagram shows such a system and the components involved:

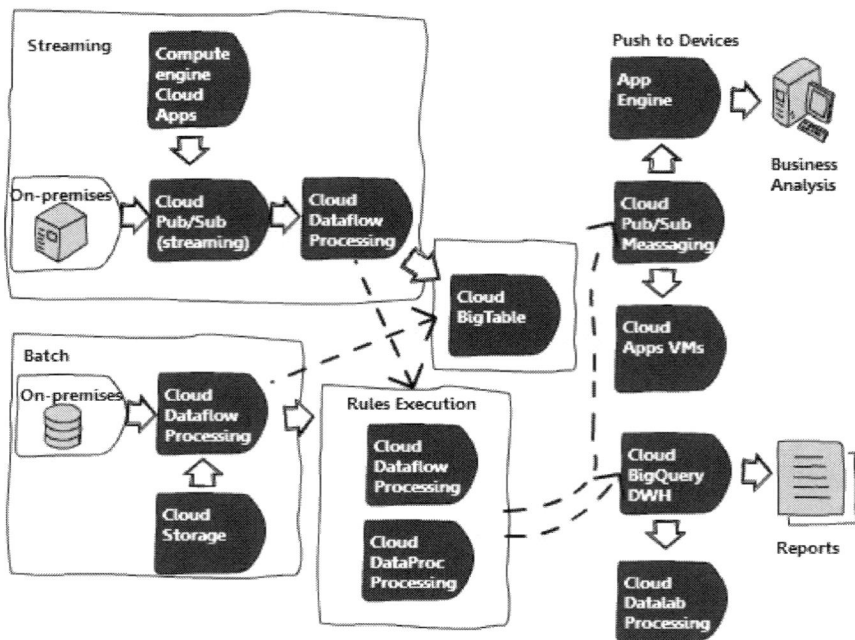

Architectural Overview

To understand how you build streaming architecture in GCP we need to consider the architecture shown in the diagram above. The architecture is designed to support both STREAMING INPUT, which can handle a continuous data flow, and also BATCH INPUT, which handles data as sizable but bounded chunks.

Streaming input

Streaming input is the mode required when you are handling data for use cases that necessitate immediate action based on close to real-time. If your use case matches these requirements then you need to use a streaming architecture to handle and process the complex events output by app, user or machine generated events.

Applications

App and User-generated events often come from the same source i.e. from interactions within applications. The user actions that create the events such as adding items to a shopping cart, clickstreams or performing a financial transaction are typically performed on apps hosted on-premises or in the cloud. On the other hand, Machine-generated events can be in the form of mobile or other IoT devices that are reporting presence, diagnostic, or similar types of data.

Transport

Regardless of where the apps or devices are hosted, the events they generate must be handled by a highly available messaging layer. In GCP this function is handled by Cloud Pub/Sub, which is a globally durable message-transport service. It also supports native connectivity to other Cloud Platform services, making it the interface between your applications, devices and the downstream processing services.

Batch input

In many cases real-time processing of data is neither required nor even preferable as in some use cases you may be processing large amounts of historical data stored in on-premises or cloud databases. In this case you can use a batch-oriented processing approach to import and process complex events.

Data sources

The data sources that generate events to be batch processed can be located on-premises or on the Cloud Platform. For on-premises data sources, you can export data and subsequently copy it to Cloud Storage as a staging post for downstream processing. Alternatively, you can directly access data stored in cloud-hosted databases by using downstream processing tools, and there are several different platforms you can use to store unprocessed event data on Cloud Platform:

- Google Cloud Storage provides object storage for flat files or unstructured data.
- Google Cloud SQL stores relational data.
- Google Cloud Datastore is a NoSQL database that supports dynamic schemas and full data-indexing.

Streaming - Processing and Storage

Data processing

When handling event data streams from applications using Cloud Pub/Sub or from other cloud data sources, such as Cloud Storage, Cloud SQL, Cloud Datastore, you might need to transform it before delivery to the processing service. Cloud Dataflow is a service built to perform tasks such as transform, enrich, aggregate or carry out some general computation on data that is streaming or batched processed. It accomplished these things by using a pipeline-based programming model. Cloud Dataflow builds and executes these pipelines as a managed service that elastically scales, as needed. In CEP workloads, you can use Cloud Dataflow to normalize data from multiple heterogeneous sources and transform it into a consistent and unified format.

Event storage

In the architecture diagram for stream and batch processing, we are using Cloud Dataflow to handle and process event data. It also normalizes the data into a single, consistent, time-series format, before storing it into a fully managed, NoSQL database service, Cloud Bigtable. In this scenario Cloud Bigtable is useful for downstream processing and analytical workloads as it provides a consistent, low-latency, high-throughput method for data access.

Rules execution

Typically in CEP systems there will be rules that must be executed across the incoming event streams. The application and management of rules necessitates the presence of a RULES ENGINE, which can be deployed in a distributed fashion using either Cloud Dataflow or Cloud Dataproc, which is a managed service for running Hadoop or Spark clusters. Using either of these systems, you can execute complex rules across large amounts of time series events, and then use the results of these rules evaluations to drive outbound actions.

Outbound actions

After inbound events have been processed by the rules engine and turned into a series of OUTBOUND ACTIONS THEY CAN BE USED TO TRIGGER THINGS SUCH AS PUSH NOTIFICATIONS for mobile devices, notifications for other applications, or sending an email to a user. To handle these outbound actions requires that you send messages through Cloud Pub/Sub via topic/subscriptions to downstream applications hosted on-premises or on Google Cloud Platform.

Streaming Analysis

However you can also store the results of the rules execution across inbound events in Google BigQuery in order to perform exploration and analysis for business intelligence or reporting purposes. BigQuery being a data warehouse designed for data processing also has connectivity to additional downstream analytical tools. For example, you can use Google Cloud Datalab, which is based on Jupyter notebooks for data exploration purposes. You could also use Google Data Studio 360 for reporting or dashboard use cases as it supports creating customizable and shareable reports.

Architecture: Optimizing Large-Scale Ingestion of Analytics Events and Logs

Let us now consider an alternative architecture, which is designed for optimizing large-scale analytics ingestion on Google Cloud Platform (GCP). As a definition of 'large-scale' in the context of this architecture we mean greater than 100,000 events per second, or having a total aggregate event payload size of over 100 MB per second.

The use case for such large-scale data ingestion architecture could well be an IoT regional connection portal that is the hub for all the tens of thousands of devices in the field. The benefit of this architecture is that it allows you to leverage GCP's elastic and scalable managed services. We need this elasticity and scalability to collect the large amounts of incoming log and analytics events, before we process them for entry into the Cloud BigQuery data warehouse.

Any architecture that is designed to handle large scale ingestion of analytics data should be able to identify and handle real-time data as well as identify data that is less urgent and can be processed after a short delay and separate them appropriately. Therefore we need to take a segmented approach whereby some events will be fast tracked and handled as real-time data but other events can wait. A segmented approach has these benefits:

- Log integrity - No logs are lost due to streaming quota limits or sampling delays so you get complete records of all logged events.

- Cost reduction – By limiting the number of urgent streaming events and logs you can reduce costs as streaming real-time events are billed at a higher rate than those inserted from Cloud Storage using batch jobs.
- Reserved query resources – By processing lower-priority logs as a batch job prevent them from having an impact on the reserved query resources needed by the real-time streaming processes.

The following architecture diagram shows such a system, and introduces the concepts of hot paths and cold paths for ingestion:

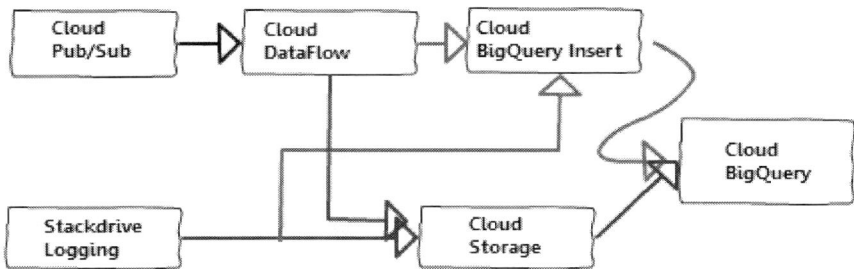

Architectural Overview

In the large-scale ingestion architecture shown above, you can see that the data originates from two possible sources:
- Analytics events are published to a Cloud Pub/Sub topic.
- Logs are collected using Stackdriver Logging.

After ingestion, regardless of the source, the next stage is to determine the path based on the latency requirements of the message. In this case the data is put either into the hot path or the cold path. The hot path is used for streaming real-time data input so it is designed to handle a continuous dataflow. On the other hand, the cold path is designed to handle a batch process, whereby it is loading the data on a schedule you determine from Cloud Storage.

Logging events

You can use Stackdriver Logging to ingest logging events generated by standard operating system logging facilities. Stackdriver logging is available in a number of Compute Engine environments by default, including the standard images, and can also be installed on many operating systems by using the Stackdriver Logging Agent. The logging agent is the default logging sink for App Engine and Kubernetes Engine.

Hot path logging

In the hot path, critical logs are selected by specifying a filter in the Stackdriver Logging sink and then streamed to multiple BigQuery tables. It is a best practice to use separate tables for ERROR and WARN logging levels, and then split them further by service if high volumes are expected. This best practice keeps the number of inserts per second per table under the 100,000 limit and keeps queries running efficiently.

Cold path logging

For the cold path, which is for non-urgent logs that don't require near real-time analysis the logs are batched and written to log files in Cloud Storage hourly batches. These logs can then be batch loaded into BigQuery using the standard Cloud Storage file import process. Batch loading does not impact the hot path's streaming ingestion or its query performance. Typically, it will be best to merge the hot and cold path logs directly into the same BigQuery tables in order to aggregate the logs, which will significantly simplify troubleshooting and report generation.

Analytics events

The source of the analytics events can be your app's services in GCP or they can be sent from remote clients. An alternative design could be to send the hot and cold analytics events/logs to two separate Cloud Pub/Sub topics. However, it is considered best practice to instead use two separate Cloud Dataflow jobs to provide the low latency separation. This is because you can change the path an analytics event follows more easily by updating the Cloud Dataflow jobs, which is simpler than having to deploying a new app.

Now let's breakdown this stream pipeline and look at the individual components. First off all we need to consider the ingest process performed by Cloud Pub/Sub.

Cloud Pub/Sub

Cloud Pub/Sub provides the real-time messaging service as it allows you to efficiently send and receive messages between independent applications. Also the Cloud Pub/Sub service guarantees – if it is feasible - the delivery of all messages. However, despite its efficiency and its storing of undelivered messages for 7 days it does not guarantee messages will be delivered on a first in first out basis. Not only are you not guaranteed to get messages delivered in order you may get duplicate messages. Despite those caveats Cloud Pub/Sub is important to data engineers because it can act as a single ingest for many diverse data sources. This is a valuable design building-block in many modern cloud architectures. For example, Cloud Pub/Sub can be deployed to interconnect and service many diverse IoT devices as data sources. All those IoT devices could publish data to the Cloud Pub/Sub Topic service, and the subscribing applications would pull down these messages as they become available. Here are some of the benefits of cloud Pub/Sub;

- It is a globally managed service with extremely low latency.
- You can dynamically rate limit, so you can throttle exactly how often or how much Pub/Sub will push those messages.
- Pub/Sub provides end-to-end reliability because we're going to acknowledge at least one guaranteed delivery and receipt of each individual message.

- Everything is completely encrypted,
- it's maintenance is free and,
- You simply just pay for exactly what you use

The way that Cloud Pub/Sub works is that it uses two levels of abstraction between the publisher and the subscriber. This deliberately de-couples the sender's transmission of the message from the receiver's receipt of the message.

Let's take a look at how publishers and subscribers interact in theory.

- A publisher in our example an IoT device wishes to publish a message.
- A message consists of a payload and optional attributes that describe the payload.
- The Pub/Sub service that receives the message from the publisher on behalf of the topic is called the publishing forwarder. A topic is a feed of a category of messages.
- The topic stores the message ensuring availability and reliability. The message is transmitted to one or more subscriptions.
- The Pub/Sub service that receives the message from the publishing forwarder and ensures delivery to subscribers is the subscribing forwarder.
- A subscription is an entity that represents interests in receiving messages.
- The Pub/Sub subscribing forwarder determines which subscribers are registered to receive the message and queues up the messages to be sent.
- Subscribers can either receive the message through pull or push.
- The subscribers either receive messages by Pub/Sub pushing them to the subscriber's endpoint or by pulling them from the service. Pull subscribers use HTTPS requests to Google APIs. Push subscribers use web hook endpoints that can accept post requests over HTTPS.
- The message arrives at the subscriber where it is consumed and an acknowledgment sent back to the subscribing forwarding service.

- The Pub/Sub subscribing forwarding service receives the acknowledgement and registers each delivery. When all of the deliveries are complete, it removes the message from the queue.

There are many common cloud Pub/Sub use cases, such as in deploying IoT or in balancing workloads in network clusters, for example, a large queue of tasks can be efficiently distributed among multiple workers such as Google Compute Engine instances. But there are myriad other use case;

- Implementing asynchronous workflows, for example, an order processing application can place an order on a topic from which it can be processed by one or more workers.
- Distributing event notifications, for example, a service that accepts user sign-ups can send notifications whenever a new user registers and a downstream service can subscribe to receive notifications of the event.
- Refreshing distributed caches, for example, an application can publish invalidation invents to update the ID's of objects that have changed.
- Logging into multiple systems, for example, a Google Compute Engine instance can write logs to the monitoring system, to a database for later querying and so on.
- Data streaming from various processes or devices, for example, a residential sensor can stream data to back-end services hosted in the cloud. Also
- Reliability improvement, for example, a single-zone Compute Engine service can operate in additional zones by subscribing to a common topic to recover from failures in a zone or region.

Using Cloud Pub/Sub to send and receive real-time messages

This is a brief introduction to the command-line interface for Cloud Pub/Sub, using the gcloud command-line tool.

Creating a topic

In Cloud Pub/Sub a topic is a named resource to which you send messages. Create your first topic with the following command:

```
gcloud pubsub topics create 'my-
topic'
```

Add a subscription

To read messages from a topic, you will need to first create a subscription to the topic. Create your first subscription to a topic – 'my-topic' with the following command:

```
gcloud pubsub subscriptions \
    create my-sub --topic my-topic \
    --ack-deadline=60
```

This command creates a subscription named my-sub attached to the topic my-topic. Any messages published to my-topic will be delivered to the subscription my-sub. The ack-deadline option sets an acknowledgement deadline of 60 seconds for this subscription.

List topics and subscriptions

Before sending your first message, you should first check that your topic and the corresponding subscription have been successfully created. List your topic and subscription using the following commands:

```
gcloud pubsub topics list
gcloud pubsub subscriptions
list
```

Publish messages to the topic

You can send two messages to the topic my-topic using the following commands:

```
gcloud pubsub topics publish my-topic --message hello
gcloud pubsub topics publish my-topic --message
goodbye
```

Each of these commands sends a different message. The first message is hello and the second is goodbye. When you successfully publish a message, you should see the Message_ID returned from the server. This is a unique ID automatically assigned by the server to each message.

Pull messages from the subscription

Now, that you have successfully sent two messages to my-topic you can pull the messages with the following command:

```
gcloud pubsub subscriptions \
    pull --auto-ack --limit=2 my-
sub
```

This should return the two messages that you have just published. The messages have the data, hello and goodbye, as well as MESSAGE_ID.

Acknowledging messages

After you pull a message and process it, you must notify Cloud Pub/Sub that you successfully received the message. This action is called acknowledgement.
If you do not acknowledge the message before the acknowledgement deadline has passed, Cloud Pub/Sub will re-send the message.
The --auto-ack flag passed with the pull command automatically acknowledges a message when it is pulled.

Manual acknowledgement

Send a new message with the following command:

```
gcloud pubsub \
    topics publish my-topic --message thanks
```

Pull the messages with this command:

```
gcloud pubsub subscriptions \
    pull my-sub
```

This should display the thanks message, as well as the unique MESSAGE_ID and the ACK_ID. The ACK_ID is an ID that you can use for acknowledging the message. Copy the ACK_ID value, which you will paste into an acknowledgement in the next step.

Manually Acknowledge the message

You can manually acknowledge the message with the following command, replacing [ACK_ID] with the ID that you copied in the previous step:

```
gcloud pubsub subscriptions ack \
    my-sub --ack-ids [ACK_ID]
```

As the Cloud Pub/Sub subscriber data APIs provide only limited access to message data the acknowledged messages are typically inaccessible to subscribers. However this may cause a problem as subscriber clients must process and acknowledge every message in a subscription even if only a subset is needed.

The way that you can work around this is to use the **Seek** feature in Cloud Pub/Sub, which extends the subscriber functionality by allowing you to replay previously acknowledged messages or discard messages in bulk. Recovering acknowledged messages generally requires the source subscription to be configured in advance so that acknowledgements are stored but this can result in additional storage fees in billing.

Cloud Pub/Sub Seeking

Seeking to a timestamp

You can seek to a time reference so that every message received by Cloud Pub/Sub before the time will be acknowledged, and all messages received after the time will be considered to be unacknowledged. If you need to replay and reprocess previously acknowledged messages, then you can seek to a prior time. Similarly, you can also seek to a time in the future to discard messages. However as the message publication time is generated by the Cloud Pub/Sub servers this approach can be imprecise due to:

- Possible clock skew among Cloud Pub/Sub servers.
- The fact that Cloud Pub/Sub has to work with the arrival time of the publish request rather than when an event occurred in the source system.

To seek to a prior time, you must first configure your subscription to retain acknowledged messages:

- An acknowledged message is only retained in a subscription if the subscription's retain_acked_messages property is set to true - the default is false. Also it will only be retained up to the message_retention_duration value after it is published - the default is 7 days. If you want to store any acknowledged messages you have to preconfigure the subscriptions retain_acked_messages and set it to true.
- Both the retain_acked_messages and the message_retention_duration properties of a subscription can be specified at subscription creation, or updated for an existing subscription.

Note: When you modify the message retention duration – default 7 days or the subscription expiration policy – default 31 days, you must ensure that the subscription expiration duration is set to a higher value than the message retention duration.

Seeking to a snapshot

The snapshot feature allows you to capture the message acknowledgment state of a subscription. Once a snapshot is created, it retains:

- All messages that was unacknowledged in the source subscription at the time of the snapshot's creation.
- Any messages published to the topic thereafter.

You can replay these unacknowledged messages by using a snapshot to seek to any of the topic's subscriptions.

Unlike with seeking to a time, you don't need to perform any special subscription configuration to seek to a snapshot. You just need to create the snapshot ahead of time. For example, you might create a snapshot when deploying new subscriber code, in case you need to recover from unexpected or erroneous acknowledgements.

Snapshots expire and are deleted in the following cases (whichever comes first):

- The snapshot reaches a lifespan of seven days.
- The oldest unacknowledged message in the snapshot exceeds the message retention duration.

For example, consider a snapshot of a subscription with a backlog where the oldest unacknowledged message is a day old. The snapshot expires after six days, rather than seven. This timeline is necessary for snapshots to offer strong at-least-once delivery guarantees.

Eventual consistency

Seek operations are strictly consistent in regard to message delivery guarantees. This means that any message that is to become unacknowledged based on the seek condition is guaranteed to be eventually delivered at least once after the seek operation succeeds.

However, delivered messages do not instantly become consistent with the seek operation. So a message that was published before the seek timestamp or that is acknowledged in a snapshot might be delivered after the seek operation. In a sense, message delivery operates as an eventually consistent system with respect to the seek operation: it might take as long as a minute for the operation to take full effect.

Cloud Pub/Sub Seek use cases

- **Update subscriber code safely.** A concern with deploying new subscriber code is that the new executable may erroneously acknowledge messages, leading to message loss. Incorporating snapshots into your deployment process gives you a way to recover from bugs in new subscriber code.
- **Recover from unexpected subscriber problems.** In cases where subscriber problems are not associated with a specific deployment event, you might not have a relevant snapshot. In this case, if you have enabled ACKNOWLEDGED MESSAGE RETENTION for a subscription, seeking to a past time gives you a way to recover from the error.
- **Save processing time and cost.** Perform a bulk acknowledgement on a large backlog of messages that are no longer relevant.
- **Test subscriber code on known data.** When testing subscriber code for performance and consistency, it is useful to use the same data in every run. Snapshots enable consistent data with strong semantics. In addition, snapshots can be applied to any subscription on a given topic, including a newly created one.

Cloud Pub/Sub in Streaming Pipelines

As we have seen Cloud Pub/Sub plays an important role when handling the ingress of vast quantities of streaming data. This makes Cloud Pub/Sub an integral part of any real-time streaming data pipeline. However, it is not without some glaring flaws most notably its guarantee to deliver at least once. The issue here is the qualifier once as it implies that Cloud Pub/Sub may deliver messages more than once and in some applications that would be a major issue. For example in ecommerce sending a client a product two or three times for a single transaction would be financially ruinous. Indeed, for many applications receiving duplicate or triplicate copies of the same message is unwelcome as it plays havoc with averages, totals, or any other statistics they may rely upon. Therefore there is a definite requirement to make Cloud Pub/Sub work so that it delivers exactly once. Only then can it be considered a viable messaging service for most production applications. The problem is how do we accomplish this?

Fortunately there is a method of ensuring Cloud Pub/Sub delivers exactly once and that is to couple it with Cloud Dataflow, which we will discuss in the next chapter. The way this works is that the duplicate messages are the result of one of two sources; the first is they are actually the product of Cloud Pub/Sub in which case the messages will have identical event IDs. Now these event IDs are supposed to be unique and they are embedded into the message headers so they can be promoted and used as a message attribute. An attribute is simply a key value pair that is contained within the message. If every message has its eventId set as an attribute then we can inform Cloud Dataflow to examine the attributes within the PubSubIO. This means that duplicates can be identified at the point where they are input to the Cloud Dataflow pipeline and de-duplicated and quietly dropped.

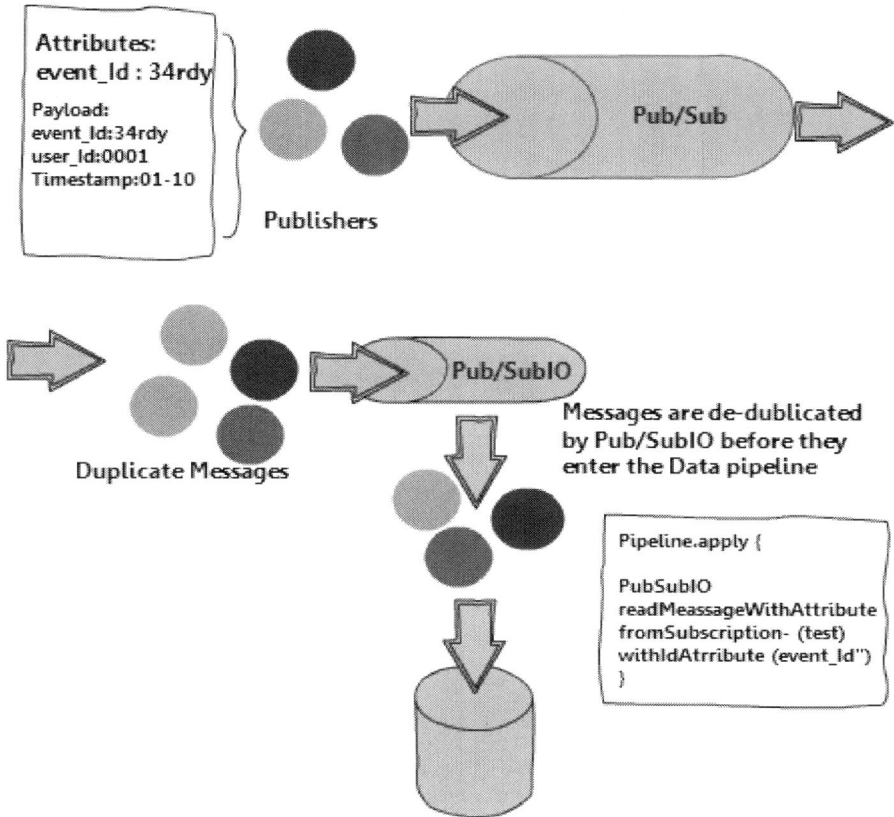

Attributes:
event_Id : 34rdy

Payload:
event_Id:34rdy
user_Id:0001
Timestamp:01-10

Publishers

Pub/Sub

Duplicate Messages

Pub/SubIO

Messages are de-dublicated
by Pub/SubIO before they
enter the Data pipeline

Pipeline.apply {

PubSubIO
readMeassageWithAttribute
fromSubscription- (test)
withIdAtrribute (event_Id")
}

The second way that duplicate messages can be produced via Cloud Pub/Sub is that the application that produce the events that feeds the topics may be sending the duplicate messages. Therefore we need to take a slightly different approach. The way it works is that at the egress of Cloud Pub/Sub and before the ingress into Cloud Dataflow i.e. at the PubSubIO every new message will be copied into a buffer table and subsequent messages arriving are checked against the entries in the table for exact duplicates. In this scenario the event IDs will be caught in the same manner as before but only if they occur within 10 minutes of each other. This is because the eventId buffer table is only kept for that length of time.

Kafka

Google's Cloud Pub/Sub cloud-native messaging service is not the only option as GCP also supports the popular open source streaming platform Kafka. Indeed for most on-premises systems migrating to the cloud retaining Kafka as the primary messaging a streaming platform is a top priority. To understand why and to see how data engineers can incorporate Kafka into the cloud ecosystem we need to take a look at Kafka and its unique capabilities.
Kafka has three key capabilities:

- Publish and subscribe to streams of records, similar to Cloud Pub/Sub or a message queue or enterprise messaging system.
- It has the capability to store streams of records in a fault-tolerant durable way for a configurable time period.
- It processes streams of records as they occur and guarantees order of delivery and exactly-once

Kafka is generally used for two broad classes of applications:

- Building real-time streaming data pipelines that reliably move data between systems or applications
- Building real-time streaming applications that transform or react to the streams of data

Kafka Infrastructure

Kafka can be run on-premises so it traditionally is run as a cluster on one or more servers that can span that can if necessary be distributed across multiple data centres. Similar to Cloud Pub/Sub messaging the Kafka cluster stores streams of records in categories called topics. Each record consists of a key, a value, and a timestamp. Interested parties subscribe to these topics using the Consumer and Producer APIs- this is a standard pub/sub pattern.
Where Kafka starts to differ is that it has other capabilities enabled by its other two core APIs:

- The Streams API allows an application to act as a stream processor, consuming an input stream from one or more topics and producing an output stream to one or more output topics, effectively transforming the input streams to output streams.

- The Connector API allows building and running reusable producers or consumers that connect Kafka topics to existing applications or data systems. For example, a connector to a relational database might capture every change to a table.

Kafka as a Streaming Platform

One of the main advantages of Kafka as a messaging service is that it acts as both a traditional queuing service and a Sub/pub messaging service. This means that it can divide up processing to scale over multiple consumer instances yet still broadcast to consumer groups. Kafka can also guarantee the order of delivery.

As a storage service Kafka can retain messages (records) as they are publish rather than consumed. This means that Kafka stores the messages to persistent disk for a configurable time period so it acts as a distributed filesystem dedicated to high-performance, low-latency commit log storage, replication, and propagation.

In general a stream processor is anything that takes a continuous stream of data as input performs some processing, and then produces an output as a continuous stream of data. Other messaging services make it possible to do simple processing directly using the topic/subscriber pattern as they can handle vast amounts of incoming messages and Kafka can do the same using its producer and consumer APIs. However for more complex transformations Kafka provides a fully integrated Streams API. This specialist streaming API allows building applications that do complex processing such as compute aggregations of data streams or join streams together. This API also enables Kafka to handle out-of-order data as well as the reprocessing of input as code changes or performing stateful computations, etc.

This combination of messaging, storage, and stream distinguishes from Cloud Pub/Sub as Kafka's is a true streaming platform.

Customers that want to deploy Kafka can always build their clusters in Compute Engine or Kubernetes Engine but for convenience there is also a managed serverless solution – Confluent on GCP – which is now available as a managed Kafka service on GCP.

Chapter 28 - Working with Cloud Dataflow SDK (Apache Beam)

Cloud Dataflow (Apache Beam) can be considered as a unified API that integrates with all the other frameworks such as Hadoop and Spark and binds them together with their data sources. Therefore, we can consider that the Dataflow SDK provides an abstraction of the application logic from the underlying big data ecosystem. Hence, you are free to ignore when you are writing your data processing application the complexities associated with:

- Data Sources — You are not constrained by the type of data source - as you can handle batches, micro-batches, streaming data or streaming-files
- SDK — You are free to choose your preferred programming SDK (Java, Python)
- Runners — you are free to choose one of the available runners (Apache Spark, Apache Flink, or Google Cloud Dataflow, amongst others) to run your application.

Beam abstracts the application logic from the processing framework and this allows you to write your application logic once, and then reuse without having to worry about runner specific parameters. However, before we delve into Dataflow/Beam we need to get an understanding of some unique terminology and some of the core concepts.

Dataflow Core Concepts

There are five main conceptions in Beam: Pipeline, PCollection, PTransform, ParDO, and DoFn.

- Pipeline: A Pipeline encapsulates the workflows, which are the sequential steps that make up your entire data processing journey from start to finish. This journey includes the initial reading of input data from a source, transforming that data, and then finally writing output data to a sink. The concept of a pipeline is fundamental so you must create the Pipeline with the execution options that tells Beam where and how to run it.

- PCollection: A PCollection represents a distributed data set that your Beam pipeline operates on. The data set can be either bounded, meaning it comes from a fixed source like a file (batch), or unbounded, meaning it comes from a continuously updating source (streaming) via a Pub/Sub or Kafka subscription or some other streaming mechanism

- PTransform: A PTransform is the operational process that transforms the dataset within an input PCollection into the new dataset that is the output PCollection. A PTransform occurs between every step in your pipeline. Every PTransform takes one or more PCollection(s) and transforms it using an operator to create an output. However a PTransform does not consume a PCollection instead it produces zero or more new output PCollection objects.

- ParDo: ParDo is a Beam transform for generic parallel processing. It is similar to the "Map" phase of a Map/Shuffle/Reduce-style algorithm in so much as a ParDo transform takes each data element in the input PCollection and produces zero or more data elements to an output PCollection.

- DoFn: A DoFn is the operational logic wrapped in a ParDo that applies your PTransform application code to each element in the input PCollection and produces the elements of an output PCollection.

- Runner: The runner is the process that will upload your application code along with any the dependencies then run them as a job. For example, if you run your pipeline using Cloud Dataflow, the runner will upload your executable code to a Google Cloud Storage bucket and then it will create a Cloud Dataflow job. The job is run, which duly executes your pipeline on the managed resources in Google Cloud Platform.

Creating Pipelines

When creating a Dataflow pipeline there are a few things that you need to consider:

- **What are your data sources?** It is important to understand how many sets of input data you have. This is because the first stage of the pipeline will be a Read transform so you will need to know how many and what type you are going to need.
- **What format is your data in?** Your data might be log files or from a database table however some Beam transforms work exclusively on PCollections of key/value pairs. In that case you'll need to determine how your data can be keyed in your pipeline's PCollection(s).
- **What are you doing with the data?** The core transforms available in the Apache Beam SDKs are for general purpose use. So you will need to know if you can use the pre-written transforms included with the Beam SDKs or if you will have to change or manipulate your data when building core transforms like ParDo.
- **What is your output data, and where does it go?** The answer to this question will let you know what kinds of Write transforms you'll need to apply at the end of your pipeline.

A basic Dataflow pipeline

The simplest pipelines represent a linear flow of operations, as shown in figure 1.

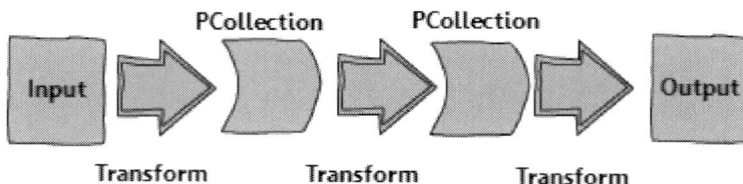

However, it's very likely that your pipeline will be more complex. Nonetheless, all pipelines will represent a Directed Acyclic Graph of steps. Hence a pipeline can have multiple input sources, multiple output sinks, and its intermediary operations (PTransforms) can both read and output multiple PCollections.

Branching PCollections

An important thing to understand is that the pipeline transforms do not consume the PCollections. Instead, the transforms handle each individual element of a PCollection and then create a new PCollection as the output. Because of this you can perform different transforms to different elements in the same PCollection.

Multiple transforms process the same PCollection

As the PCollection is not consumed by the transforms you can use the same PCollection as input for multiple transforms without consuming the input or altering it in any way.

For example in a branching pipeline that reads its input – in this example a table of first names that are represented as strings - and then creates a PCollection of table rows. Then, the pipeline applies multiple transforms to the **same** PCollection. For example, in the diagram below we can see that the Transform A extracts all the names in that PCollection that have the initial 'A', and Transform B extracts all the names in that PCollection that have the initial 'B'. However both transforms A and B have the same input PCollection.

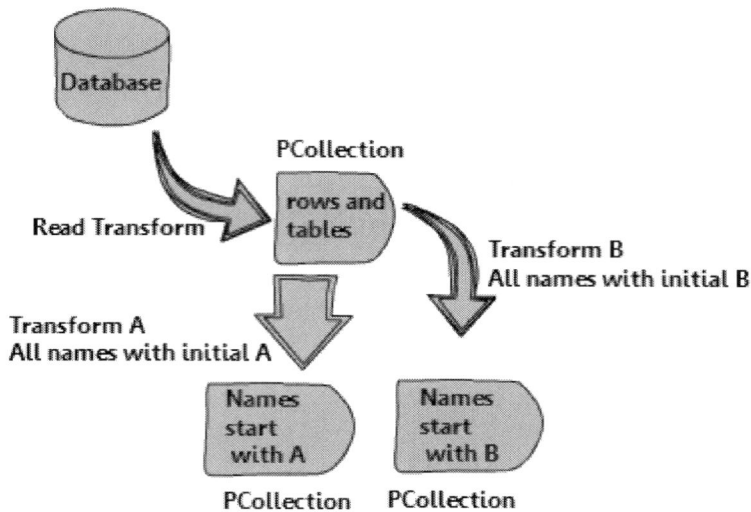

A BRANCHING PIPELINE WHERE TWO TRANSFORMS ARE APPLIED TO A SINGLE PCOLLECTION OF DATABASE TABLE ROWS.

The following example code applies two transforms to a single input collection.

- Java

```java
PCollection<String> dbRowCollection = ...;
PCollection<String> aCollection = dbRowCollection.apply("aTrans",
ParDo.of(new DoFn<String, String>(){
 @ProcessElement
 public void processElement(ProcessContext c) {
  if(c.element().startsWith("A")){
   c.output(c.element());
```

```java
 }
 }
}));
PCollection<String> bCollection = dbRowCollection.apply("bTrans",
ParDo.of(new DoFn<String, String>(){
 @ProcessElement
```

```
public void processElement(ProcessContext c) {
  if(c.element().startsWith("B")){
    c.output(c.element());
  }
}
}));
```

Alternatively, we can have a branch in a pipeline where a **single** transform output is used as input to multiple PCollections by using tagged outputs. These types of transforms will produce more than one output process as each element of the input is processed once, and then output to one or more PCollections.

Figure 3 illustrates the same example described above, but with one transform that produces multiple tagged outputs. Names that start with 'A' are added to the main output

PCollection and names that start with 'B' are added to an additional output PCollection.

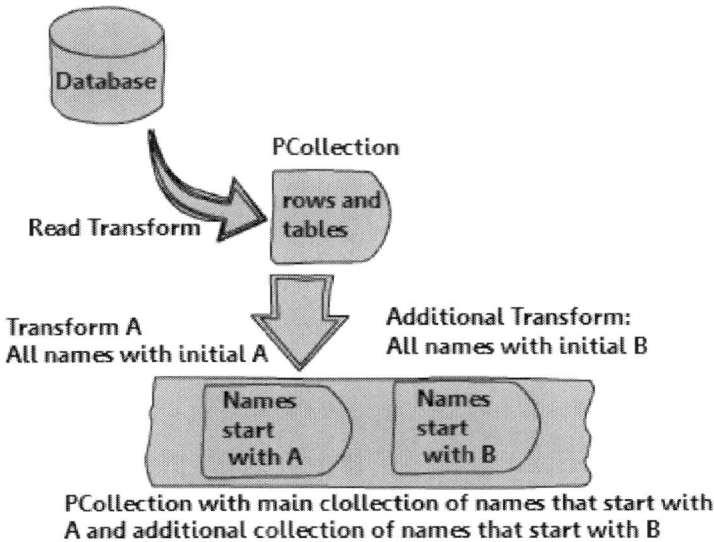

PCollection with main clollection of names that start with A and additional collection of names that start with B

A PIPELINE WITH A TRANSFORM THAT OUTPUTS MULTIPLE PCOLLECTIONS

If we compare the pipelines in figure 2 and figure 3, you can see they perform the same operation but using different logic. For example, the pipeline in figure 2 contains two transforms and each processes the same elements in the same input PCollection. One transform uses the following logic:

if (starts with 'A') { outputToPCollectionA }

While the other transform uses:

if (starts with 'B') { outputToPCollectionB }

Because each transform reads the entire input PCollection, each element in the input PCollection is processed twice.
However, when we consider the method used in the pipeline in figure 3 it performs the same operation with only one transform that uses the following logic:

if (starts with 'A') { outputToPCollectionA } else if (starts with 'B') { outputToPCollectionB }

The notable difference is that each element in the input PCollection is processed only once.
The following example code in Java shows how to apply one transform on a PCollection that processes each element once and produces two different outputs.

- Java

```java
// Define two TupleTags, one for each output.
final TupleTag<String> startsWithATag = new TupleTag<String>(){};
final TupleTag<String> startsWithBTag = new TupleTag<String>(){};
PCollectionTuple mixedCollection =
  dbRowCollection.apply(ParDo
    .of(new DoFn<String, String>() {
```

```java
    @ProcessElement
    public void processElement(ProcessContext c) {
      if (c.element().startsWith("A")) {
        // Emit to main output, which is the output with tag
startsWithATag.
        c.output(c.element());
      } else if(c.element().startsWith("B")) {
        // Emit to output with tag startsWithBTag.
        c.output(startsWithBTag, c.element());
      }
     }
    })
    // Specify main output. In this example, it is the output
    // with tag startsWithATag.
    .withOutputTags(startsWithATag,
    // Specify the output with tag startsWithBTag, as a TupleTagList.
          TupleTagList.of(startsWithBTag)));
// Get subset of the output with tag startsWithATag.
mixedCollection.get(startsWithATag).apply(...);
// Get subset of the output with tag startsWithBTag.
mixedCollection.get(startsWithBTag).apply(...);
```

There is no hard and fast rule that determines which method you can use so you are free to choose either method to produce multiple output PCollections. However, you should be aware that using additional outputs method will make more sense if the transform's computation per element is time-consuming.

Merging PCollections

Typically, after you've separated your PCollection into multiple PCollections via multiple transforms, you'll often want to merge some of those PCollections back together again. You can do so by using one of the following techniques:

- **Flatten** - You can use the Flatten transform in the Beam SDKs to merge multiple PCollections if they are the same type
- **Join** - You can use the CoGroupByKey transform in the Beam SDK to perform a relational join between two PCollections. However, a constraint is that the
PCollections must be key/value pairs and they must share the same key type.

For example if we look at figure 4, we can see that after branching into two PCollections, one with initial 'A' and one with initial 'B', the pipeline merges the two together into a single PCollection. The resulting PCollection contains all names with either initial 'A' or 'B'. In this example it makes sense to use the Flatten technique because the PCollections being merged are the same type.

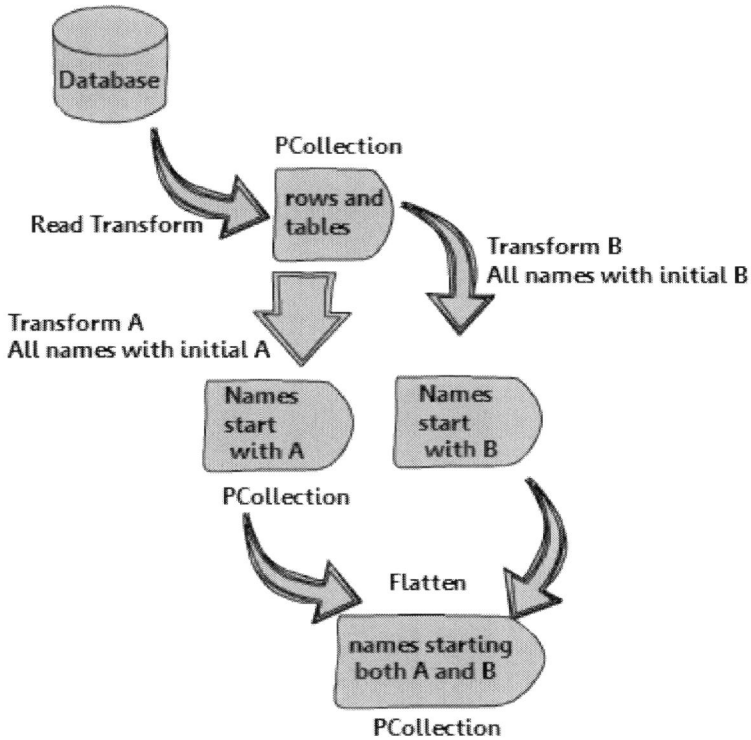

A PIPELINE THAT MERGES TWO COLLECTIONS INTO ONE COLLECTION
WITH THE FLATTEN TRANSFORM

The following example code applies Flatten to merge two collections.

- Java

```
//merge the two PCollections with Flatten
PCollectionList<String> collectionList =
PCollectionList.of(aCollection).and(bCollection);
PCollection<String> mergedCollectionWithFlatten = collectionList
   .apply(Flatten.<String>pCollections());
// continue with the new merged PCollection
mergedCollectionWithFlatten.apply(...);
```

Multiple sources

Your pipeline can read its input from one or more sources. If your pipeline reads from multiple sources and the data from those sources is related, it can be useful to join the inputs together. In the example illustrated in figure 5 below, the pipeline reads names and addresses from a database table, and names and order numbers from a Kafka topic. The pipeline then uses CoGroupByKey to join this information, where the key is the name; the resulting PCollection contains all the combinations of names, addresses, and orders.

A PIPELINE THAT DOES A RELATIONAL JOIN OF TWO INPUT COLLECTIONS

However, if we contemplate merging PCollections using the Join as they are relational – names, addresses, and order numbers - you can see the difference in the required code.

- Java

```
PCollection<KV<String, String>> userAddress =
pipeline.apply(JdbcIO.<KV<String, String>>read()...);
```

```
PCollection<KV<String, String>> userOrder =
pipeline.apply(KafkaIO.<String, String>read()...);
final TupleTag<String> addressTag = new TupleTag<String>();
final TupleTag<String> orderTag = new TupleTag<String>();
// Merge collection values into a CoGbkResult collection.
PCollection<KV<String, CoGbkResult>> joinedCollection =
  KeyedPCollectionTuple.of(addressTag, userAddress)
           .and(orderTag, userOrder)
           .apply(CoGroupByKey.<String>create());
joinedCollection.apply(...);
```

Building a Beam Pipeline using the SDK Classes

When you build a pipeline you need to express the data processing steps involved from start to finish. To construct a pipeline using the classes in the Beam SDKs, your program will need to perform the following general steps:

- Create a Pipeline object.
- Use a **Read** or **Create** transform to create one or more PCollections for your pipeline data.
- Apply **transforms** to each PCollection. Transforms can change, filter, group, analyse, or otherwise process the elements in a PCollection. Each transform creates a new output PCollection, to which you can apply some other transforms until all the processing steps are complete.
- **Write** transform the final output, for the transformed PCollections.
- **Run** the pipeline.

Creating Your Pipeline Object

A Beam program often starts by creating a Pipeline object. In the Beam SDKs, each pipeline is represented by an explicit object of type Pipeline. Each Pipeline object is an independent entity that encapsulates both the data the pipeline operates over and the transforms that are applied to that data.

To create a pipeline, you must first declare a Pipeline object, and then pass it some specific configuration options.

- Java

```java
// Start by defining the options for the pipeline.
PipelineOptions options = PipelineOptionsFactory.create();
// Then create the pipeline (p) as this is the entry point into your program
Pipeline p = Pipeline.create(options);
```

Reading Data into the Pipeline

To create your pipeline's initial PCollection, you will have to apply a root transform to your pipeline object. A root transform will create an initial PCollection from either an external data source or some local data source such as a file that you can specify.

There are basically two kinds of root transforms in the Beam SDKs: Read and Create.

A Read transform will as the name suggests read data from an external source, such as a text file or a database table. On the other hand, a Create transform will make a new PCollection from an in-memory java.util.Collection.

The following example code shows how to use a TextIO.Read root transform to read data from a text file - "gs://some/inputData.txt". Then the transform is applied to a Pipeline object p, and it will subsequently output data set in the format of a PCollection<String>:

- Java

```
PCollection<String> lines = p.apply(
  "ReadLines", TextIO.read().from("gs://some/inputData.txt"));
```

Applying Transforms to Process Pipeline Data

You can build your pipeline logic by manipulating your data using the various transforms that are inbuilt in the Apache Beam SDKs. To accomplish this task, you would **apply** the transforms to your pipeline's PCollection by calling the apply method on each PCollection. By doing so you would process the PCollection and then output the desired transform object as an argument.

The following example code demonstrates how the popular word-reverse demo pipeline works in practice and we can see how to apply a transform to a PCollection of strings.

The transform is a user-defined custom transform that reverses the contents of each string and outputs a new PCollection containing the reversed strings.

The input is a PCollection<String> called words; the code passes an instance of a PTransform object called ReverseWords to apply, and then it saves the returned value as the PCollection<String> called reversedWords.

- Java

```
PCollection<String> words = ...;
PCollection<String> reversedWords = words.apply(new ReverseWords());
```

Writing or Outputting the Output Pipeline Data

Once your pipeline has stepped through from start to finish and applied all of its transforms, you'll need to somehow output the results. To accomplish this typical means that you output your pipeline's final PCollections by applying a Write transform to that PCollection.

A Write transform can output the elements of a PCollection to an external data sink, such as a database table. You can actually apply a Write transform to the output of a PCollection at any stage in your pipeline, but typically you would write out data at the end.

The following example code shows how to apply a TextIO.Write transform to write a PCollection of String to a text file ("gs://some/outputData.txt") :

- Java

```
PCollection<String> filteredWords = ...;
filteredWords.apply("WriteMyFile",
TextIO.write().to("gs://some/outputData.txt"));
```

Running Your Pipeline

Finally once you have built your pipeline and tested the logic using some local unit-testing you would then use the run method to run the pipeline. Notably, when you run Pipelines they are executed asynchronously: the program you create sends a specification for your pipeline to a **pipeline runner**, which then constructs and runs the actual series of pipeline operations.

- Java

```
p.run();
```

As we have just learned the run method is executed asynchronously. However, if you'd like a blocking execution instead you could run your pipeline appending the waitUntilFinish method:

- Java

```
p.run().waitUntilFinish();
```

Testing and Debugging a Pipeline

 It is important to test your pipeline locally first before running it in GCP as it will make troubleshooting easier and prevent running up accidental charges. Therefore, before you consider running your pipeline in the cloud, you should unit testing your pipeline code locally using your familiar/favourite local debugging tools to identify and fix bugs in your pipeline code. For this you could use DirectRunner, which is a local runner useful for testing the pipeline as it validates that the code reflects the Beam model as closely as possible. After you test your pipeline and validated the code you can always revert to using a runner of your choice to test on a small scale. For example, you could use the Apache Flink runner with a local or remote Flink cluster. However remember that it is always easier, faster and potentially less expensive to troubleshoot and debug a local rather than a cloud based cluster.

In addition, in order to support unit testing, the Beam SDK for Java provides a number of test classes in the testing package. These provide a number of helpful ways to unit test your pipeline code, such as:

- Test the individual function objects, such as **DoFn**s, inside your pipeline's core transforms.
- Test an entire Composite Transform as a unit.
- Perform end-to-end testing of an entire pipeline.

Handling Bad Messages

When we are using Cloud Dataflow for streaming data we need to ensure that the pipeline can identify bad messages and take some sort of appropriate action. If we do nothing then a bad message will get caught within an infinite loop in the pipeline transform.

Attributes:
event_Id : 34rdy

Payload:
event_Id%%%$F#
user_Id:0001
Timestamp:01-10

Publishers

Malformed
Messages

Pub/SubIO

Bad Messages would be
reprocessed for ever

DataFlow
Pipeline

Parse Messages to catch
malformed messages

```
@ProcessElement
void processElement(ProcessContext c) {
  try {
      c.output(process(c.element()));
  } catch (Exception e) {
    // Re-route failed messages
    c.sideOutput(deadLetterTag, c.element());
  }
}
```

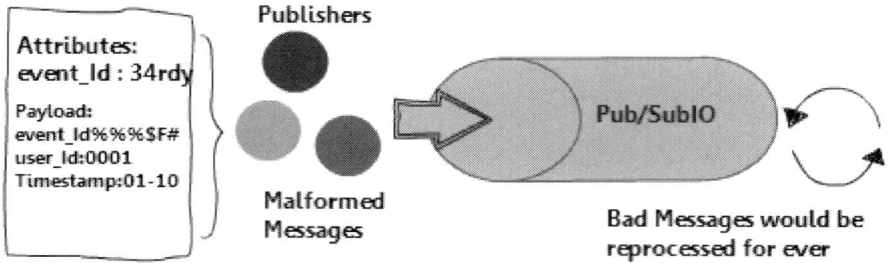

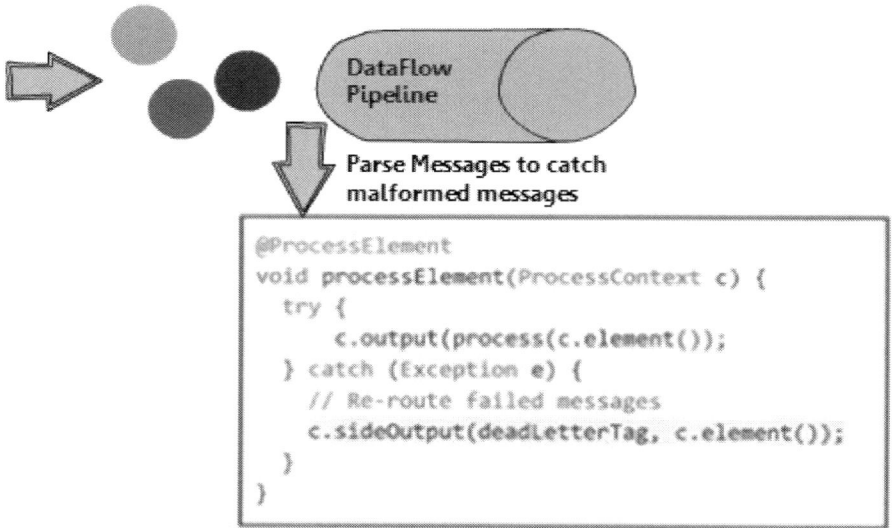

This is because Cloud Dataflow doesn't want to drop messages by default so it will retry to process them until you manually intervene and tell it what to do. The way we can resolve this issue is by adding a try-catch block with a side output as shown below:

To handle this issue we will need to change our architecture to be able to handle bad or malformed messages sent to the side output and delivered to the dead letter sinks:

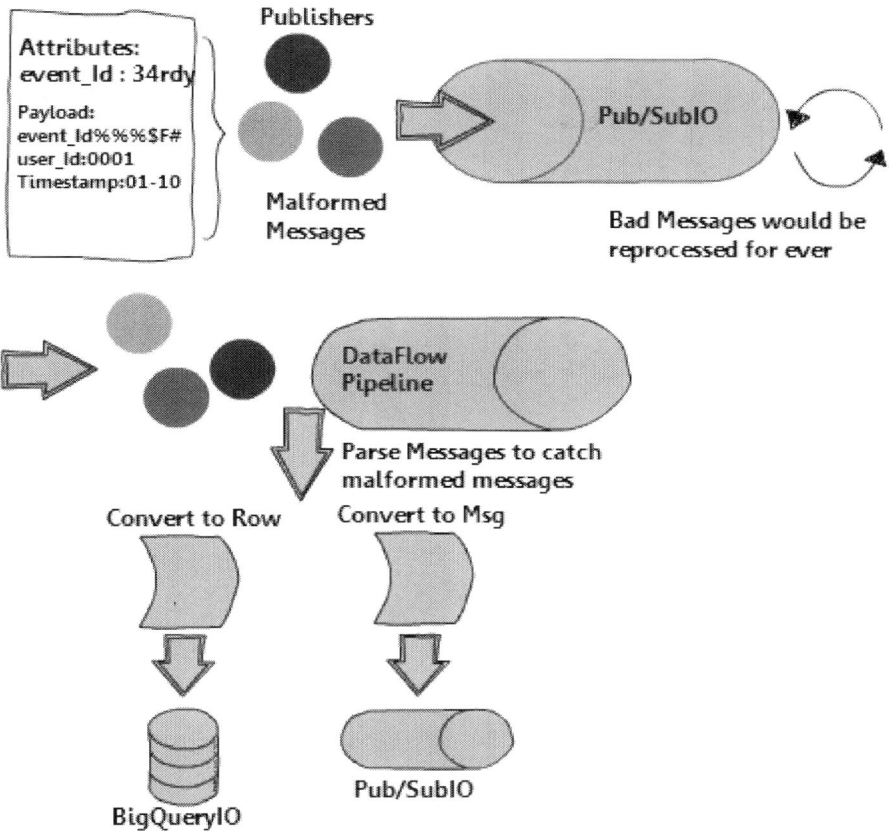

Using Stackdriver Monitoring for Cloud Dataflow pipelines

A feature of Dataflow is that it is tightly integrated with other GCP services such as Stackdriver, which provides you with powerful capabilities in monitoring, logging, and diagnostics. As a result of Cloud Dataflow's integration with Stackdriver you have the tools to access Cloud Dataflow job metrics. Hence you are able to monitor the Job Status, Element Counts, and User Counters or in the case of streaming data the system lag all from the inbuilt Stackdriver dashboards. In addition, you can deploy Stackdriver's inbuilt alerting capabilities for automated notification through several channels of a variety of pre-configured conditions, such as increasing system lag or in the event of a failed job.

Explore Metrics

In order to get a list of all the Cloud Dataflow metrics used by Stackdriver you can follow the steps below to explore the standard metrics provided for each of your Apache Beam pipelines.

1. In the Google Cloud Platform Console, select **Stackdriver Monitoring**:
2. If the **Add your project to a Workspace** dialog is displayed, create a new Workspace by selecting your GCP project under **New Workspace** and then clicking **Add**.
3. In the **Resource** menu, select **Metrics Explorer**.
4. In the **Find a resource type and/or a metric** pane, select the dataflow_job resource type.
5. From the list that appears, select a metric you'd like to observe for one of your jobs.

Create alerts and dashboards

Stackdriver provides you with access to a comprehensive set of Cloud Dataflow-related metrics. It also allows you to create dashboards and alerts so you can chart and be notified when these metrics reach specified values.

Create groups of resources

In addition to being able to set alerts and build dashboards you can also create resource groups that include multiple Apache Beam pipelines of interest.

1. In the Google Cloud Platform Console, select **Stackdriver Monitoring**:
2. In the **Groups** menu, select **Create Groups**.
3. Add filter criteria that define the Cloud Dataflow resources included in the group. For example, one of your filter criteria can be the name prefix of your pipelines.
4. After the group is created, you will be able to see the basic metrics related to resources in that group.

Create alerts for Cloud Dataflow metrics

Stackdriver gives you the ability to create alerts and be notified when a certain metric crosses a specified threshold for example, when **System Lag** of a streaming pipeline increases above a predefined value.

1. In the Google Cloud Platform Console, select **Stackdriver Monitoring**:
2. In the **Alerting** menu, select **Policies Overview**.
3. Click on **Add Policy**.
4. In the **Create new alerting policy** page, you can define the alerting conditions and the channels of communication for alerts.
5. After you've created an alert, you can review the events related to Cloud Dataflow by navigating to **Alerting** > **Events**. Every time an alert is triggered by a **Metric Threshold** condition, an **Incident** and a corresponding **Event** are created in Stackdriver. If you specified a notification mechanism in the alert (email, SMS, etc), you will also receive a notification.

Build your own custom monitoring dashboard

You can build Stackdriver monitoring dashboards with the most relevant Cloud Dataflow-related charts.

1. Go to the Google Cloud Platform Console, and select **Stackdriver Monitoring**:
2. Select **Dashboards** > **Create Dashboard**.
3. Click on **Add Chart**.
4. In the **Add Chart** window, select "Dataflow Job" as the **Resource Type**, select a metric you want to chart in the **Metric Type** field, and select a group that contains Apache Beam pipelines in the **Filter** panel.

You can add as many charts to the dashboard as you like.

Receive worker VM metrics from Stackdriver Monitoring agent

You can do a lot more with Stackdriver and if you are interested in monitoring the underlying infrastructure such as the cluster workers you can do so. However you have to enable the Stackdriver Monitoring agent. For example, if you are interested in monitoring the persistent disks, CPU, network, and process metrics regarding your Cloud Dataflow worker VM instances, then you can enable the Stackdriver Monitoring Agent when you run your pipeline.

To enable the Monitoring agent:

You use the --experiments=enable_stackdriver_agent_metrics option when running your pipeline.

To disable the Monitoring agent without stopping your pipeline, update your pipeline by launching a replacement job and without specifying the --experiments=enable_stackdriver_agent_metrics parameter.

Stopping a running pipeline

Despite all your diligent testing and validation there will likely be times when you need to manually intervene and stop a running Cloud Dataflow job. The way that you can do so is through issuing a command via either the Cloud Dataflow Monitoring Interface or the Cloud Dataflow Command-line Interface. There are two available commands that you can use to stop your job depending on the circumstances: **Cancel** and **Drain**. You would select and use the **Cancel** option to cancel your job immediately. Upon receiving a Cancel command the Dataflow service will immediately halt all data ingestion and processing as soon as possible. In addition it will begin cleaning up the Google Cloud Platform (GCP) resources attached to your job such as shutting down Compute Engine worker instances and closing active connections to I/O sources or sinks. However as the Cancel command does immediately halt processing, this means you may lose any "in-flight" data i.e. data that is actively being processed by your pipeline. However, the data already written from your pipeline may still be accessible on your output sink.

You should use the Cancel option to stop your pipeline and to ensure the GCP resources associated with your job are shut down as soon as possible only if data loss is not a concern. If you do have concerns about in-flight streaming data loss then use the alternative Drain command.

Draining a job

Instead of cancelling a job with immediate effect there is the option that you can drain the job, which provides for a graceful shut-down.

Using the **Drain** option to stop your job tells the Cloud Dataflow service to stop ingesting new data from input sources but the Cloud Dataflow service will preserve any existing resources, such as worker instances, to finish processing and writing any in-flight data in your pipeline. When all pending processing and write operations are complete, the Cloud

Dataflow service will clean up the GCP resources associated with your job but this can take a few minutes.

Note: Your pipeline will continue to incur the cost of maintaining any associated GCP resources until all processing and writing has completed. Use the Drain option to stop your job if you want to prevent data loss as you bring down your pipeline.

Effects of draining a job

Issuing a Drain command will prompt the Cloud Dataflow service to immediately close any in-process windows and fires all triggers. The service will abort any outstanding time-based windows it will not wait for them to finish. For example, if you have a one hour time window running and you are 50 minutes in the service will shut it down immediately it won't wait for it to finish.

Issuing a Drain command will cause any active Cloud Dataflow windows to close and also if you are Draining a pipeline that uses a custom data source class, Cloud Dataflow will stop issuing requests for new data. In both cases it will advance the system watermark to infinity, and call your source's **finalize()** method on the last checkpoint.

Dataflow Templates

Google provides many preconfigured templates for constructing dataflow connectors that enable you to construct your own pipelines with no coding required. There are several pipeline templates available that are preconfigured and ready to run. One such template is for running a pipeline from a Cloud Pub/Sub Subscription to a BigQuery sink. This particular template is a streaming pipeline that reads JSON-formatted messages from a Cloud Pub/Sub subscription and writes them to a BigQuery table. You can use the template as a quick solution to move

JSON-formatted messages from Cloud Pub/Sub and convert them to BigQuery elements.

Creating a pipeline using a Google template

Run a streaming pipeline using the Google-provided Cloud Pub/Sub Topic to BigQuery template.

- Go to the Cloud Dataflow Web UI.
- Click Create job from template.
- Enter a Job name for your Cloud Dataflow job.
- Under Cloud Dataflow template, select the Cloud Pub/Sub Topic to BigQuery template.
- Under Cloud Pub/Sub input topic, enter your topic details such as "projects/pubsub-public-data/topics/test-topic-realtime. The pipeline then ingests incoming data from the input topic.
- Under BigQuery output table, enter <myprojectid>:testtopic.realtime
- Under Temporary Location, enter gs://<mybucket>/tmp/. This is a subfolder for storing temporary files, like the staged pipeline job.
- Click the Run job button.

Requirements for this pipeline:

- The Cloud Pub/Sub messages must be in JSON format, described here. For example, messages formatted as {"k1":"v1", "k2":"v2"} may be inserted into a BigQuery table with two columns, named k1 and k2, with string data type.
- The output table must exist prior to running the pipeline.

Template parameters

Parameter	Description
inputSubscription	The Cloud Pub/Sub input subscription to read from, in the format of projects/<project>/subscriptions/<subscription>.
outputTableSpec	The BigQuery output table location, in the format of <my-project>:<my-dataset>.<my-table>

Running the Cloud Pub/Sub Subscription to BigQuery template

Run from the gcloud command-line tool

When running this template, you'll need the Cloud Storage path to the template:

```
gs://dataflow-
templates/VERSION/PubSub_Subscription_to_BigQuery
```

You must replace the following values in this example:

- Replace *YOUR_PROJECT_ID* with your project ID.
- Replace *JOB_NAME* with your job name
- Replace *YOUR_SUBSCRIPTION_NAME* with your Cloud Pub/Sub subscription name.
- Replace *YOUR_DATASET* with your BigQuery dataset, and
- Replace *YOUR_TABLE_NAME* with your BigQuery table name.

```
gcloud dataflow jobs run JOB_NAME \
  --gcs-location gs://dataflow-
templates/latest/PubSub_Subscription_to_BigQuery \
  --parameters \
inputSubscription=projects/YOUR_PROJECT_ID/subscriptions/

YOUR_SUBSCRIPTION_NAME,\
outputTableSpec=YOUR_PROJECT_ID:

\YOUR_DATASET.YOUR_TABLE_NAME
```

Connecting to BigQuery

The Beam SDKs include built-in transforms that can read data from and write data to Google BigQuery tables. These transforms are bundled under the Google BigQuery I/O connector. To use BigQueryIO, you must install the Google Cloud Platform dependencies by running:

```
pip install apache-beam[gcp]
```

BigQuery IO basics

To read or write from a BigQuery table, you must provide a fully-qualified BigQuery table name (for example, bigquery-public-data:github_repos.sample_contents).
A fully-qualified BigQuery table name consists of three parts:

- **Project ID**: The ID for your Google Cloud Project. The default value comes from your pipeline options object.
- **Dataset ID**: The BigQuery dataset ID, which is unique within a given Cloud Project.
- **Table ID**: A BigQuery table ID, which is unique within a given dataset.

Chapter 29 - Working with BigQuery
Big Query – GCP's Data Warehouse

BigQuery is an enterprise data warehouse that solves the problem of storing and querying massive datasets by enabling super-fast SQL queries that leverage the processing power of the GCP infrastructure. BigQuery is a fully managed service so there is next to zero-ops as it is serverless and this means you don't even need to provision VMs or disks. All that is required is you simply move your data into BigQuery and Google will do the rest. Security is a shared responsibility so you control access to both the project and your data via IAM. You can give others the privileges to view or query your data based upon your business requirements.

You can access BigQuery by using the GCP Console or the browser UI, by using a command-line tool, or by making calls to the BigQuery REST API using a variety of client libraries such as Java, .NET, or Python. There are also a plethora of third-party tools available that you can use to interact with BigQuery, such as when visualizing the data or to assist in loading the data.

There are three typical purposes for interacting with BigQuery;

- Loading and exporting data
- Querying and viewing data
- Managing data

Loading and exporting data

In most cases, you load data into BigQuery storage. If you want to get the data back out of BigQuery, you can export the data. Alternatively, you can set up a table as an external data source, which allows you to query data stored outside of BigQuery.

Querying and viewing data

After you load your data into BigQuery, you can query or view the data in your tables. For example, you can perform the following tasks:
- Run interactive queries
- Run batch queries
- Create a view, which is a virtual table defined by a SQL query
- Use partitioned tables to query a subset of your data

Managing data

In addition to querying and viewing data, you can manage data in BigQuery in the following ways:
- Listing projects, jobs, datasets, and tables
- Getting information about jobs, datasets, and tables
- Defining, updating, or patching datasets and tables
- Deleting datasets and tables
- Managing table partitions

Running BigQuery jobs

BigQuery jobs are actions that it runs on the data warehouse on your behalf typically to load, export, query, or copy data.
When you run a job BigQuery resources are automatically created, scheduled, and run. However you are not restricted to running jobs interactively through the console or the command-line as you can also programmatically run a job. In this case BigQuery schedules and runs the job for you.
Because by their size and nature BigQuery jobs can potentially take a long time to complete, they are executed asynchronously and managed by a dedicated job resource but they can still be polled for their status. Not all jobs will have a job resource as some smaller tasks such as listing resources or getting metadata do not require management.

BigQuery IAM permissions

At a minimum, to run a job, you must have bigquery.jobs.create permissions. bigquery.jobs.create permissions are required for jobs that are automatically created by BigQuery, and they are required for jobs that you run programmatically.
The following predefined Cloud IAM roles include bigquery.jobs.create permissions:
- bigquery.user
- bigquery.jobUser

Every job is associated with a specific project that you specify. The billing account attached to the associated project is billed for any usage incurred by the job. If you share access to a project, any jobs run in the project are billed to the attached billing account.
As BigQuery jobs can take some time to complete and use considerable resources it is necessary to have some safety measures in place to prevent accidental over-run. BigQuery jobs have strict quotas applied to many BigQuery actions to prevent accidental over-billing.
When you run a job programmatically you will need to access the BigQuery API and call the jobs.insert method. To run the BigQuery jobs, you must be granted bigquery.jobs.create permissions. The following predefined Cloud IAM roles incude bigquery.jobs.create permissions:
- bigquery.user
- bigquery.jobUser
- bigquery.admin

When you call the jobs.insert method, include a job resource representation that contains:
- Your location in the location property in the jobReference section.
- The job ID generated by your client code. The server generates a job ID for you if you omit it, but it is a best practice to generate the job ID on the client side to allow reliable retry of the jobs.insert call.

Generating a job ID

As a best practice, generate a job ID using your client code and send that job ID when you call jobs.insert. If you call jobs.insert without specifying a job ID, BigQuery will create a job ID for you, but you will not be able to check the status of that job until the call returns. Also, it might be difficult to tell if the job was successfully inserted or not. However, if you use your own job ID, you can check the status of the job at any time, and you can retry on the same job ID to ensure that the job starts exactly one time. Job IDs must be unique within a project. A common approach to generating a unique job ID is to use a human-readable prefix and a suffix consisting of a timestamp or a GUID. For example:
daily_import_job_1447971251
For example:

```
{
 "jobReference": {
  "projectId": "my_project",
  "jobId": " daily_import_job_1447971251",
  "location": "asia-northeast1"
 },
 "configuration":
 {
  // ..
 },
}
```

In the configuration section of the job resource, include a child property that specifies the job type — load, query, extract, or copy.
After calling the jobs.insert method, check the job status by calling jobs.get with the job ID and location, and check the status.state value to learn the job status. There are some other methods such as jobs.query that you can run to automate the process of checking the job status as it periodically polls the job on your behalf for the status of DONE. When status.state is DONE, the job has stopped running; however, a DONE status does not mean that the job completed successfully, only that it is no longer running.

You will know if the job completed successfully if there is no status.errorResult property. To check the reason for job failure you need to look at the errorResult property as it holds information describing what went wrong.

Introduction to loading data

Typically you must first load your data into BigQuery before you can run queries.
You can load data from Cloud Storage into BigQuery using a Cloud Dataflow pipeline, using DML statements, via streaming inserts, amongst many other ways. Alternatively, you can store the data locally in Cloud BigQuery as the storage costs are much the same as with the other storage options.
When you load data into BigQuery, you can supply the table or partition schema, or, for supported data formats, you can use schema auto-detection.

Supported data formats

BigQuery supports loading data from Cloud Storage and other readable data sources, the default source format for loading data is CSV. To load data that is stored in one of the other supported data formats, such as JSON you need to specify the format explicitly. When your data is loaded into BigQuery, it is converted into columnar format for Capacitor (BigQuery's storage format).

Choosing a data ingestion format

You can load data into BigQuery in a variety of formats. When you are loading data, choose a data ingestion format based upon the following factors:
- Your data's schema - Avro, CSV, JSON, ORC, and Parquet all support flat data. Avro, JSON, ORC, Parquet, Cloud Datastore exports, and Cloud Firestore exports also support data with nested and repeated fields. Nested and repeated data is useful for

expressing hierarchical data. Nested and repeated fields also reduce duplication when denormalizing the data.

- Embedded newlines - When you are loading data from JSON files, the rows must be newline delimited. BigQuery expects newline-delimited JSON files to contain a single record per line.
- Loading encoded data - BigQuery supports UTF-8 encoding for both nested or repeated and flat data. BigQuery supports ISO-8859-1 encoding for flat data only for CSV files.
- Character encodings - By default, the BigQuery service expects all source data to be UTF-8 encoded. Optionally, if you have CSV files with data encoded in ISO-8859-1 format, you can explicitly specify the encoding when you import your data so that BigQuery can properly convert your data to UTF-8 during the import process. Currently, it is only possible to import data that is ISO-8859-1 or UTF-8 encoded. Keep in mind the following points when you specify the character encoding of your data:
- If you don't specify an encoding, or explicitly specify that your data is UTF-8 but then provide a CSV file that is not UTF-8 encoded, BigQuery attempts to convert your CSV file to UTF-8. Generally, your data is imported successfully, but it may not match byte-for-byte what you expect. To avoid this, specify the correct encoding and try your import again.
- Delimiters must be encoded as ISO-8859-1. Generally, it's a best practice to use a standard delimiter, such as a tab, pipe, or comma.
- If BigQuery can't convert a character, it's converted to the standard Unicode replacement character: �.
- JSON files must always be encoded in UTF-8.
- If you plan to load ISO-8859-1 encoded flat data using the API, specify the encoding property in the load job configuration.

Loading compressed and uncompressed data

The Avro binary format is the preferred format for loading both compressed and uncompressed data. Avro data is faster to load because the data can be read in parallel, even when the data blocks are compressed. Compressed Avro files are not supported, but compressed data blocks are. BigQuery also supports the DEFLATE and Snappy codecs for compressed data blocks in Avro files.

Parquet binary format is also a good choice because Parquet's efficient, per-column encoding typically results in a better compression ratio and this results in smaller files. Moreover, Parquet also leverages compression techniques that allow files to be loaded in to BigQuery in parallel. Similar to Avro, compressed Parquet files are not supported, but compressed data blocks are. BigQuery supports Snappy, GZip, and LZO_1X codecs for compressed data blocks in Parquet files.

The ORC binary format offers benefits similar to the benefits of the Parquet format. Data in ORC files is fast to load because data stripes can be read in parallel. The rows in each data stripe are loaded sequentially. To optimize load time, use a data stripe size of approximately 256 MB or less. Compressed ORC files are not supported, but compressed file footer and stripes are. BigQuery supports Zlib, Snappy, LZO, and LZ4 compression for ORC file footers and stripes.

For other data formats such as CSV and JSON, BigQuery can load uncompressed files much faster than compressed files because uncompressed files can be read in parallel. However, as uncompressed files are larger, using them can lead to bandwidth limitations and higher Cloud Storage costs for data staged in Cloud Storage prior to being loaded into BigQuery. Also, keep in mind that line ordering isn't guaranteed for compressed or uncompressed files. It's important to weigh these trade-offs depending on your use case.

In general, if bandwidth is limited, compress your CSV and JSON files by using gzip before uploading them to Cloud Storage. Currently, when you load data into BigQuery, gzip is the only supported file compression type for CSV and JSON files. If loading speed is important to your app and you have a lot of bandwidth, then it might be better to leave your files uncompressed.

Loading denormalized, nested, and repeated data

Many developers are accustomed to working with relational databases and normalized data schemas. In short, normalization eliminates duplicate data from being stored, and provides consistency when regular updates are made to the data.

However, BigQuery performs best when your data is denormalized. Rather than preserving a relational schema, such as a star or snowflake schema, you can improve performance by denormalizing your data and taking advantage of nested and repeated fields. Nested and repeated fields can maintain data relationships without the performance impact of preserving a relational (normalized) schema.

Today, one of the main drivers for normalisation is no longer valid as storage savings from using normalized data has less relevance. Storage is now cheap so increases in storage volume hardly affect the costs so are worth the performance gains of using denormalized data. Similarly performing table Joins require data coordination (communication bandwidth) and memory and CPU cycles. On the other hand denormalization localizes the data to individual slots, so that execution can be done in parallel without any table joins.

Schema auto-detection

When auto-detection is enabled, and you can use schema auto-detection when you load JSON or CSV files into BigQuery. Then BigQuery will start the inference or discovery process by selecting at random a file in the data source and scanning up to 100 rows of data, which it uses as a representative sample. BigQuery will then examine each field in the sample and attempt to discover the schema by assigning a data type to each field based on the values in the sample.

Schema auto-detection is not available for Avro files, ORC files, Parquet files, Cloud Datastore exports, or Cloud Firestore exports because schema information is self-described for these formats.

Alternatives to loading data to query

There are many situations where you can query data without loading it into BigQuery such as when running external queries or in the following situations:

- Public datasets - Public datasets are datasets stored in BigQuery and shared with the public.
- Shared datasets - You can share datasets stored in BigQuery. If someone has shared a dataset with you, you can run queries on that dataset without loading the data.
- External data sources - You can skip the data loading process by creating an external table that is based on an external data source.

BigQueryIO – Beam Connector basics

The Beam SDKs include built-in transforms that can read data from and write data to Google BigQuery tables via the BigQueryIO connector for Beam. In order to read or write from a BigQuery table, you must first provide a fully-qualified BigQuery table name (for example, bigquery-public-data:github_repos.sample_contents).
A fully-qualified BigQuery table name consists of three parts:

- **Project ID**: The ID for your Google Cloud Project. The default value comes from your pipeline options object.
- **Dataset ID**: The BigQuery dataset ID, which is unique within a given Cloud Project.
- **Table ID**: A BigQuery table ID, which is unique within a given dataset.

To specify a BigQuery table in BigQueryIO, you can use either the table's fully-qualified name as a string, or use a TableReference object.

Using a string

To specify a table by using a string, then you will use the format:

```
[project_id]:[dataset_id].[table_id]
```

in order to specify the fully-qualified BigQuery table name. For example:

- Python

```
# project-id:dataset_id.table_id
table_spec = 'clouddataflow-readonly:samples.weather_stations'
```

You may omit project_id and just use the abbreviated format [dataset_id].[table_id]. In that case if you choose to omit the project ID, Beam uses the default project ID you configured in pipeline options.

- Python

```
# dataset_id.table_id
table_spec = 'samples.weather_stations'
```

Using a TableReference

An alternative is to specify a table using a TableReference, in which case you need to first create a new TableReference using the three parts – projectId, datasetId and tableId - of the specific BigQuery table name you wish to reference. For example:

- Python

```
from apache_beam.io.gcp.internal.clients import bigquery
table_spec = bigquery.TableReference(
    projectId='clouddataflow-readonly',
    datasetId='samples',
```

```
tableId='weather_stations')
```

Data types

BigQuery supports the following data types: STRING, BYTES, INTEGER, FLOAT, NUMERIC, BOOLEAN, TIMESTAMP, DATE, TIME, DATETIME and GEOGRAPHY. BigQueryIO allows you to use all of these data types. The following example shows the correct format for data types used when reading from and writing to BigQuery:

- Python

```
bigquery_data = [{
    'string': 'abc',
    'bytes': base64.b64encode(b'\xab\xac'),
    'integer': 5,
    'float': 0.5,
    'numeric': Decimal('5'),
    'boolean': True,
    'timestamp': '2018-12-31 12:44:31.744957 UTC',
    'date': '2018-12-31',
    'time': '12:44:31',
    'datetime': '2018-12-31T12:44:31',
    'geography': 'POINT(30 10)'
}]
```

Reading from BigQuery

The Beam SDK connector BigQueryIO allows you to read from a specified BigQuery table, or read the results of an SQL query. By default, Beam will invoke a BigQuery export request as a result of you applying a BigQueryIO read transform. This is because BigQuery outputs data via exports.

On the other hand to read from a BigQuery table using the Beam SDK, you would apply a Read transform on a BigQuerySource. When you apply a Read transform to BigQueryIO it returns a PCollection, where each element in the PCollection represents a single row in the BigQuery table. Similarly, a single row in a BigQuery table also corresponds to an element in a PCollection. In addition, integer values in the TableRow objects are encoded as strings to match BigQuery's exported JSON format.

Reading from an entire table

If you would like to use BigQueryIO to read an entire BigQuery table, then you would use the table parameter with the BigQuery table name. For example: To read the entire table in BigQuery you would use the following code. In this example the BigQueryIO code reads an entire table that contains weather station data and extracts the max_temperature column.

- Python

```
max_temperatures = (
  p
  | 'ReadTable' >> beam.io.Read(beam.io.BigQuerySource(table_spec))
  # Each row is a dictionary where the keys are the BigQuery columns
  | beam.Map(lambda elem: elem['max_temperature']))
```

Reading with a query string

On the other hand if you do not wish to read an entire table you can simply supply a query string to BigQuerySource specifying the query parameters for the data of interest.

The following code uses a SQL query to only read the max_temperature column.

- Python

```
max_temperatures = (p

  | 'QueryTable' >> beam.io.Read(beam.io.BigQuerySource(
      query='SELECT max_temperature FROM '\
         '[clouddataflow-readonly:samples.weather_stations]'))
  # Each row is a dictionary where the keys are the BigQuery columns
  | beam.Map(lambda elem: elem['max_temperature']))
```

You can also use BigQuery's standard SQL dialect with a query string, as shown in the following example:

- Python

```
max_temperatures = (
  p
  | 'QueryTableStdSQL' >> beam.io.Read(beam.io.BigQuerySource(
      query='SELECT max_temperature FROM '\
         '`clouddataflow-readonly.samples.weather_stations`',
      use_standard_sql=True))
  # Each row is a dictionary where the keys are the BigQuery columns
  | beam.Map(lambda elem: elem['max_temperature']))
```

Using the BigQuery Storage API

The BigQuery Storage API allows you to directly access tables in BigQuery storage. As a result, your pipeline can read from BigQuery storage faster than previously possible.
The Beam SDK for Java (version 2.11.0 and later) adds support for the beta release of the BigQuery Storage API as an experimental feature. Beam's support for the BigQuery Storage API has the following limitations:

- The SDK for Python does not support the BigQuery Storage API.

- Dynamic work re-balancing is not currently supported. As a result, reads might be less efficient in the presence of stragglers.
- SDK versions 2.11.0 and 2.12.0 do not support reading with a query string; you can only read from a table.

Because this is currently a Beam experimental feature, export based reads are recommended for production jobs.

Enabling the API

The latest version of the BigQuery Storage API is distinct from the existing BigQuery API. Therefore, you must enable the BigQuery Storage API for your Google Cloud Platform project.

Integrating with Stackdriver Logging & Monitoring

Stackdriver Logging provides you with an option to export log files from application or services directly into BigQuery. Another alternative to loading data is to stream the data one record at a time as they occur. Streaming is typically used when you need the data to be immediately available or in close to real-time such as when logging critical events or alerts.

Monitoring with Stackdriver

To use Stackdriver to monitor your BigQuery project you will first have to select your project:

- In the Google Cloud Platform Console, select Stackdriver > Monitoring,
- Select the name of your project if it is not already selected at the top of the page.

To view BigQuery resources;

- Select Resources > BigQuery. On this page you'll see a list of tables, events and incident reporting that are user configurable as well as charts of project metrics or dataset metrics.

Stackdriver BigQuery dashboard

To visualize the slots available and slots allocated to your project - slots are allocated per billing account and multiple projects can share the same reservation of slots - go to the Stackdriver dashboard for BigQuery:
In the Google Cloud Platform Console;
- Select Stackdriver > Monitoring,
- Select Resources > BigQuery.

On the Stackdriver dashboard for BigQuery, scroll to the chart named Slot Utilization.
The Slot Utilization chart appears on both the main Stackdriver default dashboard and the Stackdriver dashboard for BigQuery. You can view slot utilisation based on billing account, project or job type - currently, load and export jobs are free operations and they run in a public pool of resources, so they do not use up any of your project slots. In addition you can set up your own charts and dashboards as well as set your own alerts on a wide array of BigQuery metrics.

BigQuery best practices

This section describes best practices for controlling costs and optimising performance in BigQuery. Because BigQuery jobs can take a long time to run and use many resources it is critical that we adhere to some best practice with regards to BigQuery billing and performance so that we can avoid any nasty surprises.

Controlling costs and Optimising performance

1) Best practice: Query only the columns that you need.
Avoid using SELECT * as it is the most expensive way to query data. When you use SELECT *, BigQuery does a full scan of every column in the table.
2) Best practice: Don't run queries to explore or preview table data.
If you are experimenting with or exploring your data, you can use table preview options to view data for free and without affecting quotas.

BigQuery supports the following data preview options:
- In the GCP Console or the classic web UI, on the table details page, click the Preview tab to sample the data.
- In the CLI, use the bq head command and specify the number of rows to preview.
- In the API, use tabledata.list to retrieve table data from a specified set of rows.
- Price your queries before running them

3) Best practice: Before running queries, preview them to estimate costs. Queries are billed according to the number of bytes read so you need to estimate the costs before running a query:
- View the query validator in the GCP Console
- Use the Google Cloud Platform Pricing Calculator
- Perform a dry run by using the: --dry_run flag in the CLI dryRun parameter when submitting a query job using the API

Using the query validator

When you enter a query in the GCP Console, the query validator verifies the query syntax and provides an estimate of the number of bytes read. You can use this estimate to calculate query cost in the pricing calculator. To perform a dry run:
1. Enter a query like the following using the --dry_run flag.

```
bq query \
--use_legacy_sql=false \
--dry_run \
'SELECT COUNTRY, AIRPORT, IATA FROM `project_id`.dataset.airports
LIMIT 1000'
```

The command produces the following response:

```
Query successfully validated. Assuming the tables are not modified,
running this query will process 10918 bytes of data.
```

Using the pricing calculator

To estimate query costs in the Google Cloud Platform Pricing Calculator, enter the number of bytes that are processed by the query as MB, GB, TB, or PB. If your query processes less than 1 TB, the estimate is $0 because BigQuery provides 1 TB of on-demand query processing free per month. Note: If your query processes a small amount of data, you might need to convert the bytes that are processed from KB to MB. MB is the smallest measure used by the pricing calculator.

4) Best practice: Use the maximum bytes billed setting to limit query costs.

You can limit the number of bytes billed for a query using the maximum bytes billed setting. When you set maximum bytes billed, if the query will read bytes beyond the limit, the query fails without incurring a charge.

If a query fails because of the maximum bytes billed setting, an error like the following is returned:

```
Error: Query exceeded limit for bytes billed: 1000000. 10485760 or higher required.
```

To set the maximum bytes billed:

- In the BigQuery web UI, enter an integer in the Maximum Bytes Billed field in the query options. Currently, the GCP Console does not support the Maximum Bytes Billed option.
- In the CLI, use bq query command with the --maximum_bytes_billed flag.

```
bq query --maximum_bytes_billed=1000000 \
--use_legacy_sql=false \
'SELECT  word FROM
 `bigquery-public-data`.samples.shakespeare'
```

In the API, you can set the set the maximumBytesBilled property in the query job configuration.

5) Best practice: Do not use a LIMIT clause as a method of cost control. Applying a LIMIT clause to a query does not affect the amount of data that is read. It merely limits the results set output. You are billed for reading all bytes in the entire table as indicated by the query.

The amount of data read by the query will count against your free tier quota despite the presence of a LIMIT clause.

6) Best practice: Create a dashboard to view your billing data so you can make adjustments to your BigQuery usage. Also consider streaming your audit logs to BigQuery so you can analyse usage patterns.

You can export your billing data to BigQuery and visualize it in a tool such as Google Data Studio.

You can also stream your audit logs to BigQuery and analyse the logs for usage patterns such as query costs by user.

7) Best practice: Partition your tables by date.

You should wherever possible partition your BigQuery tables by date. Partitioning your tables allows you to query relevant subsets of data based on a date which improves performance and reduces costs.

For example, when you query partitioned tables, use the _PARTITIONTIME pseudo column to filter for a date or a range of dates. The query processes data only in the partitions that are specified by the date or range.

8) Best practice: If possible, materialize your query results in stages.

If you have to create and run a very large, multi-stage query, then be aware that every time you run it, BigQuery will read all the data that is required by the query. So be aware that you are charged for all the data that is read each time the query is run.

To avoid this pitfall break your query into stages where each individual stage writes its query results into a temporary destination table. Then you can query the far smaller destination table for aggregated results and this reduces the amount of data that is read and lowers costs. This is especially true if you plan to regularly run the query for the cost of storing the individual results in a BigQuery table is much less than the cost of processing large amounts of data.

9) Best practice: If you are writing large query results to a destination table, use the default table expiration time to remove the data when it's no longer needed.

Keeping large result sets in BigQuery storage has a cost. If you don't need permanent access to the results, use the default table expiration to automatically delete the data for you.

10) Best practice: Use streaming inserts only if your data must be immediately available i.e. required in near real-time. Be aware there is a difference between loading and streaming in so much as there is no charge for loading data into BigQuery but there is a charge for streaming data into BigQuery. Unless your data must be immediately available, load your data rather than streaming it.

Optimizing query performance

In general, queries that do less work perform better. When evaluating query performance in BigQuery, the amount of work required depends on a number of factors:

- Input data and data sources (I/O): When evaluating your input data, consider the required I/O. How many bytes does your query read? Are you properly limiting the amount of input data? Is your data in native BigQuery storage or an external data source? The amount of data read by a query and the source of the data impact query performance and cost.
- Communication between nodes (shuffling): When evaluating your communication throughput, consider the amount of shuffling that is required by your query. How many bytes are passed between stages? How many bytes are passed to each slot? For example, a GROUP BY clause passes like values to the same slot for processing. The amount of data that is shuffled directly impacts communication throughput and as a result, query performance.
- Computation: When evaluating the computation that is required by a query, consider the amount of work that is required. How much CPU time is required? Are you using functions like JavaScript user-defined functions that require additional CPU resources?
- Outputs (materialization): When evaluating your output data, consider the number of bytes written by your query. How many bytes are written for your result set? Are you properly limiting the amount of data written? Are you repeatedly writing the same data? The amount of data written by a query impacts the query

performance (I/O). If you are writing results to a permanent (destination) table, the amount of data written also has a cost.

- Query anti-patterns: Are your queries following SQL best practices and good business logic?

Chapter 30 - Working with Dataprep

Data analysts and data engineers spend almost 80% of their time cleaning, preparing and turning raw data into a useable condition. Any tools that can help reduce this tiresome process is appreciated as it also reduces the time to achieving insights. Furthermore these tools add value to the analytical process as it makes businesses more responsive due to quicker and more informed decision making.

In Google Cloud Platform the service for cleaning, preparing and transforming data is called Cloud Dataprep, which is an intelligent data service for exploring, cleaning, and preparing structured and unstructured data for analysis. Cloud Dataprep is a managed service, which is browser based and serverless so there is no infrastructure to deploy or manage. This makes getting started with Cloud Dataprep quick and easy. Despite this simplicity Cloud Dataprep is powerful and flexible as it natively integrates with GCP's Cloud BigQuery, Cloud Storage, as both data sources and sinks. Furthermore, Cloud Dataprep can also support the uploading of local files so you can use common file types, like CSV and JSON.

The typical use cases for Cloud Dataprep are:

- Data onboarding – this where data engineers need to source external data that perhaps doesn't conform to internal formats or standards

- Data Science & Machine Learning – ML models require clean and well formatted data in order to get best training results

- Marketing & Business Analytics – Data typically comes from several sources, sales, engineering, finance, support and these diverse datasets need to be aggregated and manipulated to provide the business insights

The Dataprep Lifecycle

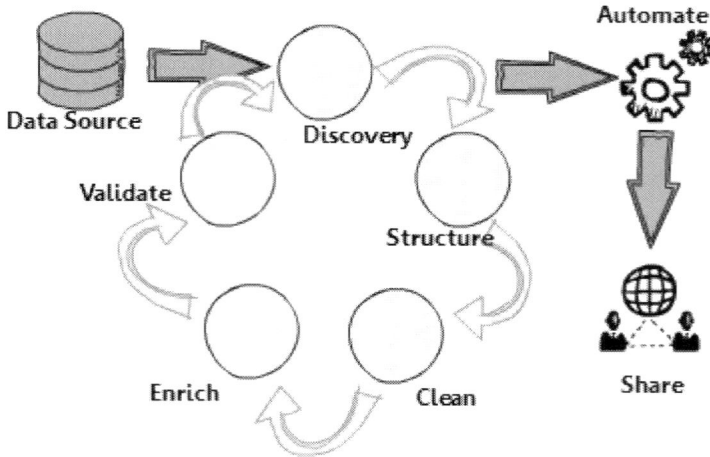

The Dataprep lifecycle is an iterative process by design whereby the ultimate goal is to construct a pipeline or data flow that can be automated to provide a consistent process for handling raw data. This includes handling nested data, cleaning and normalising, transforming and enriching and then finally validating that the data is acceptable to the end data sink.

Therefore as part of the Dataprep lifecycle we have to ensure the following happens in a consistent manner:

- Nested data is handled competently – i.e. undertaking the task of separation of data that is held or embedded in several formats such as CSV, Avro.XLS, or JSON or different types such as structured or unstructured data
- Data cleansing – after you have structured the data then you need to normalise and standardise it as well as set the format so that all the erroneous data such a removing nulls or incorrect dates are removed and only valid data entries remain
- Validation – in this final step we need to ensure that the downstream analytic systems or models will accept the data in the current format, pattern or order

Understanding Nested Data

Dataprep handles nested data in this type of scenario by being able to infer the data schema and present you with a visual row by column representation. But it doesn't just recognise the data format it can also identify nested data and elements and break them out (un-nest them) into their own columns by expanding the rows and columns for you. This then makes it easy to aggregate and join similar types of data in the expanded rows and columns.

Of course often the goal is to only extract a small part of the data such as some embedded values or elements and disregard the rest. In this scenario we can achieve this as Dataprep can dig deep into the body of the data and extract only the key data that is of interest to you. Finally you can also perform metadata operations or extract only substring from a body of text. This is possible because of Dataprep's understanding of the embedded data structures and its ability to present you with a visualised map of the data.

Identifying data patterns

One of the biggest issues yow will have when dealing with data from multiple sources or geographies is getting the data into a standard format that you can use. The most common examples of anomalies are mismatched formats for date and time, telephone numbers, zip/post codes, and timestamps. Fortunately Dataprep comes with in-build tools specifically to recognise and transform these types of pattern mismatches. It does this by profiling the data for common patterns, then inspecting the cardinality of the patterns and identifying the preferred pattern. It can then generate an array of possible options for you to select the correct syntax.

Dealing with inconsistent data

Where humans are entering data into a system such as a data base there are often many inconsistencies – spelling mistakes, non-standard format, and the misuse of acronyms, especially if the record fields are not validated. The result is data that is basically rubbish and unidentifiable even to Dataprep's pattern recognition algorithms. The goal however is still to be able to standardise these data fields. Dataprep however can make sense of these data inconsistences by using clustering algorithms to review and find the closest neighbour and exclude only the outliers or exceptions. Dataprep uses several clustering algorithms to identify and group similar data records such as by closest spelling, pronunciation or format. You can then see the group of similar data records and decide which to include and which to exclude and this allows you to standardise the data as it learns over time.

Data Validation

The final step is to validate the data is actually in a useable structure, order and format that is acceptable to the target systems i.e. BigQuery. Dataprep can do this for you as it knows the specific structures, standards and rules that many types of data sinks demand. The way that this works is Dataprep can import the target on top of the dataset so that you can compare the relative structure. For example, correct matches will be highlighted in green, slight mismatches in blue and significant errors in red. If there are any significant mismatches Dataprep will make suggestions on a suitable transformation that will fix the issue based on the targets schema and your data.

However what makes Cloud Dataprep so easy to work with is that it not only automatically detects schema, type, and mismatched or missing data it allows you easy ways to filter and slice and dice your data graphically much like in Excel. This makes it very intuitive to learn and use as you can understand and pivot the data in a few clicks. For example, you simply highlight a selection of data such as some columns and Dataprep will predict the likely transformations you might want. In this way you can filter or join data sets very easy because it is visual and intuitive. Also any common keys are automatically detected, and a visual preview of the join is generated. You can edit the join as you like, filter or select the required fields, and of course, visualise the results.

Cloud Dataprep transformations are serverless, powerful, and fully managed so they require no infrastructure, configuration or management. In addition, you can build data analytic pipeline without any knowledge of Java or Python as Dataprep handles all the code for you. Indeed, the transformations are constructed and then run as Cloud Dataflow pipelines in the background, which gives Cloud Dataprep tremendous scalability.

Cloud Dataprep use-case

To demonstrate how well Dataprep integrates with the other data processing services in GCP let us take a look at how it works alongside Cloud Storage and Cloud BigQuery. In this scenario we will simply look at ingesting data from a Cloud Storage bucket which we are using as our data source. In this bucket we will create a sample dataset, for example an SQL dump from an ecommerce website. Then we will use Dataprep to filter, clean, transform and prepare our data the way we want it before outputting it to Cloud BigQuery data warehouse. This way we will construct a repeatable scheduled data pipeline that's going to run automatically whenever any updates comes into that Cloud Storage bucket and ultimately output to our data table in BigQuery. So, to summarise we are going to do four things, first we will upload and explore the sample of our ecommerce data into Cloud Storage; Second we will clean it, transform and enrich it; thirdly we will output it to BigQuery; fourth we want to update our e-commerce dataset tables.

When you first open Cloud Dataprep it will prompt you for a data source such as our Cloud Storage staging bucket and it will connect automatically to this. Then we will be asked to create a Dataprep data flow, which is the term for a pipeline. However to create a flow, we're going to need to know the purpose and the business logic to construct the data flow. In this scenario we want to be able to report on revenue so we will call the Dataprep flow – Ecommerce Revenue Analytics Pipeline. This is going to be output to a BigQuery revenue reporting table for sportswear so we only care about all the original ecommerce data that has transactions and revenue associated with the sportswear product category. We can then select the relevant columns (sportswear, transactions and revenue) in Dataprep and this sets the flow we're going to create – we effectively tell Dataprep to filter everything else. Now we will need to create a table in BigQuery but we don't need to create a schema as BigQuery will handle that for us. All we have to do is run the data flow, which will take a subset, just one sample of data from the ecommerce dataset and ingest it into our raw Dataprep. Now when we select the target as BigQuery this creates the Cloud Dataprep dataset. It starts to pull in a preview automatically. It's often faster and easier to load a sample of it into Cloud Dataprep this way than to use SQL in BigQuery for a preview. So now that we have transformed and enriched the dataset (revenue table) that we are interested in we can automate this process so that the Dataprep flow is activated and our BigQuery table is updated every time the cloud storage dataset is updated giving us an always up-to-date view of this data.

Moreover, Dataprep flows also allow us to integrate other services into the pipeline for example by calling a ML platform service. We might want to add this functionality if we wanted to not just report on historical revenue but to try and make predictions on future revenue generation. In this case we would have a upgraded data processing architecture resembling something like this:

The interesting thing about this Dataprep data flow – albeit a very simple use case -is that we did not need to use any coding for data transformation nor for the system integration interfaces. In short we used Cloud Pub/Sub to ingest a huge stream of data at scale. We used Dataflow to build a pipeline to give us a good analytics system. We used BigQuery so that we always had the complete historical data available so we never had to deal with sampled data. At the end, we use Cloud ML and Dataprep to build, train and scale the model. This production ready architecture is completely serverless and a fully managed service that required no code – not even SQL- to build.

Chapter 31 - Working with Datalab

In the previous chapters we have covered the stages of data engineering from collection to storage to data processing, now we turn our attention to data exploration, analysis and visualisation. Hence, in this chapter we will investigate another Google Cloud Platform service called Cloud Datalab, which is a powerful interactive tool created to explore, analyse, transform, and to visualize data and it can even be used to build machine learning models. Cloud Datalab runs on Compute Engine and integrates well with multiple cloud services.

What is Cloud Datalab?

Cloud Datalab is an open source version of the popular Jupyter Notebook (formerly IPython), which has a thriving ecosystem of extensions, modules, knowledge and an active developer community. Cloud Datalab is integrated into GCP so it enables easy connection to BigQuery, Cloud Machine Learning Engine, Compute Engine, and Cloud Storage using Python, SQL, and JavaScript for analysis of your data.

Furthermore, Cloud Datalab is versatile and scalable so you can operate at low or vast scale across several platforms. For example, you can analyse terabytes of data in Cloud Datalab due to its connectors that allow it to query data in BigQuery, or alternatively to run local analysis on megabytes of sampled data from a local file.

With its tight integration with the other Cloud Platform services this enables you to manage your data as well as to perform exploration and visualization to gain valuable insights. With Datalab you can interactively explore, transform, analyse, and visualize your data using connections to BigQuery, Cloud Storage, and Cloud Machine Learning engine.

Indeed in the case of the latter Datalab has full Cloud Machine learning lifecycle support. This means that you can easily start to go beyond basic or even advanced data analysis and start to deploy machine learning (ML) models that are ready for prediction. Indeed, you can begin to explore, build, evaluate, and optimize machine learning models using TensorFlow in the Cloud Machine Learning Engine.

Datalab's extensive set of features includes:

- Integration - Cloud Datalab simplifies data processing through its tight integration with Cloud BigQuery, Cloud Machine Learning Engine, Cloud Storage, and Stackdriver Monitoring. In addition, authentication, cloud computation, and source control are in-built and supported natively.
- Multi-language support - Cloud Datalab currently supports Python, SQL, and JavaScript (for BigQuery user-defined functions).
- Notebook format- based upon Jupyter the Cloud Datalab notebook format combine your code, documentation, results, and visualizations.
- Pay-per-use pricing - Only pay for the cloud resources you use: Compute Engine VMs, BigQuery, and any additional resources you decide to use, such as Cloud Storage.
- Interactive data visualization - Use Google Charting or matplotlib for easy visualizations.
- Machine learning – supports native TensorFlow-based deep ML models in addition to Scikit-learn. It also scales training and prediction via specialized libraries for Cloud Machine Learning Engine.
- IPython support- Datalab is based on Jupyter (formerly IPython) so there are many existing packages available for statistics, machine learning, etc. You can also benefit and learn from a vast collection of published notebooks and swap tips with a thriving IPython developer community.
- Open source- Developers wishing to extend Datalab can fork and/or submit pull requests on the GitHub hosted project.
- Easy and quick start up.

Steps to set up and open Cloud Datalab

From a terminal window on your local machine:
1. Update your gcloud command-line tool components:

2. gcloud components update

If you installed the gcloud command-line tool through apt or yum, use those package managers to update the components:

```
sudo apt update && sudo apt upgrade google-cloud-sdk

sudo yum upgrade google-cloud-sdk
```

3. Install the datalab component for the gcloud command-line tool:

```
gcloud components install datalab
```

If you installed the gcloud command-line tool through apt or yum, use those package managers to update the components:

```
sudo apt update && sudo apt install google-cloud-sdk-datalab

sudo yum install google-cloud-sdk-datalab
```

4. Create a Cloud Datalab instance. The name of the instance must start with a lowercase letter, followed by up to 62 lowercase letters, numbers, or hyphens, and cannot end with a hyphen.

```
datalab create datalab-instance-name
```

If the command returns an error, re-run the command with the following debug flag to help diagnose the problem:

```
datalab create --verbosity=debug datalab-instance-name
```

By default, the datalab create command connects to the newly created instance. To create the instance but not connect to it, pass in the --no-connect flag:

```
datalab create --no-connect instance-name
```

Cloud Datalab runs inside of a Google Compute Engine VM with an attached persistent disk that is used to store notebooks. Cloud Datalab VMs are connected to a special network in a project called datalab-network. The default configuration of this network limits incoming connections to SSH connections.
The datalab create command also creates the following Google Cloud Platform resources (if not already available):

- The datalab-network network
- A firewall rule on the datalab-network allowing incoming SSH connections
- The datalab-notebooks Google Cloud Source Repository
- The persistent disk for storing Cloud Datalab notebooks

Choosing a machine type

You choose a machine type for your Cloud Datalab VM instance when you create the instance. Here's an example:

```
datalab create --machine-type n1-highmem-2 instance-name
```

At the time of creation of a Datalab VM instance, the default machine type used is the n1-standard-1 but you are free to select a different machine type. Your decision may be based on performance and cost characteristics or to suit your data analysis specific needs. Here are a few key considerations to keep in mind when selecting a machine type:
- Depending on your projected workloads you should be aware that each active notebook instance uses a Python kernel to run code

within its own process. For example, if you have N notebooks open, there are at least N processes open.

- Each kernel is single threaded. However, unless you are planning on running multiple notebooks at the same time, multiple cores may not provide a significant benefit.
- You may be better to select a machine-type with additional memory depending on your usage pattern and the amount of data you intend to process.
- Bear in mind that execution is cumulative so running three Cloud Datalab notebook cells in a row will result in high memory usage and the accumulation of corresponding state.
- Processing large amounts of data in memory (for example, using Pandas Dataframes) causes proportional memory allocation. However, when you finish running a notebook, you can stop the session and shutting down the session releases the memory.
- Cloud Datalab utilizes disk-based swap file to provide overhead for additional memory requirements. But relying on the swap file is likely to slow down processing. Therefore, it's best to estimate memory needs appropriate to the workload and then pick a machine type which at least meets the estimated amount of memory per job.

For example, to change the default setting and create a Cloud Datalab instance with one K80 GPU use the following command:

```
datalab beta create-gpu datalab-instance-name
```

If you need more that on GPU you can specify other K80 GPUs, use the --accelerator-count *number* flag.

```
datalab beta create-gpu --accelerator-count number
```

5. To connect securely from your local machine to the Datalab instance in GCP you will need to have a secure SSH connection. The Datalab tool can create a persistent SSH tunnel to your Cloud Datalab instance you that will allow you to connect to the

instance from your local browser as though Cloud Datalab was running on your local machine. To create this connection, use the datalab connect command:

```
datalab connect instance-
name
```

You can list your instance-names via the Datalab list command. The datalab connect command will restart your instance if it is not running. The command continues to run until you stop it (the connection remains available for as long as the command is running). By default, the local port used for the connection is 8081. To change to a different port, pass in the --port flag. For example, to use local port 8082, run the following:

```
datalab connect --port 8082 instance-name
```

6. Once you have provisioned the Datalab VM and secured the connection all that remains is to open the Cloud Datalab home page in your browser.

```
http://localhost:8081
```

The connection to your Datalab instance remains open while the Datalab notebook is active. If the terminal command window is closed or interrupted, the connection will terminate, if this occurs you will need to run the following command to re-establish the connection:

```
datalab connect instance-name
```

Adding Python libraries to a Cloud Datalab instance

Cloud Datalab includes a set of libraries intended to support common data analysis, transformation, and visualization scenarios. However, you can add your own Python libraries using one of the following ways:

- Add a code cell in a notebook to pip install the library, this is the easiest way to add addition libraries.
- Create a new notebook and add a code cell with the following content after substituting lib-name:

```
%%bash
echo "pip install lib-name" >> /content/datalab/.config/startup.sh
cat /content/datalab/.config/startup.sh
```

You then have to run the cell and restart the Cloud Datalab instance

- The other way you can add additional libraries is to inherit them from a Cloud Datalab Docker container using a Docker customization mechanism. This option is much more heavyweight compared to the other options listed above. However, it provides maximum flexibility for those who intend to significantly customize the container for use by a team or organization. To use this method you need to build your own container. For example you could make one called "Dockerfile-extended-libraries", then in the Dockerfile-extended-libraries.in:

```
FROM datalab
...
pip install lib-name
...
```

This approach requires that you do a lot more work such as building and maintaining your own image and it is not a one off event as the underlying Datalab container will evolve over time. Therefore, it is recommended that you use this method only if the other ways are not suitable.

Source control

When you run Datalab it adds a Datalab-notebooks Cloud Source Repository inside the project. You can browse the cloud source repository from the Google Cloud Platform Console Repositories page.

Repositories

Repository Name ∧	Clone URL
datalab-notebooks	https://source.developers.google.com,

Stopping an instance

Run the following command to stop your Cloud Datalab instance to avoid incurring unnecessary costs.

```
datalab stop instance-
name
```

When you are ready to start using Cloud Datalab again, run the datalab connect command to restart the instance.

Clean up

You should be aware that you will incur charges from the time of creation to the time of deletion of the Cloud Datalab VM instance. Therefore you are also charged for the Persistent Disk where notebooks are stored. The Persistent Disk however remains after the deletion of the VM until you specifically delete it. The following command deletes both the VM instance and its Persistent Disk.

```
datalab delete --delete-disk instance-
name
```

Updating the Cloud Datalab VM without deleting the notebooks disk
To update to a new Cloud Datalab version, or to change VM properties such as the machine type or the service account, you can delete and then re-create the Cloud Datalab VM without losing your notebooks stored on the persistent disk.

```
datalab delete --keep-disk instance-name
datalab create instance-name
```

Notebooks are not copied between zones. Cloud Datalab VMs are zonal. If you change zones when you re-create the VM, the new VM will get a new Persistent Disk (PD). Your notebooks will not be copied from the PD in the previous zone to the PD in the new zone.

Reducing usage of compute resources

Google compute engine VMs do incur costs and so you will be charged for the time that a cloud datalab instance is running whether or not you are using it. You can reduce cloud datalab VM charges by stopping the instance when you are not using it. However, you will continue to incur charges for the resources attached to the VM (such as the persistent disk and the external IP address), but the VM instance itself will not incur charges while it is stopped.
When you need to use your stopped instance again, run datalab connect instance-name to connect to your instance, and the datalab tool will restart the instance before attempting to connect to it.

Copying notebooks from the Cloud Datalab VM

You can copy files from your Cloud Datalab VM instance using the gcloud compute scp command. For example, if you want to copy the contents of your Cloud Datalab VM's datalab/notebooks directory to an *instance-name*-notebooks directory on your local machine, run the following command:

```
gcloud compute scp --recurse \

 datalab@instance-name:/mnt/disks/datalab-
pd/content/datalab/notebooks \

 instance-name-notebooks
```

Cloud Datalab backup

Cloud Datalab instances will periodically and automatically back up your user content to a Google Cloud Storage bucket in your project. This is done to prevent accidental loss of your content if your VM disk be deleted or be otherwise unavailable. By default, a Cloud Datalab instance will store all of the user's content on an attached disk, and the backup utility works on this disk's root. The backup job is run by default every ten minutes, and this creates a zip file of the entire disk initially but only copies changed files in later backups. Cloud Datalab uploads the backup files to Google Cloud Storage.

Cloud Datalab retains in Cloud Storage only the last 10 hourly backups, 7 daily backups, and 20 weekly backups, all other backup files are deleted to preserve space. Automatic backups can be switched off by passing the --no-backups flag when creating a Cloud Datalab instance with the datalab create command.

Restoring backups

To restore a backup, the user selects the backup file from Google Cloud Storage by examining the VM zone, VM name, notebook directory, and the human-readable timestamp. For example, a sample backup file path would look like this :

gs://myproject/datalab-backups/us-central1-a/datalab0123/content/daily-20190328113922 /tmp/backup0127.zip

We can deduce from this path that this sample backup was created for the VM datalab0123 in zone us-central1-a, and it contains all content under the notebook's/content directory. It was created as a daily backup point on 03/28/2019 at 11:39:22.

A backup zip file can be downloaded from the browser or by using the gsutil tool.

- To use the browser, navigate to Google Cloud Platform Console, then select **Storage** from the left navigation sidebar. Browse to the Cloud Datalab backup bucket, then select and download the zip file to disk.
- To use gsutil to download the backup file, run gsutil cp gs://backup_path destination_path. For example, to backup and extract the sample zip file discussed above:

```
gsutil cp
gs://myproject/datalab-backups/us-central1-
a/datalab0123/content/daily-20190328113922 /tmp/backup0127.zip


unzip -q /tmp/backup0127.zip -d /tmp/restore_location/
```

Working with data

Cloud Datalab can access data located in any of the following places:

- Google Cloud Storage: files and directories in Cloud Storage can be programmatically accessed using the datalab.storage APIs (see the /datalab/docs/tutorials/Storage/Storage APIs.ipynb notebook tutorial)
- BigQuery: tables and views can be queried using SQL and datalab.bigquery APIs (see the datalab/docs/tutorials/BigQuery/BigQuery/BigQuery APIs.ipynb notebook tutorial)
- Local file system on the persistent disk: you can create or copy files to the file system on the persistent disk attached to your Cloud Datalab VM.

Local files are not backed up (compare to Cloud Datalab backup to Cloud Storage), and will be lost if you delete the VM running Cloud Datalab. Also, the default size of persistent disk is not sufficient to store large amounts of data. Therefore, using Cloud Storage instead of the local file system for data is strongly recommended.

If your data is in a different location—on premise or in another cloud—you can transfer the data to Cloud Storage using the gsutil tool or the Cloud Storage Transfer Service.

Cloud Datalab uses the Cloud Datalab VM service account to access data and to execute code using Google Cloud services such as Google BigQuery, Google Cloud Machine Learning Engine, Google Cloud Storage, and Google Cloud Dataflow. The service account must be granted appropriate authorization to access or execute code before the corresponding notebook is run.

Chapter 32 – Integrating BigQuery BI Engine with Data Studio

BI Engine

Integrating GCP's data warehouse and analytical workhorse BigQuery with data visualisation tools such as Tableau or Cloud Data Studio is fast and easy. This is thanks to BigQuery's array of inbuilt connectors and integration tools but more specifically the BI Engine. By using BI Engine's fast, in-memory analysis service you can analyse data stored in BigQuery with sub-second query response time and with high concurrency.
BI Engine integrates with and supports many of the familiar visualisation tools like Google Data Studio to accelerate data exploration and analysis. By utilising the BI Engine service, you can easily and quickly visualise and present your data analysis via rich presentation, graphs, interactive dashboards and reports using Data Studio. This is readily achievable without any graphic skills and without compromising quality or performance.
When you are using operational and prescriptive business intelligence to help steer the decision making process in your business then the BI visualisation and analysis tools you deploy have to be intuitive to use and fast. BI Engine performance matches the speed of business as it delivers sub-second query response time with minimal load times and improved concurrency. When you integrate BI Engine with BigQuery streaming and Data Studio, you can realise real-time data analysis over streaming data and also materialise data visualisation without sacrificing data freshness. This is because unlike other traditional data integration solutions Data Studio and BI Engine have no complex data pipelines or additional servers as it is built upon an entirely serverless architecture.

The core issue that BI Engine and Data Studio addresses is that traditional BI systems that move data from data warehousing platforms to BI platforms to support fast interactive analysis and visualisation typically requires complex ETL pipelines for data movement. The problem is that the time introduced by these ETL periphery services and jobs can often introduce delays into your reporting and compromise the freshness of data. This is not acceptable today for critical decision support systems. In contrast to the pipeline technique BI Engine performs in-place analysis within BigQuery. This eliminates the need to move or transform data or to build and deploy any complex data pipelines.

In addition BI Engine's is intuitive to learn and to operate as it is almost entirely self-tuning. It is designed to automatically tune queries by transferring data between BI Engine's in-memory storage, the BigQuery query cache, and BigQuery storage. This ensures optimal performance and load times for dashboards and near-real time interactive reports. However there are some things you can manually tune such as the BigQuery administrator can add or remove BI Engine memory capacity by using the BigQuery UI in the GCP Console.

Getting Started with Data Studio & BI Engine

The first step in getting started with BigQuery BI and Data Studio is to create a BigQuery dataset to store your data that we can later use in the BI Engine-managed table. To create your BigQuery dataset:

1. Go to the BigQuery web UI in the GCP Console.
2. In the navigation panel, in the **Resources** section, click your project name.
3. On the right side, in the details panel, click **Create dataset**.

On the **Create dataset** page:

4. For **Dataset ID**, enter biengine_tutorial.
5. For **Data location**, choose **United States (US)**. We select the US as currently, the public datasets are stored in the US multi-region location. Hence, for convenience and

simplicity, you should place your dataset for this demo in
the same location.

Create dataset

Dataset ID

biengine_tutorial

Data location (Optional) @

United States (US) ▼

Default table expiration @

● Never
○ Number of days after table creation:

6. Leave all of the other default settings in place and
click **Create dataset**.

Create a table by copying data from a public dataset

In this case we will use a dataset available through the Google Cloud
Public Dataset Program. A public dataset is any dataset that is stored in BI
Engine and Google makes available to the general public. These
collections of public datasets are hosted within BI Engine and you are free
to integrate them into your applications.
In this section, we will create a table by copying data from the San
Francisco 311 service requests dataset. You can explore the dataset by
using the BigQuery web UI in the Google Cloud Platform Console.
Create your table
To create your table:
1. Open the SF 311 dataset in the BigQuery web UI.
2. In the navigation pane, expand **san_francisco_311** and click
the **311_service_requests** table.
3. On the right side of the window, click **Copy table**.

4. In the **Copy table** dialog, in the **Destination** section:

- For **Project name**, choose your project.
- For **Dataset name**, verify **biengine_tutorial** is selected.
- For **Table name**, enter **311_service_requests_copy**.
- Click Copy

Copy table

Source

Project name	Dataset name	Table name
bigquery-public-data	san_francisco_311	311_service_requests

Destination

Project name		Dataset name	
I▒▒▒▒▒▒▒	▼	biengine_tutorial	▼

Table name

311_service_requests_copy

5. When the copy job is complete, you can verify the table contents by expanding **[PROJECT] > biengine_tutorial** and clicking **311_service_requests_copy > Preview**.

Step three: Create your BI Engine reservation

1. Go to the BI Engine page in the BigQuery Admin Console.
2. Click **Create reservation**.
3. On the **Create reservation** page, verify your project name is correct
4. Choose your location. The location should match the location of the datasets you are querying.

5. Adjust the slider to select the amount of memory capacity you're reserving. The following example will set the Memory capacity to 2 GB. The current maximum is 10 GB.

① Configure

BigQuery BI Engine reservation will be assigned to your current project.

Project
[▬▬▬▬▬▬]   ▼   ❓

Location *
United States (US)   ▼   ❓

GB of Capacity   ❓

        ②
1 ─────────────── 10 Total: 2 GB

6. Click **Next**.
7. Review your reservation details and then click **Next**.
8. You are asked to review the agreement and then click **Create**.
9. After confirming your reservation, the details are displayed on the reservation page.

⦿ BigQuery   ← BI Engine BETA   + CREATE RESERVATION

Reservations

☰ Filter table

Project ↑	Size ❓	Location	Monthly Cost	Actions
▬▬▬▬	2 GB	United States (US)	$60.00	⋮

Create a data source connection in Data Studio

Before you can get started and create a report in Google Data Studio, you must create a data source or sources for the report.. When you create a data source for BI Engine, Google Data Studio uses the BigQuery connector.

When you define your data source connection in Data Studio, BI Engine uses the table and columns you configure to determine what data to cache. BI Engine only caches the columns that you select to be in your report.

Required IAM permissions

To be able to add a connector to BigQuery you need to have the prerequisite privileges to add a BigQuery data source to a Google Data Studio report. In addition, the IAM permissions applied to BigQuery datasets will also apply to the reports, charts, and dashboards you create in Google Data Studio. It is important to know that a Google Data Studio reports are not visible to anyone else unless you share them. When shared, the reports are visible only to users who you have granted the appropriate permissions.

The permissions that you will need to run a query job to populate a report requires the BigQuery permission - bigquery.jobs.create. However, in order for the query job to complete successfully, the user or group must have access to the dataset containing the tables referenced by the query. The minimum access level required is the 'Can view' permission, which maps to the bigquery.dataViewer role for that dataset.

If you are the person who created the dataset then you are automatically granted the owner access to the dataset which gives you complete control over it. As well, since you created the project you have Owner access at the project level. Owner access also gives you the ability to run jobs in the project.

Permission details

You can set bigquery.jobs.create permissions at the project level by granting any of the following predefined IAM roles:

- bigquery.user
- bigquery.jobUser
- bigquery.admin

Note: Most users such as data analysts and data scientists should be granted **bigquery.user**
or **bigquery.jobUser**. You should not grant **bigquery.admin** unless it is to an administrator as it has full permissions across all datasets in a project.

Granting a user or group the bigquery.user role at the project level, by default, provides no access to any of the datasets, tables, or views in the project. The permission granted through the bigquery.user role only gives users the ability to create their own datasets and to run query jobs against datasets they have created themselves or have been given explicit access to. Therefore, If you assign
the bigquery.user or bigquery.jobUser role, you must also grant
them access to each dataset the user or group needs to access.
When you assign access to a dataset, there are 3 options:

- **Can view** maps to the **bigquery.dataViewer** role for that dataset.
- **Can edit** maps to the **bigquery.dataEditor** role for that dataset.
- **Is owner** maps to the **bigquery.dataOwner** role for that dataset.

The minimum access required for a user to run a query is Can View.

Creating your data source

To create your data source:
1. Open Google Data Studio.

2. On the **Reports** page, in the **Start a new report section**, click the **Blank** template. This creates a new untitled report.
3. If prompted, complete the **Marketing Preferences** and the **Account and Privacy** settings and then click **Save**.
4. In the **Add a data source** window, click **Create new data source**.
5. In the **Google Connectors** section, look for **BigQuery** and then click **Select**.
6. For **Authorization**, click **Authorize**. This allows Google Data Studio access to your GCP project.
7. In the **Request for permission** dialog, click **Allow** to give Google Data Studio the ability to view data in BigQuery.
8. In the **Project** pane, click the name of your project.
9. In the **Dataset** pane, click the name of your project (in this case - **biengine_tutorial**).
10. In the **Table** pane, click **311_service_requests_copy**.
11. Click **Connect**. Once Google Data Studio connects to the BigQuery data source, the table's fields are displayed to you. You can use this page to edit the field properties or to create new fields.
12. In the upper right corner, click **Add to report**.
13. In the **Request for permission** dialog, click **Allow** to give Data Studio the ability to view and manage files in Google Drive.

Creating a chart

Now that you have created you dataset and connected to your data source within BigQuery and added it to your report the next step is to create a visualization. In our demo using the 311 calls data set the bar chart you create will display the top complaints by neighbourhood:

1. Change the report name. For example, type BI Engine tutorial.
2. After the report editor loads, click **Insert > Bar chart**.
3. Using the handles, expand the size of the chart.
4. On the **Data** tab, notice the value for Data Source is 311_service_requests_copy.

Because you are charting the number of requests by neighbourhood, you need to set the Dimension to category and the Breakdown dimension to neighbourhood. Click the default dimension (likely status), and in the list, choose **category**.

5. In the **Available Fields** list, click and drag **neighbourhood** onto the **Add dimension here** box under **Breakdown dimension**.

Add a filter

Because the data includes a number of NULL values in the neighbourhood column, you add a filter that excludes NULL values from the chart.

To add a filter:

1. On the **Data** tab, click **Add a filter**.
2. In the **Create filter** dialog:
3. For **Name**, enter **Exclude nulls**.
4. Verify **Data source** is set to 311_service_requests_copy.
5. Click **Include** and choose **Exclude**.
6. Click **Select a field** and choose **neighbourhood**.
7. Click **Select a condition** and choose **Is null**.
8. Click **Save**.
9. After the filter is applied, your chart should look like the following.

Chapter 33 - Orchestrating Data Workflows with Cloud Composer

Although not strictly included within the data analytical lifecycle of collect, store, process, analyse and visualise, the final component of orchestrate is clearly missing. This is simply because precious little analytical architecture today could function without a worthy component for orchestration.

Indeed orchestration is a prerequisite for most architecture whether it is based upon traditional compute engine VMs, containers, event-driven applications or big data analytical systems such as a Hadoop ecosystem as the workflows have become so much more complex and opaque. Hence, the subtle shift in the emphasis on orchestration from rapid deployment and automated provisioning which are still very important towards managing, automating and thereby simplifying complex workflows. Google Cloud Platform addresses the requirement for orchestration through Cloud Composer, which is a fully managed workflow orchestration service. Cloud Composer by design enables you to create, schedule, and monitor data and analytical pipelines that span across on-premises data centres and hybrid cloud solutions. In order to achieve this comprehensive scope and compatibility Cloud Composer like many GCP products and services is built upon open source components. In the case of Cloud Composer it is built on Apache Airflow, which is a popular open source project that uses the Python programming language. This ensures that Cloud Composer is free from the risk of vendor lock-in and will be easy to use and support.

Under the Bonnet

For an orchestration solution to be effective it must be intuitive and easy to learn and operate. Hence, Cloud Composer is designed to build pipelines, which are configured as directed acyclic graphs (DAGs) using Python. This at first glance may not sound very intuitive or easy but building upon Python using the DAGs model does make it easy for users of any experience level to build and schedule a workflow so long as there is sufficient abstraction. Consequently Cloud Composer abstracts most of the implementation complexity by introducing a one-click deployment UI. Access to this UI gives the user access to a library of connectors as well as multiple graphical representations of their workflow. By enabling the user to visualise their pipeline in action, and thereby increasing their understanding of the underlying processes makes troubleshooting easier. It also goes a long way in making their pipelines more reliable. Furthermore, Cloud Composer's traditional role as an automatic scheduler of events ensures the synchronization of your directed acyclic graphs and keeps your jobs on schedule.

End-to-end integration for GCP workloads

As Cloud Composer is tightly integrated with the other GCP services, this provides users with the ability to orchestrate their full pipeline from end to end. Cloud Composer's built-in and robust integration with many of the building blocks for analytical platforms such as BigQuery, Cloud Dataflow, Cloud Dataproc, Cloud Datastore, Cloud Storage, Cloud Pub/Sub, and Cloud ML Engine makes designing and operating big data and machine learning platforms much easier.

Ease of use comes from Cloud Composer's managed service model, which places the burden of provisioning, scaling and maintaining the infrastructure on Google, which allows you to focus on designing, scheduling, and monitoring your workflows.
To demonstrate how simple it is to create a Cloud Composer environment using the Google Cloud Platform Console and run a simple Apache Airflow DAG (also called a workflow) you can follow the quickstart guide, which is summarised below.

Getting Started with Cloud Composer

As always when launching any GCP service you will require to have a project and a billing account and to enable the appropriate APIs – in this case the Cloud Composer API. Once you have the prerequisites in order you can continue with the deployment.

Creating an environment

1. In the GCP Console, go to the Create environment page.
2. In the **Name** field, enter the environment label such as, example-environment.
3. In the **Location**, select a region from the drop-down box for the Cloud Composer environment.
4. Use the provided defaults for the other fields.
5. To create the environment, click **Create**.
6. Wait until environment creation is completed this can take up to 25 minutes perhaps longer so be patient. When the environment is built, you will see the green check mark against the environment name.

Viewing environment details

After environment creation is completed, you can view your environment's deployment information, such as the Cloud Composer version, the URL for the Airflow web interface, and the DAGs folder in Cloud Storage.
To view deployment information:

1. In the GCP Console, go to the Environments page.
2. To view the Environment details page, click on the environment of interest – in this case - example-environment. The following page will be displayed:

✎ EDIT

Name	example-environment
Zone	us-central1-c
Service account	@developer.gserviceaccount.com
Google API scopes	https://www.googleapis.com/auth/cloud-platform
GKE cluster	
Details	None
Workloads	None
Image version	composer-1.7.2-airflow-1.9.0
Python version	2
Network tags	None
Worker nodes	
Node count	3
Disk size (GB)	100
Machine type	n1-standard-1
Network configuration	
Network ID	projects/composer-test-1/global/networks/default
Subnetwork ID	-
DAGs folder	None
Airflow web UI	None
Stackdriver	view logs
Created	Thu Jun 27 2019 15:54:09 GMT-0700 (Pacific Daylight Time)
Updated	Thu Jun 27 2019 15:54:09 GMT-0700 (Pacific Daylight Time)

Now that you have complete building your environment the next step is to construct your DAG. A DAG is simply a graphical representation of the organisational steps required to run a job or accomplish a task.

Creating a DAG

Cloud Composer is built upon the open source orchestration application Airflow so it is fully compatible with Airflow DAGs, which are a collection of organized tasks that you want to schedule and run. Just like in Airflow the DAGs are defined in standard Python files.

For example; the Python code in quickstart.py will:

1. Create a DAG, 'composer_sample_dag' that will run once per day.
2. Execute one task, print_dag_run_conf. This task will print the DAG run configuration.
3. To create a DAG, you need to copy the Python quickstart.py file to your local machine.

Uploading the DAG to Cloud Storage

One thing that you need to be aware of is that Cloud Composer only schedules DAGs that are in the DAGs folder in the environment's Cloud Storage bucket.

Therefore to schedule your DAG within GCP, you must move quickstart.py from your local machine to your environment's DAGs folder on Cloud Storage:

1. In the GCP Console, go to the Environments page.
2. Open the /dags folder, and click the **DAGs folder** link for example-environment.
3. On the Bucket details page, click **Upload files** and then select your local copy of quickstart.py.
4. To upload the file, click **Open**.

After you have successfully uploaded your DAG – the quickstart.py file - Cloud Composer will add the DAG to Airflow and automatically provision the DAG. However, it might take a few minutes for the DAG to show up in Cloud Composer's web interface.

You can also use gcloud composer commands to interact with your environment. For example, to upload a DAG:

```
gcloud composer environments storage dags import \

  --environment my-environment  --location us-central1 \

  --source test-dags/quickstart.py
```

Viewing the DAG in the Airflow web interface

Each Cloud Composer environment has a web server that runs the Airflow web interface that you can use to manage DAGs.
To view the DAG in the Airflow web interface:

1. In the GCP Console, go to the Environments page.
2. To open the Airflow web interface, click the **Airflow** link for example-environment. The interface opens in a new browser window.
3. In the Airflow toolbar, click **DAGs**.
4. To open the DAG details page, click composer_sample_dag.

The page for the DAG shows the Tree View, a graphical representation of the workflow's tasks and dependencies.

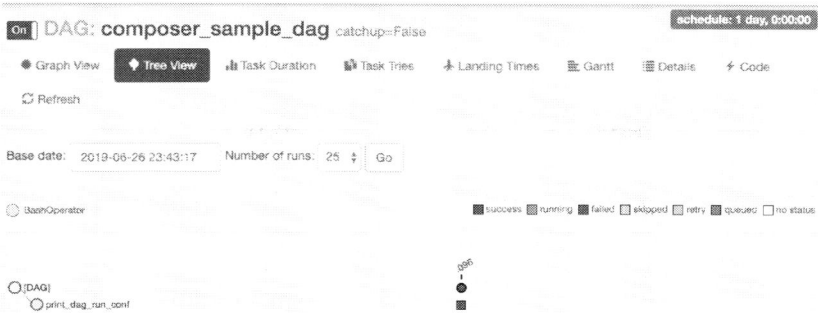

Viewing task instance details in the Airflow logs

The DAG that you scheduled via the quickstart.py file only includes one task, which you can see in the tree is the 'print_dag_run_conf' job. This particular task as we saw earlier simply prints the DAG run configuration, which you can see in the Airflow logs for the task instance.

To view the task instance details click on the DAG's tree view: If you hover over the graphic for the print_dag_run_conf task, its status is displayed – i.e. whether it is running or not (Green border).

You can also view the Task Instance Context Menu which displays job metadata and lets you perform some actions. In addition as Clod Composer (Airflow) is so deeply integrated with Stackdriver Logging you can view the log details within the Stackdriver logs.

Chapter 34 - Working with Cloud AI Platform

Google Cloud Platform is a rapidly developing ecosystem and Google are constantly updating, enhancing existing as well as delivering new products and services to the portfolio. Therefore it can be difficult to stay abreast of the new features and the shifting emphasis from one service to another. An example of this is the shift in emphasis from Cloud Datastore to the latest Cloud Firestore NoSQL storage service. However, it is not just single services which eventually require to be depreciated by a newer enhanced version but sometimes an entire platform – a portfolio of services – needs to be introduced. Such was the case with Cloud AI Platform. This is now a portfolio of AI and ML assets bundled together as they have close symmetry to create a new platform – Cloud AI Engine - which was previously known as Machine Learning Engine or Cloud ML Engine. That collection of ML services and tools are now under the umbrella platform called the Cloud AI Platform.

When it comes to understanding GCP's new Cloud AI Platform it is probably better to view just where it fits into to Google's ever expanding catalogue of AI and Machine Learning assets.

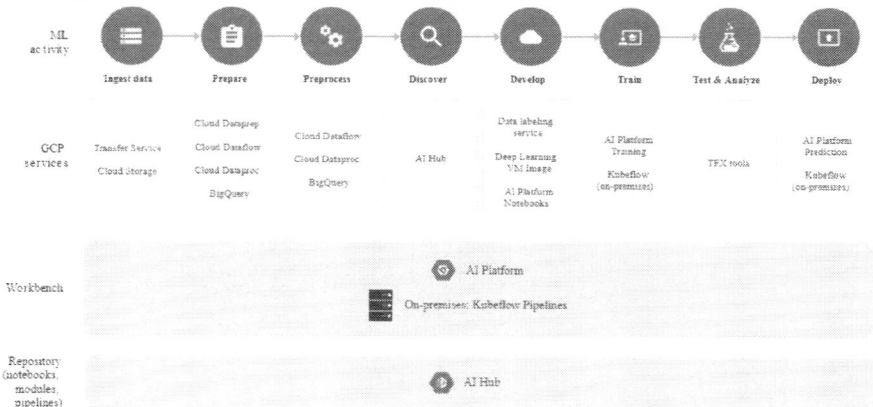

As shown in the diagram the Cloud AI Platform hosts a plethora of AI and ML services to provide a comprehensive end-to-end solution for all your data engineering activities.

Overview of Cloud AI Platform

At Cloud Next 2019, Google announced the launch of AI Platform, formerly the Cloud ML Engine. The rational for the name change is that Google has many machine learning and artificial intelligence tools and services in GCP that go beyond the boundaries of Cloud ML Engine a platform for training and deploying ML models. For example, Google introduced in 2017, an open source project called Kubeflow that aims to bring containerized distributed machine learning to Kubernetes. Kubeflow is a service that enables organizations to train and deploy ML models in containers. Google is also the founder of TensorFlow, the most popular framework for building sophisticated machine learning and deep learning models. The intention therefore is to bring all its diverse ML and AI assets beneath one umbrella service – the Cloud AI Platform. This new platform supports the entire spectrum of GCP's ML services including data preparation, training, tuning, deploying, collaborating and sharing of machine learning models. There are some notable additional ML services available on Google AI Platform:

AI Hub

The AI Hub acts as a community marketplace for the sharing and deploying of ML models. Essentially, like Cloud Marketplace it is a virtual market or catalogue for the sharing of reusable ML models. The purpose is that developers can readily distribute or publish their models so that others can quickly discover and deploy any ML models of interest. The catalogue supports an array of ML models packaged in a format that can be readily deployed in either Kubeflow, deep learning VMs backed by GPU or TPU, Jupyter Notebooks, or Google's own AI APIs. AI Hub supports all popular frameworks such as TensorFlow, PyTorch, Keras, XGBoost and Scikit-learn.

Deep Learning VMs

In order to make available to developers all the most popular deep learning tools and machine learning frameworks the AI Platform has a Deep Learning VM Image. This Deep Learning VM is pre-installed with a choice of frameworks, and all drivers and dependencies, including the latest GPU and TPU drivers. Since Google maintains the VM images, they have the latest version of TensorFlow and PyTorch. As this is a VM instance it is hosted on Google Computing Engine, which makes it easy and fast to instantiate.

Kubeflow Pipelines

Kubeflow pipeline is a core component of the open source package Kubeflow. It provides support for containers running on Kubernetes. Kubeflow makes the deployment of ML workflows in containers a feasible way to deploy portable ML models to diverse infrastructures. The Kubeflow Pipelines component is a tool for building and deploying portable, scalable ML workflows that are based upon each functional block in a pipeline running on its own Docker container. Since Kubeflow is orchestrated by Kubernetes the platform is open source and designed to be flexible and portable. The concept behind Kubeflow pipelines is that GCP customers will design and train their ML models on Kubeflow pipelines on-premises and then deploy them to Google Kubernetes Engine when they need to train at scale. Kubeflow is open source and it runs on Google Kubernetes Engine. But importantly Kubeflow abstracts much of the complexity of Kubernetes from the end user.

AI Platform – Frameworks

Google Cloud AI Platform- formerly - Cloud ML Engine - is expanding to support new or to augment existing features such as in-built algorithms, custom container-based ML training, and support for PyTorch. As a managed service (PaaS), the goal of services such as Cloud ML Engine is to abstract all of the complexity of handling the provisioning, configuring and managing of the infrastructure. Indeed Cloud ML engine has been the cornerstone of GCP ML offering for several years now.

The Cloud AI Platform augments the existing Cloud ML Engine's services to developers by supporting ML training jobs created in TensorFlow, Keras, PyTorch, Scikit-learn, and XGBoost. In addition the GCP offers a more expansive catalogue of in-built algorithms for prediction, linear classification, as well as wide and deep and XGBoost models. Developers can also bring their own containers thanks to integration with Kubeflow and GKE which enables custom built container frameworks to train at scale. The AI Platform also supports hyperparameter tuning to increase the accuracy of trained models.

AI Platform – Notebooks

AI Platform Notebooks – JupyterLabs - enables developers to create and manage virtual machine (VM) instances that are pre-packaged with the latest version of JupyterLab. These AI Platform Notebooks are hosted on Compute Engine VM instances, which are easily accessible via a local browser on a laptop. Moreover, the AI Platform Notebooks are pre-configured with the core packages and dependencies required to support TensorFlow and PyTorch environments. In addition the packages come with the latest Nvidia driver for GPU-enabled instances.
The AI Platform Notebooks enable developers during development to construct, train and validate ML models by running jobs locally using their favoured tools before they are deployed on the AI Platform for production. Since Jobs can be run on the AI Platform Notebooks without provisioning any infrastructure this service can support both online and batch predictions, which make Google AI Platform a fully comprehensive set of services to train, tune and deploy machine learning models.

Deploying Deep Learning VM with AI Platform Notebooks

There are as we have just seen many good reasons for data engineers to deploy an AI Platform Notebook. The foremost is that the AI Platform Notebooks is a GCP managed service that offers an integrated JupyterLab environment integrated with BigQuery, Cloud Dataproc, and Cloud Dataflow, making it trivial to create data flows from data ingestion to exploration, and eventually to model training and deployment. Secondly, it saves a lot of time as you can deploy new JupyterLab instances with one click and then start developing models and analysing your data on your local machine. For added convenience each notebook instance comes pre-configured with optimized versions of the most popular data science and machine learning libraries like TensorFlow, PyTorch, Scikit-learn, Pandas, NumPy, SciPy, and Matplotlib. Having all these frameworks and tools at your fingertips in one integrated notebook allows you to control everything from data collection and cleansing, data transformation, pipeline/model building through to eventually leveraging AI Platform services or Kubeflow for distributed training and predictions. Furthermore it is serverless and auto-scalable; so there is no need to create and manage VMs it's all managed for you.
In addition to the ease of use there is also an easy way to deploy a marketplace solution for deploying and running the Cloud AI Notebook it is by deploying the Deep Learning model VM as this also creates the AI Platform Notebook - JupyterLab - GUI.

Deploy Deep Learning Virtual Machine

The prerequisites to deploying any GCP service are that you must have an account and a project for billing. Once you have these configured you can go ahead and deploy any of the pre-built marketplace solution.
To set up a Deep Learning VM you need to go to the marketplace solution tab, and then search for "Deep Learning VM". This should take you to the landing page for "Deep Learning VM".
Once you launch the compute engine, which will deploy your Deep Learning VM, you will be taken to the configuration page, where you can set a name for the environment, select the zone for the machines and select the number of CPUs or GPUs you would want.

When it comes to selecting your zone there may be restrictions in some zones on the number of CPUs and GPUs you can access.

As you go through the configuration by selecting your preferred options such as the number of CPU or GPU you can see the estimated billing amount change. This however, is the billing you will incur should you run the VM 24/7 for the full month.

The next thing you need to choose is the preferred size of your hard-drive. "Standard Persistent Disk" should be sufficient for any project, but if you want to optimise your configuration for more memory as perhaps you are working on a lot of data you can always optimise the memory options. Fortunately, you don't need to worry too much about getting it right first time as configurations can be easily changed later or even on a per job basis. Once you have finalised the Deep Learning VM's configuration you can hit "Deploy". It may take 5 to 10 minutes - based on your machine-type selection - for the deployment to become active. However, before you can access or run code on the Deep Learning instance from your local machine you will first need to setup SSH to secure the connection. For this you will need to download the Google SDK and install it on your local machine - you can find the Google SDK **here** or at **https://cloud.google.com/sdk/install**?

It is easy to initialize the Google SDK as all you need to enter is your Google account ID and the Project ID that you created earlier. Once you have Google SDK installed and configured, you need to go the Deployment Manager and copy the SSH key that shows up on your deployment page then paste it to the Google SDK. The SSH link will be under the header "Create an SSH connection to your machine". Once you have successfully created a SSH connection from your local machine to the Deep Learning VM instance, a PuTTY screen will pop-up, Now you can interact via the command line through PuTTY or you can use the more user friendly web GUI. To use the GUI all you have to do is to return to the deployment manager and hit the localhost:8080 button to connect to and access the Deep Learning VM through the Cloud JupyterLab GUI. While you are still in Deployment Manager and on the deployment page you might want to select – on the far right – a static IP address so that you maintain the same IP across sessions. An important thing to note here is that you should **stop all Deep Learning instances when not in use as you do not want to be billed for the time your instances are sitting idle.**

After you have configured your VM Deep Learning instance and you fine that the default instance types are not suitable you can always create a new instance and specify your preferred options. To create an AI Platform Notebooks instance and specify your preferred options follow these steps:

1. Go to the **AI Platform Notebooks** page in the Google Cloud Platform Console.
2. Select New **Instance**, → **Customize instance**.
3. On the **New Notebook instance** page, provide information for your new instance:
4. **Instance name** - provide a name for your new instance.
5. **Region** - select a region for the new instance. Select the region that is closest to you for best network performance.
6. **Zone** - select a zone within the region that you selected that supports the features you want.
7. **Environment** - select the environment based on the machine learning framework you want to use.
8. **Machine type** - select the number of CPUs and the optimal amount of RAM for your new instance. AI Platform Notebooks provides monthly cost estimates for each machine type that you select.
9. **GPUs** - select the **GPU type** and **Number of GPUs** for your new instance. Select the option to **Install NVIDIA GPU driver automatically for me**. You can modify the GPU type and number of GPUs for your instance after it is created.
10. If you want to change the default boot disk settings or encryption settings;

- Select the **Boot disk type** and **Boot disk size in GB**
- Under **Encryption**, select **Customer-managed key** to use your own customer-managed encryption. Select and enter the customer-managed key that you want to use, or enter the resource ID for your customer-managed key. The resource ID for your customer-managed key looks like this:

projects/***project-id***/locations/global/keyRings/***name-of-key-ring***/cryptoKeys/***name-of-key***

You can retrieve a resource ID by running the following gcloud command in Cloud Shell,

```
gcloud kms keys list --location global --keyring name-of-key-ring
```

If necessary, click **Grant** to give your service account permissions to encrypt and decrypt using this key.

11. If you want to change network settings, such as to select a Virtual Private Cloud, disable proxy access, or disable the external IP address, complete the following steps:

Expand the **Networking** section.

- Select either **Networks in this project** or **Networks shared with me**.

On the **Network** menu, select the network that you want. You can select a VPC network, as long as the network has Private Google Access enabled or can access the internet.

On the **Subnetwork** menu, select the subnetwork that you want.

- If you want to disable the external IP address, set the **External IP** menu to **None**.
- If you want to disable proxy access, clear the checkbox next to **Allow proxy access when it's available**.

Note: If you disable proxy access, you must use SSH to connect to your JupyterLab instance.

12. If you want to grant access to all users who have access to a specific Compute Engine service account or to a specific user, expand the **Permission** section and complete one of the following steps:

- To grant access to a specific service account, click the **Access to JupyterLab** menu, and select - **Other service account**. Then fill out the **Service account** field.
- To grant access to a single user, click the **Access to JupyterLab** menu, and select **Single user only**. Then fill out the **User email** field.

13. Click **Create**.

14.   AI Platform Notebooks creates a new instance for you with the
options that you selected and the name that you provided.

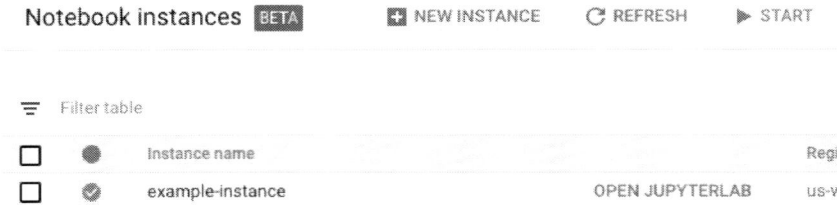

| Notebook instances BETA | ✚ NEW INSTANCE | ⟳ REFRESH | ▶ START |

☐	⬤	Instance name		Regi
☐	✓	example-instance	OPEN JUPYTERLAB	us-w

Determine who has access to the JupyterLab instance

Unless you granted access to a specific service account or a single user,
anyone that has **editor** permissions to your GCP project can access the
notebook.

If you granted access to a specific service account, anyone who has access
to that service account can access the JupyterLab instance. Note that you
will not have access to the JupyterLab instance unless you also have
access to the specified service account.

If you granted access to a single user, that user is the only one who has
access to the JupyterLab instance you will effectively lock yourself out.

To open a notebook:

Go to the **AI Platform Notebooks** page in the Google Cloud Platform
Console.

Select **Open JupyterLab** for the instance that you want to open.

☐	⬤	Instance name		Region
☐	✓	example-instance	OPEN JUPYTERLAB	us-west1-a

AI Platform Notebooks directs you to a URL for your notebook instance via
the prominent, Open JupyterLab button.

Working with the Deep Learning VM and TensorFlow

Now that we have a Deep Learning instance deployed and configured we can start to use it to build, tune and train a ML model using TensorFlow. If you are new to Machine Learning and neural networks it is highly recommended that you work through Google's ML and TensorFlow tutorial to get up to speed in the theory and concepts behind neural networks and ML models. What is an added bonus is that all the lab work is on simulations of Jupyter notebook so you can run everything from your PC without having to download or deploy any software. The short course is free and is an excellent resource aimed at the beginner. We cannot possibly do justice to it here as it would take an entire book in itself to cover the material but we will pick out some highlights and key topic in the following paragraphs regarding building and tuning TensorFlow models. The course can be found **here** at
https://developers.google.com/machine-learning/crash-course

Building and Training TensorFlow Models

The first thing that we need to understand when we discuss TensorFlow models is that they are in fact deep neural networks – i.e. neural networks with three or more layers. We can see a deep neural network in action using Google's simulator in the ML crash course. In the simulation you can build your own neural network and tune it using the hyperparameter of learning time, batch size and epochs.

Where deep neural network become of interest in Machine Learning is when we contemplate solving non-linear problems. What we mean by non-linear is that we cannot solve the problem by using a straight-line. For example; with a complex dataset such as this one:

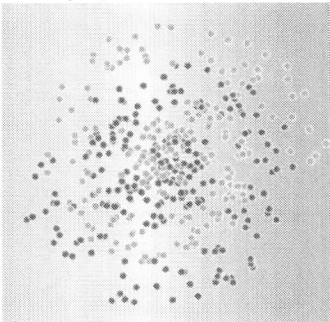

With the non-linear example shown above we need to use a deep neural network that has non-linear layers – called activation layer – introduced to provide the non-linear functions. We can visualise this by comparing the neural networks side by side.

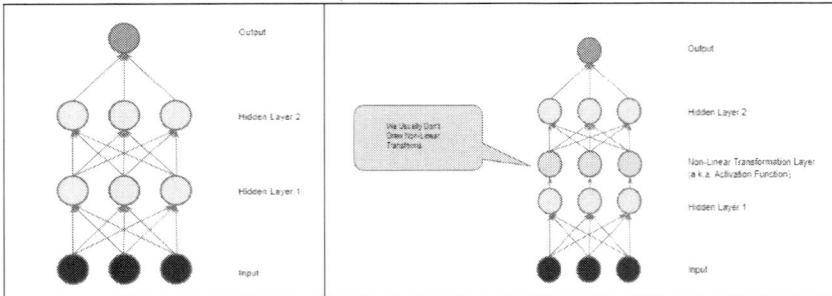

In the diagram above we see a linear neural network on the left and a non-linear neural network on the right. The core difference is the addition of a non-linear activation layer – note activation layers are not typically shown in neural network representations.

By adding activation layers we are effectively stacking nonlinearities on nonlinearities and this lets us model very complicated relationships between the inputs and the predicted outputs. Simplistically, this is because each layer is effectively learning a more complex, higher-level function based upon the raw inputs. The typical function of the non-linear activation layer is either a Sigmoid or the ReLU (rectified linear unit) function. The difference is that the sigmoid function converts a weight into a value between 0 and 1, whereas the ReLU tends to perform better in real-world scenarios and its computation is much easier.

In short a deep learning model will comprise of the following components:

- A set of nodes, organized in layers.
- A set of weights representing the connections between each neural network layer and the layer beneath it.
- A set of biases, one for each node.
- An activation function that transforms the output of each node in a layer. Different layers may have different activation functions.

If we consider how we can build a model to solve a complex non-linear problem we can clearly see that a linear neural network regardless of the number of layers is simply not going to work – see the diagram below.

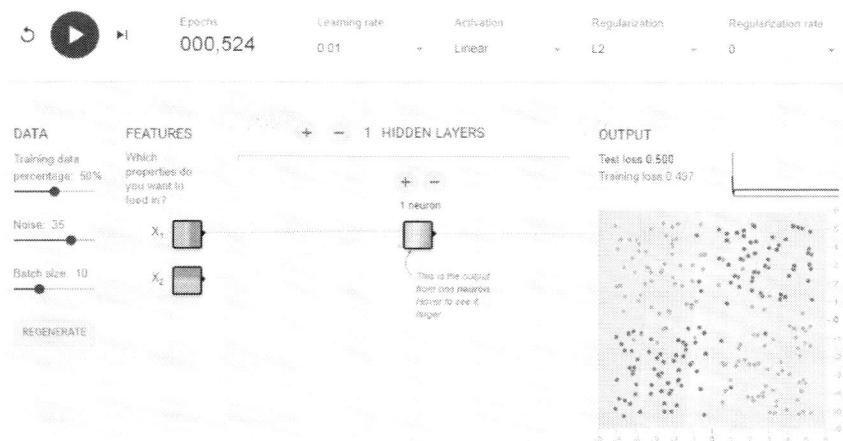

To be able to solve this non-linear problem we need to add activation layers and more hidden layers.

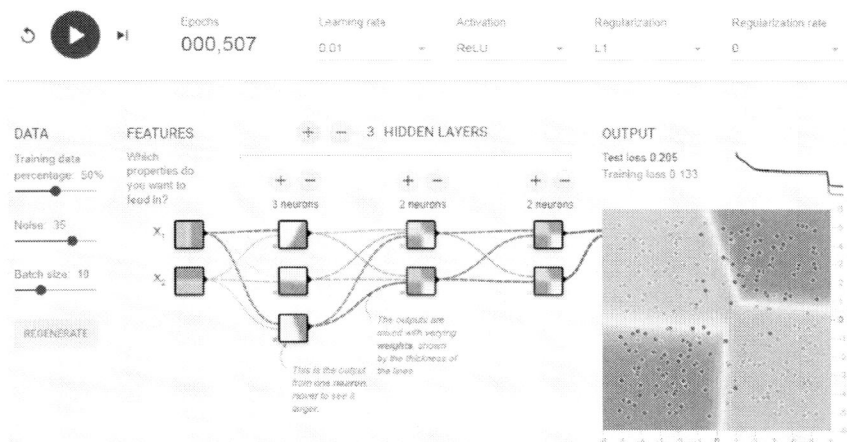

To solve the non-linear problem we have built a neural network with an additional hidden layer using ReLU as the activation function, with just this simple model we can solve the non-linear problem. However adding a second hidden layer adds redundancy and lets the model perform better. Notice the Output loss is much lower. But how can we tune this model to perform better with less loss in both training and testing?

Tuning to improve DNN performance

The first thing we have to do is split up our data set – in this example it is the California house price data – into training, validation and testing sets. We do this because we must keep the data we use for training isolated from the testing set. This is crucially important because to test for learning the model bust be tested against sample data that it has never seen before. We need a validation set because we will need to tune our model to optimise its performance hence the need for a separate validation data set that we can tune against without corrupting the testing scenario. A good split is 80% for training and 10% each for validation and testing. However, it's a bad idea to just take the first 80% or the last 10% of the dataset we need to regularize the entire data set first – i.e. shuffle the pack to distribute the data evenly across the board. This ensure that we done get lumps of very similar data that would possibly skew our training and the test results.

When building, tuning and testing with TensorFlow we follow these steps:

- First we build the TensorFlow model – the feature columns
- Then we prepare to train this neural network – by setting the features, the batch size, the number of epochs, and the tuple of features and labels for the next training batch
- Normalise all of the the features in the data using linear scaling to get input between -1 and 1
- This is followed by configuring the optimizer and training model – i.e. a regression model this is where we can define the elements that we will use to tune the model,
- Finally we run the training job – as seen below and this is where we can tune the model – see the code snippet below:

```
= train_nn_regression_model(
my_optimizer=tf.train.GradientDescentOptimizer(learning_rate=0.001),

steps=500,

batch_size=10,

hidden_units=[10, 10],
```

```
                training_examples=training_examples,

                training_targets=training_targets,

                validation_examples=validation_examples,

                validation_targets=validation_targets)
```

This results in the following output:

```
Training model...
RMSE (on training data):
  period 00 : 194.21
  period 01 : 187.09
  period 02 : 174.16
  period 03 : 182.42
  period 04 : 174.10
  period 05 : 166.52
  period 06 : 170.68
  period 07 : 165.83
  period 08 : 166.53
  period 09 : 168.87
Model training finished.
Final RMSE (on training data):   168.87
Final RMSE (on validation data): 168.87
```

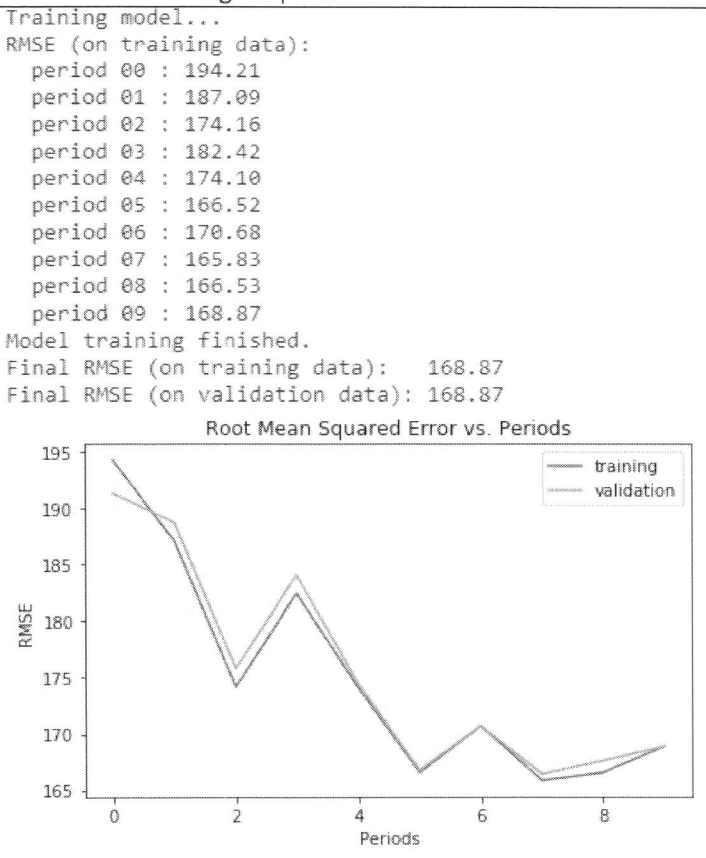

Root Mean Squared Error vs. Periods

Tuning the TensorFlow model

We can tune the model by adjusting the following parameters:
- Learning rate
- Batch size
- Steps

For example we can improve the performance and lower the training and testing losses by tuning these hyper parameters as shown below:

```
= train_nn_regression_model(
my_optimizer=tf.train.GradientDescentOptimizer(learning_rate=0.0007),

steps=5000,

        batch_size=70,

         hidden_units=[10, 10],

         training_examples=training_examples,

         training_targets=training_targets,

         validation_examples=validation_examples,

         validation_targets=validation_targets)
```

```
Training model...
RMSE (on training data):
  period 00 : 168.02
  period 01 : 164.32
  period 02 : 162.09
  period 03 : 160.22
  period 04 : 159.21
  period 05 : 158.07
  period 06 : 157.10
  period 07 : 157.34
  period 08 : 155.58
  period 09 : 155.05
Model training finished.
Final RMSE (on training data):   155.05
Final RMSE (on validation data): 154.16
```

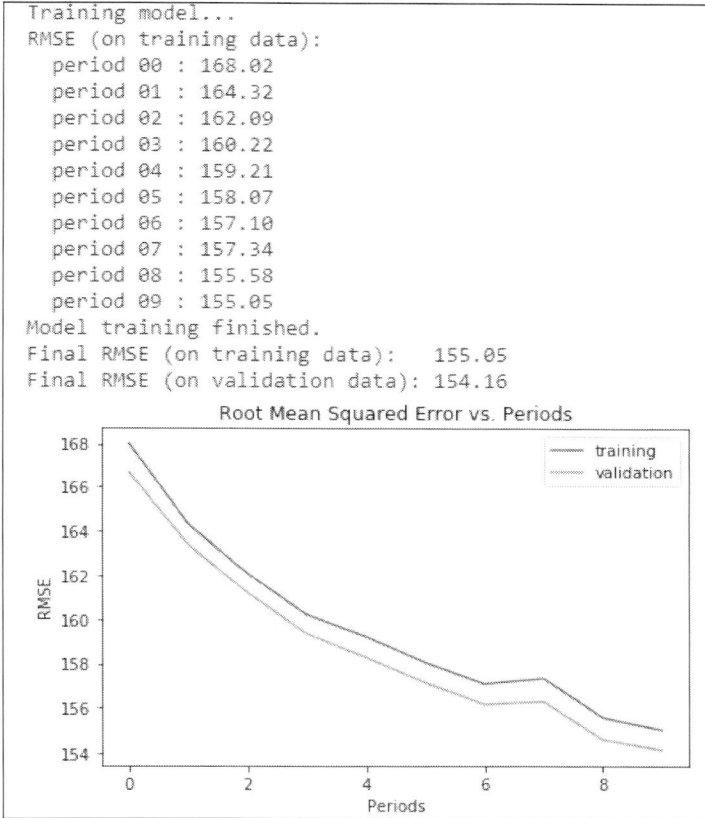

Root Mean Squared Error vs. Periods

Unfortunately there are no hard and fast rules when it comes to tuning as it varies from one dataset to another. But the rule of thumb is that typically the best formulations occur with low learning rates, large batch sizes and high number of steps – as shown in our tuning example. But that is just a generalisation as this is why we do tuning to optimise the model to our specific data set.

Kubeflow – why use containers?

When we consider big data systems we tend to think of distributed Hadoop, Spark and other big data platforms. However lately there is a growing tendency to run big data systems in containers as this is now a feasible option as they can be deployed in clusters of Docker containers managed by orchestration frameworks like Kubernetes. Applications broken down perhaps into microservices can now be automatically packaged into images and deployed onto containers. However, it's not just a new way to build big data systems as this method provides greater flexibility and agility. This is because running big data systems in containers provides improvements especially in real-time decision making.

In the context of Big Data systems deployed as containers it can be viewed as part of a continuum of infrastructure simplification. Whereby, container deployment is situated between traditional on-premise clusters or IaaS and serverless functions. Compared to container and IaaS deployments, serverless deployments deliver more agility with reduce costs and reduce the management burden. This is why serverless computing for Big Data systems has become so popular. However containers do have their benefits. For example, containers are still a better approach to refactoring monolithic applications and they provide developers with greater control over the virtual environment. For example, containers hosted on GKE can be continuously monitored, and they can rapidly scale (autoscaling) and proactively self-heal. This means that if one of the nodes in a distributed cluster is nonresponsive then the system can proactively kill the bad container and seamlessly replace it with another node.

When it comes to building streaming analytics the optimal way to create and manage data pipelines is via serverless managed services but pairing containers with open source pipeline technologies like Dataflow SDK (Beam) can rapidly transform the way we build big data systems. However there are several technological issues that need to be addressed such as security and networking. In the big data security is typically through Kerberos and short-lived job tokens, while the containers use WebAuth and certificates. Similarly, big data environments are engineered with high-throughput between nodes, racks and clusters which is not something containers can support. The concern is that containers with data-intensive workloads could adversely affect the use of CPU, memory or network resources needed by other containers. On the other hand containers have several advantages over serverless solutions.

Containers make it easier to deploy and spin up additional infrastructure resources on-demand. And Docker containers provide a consistent packaging mechanism for applications, developer code and tools like Jupyter Notebooks that can all be deployed on the same cluster. This provides consistency between development, testing, staging and production, or when working across private or public cloud environments. Containers in GCP are typically provisioned within GKE and they are managed using Kubernetes Engine. Kubernetes provides the consistent platform to run almost any big data, AI or machine learning application workload. But deploying big data systems in containers also involves more provisioning complexity, configurations and settings and all that must be managed.

In the following sections in this chapter we will look at deploying a Machine Learning system based on TensorFlow using both a serverless API solution (Keras) and a container focused solution – Kubeflow. The objective is to demonstrate the difference in provisioning and deployment complexity and highlight their respective advantages.

The objective is to demonstrate how to setup and train a neural network on the GCP AI Platform using the Keras sequential API and using prewritten Keras code to show you how to serve predictions from that model. Keras is a high-level API for building and training deep learning models - tf.keras - is TensorFlow's implementation of this API.

The goal is to show the steps required to setup and train a deep neural network (DNN) using Keras that predicts using a dataset of US census income as to whether a person makes more than $50,000 a year (target label) based on other Census information about the person (features).

There are several pre-requisites that you must have in place before you can train and deploy a model in AI Platform:

1. Set up your local development environment.
2. Set up a GCP project with billing and the necessary APIs enabled.
3. Create a Cloud Storage bucket to store your training package and your trained model.
4. Set up your local development environment

You will also need the following tools installed on your local server:

- Git
- Python 3
- virtualenv
- The Cloud SDK

The Google Cloud guide to Setting up a Python development environment provides detailed instructions for meeting these requirements.

Create a Cloud Storage bucket

When you submit a training job using the Cloud SDK, you upload a Python package containing your training code to a Cloud Storage bucket. AI Platform runs the code from this package. AI Platform also saves the trained model that result from your job in the same bucket. You can then create an AI Platform model version based on this output in order to serve online predictions.

When creating your Cloud Storage bucket you first need to assign it a unique name as an environment variable. It must be globally unique across all Cloud Storage buckets:

```
BUCKET_NAME="your-bucket-name"
```

Select a region where AI Platform training and prediction are available and create another environment variable. For example:

```
REGION="us-central1"
```

Create your Cloud Storage bucket in this region and, later, use the same region for training and prediction. Run the following command to create the bucket if it doesn't already exist:

```
gsutil mb -l $REGION gs://$BUCKET_NAME
```

Quickstart for training in AI Platform

After configuring the environment and our Cloud Storage bucket the next task is to submit a training job to the AI Platform. This job runs sample code that uses Keras to train a deep neural network on the United States Census data. The job outputs the trained model as a TensorFlow SavedModel directory in your Cloud Storage bucket.

Get training code and dependencies

First, download the training code and change the working directory:

```
# Clone the repository of AI Platform samples
git clone --depth 1 https://github.com/GoogleCloudPlatform/cloudml-samples
# Set the working directory to the sample code directory
cd cloudml-samples/census/tf-keras
```

Notice that the training code is structured as a Python package in the trainer/ subdirectory:

```
# `ls` shows the working directory's contents. The `p` flag adds trailing
# slashes to subdirectory names. The `R` flag lists subdirectories
recursively.
ls -pR
.:
README.md  requirements.txt  trainer/./trainer:__init__.py  model.py
task.py  util.py
```

Next, install Python dependencies needed to train the model locally:

```
pip install -r requirements.txt
```

When you run the training job in AI Platform, dependencies are preinstalled based on the runtime version you choose.

Train your model locally

Before training on AI Platform, it is advisable to train the job locally to verify the file structure and packaging is correct. Similarly if you plan to run any complex or resource-intensive job, you should train locally to start with using a small sample of your dataset to verify your code. When you are confident it is working okay then you can run the job on AI Platform to train on the whole dataset.

This sample runs a relatively quick job on a small dataset, so the local training and the AI Platform job run the same code on the same data. Run the following command to train a model locally:

```
# This is similar to `python -m trainer.task --job-dir local-training-output`
# but it better replicates the AI Platform environment, especially
# for distributed training (not applicable here).
gcloud ai-platform local train \
  --package-path trainer \
  --module-name trainer.task \
  --job-dir local-training-output
```

Observe training progress in your shell. At the end, the training application exports the trained model and prints a message like the following:

```
Model exported to: local-training-output/keras_export/1553709223
```

Train your model using AI Platform

Next, submit a training job to AI Platform. This runs the training module in the cloud and exports the trained model to Cloud Storage.

First, give your training job a name and choose a directory within your Cloud Storage bucket for saving intermediate and output files. Set these as environment variables. For example:

```
JOB_NAME="my_first_keras_job"
JOB_DIR="gs://$BUCKET_NAME/keras-job-dir"
```

Run the following command to package the trainer/ directory, upload it to the specified --job-dir, and instruct AI Platform to run the trainer.task module from that package.

The --stream-logs flag lets you view training logs in your shell. You can also see logs and other job details in the GCP Console.

```
gcloud ai-platform jobs submit training $JOB_NAME \
  --package-path trainer/ \
  --module-name trainer.task \
  --region $REGION \
  --python-version 3.5 \
  --runtime-version 1.13 \
  --job-dir $JOB_DIR \
  --stream-logs
```

This may take longer than local training, but you can observe training progress in your shell in a similar fashion. At the end, the training job exports the trained model to your Cloud Storage bucket and prints a message like the following:

```
Model exported to:  gs://your-bucket-name/keras-job-
dir/keras_export/1553709421


INFO    2019-03-27 17:57:11 +0000   master-replica-0      Module
completed; cleaning up.


INFO    2019-03-27 17:57:11 +0000   master-replica-0      Clean up
finished.


INFO    2019-03-27 17:57:11 +0000   master-replica-0      Task completed
successfully
```

Training a TensorFlow model with Kubeflow

 In order to show the potential of Kubeflow we will setup and train a TensorFlow model on the MNIST dataset, which is the HELLO WORLD equivalent for machine learning. The MNIST dataset we will use contains a images of hand-written digits (0 to 9), as well as the supervised learning labels which identify the digit in each image.

The objective is to train a TensorFlow model using Kubeflow in a GKE cluster. We will then build and test the code locally on a Jupyter notebook. When it comes to training the TensorFlow model we will build a package in a Kubernetes container and upload it to the GCP's Container Registry before running a tf.train job. After training, the model will be able to classify incoming images into 10 categories (0 to 9) based on what it's learned through the training process.

Once the TensorFlow model has been trained we can then use it for making predictions (inference) against test data. For this part of the task we will save the trained model to a Cloud Storage bucket. Then we will use TensorFlow Serving to serve our model. We can then send a prediction request to the model and display the model's output – the prediction result.

Set up your environment

As always we need to first set up our environment as we discussed in the previous chapter but for the sake of brevity we can use a pre-prepared set of files that includes a TensorFlow app, a web UI to interact with our model and the Docker files to build our containers that will host the training and prediction applications. The files that you need are available **here**.

To get hold of the project data we will need to either clone the project files within the directory containing the MNIST example:

```
cd ${HOME}
git clone https://github.com/kubeflow/examples.git
cd examples/mnist
WORKING_DIR=$(pwd)
```

Or, an alternative is that you can download the **Kubeflow examples repository zip file**.

Set up your GCP account and SDK

The next step is to set up your GCP environment:

1.   Select or create a project
2.   Enabling Billing
3.   Installing the latest version of the SDK tools by running: gcloud components update
4.   Install Docker
5.   Install kubectl
6.   Install the kubectl command-line tool for Kubernetes: gcloud components install kubectl
7.   Install kustomize v2.0.3 - Kubeflow uses kustomize to help manage deployments.

Once you have set up this environment – much of this is already preconfigured if you are using a Cloud Environment in GCP- then you can start to tune the environment variables:

1.   Set your GCP project ID. In the command below, replace <YOUR-PROJECT-ID> with your project ID:

```
export PROJECT=<YOUR-PROJECT-ID>
gcloud config set project ${PROJECT}
```

2.   Set the zone for your GCP configuration.

```
export ZONE=us-central1-c
gcloud config set compute/zone
${ZONE}
```

Choose a zone that offers sufficient resources for example:

o   Ensure you have enough Compute Engine regional capacity. By default, the GKE cluster we need requires 16 CPUs.
o   If you want a GPU, ensure your zone offers GPUs.

3. If you want to set your own name for your Kubeflow deployment, set the DEPLOYMENT_NAME environment variable the default name is kubeflow:

```
export DEPLOYMENT_NAME=Kubeflow
```

Deploy Kubeflow

Follow the instructions in the guide to **deploying Kubeflow on GCP**, (https://www.kubeflow.org/docs/gke/deploy/), when the deployment finishes, check the resources installed in the namespace kubeflow in your new cluster. To do this from the command line, first set your kubectl credentials to point to the new cluster:

```
gcloud container clusters get-credentials ${KFAPP} --zone ${ZONE} --project ${PROJECT}
```

Then see what's installed in the kubeflow namespace of your GKE cluster:

```
kubectl -n kubeflow get all
```

Create a Cloud Storage bucket

The next step is to create a Cloud Storage bucket to hold your trained model.
Use the gsutil mb command to create a storage bucket. Your BUCKET NAME must be unique across all of Cloud Storage:

```
export BUCKET_NAME=${PROJECT}-${DEPLOYMENT_NAME}-bucket
gsutil mb -c regional -l {ZONE} gs://${BUCKET_NAME}
```

(Optional) Test the code in a Jupyter notebook

It is highly recommended that you experiment, test and validate the code in a Jupyter notebook before you run it on GKE. To test the code in the notebook do the following:

1. Create a Jupyter notebook VM instance and open the Jupyter UI. Accept the default settings as this gives you a standard CPU image with a recent version of TensorFlow.
2. Create a new notebook by clicking **New > Python 2** on the Jupyter dashboard.
3. Copy the code from your sample model at ${WORKING_DIR}/model.py and paste the code into a cell in your Jupyter notebook.
4. Run the cell in the notebook.

Prepare to run your training application on GKE

When you downloaded the project files into your ${WORKING_DIR} directory you also downloaded the TensorFlow code for your training application. The code is in a Python file, model.py, in your ${WORKING_DIR} directory.
The model.py program does the following:

- Downloads the MNIST dataset and loads it for use by the model training code.

- Offers a choice between two models:

    - A two-layer convolutional neural network (CNN), which is the default model in model.py.
    - A linear classifier, which we do not use here

- Defines TensorFlow operations to train and evaluate the model.
- Runs a number of training cycles or epochs as they are called in ML circles.
- Saves the trained model to a specified location, such as your Cloud Storage bucket.

Build the container for your training application

To deploy your code to Kubernetes, you must first build your local project into a Docker container image and push the image to Container Registry so that it's available in the cloud.

1. Create a version tag from the current UNIX timestamp, to be associated with your model each time it runs:

```
export VERSION_TAG=$(date +%s)
```

2. Set the path in Container Registry that you want to push the image to:

```
export TRAIN_IMG_PATH=gcr.io/${PROJECT}/${DEPLOYMENT_NAME}-train:${VERSION_TAG}
```

3. Build the Docker image for your working directory:

```
docker build $WORKING_DIR -t $TRAIN_IMG_PATH -f $WORKING_DIR/Dockerfile.model
```

> Your program is now encapsulated in a new container. The container is tagged with its eventual path in Container Registry, but it hasn't been uploaded to Container Registry yet.

4. Test the container locally:

```
docker run -it ${TRAIN_IMG_PATH}
```

> You should see training logs start appearing in your output:

```
Train and evaluate
INFO:tensorflow:Running training and evaluation locally (non-distributed).
INFO:tensorflow:Start train and evaluate loop. The evaluate will happen after 1 secs (eval_spec.throttle_secs) or training is finished.
INFO:tensorflow:Calling model_fn.
INFO:tensorflow:Done calling model_fn.
...
INFO:tensorflow:Saving checkpoints for 7 into /tmp/tmph861eL/model.ckpt.
INFO:tensorflow:Loss for final step: 2.2834966.
...
```

5. When you see log entries similar to those above, your model training is working. You can terminate the container with **Ctrl+c.**

Now that you have successfully run and tested your model locally the next step is to upload the container image to Container Registry so that you can run it on your GKE cluster.

1. Run the following command to authenticate to Container Registry:

```
gcloud auth configure-docker –quiet
```

2. Push the container to Container Registry:

```
docker push
${TRAIN_IMG_PATH}
```

3. You should now see your new container image listed on the Container Registry page on the GCP console.

Prepare your training component to run on GKE

1. Enter the training/GCS directory:

```
cd ${WORKING_DIR}/training/GCS
```

2. Give the job a name so that you can identify it later:

```
kustomize edit add configmap mnist-map-training   --from-
literal=name=mnist-train-dist
```

3. Configure your custom training image:

```
kustomize edit set image training-image=${TRAIN_IMG_PATH}
```

4. Configure the image to run distributed by setting the number of parameter servers and workers to use. The numPs means the number of Ps (parameter server) and the numWorkers means the number of worker:

```
../base/definition.sh --numPs 1 --numWorkers 2
```

5. Set the training parameters (training steps, batch size and learning rate):

```
kustomize edit add configmap mnist-map-training   --from-
literal=trainSteps=200
```

```
kustomize edit add configmap mnist-map-training  --from-
literal=batchSize=100
kustomize edit add configmap mnist-map-training  --from-
literal=learningRate=0.01
```

6. Configure parameters and save the model to Cloud Storage:

```
kustomize edit add configmap mnist-map-training  --from-
literal=modelDir=gs://${BUCKET_NAME}/
kustomize edit add configmap mnist-map-training  --from-
literal=exportDir=gs://${BUCKET_NAME}/export
```

Check the permissions for your training component

You need to ensure that your Python code has the required permissions to read/write to your Cloud Storage bucket. Kubeflow solves this by creating a user service account within your project as a part of the deployment. You can use the following command to list the service accounts for your Kubeflow deployment:

```
gcloud iam service-accounts list | grep ${DEPLOYMENT_NAME}
```

Kubeflow granted the user service account the necessary permissions to read and write to your storage bucket. Kubeflow also added a Kubernetes secret named user-gcp-sa to your cluster, containing the credentials needed to authenticate as this service account within the cluster:

```
kubectl describe secret user-gcp-sa
```

To access your storage bucket from inside the train container, you must set the GOOGLE_APPLICATION_CREDENTIALS environment variable to point to the JSON file contained in the secret. Set the variable by passing the following parameters:

```
kustomize edit add configmap mnist-map-training --from-
literal=secretName=user-gcp-sa
kustomize edit add configmap mnist-map-training --from-
literal=secretMountPath=/var/secrets
kustomize edit add configmap mnist-map-training --from-
```

```
literal=GOOGLE_APPLICATION_CREDENTIALS=/var/secrets/user-gcp-
sa.json
```

Train the model on GKE

Now you are ready to run the TensorFlow training job on your cluster on
GKE.
Apply the container to the cluster:

```
kustomize build . |kubectl apply -f -
```

When the command finishes running, there should be a new workload on
the cluster, with the name mnist-train-dist-chief-0. If you set the option to
run a distributed workload, the worker workloads show up on the cluster
too. You can see the workloads on the GKE Workloads page on the GCP
console. To see the logs, click the **mnist-train-dist-chief-0** workload, then
click **Container logs**.

View your trained model on Cloud Storage

When training is complete, you should see the model data pushed into
your Cloud Storage bucket, tagged with the same version number as the
container that generated it. To explore, click your bucket name on
the Cloud Storage page on the GCP Console.
The output from the training application includes the following:

- A set of checkpoints that you can use to resume training from a
  given point later.
- An export directory that holds the trained model in a format that
  the TensorFlow Serving component can read.

Serve the trained model

Now you can put your trained model on a server and send it prediction
requests.

1. Enter the serving/GCS directory:

```
cd $WORKING_DIR/serving/GCS
```

2. Set a name for the TensorFlow Serving job:

```
kustomize edit add configmap mnist-map-serving   --from-
literal=name=mnist-gcs-dist
```

3. Set your model path:

```
kustomize edit add configmap mnist-map-serving   --from-
literal=modelBasePath=${EXPORT_DIR}
```

4. Deploy the model, and run a service to make the deployment accessible to other pods in the cluster:

```
kustomize build . | kubectl apply -f -
```

5. You can check the deployment by running the following command:

```
kubectl describe deployments mnist-gcs-dist
```

6. The service makes the mnist-gcs-dist deployment accessible over port 9000. Run the following command to get the details of the service:

```
kubectl describe service mnist-gcs-dist
```

You can also see the **mnist-gcs-dist** service on the GKE Services page on the GCP Console. Click the service name to see the service details. You can see that it listens for connections within the cluster on port 9000.

Send online prediction requests to your model

Now you can deploy the final piece of your system: a web interface that can interact with a trained model server.

Deploy the sample web UI

When you downloaded the project files at the start of the tutorial, you downloaded the code for a simple web UI. The code is stored in the ${WORKING_DIR}/web-ui directory.
The web UI uses a Flask server to host the HTML, CSS, and JavaScript files for the web page. The Python program, mnist_client.py, contains a function that interacts directly with the TensorFlow model server.
The ${WORKING_DIR}/web-ui directory also contains a Dockerfile to build the application into a container image or you can deploy it directly to the cluster.

Access the web UI in your browser

Follow these steps to access the web UI in your web browser. It may take a few minutes for the IP address to become available:

1. Find the IP address assigned to the service:

```
kubectl get service web-ui
```

2. Copy the value shown under EXTERNAL-IP and paste it into your web browser's address bar. The web UI should appear.
3. The web UI offers three fields to connect to the prediction server:
4. By default, the fields on the above web page are pre-filled with the details of the TensorFlow server that's running in the cluster: a name, an address, and a port. You can change them if you used different values:
    - **Model Name:** mnist - The name that you gave to your serving component.
    - **Server Address:** mnist-service - You can enter the server address as a domain name or an IP address. Note that this is an internal IP address for the mnist-service service within your cluster, not a public address. Kubernetes provides an internal DNS service, so you can write the name of the service in the address field. Kubernetes

routes all requests to the required IP address automatically.

- o **Port:** 9000 - The server listens on port 9000 by default.

5. Click **Connect**. The system finds the server in your cluster and displays the classification results.

Clean up your GCP environment

Run the following command to delete your deployment and related resources:

```
gcloud deployment-manager --project=${PROJECT} deployments delete ${DEPLOYMENT_NAME}
```

Delete your Cloud Storage bucket when you've finished with it:

```
gsutil rm -r gs://${BUCKET_NAME}
```

Delete the container images uploaded to Container Registry:

```
// Find the digest id for each container image:
gcloud container images list-tags
gcr.io/${PROJECT}/${DEPLOYMENT_NAME}-train
gcloud container images list-tags
gcr.io/${PROJECT}/${DEPLOYMENT_NAME}-web-ui
// Delete each image:
gcloud container images delete gcr.io/$PROJECT/${DEPLOYMENT_NAME}-train:$DIGEST_ID
gcloud container images delete gcr.io/$PROJECT/${DEPLOYMENT_NAME}-web-ui:$DIGEST_ID
```

An alternative would be to delete the various resources using the GCP Console.

Chapter 27 – Cloud Migration

Migration from an on-premises data center to the Google cloud might not make sense for everyone and for successful migration you will really need to get everyone onside. This typically requires an in-depth sales pitch that covers all the business areas such as; costs, security, governance, regulatory compliance, data privacy and lack of talent, among other considerations. This means that to be successful in getting your colleagues backing you will have to sell them on the benefits behind Google cloud migration, be open and address the challenges, and stress Google cloud's major selling points.

It is unlikely there will be a consistent response to a proposed cloud migration across all the business units. Typically, the business orientated departments will have a focus in terms of costs where as others may have governance and regulatory compliance as their area of priority. There will also be application developers and traditional support teams that feel a move to the cloud would be both detrimental to operational performance and maintenance efficiency. However, what most people will not pick up on is its more about digital transformation of the business and modernizing the workflows and processes that are the major business drivers.

However modernization of the business is only one of the major drivers behind cloud migration. Hence, you should be aware of the other key business drivers and cloud benefits that will have appeal across the business.

1. **Scalability and agility**

The ability to scale up and down as required is very appealing to nearly all teams across the organisation at it eliminates the burden of carrying surplus capacity, as well as overprovisioning resources and provides more agility.

2. **Visibility and governance**

Despite existing concerns with governance in the cloud in general, GCP's features and tools can offer even more visibility, and thus provide better governance into the IT ecosystem. Indeed increased visibility saves on the proliferation of storage buckets and unnecessary running instances.

3. Cost effectiveness

The major cost benefits that a cloud migration could bring a company, particularly start-ups is well understood as it can significantly reduce capital expenditure on hardware but so can virtualisation however it is the operation expenditure that is not so easily understood. Virtualisation does not reduce the operational, maintenance, management and provisioning cost overheads. Cloud environments do significantly reduce these and sometimes significantly if you opt for a fully managed service. Google cloud also provides you with the visibility into billing and offers tools and advise via reports on how to reduce unnecessary expenditure due to over-sizing.

4. Talent and innovation

Google cloud managed services allow IT pros to be less burdened by tedious tasks and housekeeping, which allowed them more time for involvement in projects that produced real business value.

5. Modernisation

The migration of systems and data to the cloud is a major project that gives you the chance to re-evaluate applications and their databases. Perhaps some of these are now legacy or even if they still are mission critical systems they could perhaps be due a modernisation. During any system migration project there will be some systems that will require be re-architecting or re-factoring to make them suitable for the cloud. This is a tremendous opportunity to address some long term issues with existing systems whether you decide to move them to the cloud or not.

Planning the Workload Migration

The task of moving enterprise data and applications from inside the secure data center outside into the cloud can be particularly daunting. That is why it must be entered into iteratively in manageable steps following a fully prepared migration strategy. The strategy will differ from organisations in other industry but the core steps should be much the same.

1. Consider the applications suitability for the cloud

Unfortunately not every application is suitable for the cloud and it might require refactoring. It's also important to consider the amount of resources each application uses. The public cloud is a multi-tenant environment, which means applications share resources. And while autoscaling in the public cloud scales resources up or down based on demand, noisy neighbours can be an issue. High spikes in demand can also run up bandwidth costs and hinder an app's performance.

2. Evaluate costs

Many organizations move to the cloud on the basis that it's more cost efficient. However, cloud migrations are not cheap and although they may eventually reduce hardware and some IT overheads they actually increase operational expenses. Moreover, the increase in application OpEx will differ for each application. This is why it is critical to evaluate applications suitability for the cloud not just on architecture but on cost efficiency. Some modern applications with volatile demand such as mobile applications will tend to be very cost efficient if you move them to the cloud. But some older monolithic applications or earlier versions of an Oracle database may well be more expensive to run in the cloud. To assist you with this Google has a cloud calculator but you must still factor in network and bandwidth costs.

4. Rethink governance and security

As organizations move data to the cloud, IT's control diminishes as more responsibility is passed onto Google. Therefore, organizations must shape their governance strategies to rely less on internal security and control, and more on Google.

5. Prepare for cloud-to-cloud migration challenges

Cloud migrations aren't just a transition from on-premises technology to the cloud; they can also migrate data from one cloud to another. Additionally, cloud-to-cloud migrations involve considerable manual labour. To prepare for migration from one provider to another, enterprises need to test their applications and make all necessary configurations for virtual machines, networks, operating systems and more.

6. Define your cloud migration strategy

Once you've considered your data, costs, security and the challenges of cloud-to-cloud migrations, it's time to come up with a migration game plan. Organizations also need to determine migration timeframes for their data and applications. While some choose to migrate everything to the cloud all at once, this can be a challenging -- and risky -- proposition. It's often more effective to break the migration down by workload, starting with less critical applications.

Developing a Migration Strategy

Some suggestions for a viable migration strategy are:

1 - Leverage cloud resources for legacy applications when there is opportunity for cost savings for example, Backup, DR, Business Continuity, or for global reach.

2 - Focus your cloud strategy on new applications that will drive greater agility for the business and contribute to the bottom-line.

3 – Leverage cloud resources to fill gaps in your on-premises technologies and skills, for example machine learning.

Building a Cloud Migration Plan

When we come to build our cloud migration plan there are three key factors that should guide you through the process. These factors will help determine whether to move on-premises workloads to the public cloud or leave them where they are.

1. Evaluate current infrastructure

When it comes to evaluating an application for suitability for the cloud one must consider the existing investment. There is likely to be significant costs associated with servers and support infrastructure. The migration of a server's functionality to the cloud may leave it defunct and a wasted business investment unless the business can somehow repurpose the servers.

Servers are likely to be on a hardware lifecycle roadmap whereby they are refreshed every 3-5 years so that may be the ideal time to migrate on-premises resources to the cloud.

2. Consider application performance and portability

In the case of application servers, we must consider whether the application can function in the cloud. Compatibility and application performance are not likely to be a problem in the GCP environment but you must consider two important aspects.

The first is latency or delay because even though you can provision the virtual instance for the application server with nearly unlimited compute and memory resources if there is limited internet bandwidth then that may well be detrimental to the application performance.

The second aspect to consider will be the applications portability. In this case migrate a virtualized application server to the cloud will not be a problem but the application might have some important external dependencies. For example, a MySQL database may have several partner data source connections that are co-located or rely on direct connections.

3. Assess the network

When building a cloud migration plan you must consider the on-premises network and how it will integrate with the cloud. If an organization wants their users to be able to access applications in the cloud or if they wish to keep some of their resources on premises and some in the cloud, the cloud network must function as an extension of the on-premises network and vice versa.

This is even more complex if you are using windows as you will typically have to deploy cloud-based AD domain controllers, DNS servers as well as maintaining a secure communications path between the cloud and the on-premises network.

It is important to understand that when you build your migration plan that you do not usually need to move everything at the same time. Therefore you should strive for a lift and shift of easy applications and like for like databases early on. This is the low hanging fruit. Then as you build experience and confidence you can start to use Compute Engine VMs to migrate virtualisation of other legacy application or databases that aren't directly supported in GCP. For example MYSQL and PostgreSQL can be considered straightforward as GCP supports these databases natively. This is what would be described as a homogenous migration however if you need to later move a Microsoft SQL Server cluster or an Oracle server to the cloud you could run it within a VM on Compute Engine or a container in Kubernetes. The point being you don't need to lift and shift everything at once so take you time and look for the best deployment methods on an application to application basis.

Lift-and-Shift Vs. Refactoring

Unfortunately in many cases IT teams will often face time or budget constraints, so they believe they have no other option but to go for a lift and shift approach. But refactoring can often be the better path as it has significant benefits to basic lift-and-shift migration.

One issue is that although it may be easier and seemingly cheaper to virtualise your applications and their stacks in the cloud as-built on-premises as you are basically just replicating the on-premises set-up. However this approach could ultimately cost more than it would to run a cloud-native app. Indeed there may well be an inability to properly utilize Google's services for monitoring, security and governance.

Therefore many believe that it is a better option to refactor an application as part of a migration. This is because they have had to do so many times retrospectively due to an applications performance failing to meet benchmarks after a lift and shift migration. There are also issues when migrated applications because they are not cloud-native so they cannot integrate with some of Google's security systems, such as the identity and access management (IAM) service.

However most IT departments don't want to go through unnecessary refactoring because it adds delays and expense so how do you know when to refactor an application? Application developers need to contemplate several factors when evaluating their apps and most important is cost. This is simple business logic - do not spend more money refactoring an app than will be saved in running costs. Therefore you must consider the cost as well as enhanced performance and security benefits when you evaluate the return on your investment (ROI). Remember the ROI isn't all about money.

There's a wide variety of refactoring tools available, and an application's needs will vary depending on what programming languages and databases that it uses. Today the categories of tools lean towards refactoring in building microservices that are designed to consume cloud-native APIs. On the other hand, lately there is a shift towards container development and Kubernetes engine deployment so these tools are also becoming a very popular way to refactor an application for the cloud.

Refactoring Strategies

There are two ways to go about refactoring. There is the complete refactor of the application and this is where over 50% of the code is edited and the database is also updated so it can benefit from many cloud-native features. This is a high risk and reward strategy as it can significantly enhance performance and features to meet the evolving requirements of the business. However, the draw-back is that the refactor process can be expensive or just too complex.

On the other hand we have the option of a minimum viable refactoring process. In this case we prioritize speed and efficiency. A minimal refactor only requires minor code changes to the application. This approach to refactoring often results in integrating the app with some cloud-native security controls and a cloud database.

However, there is another method and that is to use a technique called containerization refactoring. This method is followed by moving the applications into containers with minimal modification. The concept behind this is that the applications execute within the containers. The container however also enables developers to insert cloud-native features and it also improves the portability. The costs and refactoring times also go down due to the wide acceptance of containers within IT.

There is another modern trend towards serverless application refactor but this has similar issues to containerization such as in having to learn new tools and technologies. However, with serverless refactoring there will be some code modifications required to make the application work. This is because although the serverless platforms support most languages and databases they don't yet support all of them.

In summary, you should be aware that in migration to the cloud most applications and data sets will require at least some refactoring if they are to reap the clouds benefits. However, this should be economically viable with some firm deadlines in place to ensure that most of the refactoring work will have a faster return on the investment.

Technical Issues

Now that we have covered the business and project details regards on-premises to cloud migration we will need to address some of the typical technical tasks that we will be expected to achieve.

The first technical challenge is going to be in migrating applications and webservers. Many open source applications will work on the LAMP stack, which we can readily deploy using a preconfigured image in Cloud Launcher. Similarly we can do the same with Windows Server instances so deploying applications and services directly into VM instances is straightforward but what about the workflows and the database?

Workflow Migration

When first planning workflow migration you need to prioritize the machines you want to move. In order to do this with confidence you will need to understand your application's dependencies. Then, you need to batch these dependencies within the same migration stage. For example: If an application depends on multiple VMs, migrate all of those VMs at the same time. However if that is not feasible then move the components logically. For example; if an application requires a database and a web server, then you can move the database before the web server.
In order to verify your migration strategy and tactics you could clone an on-premises workload and run it in Google Cloud Platform (GCP). This enables you to test the migration process without disrupting production. Nonetheless, the points you must consider when migrating workflows are:

- Move the VM to GCP and once this is done perform validation testing and resolve any issues.
- Migrate the application storage to GCP
- After determining that you can rely on the VMs in the cloud, schedule downtime to cut over your application to GCP. This happens in two stages:
  1. Detach the VM.
  2. Test the application to verify that it functions accurately post-migration.

Migrate for Compute Engine

Cloud migration can be complex especially if you are to be moving 100s of applications and their VMs to the GCP. Consequently, Google provides a migration service called Migrate for Compute Engine (formerly Velostrata) to assist you in a seamless transition.

Some of the features that Migrate for Compute Engine (MCE) provides are that as an agentless service there is no impact to the workload indeed you don't need to have your source instances running to migrate them to GCP. As for access to the application as its agentless you do not need to change or reconfigure your apps, VMs or network. In addition there are extensive pre-migration checklists and pre-migration testing to ensure your instances are validated before you move them to GCP

Many enterprises find MCE valuable due to its speed and scale. This is because MCE can rapidly migrate single applications saving potentially hours of time and labour yet scale to 100s of apps using several migration waves that have your stateful workloads running in the cloud within minutes rather than days. While your application starts running in Google Cloud very quickly, its remaining data will continue to synchronise and upload in the background. This means apps are live up to 100x faster, and migrations complete up to 10x quicker, as compared with traditional migration strategies.

How MCE works

The migration strategy that you use when deploying Migrate for Compute Engine is that you follow a typical workflow such as:

1. Validate and perform in-cloud testing on clones so that live applications are unaffected
2. Build your migration waves – these are pre-planned migration jobs that typically contain an application and all its dependencies so they are migrated all at once
3. Deploy the workloads to GCP

4. Background data synchronisation and transfer to GCP, which is transparent to end-users and results in near zero downtime
5. Detach and verify but if something goes wrong you can roll back with no loss of data or project time.

Migrate for Compute engine provides for automatic and seamless transitions between on-premises and the GCP for VMs and physical servers. To assist you further MCE also provides a right-sizing analytical tool so that you can provision and deploy the most optimal cloud instances for cost and performance.

Manually Migrating Databases

The task of moving databases to the cloud without incurring downtime is a tricky business as there are several problems to be overcome. The first is in physically transporting the schema and data into the cloud. Another is in keeping the databases synchronised as you do this. The following sections provide some suggestions as to how you can accomplish these tasks.

Migrating MySQL and PostgreSQL

Google Cloud Platform natively supports MySQL and PostgreSQL within its Cloud SQL service. Moreover, these are not just compatible versions they are the actual databases that you would deploy on-premises. This means that migrating either of MySQL or PostgreSQL to the cloud is going to be reasonably straightforward.
Typically, all that is going to be required is that you build your database engine instance in GCP, copy across the on-premises schema and data and then switch over. In more detail these are the steps you would take for moving an on-premise MySQL or PostgreSQL DB instance to the cloud SQL.
1. Select the project you wish to use.

2. From the navigation menu, select the "Storage -> SQL" menu item.
3. click the "Create instance" button.
4. Choose between a "First Generation" or "Second Generation" instance. (2nd is advisable as it has better performance at a lower cost but doesn't support Mysql version older than 5.6)
5. Create a DB instance ID
6. Choose a location where you was your database to reside
7. Choose a VM type
8. Choose the storage capacity
9. Click create
10. From the instance page click on the DB instance ID
11. click the "Access control" tab and the "Authorization" sub-tab. Click the "Add network" button and enter the public IP address of the server
12. On the same page, select the "Users" sub-tab. Click the "Change root password" button and enter a new password for the MySQL root user.
13. You can now migrate your application database to Google Cloud SQL. However, before you do this, you must disable write access to the application so that the original and new databases stay in sync.

The way that you copy over your data schema and data is to do a sqldump and then copy that up to a storage bucket in Cloud Storage. Then you can reference that bucket as the source for the data schema.
However, if you cannot take the on-premises SQL server offline during the SQLdump transfer then you will need to create a replication session on the master on-premises SQL server and make the cloud SQL server the slave. This will ensure that eventually the two will synchronise. You then can stop the replication session or simply promote the cloud slave to a stand-alone instance.
This procedure requires you to complete the following high-level steps:
1. Configure your source on-premises database server for replication to Cloud SQL.

2. Make the on-premises SQL server the master and the cloud SQL the slave (replica)
3. When the cloud based slave is fully synchronized with the source database server, take your applications offline, and update the applications to point to the cloud SQL database instance.
4. Disconnect the replication from master to slave.
5. Restart your applications, which should now be pointing to the Cloud SQL instance.

Migrating Database Clusters

In this section we will look at a more challenging issue with database migration than moving clusters or high availability configurations to the cloud.

Migrating a PostgreSQL Cluster to the Cloud

To begin, you perform the following tasks:

1. Set up PostgreSQL in GCP.
2. Set up replication on Compute Engine.
3. Then, you'll seed the data to a new instance before you start replicating the master.

Set up PostgreSQL in GCP

1. You configure PostgreSQL on an Ubuntu virtual machine instance on Compute Engine.
2. Set up replication on Compute Engine
3. Configure PostgreSQL to run in Hot Standby mode on Compute Engine by using two Compute Engine instances. One instance will run the primary PostgreSQL server and the other instance will run the standby server.

Seed the data

Because the master database contains a capped transaction log, most PostgreSQL migrations require the data to be seeded to a new instance before you can start replicating the master. You can seed the data in one of the following ways:

1. Dump a single database into a script or archive file using Pg_dump.
2. Take a binary copy of a running database cluster using Pg_basebackup.
3. Replicate the data folder to the replica using rsync.
4. Restore a previous backup to the replica.

After the initial seeding of the database, you can use the rsync command to feed changes to the replica that have occurred since the backup; the command syncs the data directories between the two instances. This step is important if the backup has fallen too far behind the master to catch up through normal replication.

Setting up the PostgreSQL cluster on GCP

You can create the PostgreSQL cluster using cascade replication.

1. Take a full data backup from the running master server
2. Transfer the backup to the bucket you just created:
3. Transfer the backup file to the GCP master:
4. Restore the backup file into the GCP master:
5. Create a recovery.conf file in the $PG_DATA directory
6. Start the PostgreSQL service:
7. Wait until the GCP master server syncs with the running master.
8. Create a subordinate database
9. Shut down the database and the server:
10. In the GCP Console, go to the Snapshots page.
11. From the PostgreSQL disk, create a new snapshot.
12. Start the GCP master server.
13. Go to the VM instances page, click master-instance-name, and then click Start.
14. Start the new server and mount the disk:

15. Configure data directory and replication values. Copy the PostgreSQL.conf file and the pg_hba.conf file from the GCP master, and edit the recovery.conf file

Migrating a Microsoft SQL Server Cluster

When you decide to move a SQL Server DB instance you can for the time being either use Cloud Launcher to build a pre-provisioned image or build it yourself. Support for SQL Server in Cloud SQL is expected in late 2019 but until then we have to run it in a VM. Deploying and instance or a high availability cluster using Cloud Launcher is by far the easiest route as all you need to do is use Google Cloud Launcher to provision a SQL Server Enterprise AlwaysOn Cluster. Cloud Launcher will automate the creation of multiple Windows virtual machines,
one Windows Server and two SQL Server instances. It will also configure Active Directory and Google's virtual private cloud network with a topology that's optimized for rapid fail over of the SQL Server AlwaysOn Cluster. The build uses premium images and comes with licences for both server and SQL.
 However, if you decide to build the cluster yourself and use your own licenses then moving a SQL Server DB instance or a cluster to the cloud will mean you will have to use Compute Engine VMs. Therefore the first step is to provision a Windows Virtual Machine in Google Compute Engine then will access it using window's Remote Desktop Protocol (RDP). Creating a Windows Server 2016 VM is just like any other VM except we have to create a Windows administrator password. When building a cluster aim for a VM of 2 CPU, 7.5Gb of memory and around 50 GB of disk storage. You can then connect to the VM using an RDP client such as Chrome to log on. That is how easy it is to provision and run Windows virtual machines on Google's global infrastructure.
Google supplies pre-configured Compute Engine images for the Express, Web, Standard, and Enterprise 2012, 2014, and 2016 versions.

Each SQL Server edition can be deployed on a variety of versions of Windows Server and the licence for both the server and SQL comes with the build. However in the case of SQL you can use your existing licence. Once your virtual machines are up and running, you will want to connect to them to perform General Systems Operations tasks, such as installing and configuring Windows features and your own applications.

When you provision your Windows virtual machines, the default network configuration is to

have a private IP address visible to the instance and a public IP address that's maintained by Compute Engine.

When a machine doesn't have a public IP address, then it's not able to connect to the Internet without configuring a separate machine as the network addressed translation (NAT) gateway.

This is important for Windows virtual machines, as they need to be able to connect to the Internet to contact the Windows license server when the machine is first provisioned, and subsequently at regular intervals.

So you'll need to ensure that your network configuration has a public IP address or it supports NAT.

It's likely that you will need to load large amounts of data into your SQL cluster and this is a resource-intensive operation. Therefore you might want to use an easier way to reduce the disk IO and CPU cycles. A higher performance way of doing bulk data uploads is to create a separate database that will be used solely as a staging and transforming point for the bulk dataset before you insert it into your production database. You could also put this new database on a local SSD drive, if you have enough space. This will reduce the resource consumption of your bulk operations, as well as the time to complete the jobs.

Oracle to Cloud Spanner

There will be times when we have to migrate heterogeneous databases, for example Oracle to PostgreSQL or to Cloud Spanner. This may be to release the business from expensive licences or simply to make the database cloud native and benefit from scale and flexibility. Regardless, the migration is going to be more challenging as you have many more factors to take into account.

The first formidable obstacle to overcome is the dissimilar schema, data types, queries and features that each support. Hence you are going to at a minimum have to convert the Oracle schema and data model to suit Cloud Spanner as well as translate queries. This will in all likelihood require some application changes so you have to be diligent in finding out what applications are using the Oracle database. This might seem trivial but today's databases can have many data connections to applications, partner system, and even ad-hoc connections to user spreadsheets.

Once you have performed the conversion of the data model and the translation of queries it will be time to contemplate how to export the data from Oracle to Cloud Spanner. For this task we can take advantage of Google's Dataflow ETL service.

Then when we have achieved data consistency between the databases it will be time to switch over and point the applications to the new Cloud Spanner database.

Converting your database and schema

When you start the conversion process you should be trying to match the existing Oracle schema as closely as possible to Cloud Spanner as this will make application changes simpler. However, changes are unavoidable due to differences in features, data types and SQL.

One such issue is the sequencing of primary keys that is inbuilt into Oracle but will be problematic in Cloud Spanner. This is because of potential hot spots arising from too many queries focusing on the same server. In addition to primary keys you should also look to benefit from using table interleafing and the creation of secondary keys to extract the most benefit from Cloud Spanners scalability.

Translate any SQL queries

You must convert any SQL queries that use Oracle-specific syntax, functions, and types to be compatible with Cloud Spanner. While Cloud Spanner does not support structured data as column definitions, structured data can be used in SQL queries using ARRAY and STRUCT types.
SQL queries can be profiled using the Cloud Spanner Query interface in the GCP Console to execute the query. In general, queries that perform full table scans on large tables are very expensive, and should be used sparingly.

Modifying the application to use Cloud Spanner

As part of the migration process, features not available in Cloud Spanner must be implemented in the application. You may want to look at using Cloud Spanner's client libraries for making read and write queries. These use Cloud Spanner-specific API calls. Using API calls may be faster as the SQL statement does not have to be translated.

Transferring your data from Oracle to Cloud Spanner

To transfer your data from Oracle to Cloud Spanner, you will need to export your Oracle database to a portable file format, for example CSV, then upload the file into a Cloud Storage bucket. From there it can be imported into Cloud Spanner using the extract, transform, and load (ETL) process in Cloud Dataflow.

Cloud Dataflow provides a service for running data pipelines in order to read and process large amounts of data in parallel over several servers. Dataflow is based upon Apache Beam and uses the Beam SDK connectors for Cloud Storage and Cloud Spanner so there is no coding necessary. You will only have to code the actual ETL process.

The next issue that you have to address is maintaining consistency between both databases during the migration process. The problem with data uploads is that we cannot, in most cases, keep the applications offline for the length of time the data import/export will take.

Unfortunately, when you are transferring the data it may already be stale as the applications continue to write new data to update the existing on-premises Oracle database. Nonetheless, you need to keep the databases synchronised and there are several ways to do this, such as by using the Oracle Change Data Capture feature, or by programmatically implementing simultaneous updates in your applications.

The final step in the migration will be switching to Cloud Spanner as your application's source of truth. When you have verified the data consistency and synchronisation of the data, you can then switch your application to point to Cloud Spanner. You should continue to keep the Oracle database up to date as this provides a rollback path should there be issues.

Printed in Great Britain
by Amazon